Architecture,
Problems,
and Purposes

ARCHITECTURE, PROBLEMS, AND PURPOSES

Architectural
Design as a Basic
Problem-Solving
Process

by JOHN W. WADE
Architect

A WILEY-INTERSCIENCE PUBLICATION

JOHN WILEY & SONS

New York ● London ● Sydney ● Toronto

Library of Congress Cataloging in Publication Data:

Wade, John William, 1925-
  Architecture, problems, and purposes.

  Includes bibliographies and index.
  1. Architectural design. 2. Problem solving.
I. Title.
NA2750.W3   729   76-27280
ISBN 0-471-91305-7

Printed in the United States of America

10 9 8 7 6 5 4 3 2 1

To Donna White Wade,
  my wife

To Alex Chisholm Wade
and Myrtle Kent Wade,
  my parents

Preface

This book is about the design process used by architects and other design professionals. It explains that process in considerable detail and shows its relation to other problem-solving processes. The book is organized in such a way that it can be skimmed for a quick understanding or studied in detail for a comprehensive view. After I say whom the book is for, I describe briefly the present condition of the architectural profession. By doing so I can explain further what the book is about and what purpose it can serve.

WHOM THE BOOK IS FOR

First, this book is intended for the *practitioner*. It is *not* to teach him his process or to say what it ought to be; it *is* intended to provide an understanding of the essential, legitimate, and useful features of the design process so that he can explain it to others; the book is intended to assist the practitioner in communicating with clients and other lay persons about design. It is intended to help the practitioner identify with his client those points in the design process that are value determined and subject to different interpretations. Those points are crucial for decision.

Second, this book is intended for the *design student*. It will not teach him to design, but it will help him understand the implications of what he has learned. It can help him to be alert for those vivid experiences in his own career that can be vital for learning. Let me emphasize that design can be learned only by engaging in design activity; it cannot be learned by reading about design.

Third, this book is also for the architecture *faculty member*. It may be of help in his articulate description of the design process. Since the book is organized to permit different levels of involvement in each topic, the faculty member can use it at whatever level of design instruction he finds most helpful.

Fourth, the book is intended for the concerned *lay person*. It can help him to have accurate expectations about design and to know what the designer can and cannot do. If a lay person is concerned as a design client, the book can help him participate usefully and fully in the design process.

THE CHARACTER OF THE ARCHITECTURAL PROFESSION

Architecture is a complicated and bewildering profession. It can be seen as an art, a business, or a relatively hard problem-solving discipline. In truth, architecture has been, is, and will be all these different things.

Once architecture was concerned only with the design and construction of buildings, but no longer. There are architects who have expanded their practice to include urban design and land development. Others have narrowed their practice to a concern only with building programming.

At one time architects designed all the important buildings in a community; they understood exactly what their clients wanted. Today the architect is not the only person who designs buildings; engineers do so, and "package-dealers" provide design services as part of their package. The architect who receives important commissions today might have difficulty in understanding his client's needs directly. He must work for an extraordinary variety of clients with widely varying points of view.

THE NEED FOR A DECISION BASE

With each passing decade the architect has had a more difficult task. To accomplish it some practitioners have turned to the behavioral sciences for information and to the management sciences for new techniques. Their practices have been revised to include persons with many different skills. Many practices have been organized as corporate enterprises, and in such a practice there is need for a strongly rational decision base.

In such a practice there is still the architect as artist, but he is not the architect-artist of old. Instead he must find ways to justify what he proposes in terms that his earlier artist counterpart would not have understood.

THE CHALLENGE FACING THE PROFESSION

If there is a recognized need for organizing the decision base within the profession, there is also a challenge to the profession from without. In recent years many persons and institutions have challenged the profession in its practice, in its registration and licensing procedures, and in its education.

The *practice* of architecture is being challenged in the character of its process, in the quality of its product, in the costliness of its service, and in its openness to competition. The *registration* of architects is being challenged in its failure to state standards, in its criteria for admitting candidates to examination, and in its subjective evaluation procedures. The *education* of architects is being challenged in the criteria by which its schools are accredited and in the criteria that its schools set for graduation.

A substantial part of this challenge by lay persons has been based on a mistrust of the subjective and inventive nature of the design process that was derived from a lack of understanding of design decision. The lack of understanding arose because the professional did not explain; and the professional did not explain because he did not know how. The challenge is not to the design process; it is to the *unexplained* nature of the process. It is a challenge to the profession to describe and defend its process.

WHAT THE BOOK IS ABOUT

If in the past the design professions have not been able to respond to external challenge, in the present there is a growing body of information that permits a response. This book undertakes to provide a part of that response. It sets out to explain the internal organization of the design process; it attempts to provide a verbal justification for design procedure.

It bases that justification on work done in a wide variety of fields. Substantial work has been done in systematic methods of design, in the collection of information about human behavior, and in the organized collection of information about building components and the functions they provide. Work has been done in studying how architects achieve their design proposals.

Thus it is possible to undertake this response, not only from some interesting theoretical standpoint, but also from the reality of practice and of business experience.

JOHN W. WADE

Milwaukee, Wisconsin
July 1976

Contents

Architecture,
Problems,
and Purposes

Introduction

The architect solves problems by making proposals for buildings. Understood in one way, that is a relatively simple thing to do. The client knows he needs a building of a certain sort, he tells the architect what it is (and what special things he wants the building to do for him), and the architect designs a building to suit.

The architect is assisted in this process by a tradition of building design in the society in which he lives. On every hand are ready-made solutions to the sort of building the client needs. Since people who use buildings sometimes object to being surprised or confused by their design, the architect must base much of his approach on what people's expectations are. One of the basic ways in which an architect learns to design buildings is by learning how other architects have designed similar buildings.

At the same time each building that might serve as a model was designed for some particular circumstance. It was designed for a specific place, time, and set of requirements. Many of these specifics might be in conflict with the present specific circumstances with which the architect must deal. Thus the architect is inclined to pay only passing attention to the design of existing buildings; his inclination is reinforced by the difficulty in getting accurate data about their circumstances. It is further reinforced by the art orientation of the design professions. Since the building is a work of art, shame is attached to a blatant copying of another person's work.

This conflict between the use of existing buildings as models for solution and the avoidance of such a use is only the beginning of the architect's difficulties. He has learned a problem solution sequence that moves through three phases: programming, planning, and designing. The phases work in an orderly fashion: use *words* to list and organize the client's requirements, use *diagrams* to develop the relationships between the requirements, and use *drawings* to develop the building spaces that can provide for those requirements. Unfortunately most architects have learned the use of these phases in a behavior-related sequence and not in their logical connectedness. Most architects have learned problem solving by engaging in it, not by understanding the organization of the process.

It is not difficult to see why the emphasis in design has been on learning the process rather than on understanding it. Since the buildings were themselves to be works of art, the assumption has always been that the drawings for buildings were direct substitutes for the buildings and communicated directly what the building would be to the client and to potential users. It would be just as if the building were already built, and everyone connected with the project could say what he liked and did not like. What was liked could be approved, and what was disliked could be changed.

There are, of course, substantial flaws in this view of client and user participation in the design and design approval process. First,

drawings do not always communicate directly to lay persons; perceiving what design drawings are intended to communicate is a learned
professional skill. Second, even if the drawings communicate directly
what the building's quality would be, most lay persons do not have a
developed critical skill that permits them to say what they like
and do not like; even if they can say what they do not like, they often
cannot say why. Third, unless the designer provides an orderly
description of the decision process by which his drawn proposal was
developed, the lay person is still unable to react intelligently, whatever
his skill in understanding drawings; the product does not usually
reveal all the details of the process that produced it. Fourth, the lay
person is also without a basis for judgment, since even a description of
this process cannot ordinarily review the alternatives *not* selected; the
design proposal often has a take-it-or-leave-it quality.

Some of these flaws are not restricted to design; several occur in all
fields where an expert must seek the agreement and approval of non-
expert lay persons. If they are sometimes more acute in design, it is
because the designer thinks he is communicating directly in a non-
professional language when he is *not* doing so.

The architect-designer has also had difficulty because he thinks
that a great many design decisions are his prerogative as designer (as
artist) and that queries by lay persons that touch on these areas can be
answered by reminding the lay person of his artist-designer status and
his supposed superior capability in perception. The architect has
begun to learn that his trained ability in perception is important only
where he shares a same-value orientation with his client. Clients with a
sufficiently different economic, social, or ethnic background can
disagree strongly with the values the architect had not previously
questioned.

What seems clear is that the design process is not faulty in itself,
but that it is not adequately supported by aids to communication. If
his design process is not adequate, it is because the architect has not
learned to organize the information *about* his process to the same
degree he has learned to use information *in* his process.

Defenders of the design process as it now exists (without a strong
organization of its information) like to compare it with the process of
riding a bicycle. No matter how much a person reads about bicycle
riding, they say, the only way to learn and to become accomplished is
simply by riding a bicycle. The same thing also used to be said about
flying an airplane, "Well, Wilbur, first I took off, then I flew awhile,
and then I came down. That's all there was to it!" But that is not the
way it still is in flying multimillion-dollar airplanes. No doubt the
basic motor skills must be learned in that way, but any reasonable
pilot requires an enormous amount of supporting information for a
flight. A comparison of the design process with bicycle riding indicates exactly where those designers are in their approach to design.

This book undertakes a description of the design process as an organized problem-solving procedure to support and justify the traditional procedure. But this book is intended to do more than that. It is intended to provide an access to additional techniques that will make the process more reasonable and more understandable. The architectural profession has reached a time when that is essential. Not only must the designer be able to design well, he must also be able to explain how he does so. He can no longer say that he just took off and flew awhile until he came down with the solution.

Other persons want to know what happened along the way. The architect has an obligation to tell them. Indeed it is more than an obligation, it is a necessity. There are clients now for whom architects work who must be told, or those architects do not fly for them again.

It is not easy to say how a bicycle or airplane or a design procedure works. There is even the possibility of harm to the process; if a person is asked to examine how a slight shift of his weight causes the vehicle to change direction, he may lose his balance altogether. It is better, after he has ridden or flown, to *remember* how it was that a shift of weight produced the effect it did. He can still learn from the experience, his next effort can profit from it, and he does not run the same risk of harm. I propose to use that technique in this book.

Since much of the character of the design process is related to the life experiences of the designer—because he learns that way—I try to relate the descriptions in this book to various career experiences the designer has had. Inevitably I rely on my own experience or on experiences I have heard about. With this approach, if the beginning design student or the lay reader is to understand what the book is about, I must also give an outline of what the typical career experience is like. I must describe how it is that the designer learns to design. I begin with that. Such a beginning also permits the professional designer to compare his own experience with mine, to know whether we have a common basis for understanding.

When I have completed that description, I shall begin to analyze the design process. Each segment of the analysis is kept as simple and uncluttered as possible. I want to get each group of ideas across directly. Each of these segments is kept as a direct descriptive part without footnotes or references. A *descriptive section* is then followed, where appropriate, by *technical discussion sections* that go into more depth or detail about some of the points covered in the descriptive section. Each technical discussion is followed by *references* to the literature on which the discussion is based.

By such an arrangement the reader is able to read directly through the descriptive sections or go into more and more depth as his needs require. For the extremely serious student I recommend that he pursue our subject to the referenced literature from which much of this material is drawn.

Such a pursuit by the serious student can contribute to the direction this book has begun. Although my literature search has been extended, it has been broad rather than deep. Where I have drawn material from disciplines other than my own, I have done so because of the material's usefulness to my field, rather than because of its contribution to its own. I have approached psychology, for example, as an architect and a design theorist, rather than as a psychologist. Since design is concerned with decision for action, I have not had so much a concern for defensible truth (which tends toward complexity of statement) as for actionable truth (which tends toward simplicity of statement).

This point of view may have caused some distortion in interpreting what writers from other disciplines have said. Since this book is an effort to bring together as much material as possible related to problem solving and design, I hope that any possible distortion of material from other fields will be excused. I believe the benefit to be gained by such an assembly is worth the risk of damage any distortion could cause.

1. The Architect's Career Experience

All the designer's experience affects the way he undertakes the solution of design problems. A review of the designer's career is vital to an understanding of the design process.

The architect's career usually moves from an educational experience in an architectural school, through an apprenticeship period in the office of a practicing architect, into his own independent practice. The collegiate school experience may last from five to eight years (depending on what university format the student follows). Most states require three years' apprenticeship before the candidate is admitted to the licensing examination, and it often takes several tries at the examination before a candidate completes all parts (the new examinations have changed this somewhat). The architect will thus have had at least eight years of exposure in the field and may have a number of years more before he is licensed to practice.

There are many variations on this basic pattern. The student designer may begin his apprenticeship experience before he ever finishes school. Some candidates for licensing have never had the collegiate school experience, but when they are licensed, they tend to work in some part of practice not directly concerned with design. Some designers never become licensed to practice and continue to work as unlicensed employees under the supervision of licensed practitioners.

Whatever the career pattern the architectural school experience seems to be vital. Within it the studio instruction method is essential, and within studio instruction, design criticism as a teaching technique has the greatest impact. This chapter describes each of these.

Having described these vital experiences in the formation of an architectural designer, it will be possible to consider what some of the learning experiences are that the student designer has.

1.1 THE IMPORTANCE OF DESIGN IN ARCHITECTURE

Design is the central focus of the architect's school experience. Architects are educated as designers even though their ultimate career experience may require a relatively light involvement in actual design processes.

When the student first enters the architectural field, he does so with the idea that he will be engaged during his professional career in building design. Design is extremely important in architecture, but it is also the distilled essence of the field; it is what the whole process is about, but there is also a great deal to the process of architecture that is not identifiable as design.

The student in a school of architecture gets a distorted view of what the field is like, because in school most design is a personal process. By contrast the practitioner experiences design (with the rare exception) as a cooperative, even as a corporate, experience. What was a personal process in school becomes an institutionalized process in professional practice.

Learning design is undoubtedly the essential thing that occurs in a school of architecture. But there is also no doubt that, in focusing on the essentials of the process, the school ignores a substantial part of what occurs in practice. The usual school instruction assumes that every person entering architecture will be a designer, or else he will be a "failed" designer. In other words those who do not have the talent to be designers must forsake the glory of giving actual shape to buildings and undertake some one or the other of those other tasks that make the design process work in an architectural firm. Presumably one of the school's roles is to help the talented designer, the "A" student, discover himself, and make him known to practitioners as a person to seek out for employment. An ancient design school aphorism may come closer to the truth; it says that the "B" student works for the "C" student, and the "A" student teaches. This aphorism recognizes the degree to which talent in design has anything to do with successful architectural practice. It suggests that design talent is not very important. It implies, without saying it, that a lack of talent is of some benefit; this comes from a time when high talent was associated with strong temperament, and lack of talent with a more plodding, prosaic approach to things. Without question it is possible to read far too much into an ancient aphorism, but what it has said is that management is far more important to successful architectural practice than talented design is. It is probably quite accurate.

Let us see why! As the student moves from school into an office, he has a very great amount to learn. It is usual for the student's first experience to be in very simple and then in more and more complex working drawings. These drawings are technical documents and must often be drawn and redrawn to bring them into accord with changes decided on in some part of the building. By doing working drawings, the young designer gradually learns what is and is not possible in design and what the conventional practices are in the firm where he works.

If his school trained him only as a designer, it was partly a waste of effort. Since there is such a comparatively small amount of work in the architectural office that resembles what the student knew as design, he might wonder if the school's emphasis on design was not a bit like trying to make bread with three cups of yeast and a tablespoon of flour. This would be especially true if he had spent three years at the Skidmore office drawing stair details (as a friend of mine once did). The leaven that his design training had provided did not make those stair details bake up any lighter. Or he might be so frustrated that he spent all of his design effort in making his working drawings works of art—at an enormous cost to his firm in time. A friend at the old Saarinen office took enormous pride in fitting some seventy-five intricate one-and-one-half-inch-scale wall and window details onto an ordinary working drawing sheet—in such a manner that the whole sheet made a beautiful texture, but, unfortunately, in such a way that the notes to one detail could not be distinguished from those to an adjacent detail. Certainly this was a misplaced design effort.

As his experience develops, the young designer is given the opportunity to start tentative design work under close supervision. If he proves capable, he is given responsibility for the design development of a building after initial design studies have already been set. As design job-captain he has responsibility for managing the execution of working drawings based on a senior designer's work. He will finally be trusted to develop and execute the design of a building on his own. These are the good years for which his training in school have prepared him.

His next career step departs from that direction. He begins to manage the design work of other persons. Young designers begin to work under his direction, and as he takes on more responsbility, he spends all his time reviewing their work and does no design himself. When he becomes a partner in his firm or enters independent practice, he can find himself so remote from design that he could be in any sort of business at all.

Nothing in his background or preparation has prepared him for making short-term loans to cover his payroll until the client's payment arrives, or for dealing with the intricacies of accounting, or for filling out federal forms on employees. Nothing at all has dealt with securing work from clients or with writing contracts for design that would prevent the client from cheating on his payments. To what use was that design skill being put?

There are exceptions to this pattern. Some enter practice and settle for the designer's role in a firm and do not attempt to go beyond that role. Others are so talented that they can become the design partner in a large firm and spend their entire effort in design and in supervising the work of other designers who assist their own design effort. There are also exceptions in the other direction: students with design training who never have an opportunity to use their design ability because they are so good as delineators, or as specification writers, or as any one of a dozen other specialists in an office.

The needs in practice are extremely varied, and design practice requires a multitude of different talents. Most schools, despite this fact, still place an enormous emphasis on design. Despite knowing that most professional design is an institutional effort requiring the organized work of many different persons, these schools still emphasize individual design skill. A need for a shift in emphasis is undoubtedly needed.

In describing the overall outline of a professional career, I have omitted considerable detail. I have omitted discussion of an extremely important event in a young designer's life: that time when he studies for and takes his examinations for licensing—a traumatic time. I have omitted mention of European or other foreign travel; such travel, since the time of the nineteenth-century Grand Tour has been considered to be a relatively essential part of the young architect's education. I have omitted mention of "name" offices, for they are probably not as important as they once were; at one time one could hardly recommend himself to a firm as a designer if he had not put in a bit of time working under a world-famous designer. I have sketched the career in outline to emphasize the relative importance of design in the career orientation of the architect.

I have emphasized repeatedly the importance of the school's orientation toward design. Although I have indicated that I believe the schools have placed an undue emphasis on design, still the fact that they have done so is critical to our discussion. Rightly or wrongly, the schools have trained all their graduates in a design-oriented problem-solving process. That orientation is pervasive in the architectural field. If I am to relate the discussion of this book to the design process, I must pursue design instruction into the schools, where it is emphasized and taught.

1.2 THE ARCHITECTURE SCHOOL EXPERIENCE

The school experience is crucial. Whatever the school's merit it defines the student's basic professional orientation. It determines the basic questions that the profession is willing to address.

When I entered architectural school, most schools were very much alike. The student was taught by the studio method. He was given a work place in a drafting room, or "studio," and was expected to inhabit it for as many of his waking hours as he could manage. To occupy his time, he was assigned design problems of various kinds that were ordinarily arranged to be more difficult and more complex as he moved through the five years of his curriculum. His studio was taught by practicing architects who came in three afternoons a week to assign problems, to discuss assignments, to criticize student efforts in solving problems, and finally, to judge (sometimes with outside help) the quality of the student's final solution. The problems assigned required as a solution a building proposal or sometimes a larger scale urban or environmental complex. The problems varied during an academic semester from a single-day "sketch" problem, through a single-week "short" problem, to a six-week or eight-week "long" problem.

There were exceptions to this scheme; several of the Ivy League schools offered programs at the graduate level. After receiving a bachelor's degree (often in a subject area apart from architecture), the student entered a three-and-one-half-year graduate program leading to a professional bachelor's degree or master's degree. These programs also used the studio format but usually made earlier and higher demands on their more mature students.

Studio instruction was consistently supplemented in all programs by more conventional academic courses and course sequences. The typical offering was in drafting, something called "basic design" (inspired by instruction at the German Bauhaus), architectural history, structural design, mechanical equipment of buildings, construction practice, and professional practice. The occasional school had supplementary offerings in urban planning and landscape. Most schools at that time, but not all, had given up the Beaux Arts tradition that required a knowledge of the Classical Orders and that used sketching from plaster casts of Roman and Greek ornament and building detail as a device for instruction. Schools that still had their "cast-rooms" were an oddity. There was not a great amount of disagreement about curricular issues. There was some worry whether "basic design" was very helpful, but the vital issue I remember as a student was whether there was to be an "open" or "closed" jury when student problems were judged. In the "open" jury the students were invited to make oral presentations and provide oral defense of their completed work. In the "closed" jury students were not even invited to be present.

When I had determined, as an undergraduate, that I wanted to enter architecture in graduate school, I had the immediate problem of determining what courses I could take in college that would contribute best to my professional studies. The question was (and still remains) whether to distribute studies over a broad area or to concentrate them into a narrow professional field. A remark attributed to Dean Joseph Hudnut of the Harvard Graduate School of Design is pertinent. When asked what courses a student needs to be a well-qualified architect, the Dean replied that the student should take every course the university had to offer. Since that number of courses at any major university could be estimated to require some fifty years, no student took his remark very seriously. But everyone took quite seriously the attitude behind his remark. There was a strong belief in a generalist preparation for entrance into a professional field, especially architecture; the belief seemed to be shared by faculty and students alike. Indeed the architect has tended to think of himself more as a generalist than as a specialist.

Part of the argument for offering architecture as a graduate program was based on this attitude. In the program I experienced there was a consistent follow-through of this attitude into the sequencing of the program. The first year of graduate study was an offering for architects, urban planners, and landscape architects. We were required to work from the larger scale and the more general to the smaller scale and the more particular. Our first set of problems was concerned with the redevelopment of a major portion of the city in which our university was located. Only later were we asked to deal with the design of individual buildings. The entire curriculum moved slowly from the more nearly to the less nearly comprehensive.

When I recall what I learned from the architectural school experience, the first things that come to mind are the vivid, concrete things.

I remember having an extraordinary perceptual experience because a professor had suggested that we "really" look at parts of the world. I could show you to this day the exact tree whose bark I really saw for the first time, even though I had been looking at the tree and its trunk every day. I remember the wife of a fellow student tearing me apart verbally because I had mistreated her husband during a team problem effort. The architectural school produced a strong, vivid experience. I remember people, I remember places, and I remember events.

But if I also try to say what I learned about problem solving in architectural school, that is somewhat more complicated. That requires a closer look at the studio instruction used in the school.

1.3 STUDIO INSTRUCTION IN ARCHITECTURAL DESIGN

Studio instruction is vital for learning the integrative design process; design is learned by designing. Studio instruction simulates the reality of practice without exposing the student to the hazards of practice.

Problems in studio were ordinarily assigned with a building program already provided. The instructors would already have determined that we should design a building of a specific kind, composed a list of requirements, and selected a site for which we were to design the building. They would provide a list of the required rooms in the building, the number of square feet required for each room, and a topographic survey of the site. After an introductory discussion during the first afternoon meeting the instructors (or as they were called, the "critics") would then make continuous rounds, seeing each student in turn. They reviewed each student's progress and discussed his approach to the problem.

During a six-week problem the first two-week period was usually spent in library "research" (looking through journals to see how other architects had solved similar problems), in drawing the required room areas to scale (and sometimes preparing cardboard cutouts to represent the rooms), in diagraming the needed relationships between the various rooms, and in recovering from the problem that had just been completed (sleeping, laundry, dating). The second two weeks were spent in evaluating different possible schemes and working out the difficulties associated with each to decide on a final scheme. During this middle two weeks the critics were most useful. The last two weeks were spent in working out the details of the final scheme; drawing the scheme in plan, elevation, section, and perspective; and organizing and executing the presentation drawings and model. This last two weeks tended to be an around-the-clock involvement that was a race toward a jury deadline. Other courses, sleeping, laundry, and dating all tended to be neglected in order that the harried but successful designer could stagger into the jury room and pin his drawings to the wall with seconds to spare before the faculty critics (now become a jury) should require of the student why he had done such and such a stupid thing as. . . .

Such an ordeal by fire required that the student be able to handle the pressure of a deadline and that he be reasonably quick and cogent in his responses to criticism. The public nature of the criticism required that the student develop his own internal beliefs about his capabilities. He had to care strongly enough to do a good job, and he had not to care when the faculty disagreed with him about how good a job he had done. Every student in the class knew how each other student was ranked, because grades were marked directly on each student's presentation drawings directly after each jury. There were even some insecure students whose friends changed according to which students had received high marks on the most recent problem.

There were some variations to this general pattern. Team problems, for example, imposed a need for cooperative effort and produced, on occasion, major conflicts between students unable to agree. Shorter problems were given to provide a variety of approach, and "sketch" problems were given as a treat, almost as a vacation from the more serious problem-solving effort in building design; they were intended to encourage creativity and flexibility of approach in the student. Although intense (if you did not get an idea in the first few hours, you would not be able to complete the problem), they were fun because their subject matter was often silly, and the faculty treated them less seriously.

Despite there having been many changes in studio instruction since the time I have described (students write their own programs, they often deal with real clients, they have more sophisticated analytic methods available to them), studio instruction still forms a vital part of the architectural education.

It is important then to say what studio instruction can teach. *First* and most simply, it teaches students about the organization of buildings. In a profession that has not yet been willing (possibly because of its art orientation) to formalize its information base it acquaints the student with what conventional practice has been. *Second*, it teaches students a specific overall problem-solving strategy applicable to architectural design. *Third*, it teaches them specific skills and techniques they must know if they are to engage in building design as professionals. *Fourth*, it prepares the way for students to enter professional practice; it provides a simulation of practice that is safe, where the student can make mistakes without injury to others or detriment to himself. If it is a good simulation, it lets students know what the principal difficulties in practice are.

The learning process in the studio is made vivid by studio criticism and the architectural jury, described next.

1.4 DESIGN CRITICISM AND JURY PRESENTATION

The public criticism to which the student designer is exposed evokes attitudes that are useful, and sometimes essential, for practice. The student must care intensely to do a good job; he must not care when he discovers other persons in disagreement with his proposals. A substantial part of the design process lies in discovering and resolving such disagreements.

In describing the sequence of student work in solving design problems I have not described the complexity of design instruction. This complexity depends on the subject matter, itself complex, but also on the richness of understanding the faculty bring to the program and its teaching. How these two are related can be seen by examining the design criticism used in instruction. It will be easier if I discuss that criticism in the formality of the design jury rather than in the informality of the studio.

Because architecture is so comparatively rich and our information is so limited and ill organized, design criticism itself has tended to be random and disordered; the quality of criticism has depended on the ability and understanding of faculty members. On the whole their criticism has tended to be "fair" and reasoned, directed at the qualities of the students' projects according to criteria the students know, and not at the quality of the student.

On the whole the criticism by architectural faculty is considerate criticism; it usually takes into account that the students have spent the last several weeks in intensive development of the proposals their drawings illustrate. The open jury makes demands on faculty for such considerateness; it displays the faculty member at his best and at his worst. Faculty members deal in student (and other faculty) respect. For the bright faculty member the architectural jury is a showcase for his brilliance and his understanding. It is a showcase in a different way for the less gifted faculty member. The student learns that some faculty can always be counted on to put their feet into their mouths, to be totally wrong and inept. The student learns that some faculty have only a single theme and that they can be counted on for a comment on that theme in every jury. The jury demonstrates how broad or how narrow, a faculty member's concern with architecture is.

A jury presentation puts the design student on display in a different manner. For a student the jury is very often intense. He is up for public recognition or for public censure, no matter how gentle the jury criticism might be. I can remember exact words I spoke as a student during intense jury presentations, when all the times of informal studio criticism have gone entirely from memory. The informal criticism undoubtedly had its effect, but it was not so intense and memorable. I remember once saying during a jury, "Professor 'Blank,' if you will just be quiet, I believe that I can explain the structural system for this building in a way that even *you* will understand!" The wonder was that he was quiet and that I did explain the structure satisfactorily. I was frightened to have been so bold and enormously pleased afterward to receive the congratulations of other students who had received similar heckling. Professor "Blank" was not ill intended, just not very sensitive. On other occasions I have seen students so intensely involved in their projects that adverse criticism produced uncontrollable tears. One of the greatest hazards in being a faculty critic is in being so harsh in criticism that the student is harmed.

Whereas criticism is generally recognized to be mostly just, both faculty and students realize that a jury that reviews a great number of projects will be unfair to some students. The first few projects receive a very thorough review; the faculty are fresh, are often seeing the finished drawings for the first time, and are exploring their own reactions to the projects. The great middle part of the projects then receive only passing interest, except when some particular project is remarkably different, brilliantly good, or atrociously bad, and so an inspiration to the faculty's capacity for high praise or weary (and sometimes vicious) sarcasm. At the end of the day the projects have all begun to look alike, all of the criticisms have already been given, and only those few students whose work has not yet been reviewed have any further interest in continuing. After experiencing this sequence a few times, students begin to argue and plot whether it is best to have their work reviewed early or late in a jury; I remember that my student group had decided that being third or fourth was best for getting a really good criticism of the merits and faults of a project. Too early, and the faculty will pick you apart in finding out what the project is like; too late, and the faculty might not even see your project.

Jury criticism has its major difficulties, but they are some of the same that afflict the architectural profession in its totality.

First, there are numerous shifts in the basis for criticism applied to a project. The jury is both a judgmental device and an instructional mode. In saying what a student has done ineffectively the faculty also address the entire student group. This is so relatively important that I have seen juries falter and be dismissed when too few students were present.

Second, there is a considerable flexibility in the weighting of critical values applied. The critics respond to the "Gestalt," the perceived totality, of the project being presented. This response can cause the same fault, appearing in different projects, to be condemned or forgiven, according to its placement within the Gestalt. It is clear that no single value (or its corresponding event) is very important but that the value mix is all-important.

Third, judgments are also confounded by the arbitrary nature of the school problem, and the arbitrary period of time given for solution; the faculty are consequently at some odds whether a presentation must show a precise solution or whether it must show that a solution is possible, given a longer solving time. I suspect that this too goes according to the Gestalt.

Fourth, in the judgmental process there is no explicit weighting of judgmental values. There is no explicit proportioning of importance among the many issues that architectural criticism addresses. As these several issues become better understood, and as more systematic criteria for criticism are organized, the process will very likely become more explicit. It can also suffer great harm; the nature of a Gestalt is that its sum is not equal to its parts.

At another level of concern one can ask what makes up the Gestalt in a jury presentation. There is usually no question in the minds of the students. Although the faculty like to say they are not influenced by the cleverness of a presentation, when I was in school all of us believed they were. They could not help it. Architects are trained in craftsmanship, and they respond to beautiful draftsmanship, to well-organized drawings, and to sensitively chosen colors and materials. All of us respond to showmanship in a presentation, to clear drawings and the well-presented drawn building, and to what our imaginations perceive that the building will be like in actuality. The Gestalt is undoubtedly composed of all these things. Students have always counted on their capability in one or the other of these areas to carry them through the jury (in my student class, one person made his reputation on meticulously detailed models, another on his painterly delineations, another on his technical capability in construction, another on his originality of building scheme, another on an extraordinarily severe presentation style, and so forth).

In each presentation a repetition of basic building schemes seems to occur. When a specific set of program requirements and constraints is given, only a limited number of basic building schemes will be chosen. When a large group of students all attempt to solve the same problem, they inevitably learn and take from each other. Their solutions then fall into a few basic patterns, and a good deal of the variation from one project to the next is in the treatment, even the superficial treatment, of details of the several building elements.

What then is being taught when any student who wishes can take over from another a scheme already worked out in its basic arrangements? Indeed some weaker students will always do so. What is being taught when after a time faculty criticism is not essential? Even if a good review is important for a good grade, a student soon learns he must not be too dependent on the criticism of the faculty. What is being taught when a student learns to evaluate his own work by comparing it with the work of other students? It would seem that in some ways faculty are not very important.

In studio instruction faculty are important, but not in the usual way of faculty in other disciplines. Students learn from architectural faculty what values the faculty hold. They learn what complexity of perception can be brought to architectural design. Students suffer from narrowly based faculty members, but they gain from faculty members who hold a broad view of the field. They learn how wide their own view of architecture can be.

Students learn most from the process itself. Solving architectural problems in interaction with other students, in a setting where architecture is an important concern of everyone, provides a learning atmosphere that only a very good faculty member can assist and that only a very bad faculty member can damage.

It is this learning that the rest of this book examines.

In saying how useful and important the studio instruction method is for teaching design, I do not also mean to say that the schools should be satisfied with exposing their students only to that process. Far from it. I believe strongly that architectural education must bring a great deal more information and method to the student than it has been bringing. I undertake this book to prepare a base to assist that process. Only when designers have truly understood what they have learned about design can they know how to relate other techniques and methods and a stronger information base to their process.

1.5 WHAT THE DESIGNER LEARNS IN SCHOOL

In school the designer learns about problem solving. He learns what many of the influences on problem solving are. He learns to engage in cooperative problem solving. He learns what architecture is about.

The student designer, in his experience of studio instruction and of both the informal and formal criticism process, learns a great deal about design and about problem solving. The learning occurs in a number of distinct areas.

First, the design student learns a great amount about the problem-solving process. He learns design in the same way that some people have supposedly learned to swim—by being thrown into the water. Learning design by being thrown into an ocean of design problems is certainly not a painless way to learn, but having learned, there is much the designer knows. Chapter 2 begins to examine what he knows.

Second, the design student learns a great amount about what things influence design solutions. He sees how different students produce different kinds of solutions and how different time limits affect the kind of solution a student is able to produce. In addition to learning how to design he learns what some of the influences on design are and can thus exert some control over the quality of solution he achieves. Chapter 3 states what some of these influences and controls are.

Third, the design student learns a great amount about cooperative problem solving. The social interactions he experiences in his first team problems are among the most intense in his school career. He learns some of the essential communication techniques required in any cooperative effort. If it is possible to say what some of these are, it may be possible to help the student take better advantage of what he has learned as he moves into practice. Cooperative problem solving is the subject of Chapter 4.

Fourth, in consequence of these other experiences the student learns what architecture is about. He is initiated into the architectural profession. He learns what questions the profession is willing to address and what questions it is willing to answer. He learns what questions, within a problem setting, the architectural profession believes must be answered. These matters are reviewed in Chapter 5.

Finally Chapter 6 summarizes the theoretical considerations developed in the other chapters and in the technical sections of those chapters.

The several design professions have undoubtedly failed to explore these subjects in any depth. In part no vocabulary that would make it possible for them to do so has been available. In part no urgency has impelled such an exploration. This urgency now exists, and a vocabulary is available.

Although the subject matter of this book is extended, it is also among the first extended efforts to unravel what the skills and techniques of the architectural design profession are. In attempting to do so, it assists in the development of a process of articulation that will permit the profession to see what some of its weaknesses are, but it will also permit it to say with conviction what are some of its very great strengths.

2. The Basic Solution Process

Whereas design is a holistic process that can be learned only by practice in design, still things can be said that will assist the designer in understanding how his process works. Since there is no scarcity of ideas in design, the emphasis in this discussion is on the development of judgment in the selection of ideas for application.

This chapter takes up the first of the topics I have just outlined—what the student designer learns about the solving process. It cannot consider the entire subject at once; the subject is too complex. As parts of the entire subject are discussed, the whole subject may be momentarily distorted.

Design is learned and practiced as a holistic procedure. No argument is possible with that fact. If the discussion needs to set that fact aside momentarily, I also do not want to forget the holistic nature of the design process.

To place the various sections of our discussion of the designer's solution process into context, the different sections are outlined in sequence below:

2.1 Kinds of Problems. Design problems are different from other formal problems. A design problem is what is usually called an ill-defined problem; there are no right or wrong answers in design, but only better or worse ones.

2.2 Kinds of Information. The factual information that accompanies the statement of a design problem is often weak and sometimes inaccurate. A substantial part of the information the designer uses is information based on the authority of the client for whom the designer works.

2.3 Forms of Information. The information with which the designer works can be organized into demand statements (which are to some degree negotiable) and supply statements (which are manipulatable). The design process is one of fitting supply with demand.

2.4 Forms of Notation. The designer uses different forms of notation to organize and understand the different kinds of information he uses. Some of his information is relatively abstract and other is relatively concrete. The forms of notation also vary in their abstractness and concreteness.

2.5 Transformation Processes. The information used in design occurs in an ends-means spectrum. The design process ordinarily transforms information in the direction of means for problem solution. A basic process used is "closure," the assumption or proposal of a means, for testing against some end.

2.6 Decomposition in Design. Usually the designer must decompose a problem statement into its parts to discover a solution. The process is not analysis-synthesis. It is analysis-proposal-analysis-fit.

2.7 Limitation and Factoring. As the designer moves across the information spectrum, more and more data are factored out of consideration. The designer assists this process of moving toward a solution by accepting and setting limits to the kinds and amounts of information he considers.

2.8 Products and Processes. The designer uses an imaging process to achieve an integration of his design effort. If the imaging process is to be useful to the designer, he must know how to get information into the process and how to get the mentally produced images out for further use.

The discussions of these topics will help the designer to understand how his process works. They may assist the process to some degree because they place some of the designer's processes in a more explicit form than he usually does. The discussions can help the student designer to understand the process he is going to use and might assist him to develop some skill in it sooner than he might otherwise do. But the discussions and the analytic processes they describe do not replace the design act. Nothing can be substituted for the development of a design proposal. The designer's imagination must supply the building proposals that are the essential features of any design process.

I say this from a design bias, because I believe my own principal orientation is as a designer. Because I have this orientation, I have always been surprised when theorists discussing design have been interested in the origination of design ideas and in how it is possible to stimulate more ideas. The difficulty seems to me to be, not in getting ideas, but in using good judgment in the selection of ideas for application.

All the discussions are from that point of view. I find as an experienced designer that ideas come easily; what is hard is knowing which ones to select for development. If this should seem to be an unfair bias to a beginning design student, for whom ideas do not come easily at all, I urge that he keep working. As he develops techniques for working in design, he will find that ideas come more and more easily.

If he learns how to make his problem information available for his mind to use, the ideas will come. If he also learns how to get those ideas onto paper for examination, he will be on his way toward being an experienced designer and will not be troubled by a scarcity of design ideas.

2.1 PROBLEM TYPES AND SOLUTION PROCEDURES

A design problem is an ill-defined problem; there are no right or wrong answers in design but only better or worse ones.

When the student first enters an architectural school, he soon discovers that design problems are different from most other formal problems he has faced. If he tries to find out from an instructor what things are "right" and what are "wrong," he is usually not able to do so. There are no right and wrong answers, because architectural problems cannot be phrased so precisely that only a single design or even a limited group of designs are proper solutions to any stated problem. Instead the architectural problem is so loosely stated (even with a well-detailed building program) that many solutions are possible.

2.1.1 Well-Defined and Ill-Defined Problems

In the problem-solving literature a problem that has criteria for identifying a proper solution is called well defined; one without such criteria is called ill defined.

In the problem-solving literature a problem with a proper answer (i.e., an answer identifiable as correct) is called well defined. One without criteria for saying whether a solution is correct is called ill defined. By this definition the architectural design problem is ill defined.

Some students have immediate difficulty with the notion that such problems exist. This is a very first hurdle, one that exists in any field where inventive or creative work is required. In an architectural problem so many decisions must be made in achieving a solution that learning what is "right" would be impossible.

I remember a student who had enormous difficulty because he knew all too well what was correct to do and what was not. Having spent some of his early years in the building trades, he knew in great detail how buildings are put together. He could not free himself from the issue of what was possible (in some particular context) to ask the larger and prior question of what was important. When a student finally realizes that anything (almost anything) is possible—for a cost—then he can set aside, for the time being, those limiting practical concerns to focus on issues of need and purpose. He can comfort himself with the realization that he will not be able to execute the impossible, even if he tries.

2.1.2 Solution Procedures: Algorithms and Heuristics

A problem-solving procedure that always produces a solution is called an algorithm; one that might or might not produce a solution is called a heuristic.

With different kinds of problems, then, there are also different solution processes useful in dealing with each kind. The problem-solving literature calls the process known to produce a solution each time it is applied an *algorithm*. It calls the process that might or might not produce a solution a *heuristic*.

2.1.3 The Strength and Applicability of Procedures

Heuristics can be ranked by their heuristic power; a strong heuristic is likely to produce a solution but is narrow in its application; a weak heuristic is less likely to produce a solution but is broader in its application to different problems.

If a very large group of problem-solving methods is considered, it is possible to think of each as placed along a scale stated in terms of *heuristic power*. A "strong" method is guaranteed to produce a solution and is like an algorithm. A "weak" method is not guaranteed to produce a solution and is what was earlier called a heuristic. At first glance it might seem that strong methods are always preferable to weak; as it turns out strong methods are applicable only in specific, limited circumstances, but weak methods can be applied very broadly in very diverse situations.

Most design problems require the use of both methods. They require the use of strong methods like addition, subtraction, and other mathematical techniques. They require the use of weaker methods like checking program data for consistency and defining the group of objects that will fulfill a specific required function. They require the use of very weak methods, indeed, like sketching the form of a room to provide a required space.

2.1.4 Time Placement in Problem Definition

Problems can be separated into research, management, and action problems according to the location of present reality within the problem structure.

Problems can also be separated into research, management, and action problems. On the whole, research problems are concerned with past, management problems with present, and action problems with future events. Design problems are a special form of action problem, but I leave until later a fuller discussion of this characteristic of design problems.

2.1.5 The Technical Discussions

In the several technical discussions that follow further detail is developed on the algorithm, the heuristic, and the heuristic power of different methods.

2.1.5.1 Algoriths and Formulas

A formula is a concise expression of one form of algorithm.

The set form of an algorithm is valuable not only because it guarantees a problem solution (Hunt, 1962, p. 198), but also because it is a basic model for a data transformation process (Lindsay and Norman, 1972, p. 513). A *formula* is a basic form of the algorithm.

In essence a formula displays a specific relation between known data and unknown but desired data. Function notation expresses this relationship, but a problem statement form that emphasizes the separate components of the algorithm (the known data, the set of transformations, and the unknown data) can also be used. The form below, though used here to represent an algorithm, is broadly applicable to many different problem-solving processes. The form is $A \Rightarrow B$, where A represents the known data, $\Rightarrow$ (pronounced "arrow") represents the transformation processes used in the algorithm, and B represents the unknown data.

The simple form of the algorithm is the form toward which all problem-solving processes aspire (Wehrli, 1968, p. 7). The algorithm guarantees a result. If the appropriate data and the appropriate process are known, an answer is sure. When the two terms are fully known, the problem is well defined. Even when the terms in a problem statement are not well defined, when the problem is ill defined, algorithms are required in its solution. Even though the overall solution process is heuristic, it is composed of a number of simple algorithmic segments that can be chained together to form the larger heuristic process.

An exact parallel exists between known, established behavior sequences that produce specific results (these can be thought of as structured sequences) and the algorithm. A parallel exists between open or nonpurposive behaviors (which are unstructured, but which invariably have short structured sequences in them) and heuristic processes.

The application of an algorithm has a specific, invariable sequence of steps:

1. Abstract. Identify the abstract property of the data that is capable of transformation.

2. Associate. Search memory for appropriate transformation processes (Newell, 1969, pp. 367-369).

3. Encode. Substitute conceptually equivalent form of data required for transformation (Eastman, 1970, p. 149).

4. Transform. Apply transformation processes (Craik, 1943, p. 50).

5. Decode. Substitute conceptually equivalent form of data desired.

6. Associate. Confirm success of transformation.

7. Display. Display the data in its desired form as a problem solution or as data for use in a sequel step.

Usually the algorithm is thought of as consisting of only step 4, that is, of the actual transformation processes used on the data. Nonetheless the use of such processes in the algorithm are always preceded and succeeded by the other steps listed here. For example, let us look at a simple problem.

A builder is thinking of purchasing a rectangular piece of land, but even though he likes its location and character, he needs to know its dimensions. Unfortunately the land salesman has a record of only the acreage, 1.73 acres. The builder can see the monuments that mark the lot corners along the road, and he has a steel measuring tape, but the depth of the lot away from the road cannot be measured because of a thick woods. How can he determine the depth of the lot?

The problem is, of course, trivial. He must measure the length along the road and divide that into the acreage measurement. But consider the steps that he must take by following the procedure outlined above:

1. Clearly the abstract property he must deal with is dimension, in two forms: linear and area measurement.

2. From memory he knows that when he has an area and can obtain the linear dimension of one side, the other side can be obtained by a division algorithm.

3. Division and other mathematical algorithms work properly only when the units of measurement are common units. He must convert the acreage measurement into units compatible with the units on his steel tape. If his tape measures in feet, then he must convert the acreage measurement to a square-foot measurement.

4. Having obtained the two compatible units, he performs the division procedure and obtains the other linear measurement of the lot in feet.

5. He might need that information in some other form. If so, he performs that conversion. He converts the data into some other conceptually equivalent form useful for his purposes.

6. He should confirm that the transformation has provided the data in the form he desired and that the transformation has been accurate.

7. Having confirmed the success of his transformation, he can display his length measurement of the depth of the lot and use it for whatever purpose he requires. He can confirm whether the lot is deep enough for his purposes.

REFERENCES

Craik, Kenneth J. W., *The Nature of Explanation,* Cambridge University Press, Cambridge, England, 1943.

Eastman, Charles M., "Problem Solving Strategies in Design," in Sanoff, Henry, and S. Cohn, Eds., *EDRA 1: Proceedings of the First Annual Environmental Design Research Association Conference, no publisher named,* 1970.

Hunt, Earl B., *Concept Learning,* Wiley, New York, 1962.

Lindsay, Peter H., and D. A. Norman, *Human Information Processing,* Academic, New York, 1972.

Newell, Allen, "Heuristic Programming: Ill-Structured Problems," in Aronofsky, Julius S., Ed., *Progress in Operations Research,* Vol. 3, Wiley, New York, 1969.

Wehrli, Robert, "Open-Ended Problem Solving in Design," unpublished doctoral dissertation, University of Utah, Salt Lake City, 1968.

2.1.5.2 Heuristics and Meta-Heuristics

Not only is there a heuristic spectrum from strong to weak, but there is also a spectrum from heuristic into metaheuristic.

According to George Polya (1957, p. 113), who aroused a new interest in heuristic procedures by his work in mathematics, "Heuristic reasoning is reasoning not regarded as final and strict but as provisional and plausible only, whose purpose is to discover the solution of the present problem." A heuristic procedure, then, is one that will help to discover a problem solution, and a heuristic is a problem-solving strategy. Lindsay and Norman (1972, p. 513), in discussing Polya's work, indicate that, whereas an algorithm is a procedure that will guarantee a result, a heuristic is more analogous to a rule of thumb; it does not guarantee success.

Among the basic distinctions between different problem-solving procedures are (1) the general applicability of a procedure and (2) the power a procedure has in generating a solution within acceptable time and cost limits. If the problem solver has endless time, patience, and resources, then the simplest of procedures (e.g., examining every possible solution in turn) becomes an algorithm that guarantees eventual success.

For this discussion, however, examining heuristic procedures as a rule-of-thumb approach to problem solving is more helpful. In examining rules that can assist problem solving, there are four useful levels of generality:

1. Rules that apply to a particular kind of problem.

2. Rules that apply to any kind of problem at all.

3. Metarules, that is, rules that apply to the application of rules.

4. Encompassing rules that are universally applicable.

An example of rules that apply to a particular kind of problem are those listed by Wilson (1952, pp. 140-144) in his text on scientific research. In treating *search* (not the procedure that has come to be called "heuristic search" but *search* as in "looking for something"), Wilson lists fourteen rules that should make a search procedure easier and more sure:

1. Know as much as possible about the object of search.

2. Prove that the object exists in the area to be searched.

3. Use the most efficient method of detection.

4. Be sure that you will see the object when you encounter it.

5. Be sure that you will not see the object when it is not there.

6. Search systematically instead of haphazardly.

7. If possible devise a way to determine the approximate location of the object during the search.

8. Convert a two-dimensional area of search to a one-dimensional path.

9. If possible mark the starting point and record the path of search.

10. Use a convergent procedure.

11. Search the most probable place first.

12. Distribute available search time, facilities, and effort in reasonable proportions.

13. Take into account the probability of missing the object.

14. Consider any effect of the search on the search object.

By contrast an organized group of rules by Polya, although intended for mathematical problem solving, is phrased generally enough to be able to apply to most kinds of problems; there are a number of points of correspondence with Wilson's search rules. The first can be seen by noting Polya's broad categories under which his rules are grouped (1957, pp. xvi-xvii):

1. Understanding the problem.
2. Devising a plan.
3. Carrying out the plan.
4. Looking back.

Very clearly Wilson's first five rules are concerned with understanding the problem of a search. Equally clearly the remainder of his rules are concerned with devising a plan of action.

A second correspondence can be seen: Polya's rules under his first broad heading, understanding the problem, has a close correspondence, albeit in a more general form of statement, with several of the rules Wilson has listed. Polya's rules and questions under his first heading are:

1. What is the unknown? What are the data? What is the condition?
2. Is it possible to satisfy the condition?
3. Is the condition sufficient to determine the unknown? Or is it insufficient? Or redundant? Or contradictory?
4. Draw a figure. Introduce suitable notation.
5. Separate the various parts of the condition. Can you write them down?

In a similar manner, there are rules and questions under Polya's second heading, devising a plan, that are equivalent with the more particular rules Wilson recites that are concerned with devising a plan for a search.

Polya also provides, in another place, a set of metarules that he lists under the heading rules of preference. By listing these rules, he attempts to provide guidance in the selection of procedures. He attempts to answer a basic question: among all the possible things available to a problem solver, which things should be of dominant concern, and which should he try first? Polya's metarules begin (1965, pp. 96-97):

1. The less difficult precedes the more difficult.
2. The more familiar precedes the less familiar.
3. An item having more points in common with the problem precedes an item having less.
4. The whole precedes the parts, the principal parts precede the other parts, less remote parts precede more remote parts.

In an entirely separate effort to develop problem-solving computer programs a number of researchers have attempted to develop even stronger, more incisive rules that are completely general in their application. M. L. Minsky (1956, pp. III-13-III-14) suggests that Solomonoff has noticed one of the most general methods of problem solving, the tendency of problem solvers to use and adapt methods and materials from the past (by contrast Newell [1969, p. 377] describes *generate and test* as the most encompassing heuristic, but this simply emphasizes a different general characteristic of problem-solving processes). Techniques that have been successful in solving problems are combined to form new trial techniques. In consequence Minsky suggests, "Given a certain collection of patterns, find a collection of smaller sub-patterns which help to efficiently describe the larger set. Then, if a new pattern is required, an efficient way to construct trial patterns . . . is . . . by combining in some way sets of the sub-patterns which have been useful in the past." Although Minsky was writing about computer use, there is no reason to suppose that such an approach would not apply equally in noncomputerized problem solving. That approach would simply be a more formal and self-aware development of procedures used for many years in the past.

Having followed a development of heuristic procedures from those pertaining to a specific kind of problem, to those pertaining broadly to any kind of problem, to a set of metarules for the application of procedures, and finally to completely general heuristic rules, it is possible to notice that these occupy a spectrum from the more specific and narrowly applicable to the more general and broadly applicable.

With this as background it is also possible to examine problem-solving procedures in disciplinary areas where problem solving is a major preoccupation and is formally organized; it will be useful to see what characteristics the different processes share. Three disciplinary areas can be examined: scientific research, managerial decision, and environmental planning and design. In each, complex and lengthy procedures are recorded by which typical pertinent problems can be solved. In each area the procedures are heuristic, since full information for problem solution is not typically available.

It will be useful to look at only the broad outlines of each procedure. They follow generally the outline proposed by Polya:

A. Scientific Research (Ackoff, Gupta, and Minas, 1962, p. 25)
   1. Observation
   2. Generalization
   3. Experimentation

. . . more sophisticated philosophical analysis has shown that observation always presupposes a criterion of relevance, and this criterion, in turn, always involves some theory. . . .

B. Social Science Research (Bruyn, 1966, pp. 268-269)
   1. Aim
   2. Method
      a discovery
      b description
      c explanation
   3. Procedures

C. Applied Research (Ackoff et al., 1962, p. 26)
   1. Formulating the problem
   2. Constructing the model
   3. Testing the model
   4. Deriving a solution from the model
   5. Testing and controlling the solution
   6. Implementing the solution

D. Production Design (Nadler, 2967, p. 36)
   1. Determining the function
   2. Developing the ideal system
   3. Gathering information
   4. Suggesting alternatives
   5. Selecting a solution
   6. Formulating the system
   7. Reviewing the system
   8. Testing the system
   9. Installing the system
   10. Measuring and controlling performance

E. Design (Murtha, 1973, p. 37)
   1. Defining the problem

2. Gathering data
3. Developing the preliminary solution
4. Detailing the solution
5. Evaluating the solution

That these examples of established problem-solving procedure are not restricted to disciplines that have a formalized approach to problem-solving can be seen by looking at even such a discipline as writing—remote, at least in some of its parts, from a formalized approach to problem solving. A well-regarded if somewhat elderly text in the field (Brooks and Warren, 1958, pp. 47, 99, 133, 142, 243-246) describes procedures for each of the kinds of writing the text defines: exposition, argument, description, and narration.

Since it is clear from the review above that there is an extremely wide range of different heuristic procedures with different ranges of applicability, it is useful to modify the original notion of heuristic as being simply a rule-of-thumb approach to problem solving. To do so, consider the comments by Walter Reitman in his study of the ill-defined problem, which are entirely appropriate here, for heuristic procedures are concerned with ill-defined problems. According to Reitman the largest percentage of human energies is devoted to problems that fail to meet the criterion of a well-defined problem (some systematic way of deciding when a proposed solution is acceptable). Without question all the procedures outlined above were concerned with ill-defined problems (Reitman, 1964, pp. 282-283).

Matters are not so simple, Reitman holds, that problems can be divided easily into the well defined and the ill defined, so that algorithms can be used to solve the one, and heuristics to solve the other. Instead there is a continuum of problems that range from well to ill defined; such definedness is not a simple attribute (Reitman, 1964, pp. 300-303). Since this is so, there is an aptness in speaking of the algorithmic properties of procedures and the heuristic power that a procedure has (here again the discussion is of computer programs, but the application of the discussion need not be restricted to computers). The degree of problem structure (between well defined and ill defined) can be defined by reference to the heuristic power of the procedure used in solution (Newell, 1969, p. 365).

REFERENCES

Ackoff, Russell L., S. K. Gupta, and J. S. Minas, *Scientific Method: Optimizing Applied Research Decisions,* Wiley, New York, 1962.

Brooks, Cleanth, and R. P. Warren, *Modern Rhetoric,* Harcourt Brace & World, New York, 1958.

REFERENCES

Bruyn, Severyn T., *The Human Perspective in Sociology,* Prentice-Hall, Englewood Cliffs, N.J., 1966.

Lindsay, Peter H., and D. A. Norman, *Human Information Processing,* Academic, New York, 1972.

Minsky, M. L., "Heuristic Aspects of the Artificial Intelligence Problem," M.I.T. Lincoln Laboratory, Lexington, Mass., December 17, 1956.

Murtha, Donald M., "A Comparison of Problem-Solving Approaches Used by Environmental Designers," unpublished doctoral dissertation, University of Wisconsin, Madison, 1973.

Nadler, Gerald, *Work Systems Design: The IDEALS Concept,* Richard D. Irwin, Homewood, Ill., 1967.

Newell, Allen, "Heuristic Programming: Ill-Structured Problems," in Aronofsky, Julius S., Ed., *Progress in Operations Research*, Vol. 3, Wiley, New York, 1969.

Polya, George, *How to Solve It,* Doubleday, Garden City, N.Y., 1957.

Polya, George, *Mathematical Discovery,* Vol. 2, Wiley, New York, 1965.

Reitman, Walter R., "Heuristic Decision Procedures, Open Constraints, and the Structure of Ill-Defined Problems," in Shelly, Maynard W., II, and G. L. Bryant, Eds., *Human Judgments and Optimality,* Wiley, New York, 1964.

Wilson, J. Bright, Jr., *An Introduction to Scientific Research,* McGraw-Hill, New York, 1952.

2.1.5.3 Limitations in Using Solution Procedures

A problem is ill defined if the heuristic power of the methods applicable to the problem lies below a certain threshold.

Both Allen Newell and Walter Reitman (Newell, 1969, pp. 366-367) have commented on the difficulty in analyzing and defining the ill-defined problem; apparently the typical ill-defined problem has less information in its statement than a well-defined problem has, and for this reason it also has less explicit criteria for determining when a solution has been achieved. The question raised, however, is whether the analysis of the forms that such problems take and the development of heuristic procedures for undertaking solutions convert them into well-defined problems. Clearly they do not. Determining what is missing in information and what the effect of this missing information might be has never been known, in itself, to supply the information lack. Defining an ill-defined structure is not another paradox to be resolved by Russell's theory of types (Kasner and Newman, 1956, pp. 1950-1953).

Walter Reitman has commented that the majority of human problem-solving effort is concerned with ill-defined problems. This fits exactly with a comment by Newell (1969, pp. 403-404) that, upon examining human problem solvers in their work on ill-structured problems, "There is less solid evidence on what methods people use than on the general absence of strong methods." (A strong method is one that is algorithmic—that has the power to deliver a solution.) In the real-world situation there are no strong methods. Any solution process presently known requires a representation of some formal aspect of a situation. Any optimization process is with respect to the formal representation of the situation and not of the situation itself (Shepard, 1964, pp. 261-262).

2.1.5.3

A collection of subpatterns derived from earlier patterns (Minsky, 1956, pp. 111-113 ff.) may well be the closest we can come to strong methods; the strong method might have to be restricted to limited, formally representable segments of the total problem situation. With these several factors in mind it is easy to appreciate Newell's ill-structured problem hypothesis: *A problem solver finds a problem ill-structured if the power of his methods that are applicable to the problem lies below a certain threshold* (1969, p. 375). If his methods do not guarantee a solution, then his problem is, perforce, ill defined.

It is worthwhile to follow Newell on this theme for some paragraphs further. He speaks not only of the power of a method but also of its generality (1969, pp. 371-373), its value (the quality of solution it produces), and the amount of resource use the method requires. Since an ultimate concern must be with efficacy, the selection of a method must involve a trade-off between, on the one hand, the power, generality, and value of a method and, on the other hand, its time costs, social costs, and monetary or other expendable-resource costs.

Finally Newell notes the inverse relationship between the power of a method and its generality. It seems intuitively clear that the broader the class of situations to which a method can be applied, the less specific and clear its operation can be, and therefore the less likely the method is to generate a solution. Whereas the method of addition (for example) can be applied only to the situation where the sum of two numbers is desired, it is a powerful method, indeed, and a solution is assured; by extreme contrast the general injunction, "Do something!", though applicable to an enormous number of problem situations, is an extraordinarily weak method. By considering this inverse relationship, Newell (1969, pp. 375, 394) makes the point that there is a full continuum of methods from extremely strong to extremely weak, and recognition of this fact demonstrates a relationship between problem approaches of differing kinds.

Arguing so broadly as this, it is easy for him to make the point that the hard mathematical core of management science can find its place in the solution of ill-structured problems (Newell, 1969, pp. 412-413). But that is simply arguing that highly structured segments can occur in highly unstructured sequences. It is like arguing that, among all the relatively organized but unpredictable movements a bride will make on her wedding day, it is possible to predict quite accurately, when the time of the ceremony approaches, what her attire, her route, her movements, her words, and even some of her emotions will be.

Such a harsh analogy might be overly ironic and cynical; after all, being able to predict the bride's movements is extremely useful and important to those involved so that they can schedule other events around so important an element in her wedding day. Newell has reinforced Shepard's reminder (1964, pp. 261-262) that a representation used for prediction only predicts the outcome of the representation, not of the real-world circumstance from which the representation was abstracted. It would not be possible, for example, to predict whether or not the bride will sneeze or trip on the carpet.

The first strong organizational efforts dealing with ill-structured problems have only recently been made. There is very far to go. Even as procedures and methods for solving ill-defined problems are developed, the information base is very weak when it has to be cast into a form other than that of personal knowledge. My suspicion is that handling the information for problem solution will be more difficult than finding the methods by which problems can be solved.

Within design-oriented problem solving the strongest methodological approach using explicit decision variables and other quantitative measures has been that of L. Bruce Archer (1968, Section 11.11). Yet his statement of method that encompasses the range of situations pertinent to design is so abstract it is difficult for the designer (more used to dealing with the concrete material of the world) to relate his multiple interests to its highly generalized statements. If, by converting those many different considerations into a single scale and language, he can place them into interaction, how can they be got back out again?

Gordon Best (1969, p. 149) makes the precise point. After commenting at length on the difficulty a researcher had in identifying when and how a decision got made in a firm of designers and on his discovery that the decision, after being made, was sometimes not followed; and after asking what the methodologist's decision variables had to do with such a process, Best comments: "Real situations are variable and idiosyncratic; professional and conceptual simplifications of these situations seem necessary because their variety cannot be understood in a definitive sense. The resulting simplifications while apparently clear, are unrealistic; they restrict, destroy, and ignore natural variety." (1969, p. 149.)

Rather than deny the usefulness of a methodological approach to ill-defined problems, we must next find ways to make the methods responsive to the variety in the situation. If a proposed method does not respond with an adequate specificity to a problem situation, it will not then produce an adequate solution.

REFERENCES

Archer, L. Bruce, *The Structure of Design Processes*, U.S. Dept. of Commerce, National Bureau of Standards, Gaithersburg, Md., 1968.

Best, Gordon, "Method and Intention in Architectural Design," in Broadbent, Geoffrey, and A. Ward, Eds., *Design Methods in Architecture, Symposium, Portsmouth School of Architecture,* Architect's Association Paper No. 4, London, 1969.

ARCHITECTURE, PROBLEMS AND PURPOSES

Kasner, Edward, and J. R. Newman, "Paradox Lost and Paradox Regained," in Newman, James R., Ed., *The World of Mathematics,,* Vol. 3, Simon and Schuster, New York, 1956.

Minsky, M. L., *Heuristic Aspects of the Artificial Intelligence Problem,* M. I. T. Lincoln Laboratory, Lexington, Mass., 1956.

Newell, Allen, "Heuristic Programming: III-Structured Problems," in Aronofsky, Julius S., Ed., *Progress in Operations Research,* Vol. 3, Wiley, New York, 1969.

Shepard, Roger N., "On Subjectively Optimum Selection Among Multiattribute Alternatives," in Shelly, Maynard W., II, and Glenn L. Bryan, Eds., *Human Judgments and Optimality,* Wiley, New York, 1964.

2.2 THE CHARACTERISTICS OF PROBLEM INFORMATION

The factual information in the statement of a design problem by a client is often weak and sometimes inaccurate. Despite this, the information provided by the client is "authoritative."

If a problem solution is to be successful, the student must know where to start, what kind of information to bring to the solution process, how much information to seek, and he must have some criteria for determining which information is acceptable and useful in problem solution and which is not.

2.2.1 Circularity Between Problems and Solutions

A problem statement has in it the seed of its solution; the statement of a design problem supposes that the problem solution is a designed object.

One of the great difficulties in architectural design is that a statement of a design problem already supposes that the solution is a building. Sometimes a client's problem is of such a kind that a building, a change in the physical environment, might not be a best solution. Trade-offs can be considered. A university does not have to build new classrooms to provide for more students; it can schedule the use of its present rooms over a longer period during the day. When a clear need is apparent for some physical change in the client's environment, it is not always the change that the client has identified.

This last point can be illustrated by a story that Russell Ackoff has told. A building owner demanded that the elevator service in his office building be improved. He had nearly constant complaints that it was too slow. When the consultants (architects or operations researchers) discovered that the elevators would be nearly impossible to modify, they began to examine alternatives. They learned that actual waiting time for the elevators was incredibly short and concluded that the character of the lobby was the problem. In short they solved the problem by placing mirrors in the lobby to provide entertainment for persons waiting for the elevator. The complaints dropped to zero.

The point is not that people are vain but that the problem that had produced complaints had been misperceived.

At what point then should the designer accept the client's description of a problem as legitimate, and at what point should he explore beyond the information provided by the client? At what point should he accept the client's view that a building is the proper solution to his problem, and at what point should he expand the problem to thinking of other possibilities?

Part of the designer's difficulty is the circularity of problem statement and solution. A problem statement almost always has in it the seeds of its solution. How else could the problem solver know where to start?

The design student faces another difficulty as well. Often he cannot question whether a building is a proper solution to the stated problem; indeed he is not solving the problem to have a solution; instead he is doing so to experience solving the problem in a particular way. With some practice at not questioning whether a building is a proper solution he can forget ever to raise that possibility and become an "expert" designer. The profession reinforces this direction because of the manner in which it charges for its services. It charges a commission for the design of buildings; it is not in the habit of charging for consulting on whether a building ought to be built (although there are some indications that this situation is changing).

It is just as though a physician were paid a fee only when he determined that an operation is the proper cure for a patient's illness and then performed the operation. Undoubtedly the physician would tend to perform a good number of operations.

2.2.2 The "Softness" of Problem Information

Persons are more adaptable than the objects designed for their use. Behavior is strongly conditioned by the objects that are part of the behavior setting. It is thus difficult to determine the effectiveness of objects for problem solution.

When a student discovers there are no right or wrong answers, he also discovers that the information available to the designer is very soft. It must not be examined very closely, because it might turn out to be incorrect. This is so because the kind of questions the designer asks has to do with whether objects are suitable for human use and behavior or whether a particular kind of behavior will accomplish a client's purposes.

There are no hard answers to these questions, because designers have not known how to ask appropriate questions (with the help of the behavioral sciences they are probably getting better at it, but they still have some way to go). How indeed can a designer answer a question about the usefulness of an object in assisting behavior when the behavior in question is adaptable to the character of the object to be used? A person can engage in almost any kind of behavior in almost any place; the design of the place simply helps that behavior to be better or worse, easier or harder. To understand this, think that a person could play a game of basketball in a bathroom (not a very good game of basketball) and that he could do in a basketball court what he ordinarily does in a bathroom (with some inconvenience).

Think also that a person's behavior is not independent of the objects designed for him but instead that his behavior is conditioned by those objects. I once decided that light switches would look better if moved down from their usual height to match the height of door knobs. When I tried, on entering the building at dusk, to locate a light switch, I could not do so. I was feeling for them at their usual height; my muscles had not learned their new height location.

Not only do people become accustomed to familiar qualities of buildings, but they also grow to prefer them. After students have learned to work in small rooms, they object to moving to larger ones; after they have learned to work in those larger rooms, they object to smaller ones.

It is difficult to discover how broadly applicable any information is. If it is about a person's behavior, does it apply only to the single person, can it be applied only to a specific group in a specific place at a specific time, or is it applicable to all persons everywhere? Information about the quality of design information has not been available.

Even when information is very carefully derived, it is still place dependent. The behavior of a person in one architectural setting does not predict how he will behave when placed in a differently configured setting, even if it has exactly equivalent functions.

Too often the student is expected to learn how people behave in the kind of building he is being asked to design by observing people in an existing building of the same kind. Observations of this kind can be helpful, but the student must learn that they are not conclusive.

When the factual information runs out, a need often arises to provide further information for design. Such information can then come only from an authority on that kind of building. In practice that authority is usually the client (sometimes in the person of a consulting specialist the client has employed). In a school problem it is sometimes a mock client, an individual associated with the kind of institution the students are designing for, by preference someone who has had the experience of being an actual client during a building project for his institution.

I remember an incident when a group of students was being conducted through an apartment housing project by the architect for the project. The students were about to design a similar project, and much emphasis had been placed by the faculty on solar orientation. What then were the students to think of this project when the four apartments on each floor faced north, south, east, and west? When a student asked what had been decided about solar orientation, the architect responded they had decided "To hell with it!". Evidently the authority of the client had determined that solar orientation was not a critical factor for him and his tenants.

2.2.3 The Technical Discussions

The discussions that follow go into considerably more detail about information circularity, the criteria by which information is brought to bear in problem solution, the basis for factual information, and the basis for authoritative information.

2.2.3.1 The Importance of Information Circularity

Although concealed circularity in argument is not helpful, circularity in investigation and in problem solution is unavoidable.

In any individual segment of the design process (indeed of any problem-solving process) the information input is of two kinds: demand and supply information. The typical demand information is probably of a firmer sort than the typical supply information, but this might only seem to be true. It seems true because it is usual to secure demand information from an authority of the best sort—the design client.

Churchman (1961, p. 100) defines "information" as "recorded experience which is useful for decision making." Churchman recognizes, of course, the difficulty in such a definition and notes the subjectiveness of information; for him information utility is directly related to the context and to the persons making decisions in that context. But the difficulty of his definition is, of course, that it is circular in its application. How can the decision-maker know what information is useful until he knows what information is useful? Circularity, contrary to the dictates of logic, is not bad in itself; it is simply not very useful when it forms an identity relationship in deductive logic; in other situations it is useful and is, in fact, essential. Evaluation, for example, is circular with classification (Peltz, 1971). Induction is circular with instance listing; definition is often circular with other definition (Ackoff, 1962, pp. 170-171); synthesis is circular with decision; and, most important for our present discussion, *information is circular with question framing.*

A question cannot be framed without some knowledge about the information desired. In part one must know the answer to ask the question. "The Baconian fallacy," writes David Fischer (1970, p. 4), "consists in the idea that a historian [and I must add, any other investigator] can operate without the aid of preconceived questions, hypotheses, ideas, . . . etc . . . ." Russell Ackoff (1962, p. 25), in discussing scientific method, says essentially the same, "The empirical tradition asserts the primacy of observation in science, but more sophisticated philosophical analysis has shown that observation always presupposes a criterion of relevance, and this criterion, in turn, always involves some theory." If the questioner's information is poor or partial, then his question may be badly framed; the information the first badly framed question generates may permit a better framed question, which in turn can generate better information. Lazarsfeld

2.2.3.1

(1972, p. 235) describes an iterative sequence of whole-part-whole-part that produces a simiiar result.

George Homans addresses a similar problem in a somewhat different form when he notes the difficulty associated with the description of any fairly complex situation (Homans, 1950, pp. 91-93). "The point that we want to make is that although these operations in fact take place in a continuing cycle, we must nevertheless, language being what it is, describe them as if they took place in a sequence having a beginning and an end. Therefore we must assume a certain state of affairs at the beginning of our exposition, the existence of which we can account for only at the end."

If I have noted that a certain circularity exists within a number of mental processes, I do not also mean by this notice to support the form of circularity in argument known as "begging the question." Begging the question assumes (in a hidden fashion) in the premises of an argument what the arguer pretends to prove in the course of his argument (Harvard, 1946, pp. 64-65). The distinction between legitimate and illegitimate circularity is between the intellectual honesty that exists when precedent information is used openly to frame a question and the intellectual dishonesty that conceals the existence of the prior information and fails to advance the amount or degree of information by the argument or questioning process. A definition of the word *gravitation* in *The Devil's Dictionary* (Bierce, no date, p. 78) scoffs at circularity of the illegitimate kind in science:

Gravitation, *n.* The tendency of all bodies to approach one another with a strength proportioned to the quantity of matter they contain—the quantity of matter they contain being ascertained by the strength of their tendency to approach one another. This is a lovely and edifying illustration of how science, having made A the proof of B, makes B the proof of A.

REFERENCES

Ackoff, Russell L., *Scientific Method: Optimizing Applied Research Decisions,* Wiley, New York, 1962.

Bierce, Ambrose, *The Devil's Dictionary,* Doubleday, Garden City, N.Y., no date.

Churchman, C. West, *Prediction and Optimal Decision,* Prentice-Hall, Englewood Cliffs, N.J., 1961.

Harvard (no author named), *Handbook for English A,* Harvard University Press, Cambridge, Mass., 1946.

Fischer, David Hackett, *Historian's Fallacies: Toward a Logic of Historical Thought,* Harper & Row, New York, 1970.

Homans, George C., *The Human Group,* Harcourt Brace, New York, 1950.

Lazarsfeld, Paul F., *Quantitative Analysis,* Allyn & Bacon, Boston, 1972.

Peltz, Richard, "Classification and Evaluation in Aesthetics: Weitz and Aristotle," *The Journal of Aesthetics and Art Criticism,* **30**(1), 1971.

2.2.3.2 The Abstractness of Problem Statement

The information useful for problem solution is an abstraction from the problem situation; the collection of information is controlled by its usefulness and by its cost.

When dealing with any substantial amount of raw data in problem solving, the designer must find some reasonable preliminary classification he can use to develop hypotheses (Lazarsfeld, 1972, pp. 226-227). There is little question that a retention of detail by some form of coding is an automatic mental process (Koestler, 1967, pp. 539-541); for any coding to be pertinent to deliberate problem-solving activities, it must become self-conscious and external, as well as subconscious and internal. Such a concern for and recognition of the need for coding of information require a review of classification.

Even before the designer is involved with the detail of classification, what is the information he must classify? Even if the designer has framed a set of basic questions or made a set of basic assumptions, how can he determine what information is needed to answer his questions? How can he know what information is needed to provide the demand and supply information for his solution? What information is pertinent? Indeed what determines the threshold of information *necessary* for attack on the problem, and what determines the limits of information *sufficient* for solution?

Of course, no exact answers are evident; there are only guides. One interesting set is provided by Homans (1950, pp. 16-17) as he identifies a set of rules for theory building, condensed below:

1. Look first at the obvious, the familiar, or the common.
2. State the obvious in its full generality.
3. Talk about one thing at a time.
4. Cut down as far as you dare the number of things you are talking about.
5. Once you have started to talk, do not stop until you are finished.
6. Recognize that your analysis must be abstract.

Homan's complete statement of his sixth rule is worth quoting exactly.

(6) Recognize that your analysis must be abstract, because it deals with only a few elements of the concrete situation. Admit the dangers of abstraction, especially when action is required, but do not be afraid of abstraction.

A very similar thought is expressed by K. J. W. Craik when he says (1943, p. 117):

. . . an explanation is not an explanation at all if it requires as many formulae as there are phenomena; the very essence of explanation is generalization.

Both writers make the point that the process of developing information is one of abstracting or generalizing from the immense data of experience and pulling from those data the important information. Jevons (1958, pp. 677-678) notes, in his *Principles of Science* published in 1873, that many different modes of classification exist and

2.2.3.2

that the only criterion for excellence is whether the classification scheme serves the classifier's purposes.

Still how much information is enough? Apparently several basic tests of information are based on pertinence to purpose:

1. A Test of Use. Must the designer have the information to make a decision? How detailed must it be? Or from past experience does he know that the information is not truly essential?

2. A Test of Redundancy. Does the designer have the information already? Is it repetitious? Is he not finding any new information in his search?

3. A Test of Cost. How badly does the designer need the information? How much does it cost to obtain by comparison with other information and by comparison with other things he needs?

REFERENCES

Craik, Kenneth J. W., *The Nature of Explanation,* Cambridge University Press, Cambridge, England, 1943.

Homans, George C., *The Human Group,* Harcourt Brace, New York, 1950.

Jevons, W. Stanley, *The Principles of Science: A Treatise on Logic and Scientific Method*, Dover, New York, 1958.

Koestler, Arthur, *The Act of Creation,* Dell, New York, 1967.

Lazarsfeld, Paul F., *Qualitative Analysis,* Allyn & Bacon, Boston, 1972.

2.2.3.3 The Influence of Classification on Problems

Classification is so powerful a device that a unique object is defined by its deviation from the characteristics possessed by an object class. Each new class member reorganizes the characteristics assigned to its class.

Classification is an extremely powerful force in the organization of perception; all perceptual experience is, in fact, the end product of categorization. It is so powerful that a unique object is ordinarily defined by its deviation from the usual characteristics of some object class (Bruner, 1968, pp. 634-662). When an object is perceived, and as it is assigned more and more firmly to a specific class, its deviation from the characteristics that an object of such a class has becomes more and more noticeable. A sour grape is all the more sour if the taster had thought he was tasting a sweet grape. Class assignment affects profoundly the kind of evaluation made of an object (Peltz, 1971, pp. 69-78).

Classification is not static. Individuals do not come to perception with hard, already formed classes into which they sort objects of perception. Instead each new experience modifies, however slightly, the set of categories by which that experience was organized. Polanyi (1958, p. 349) comments on this fact when he describes the biologist's empirical standards of classification, "Thus, every time a specimen is appraised, the standards of normality are somewhat modified so as to make them approximate more closely to what is truly normal for the species." In this way a person constantly increases the size of the sample of the entire population of objects on which his classification and his evaluation are based. The single advantage that experience and age can claim is access to a larger population in the construction of its perceptual classes.

In addition to constantly modifying his categories the individual also forms *new* ones. He does so to collect a number of separate identities or relationships under a simpler single unit. In explaining this process, George A. Miller quotes John Locke, " ' . . . the mind does three things: first, it chooses a certain number [of specific ideas] ; secondly, it gives them connexion, and makes them into one idea; thirdly, it ties them together by a name.' " (Miller, 1956, pp. 42-46.) According to Miller the organization of many separate items into a single unit is important because it reduces the load that memory must carry and leaves the mind free for further thought. Words vary enormously in the number of ideas they organize into a unit. Generally the more abstract the word, the greater the number of ideas it organizes; an abstraction ladder, a sequence from the concrete to the abstract, organizes more and more material under a single term as it proceeds (Hayakawa, 1964, pp. 177-179). Whether to choose a more concrete classification that preserves more distinctions but is more difficult to survey conveniently or a more abstract classification with a few broad groupings that combine a greater number of dissimilar elements is often a difficult decision (Lazarsfeld, 1972, pp. 227-228). The decision must depend on the purpose the classification is to serve, and the choices are very wide. According to Jevons (1958, pp. 677-678), "there must generally be an unlimited number of modes of classifying a group of objects."

Categorization is a powerful force in organizing perception; in turn each new perception reorganizes the mind's categories. Even more powerful is the ability of the mind to organize related ideas (related categories) into a single other subsuming category and thereby to deal with that structured group of categories as a unit.

REFERENCES

Bruner, Jerome S., "On Perceptual Readiness," in Haber, Ralph N., Ed., *Contemporary Theory and Research in Visual Perception,* Holt Rinehart & Winston, New York, 1968.

Hayakawa, S. I., *Language in Thought and Action,* Harcourt Brace & World, New York, 1964.

Jevons, W. Stanley, *The Principles of Science: A Treatise on Logic and Scientific Method,* Dover, New York, 1958.

ARCHITECTURE, PROBLEMS AND PURPOSES

Lazarsfeld, Paul F., *Qualitative Analysis*, Allyn & Bacon, Boston, 1972.

Miller, George A., "Information and Memory," *Scientific American,* **195**(2), 1956.

Polanyi, Michael, *Personal Knowledge: Towards a Post-Critical Philosophy,* University of Chicago Press, Chicago, 1958.

Peltz, Richard, "Classification and Evaluation in Aesthetics: Weitz and Aristotle," *Journal of Aesthetics and Art Criticism,* **30**(1), 1971.

2.2.3.4 Description by Combined Classifications

Verbal representation combines a number of classifications to develop a unique description.

Whereas classification reduces the variety and complexity of experience to a manageable size, it can also be used to generate an equally complex and varied set of statements. As Craik points out: "a small number of known facts gives rise to an enormous number of hypothetical and actual conditions." (Craik, 1943, p. 113.) By putting more and more classes into relationship, more and more possibilities are generated, but then as more specific selections from those classes are made, a more nearly unique event is determined.

William Empson (1947, p. 238) observing that the selection of one event causes the inhibition of other potentially equivalent events, comments, "to say a thing in two parts is different in incalcuable ways from saying it as a unit. . . . When you are holding a variety of things in your mind, or using for a single matter a variety of intellectual machinery, the only way of applying all of your criteria is to apply them simultaneously." The process that integrates several components into a single unit is discussed at some length by Max Black (1962, pp. 44-45) in his exposition of metaphor. He notes that, although metaphor can be viewed as a substitution or as a comparison device, the most useful description is that of an interaction between two subjects. "The metaphor selects, emphasizes, suppresses, and organizes features of the principal subject by implying statements about it that normally apply to the subsidiary subject." It appears to be equally true that any verbal statement has this same effect; it places at least two different classes (represented by words) into juxtaposition. Where Empson notes that, "Metaphor is the synthesis of several units of observation into one commanding image," it is also possible to point out that any verbal statement accomplishes a similar thing.

Empson also observes that any prose statement can be called ambiguous; it can be analyzed into a series of other statements about its component parts; as those parts are explained, the choice of terms can carry the original sentence meaning into a number of different directions (Empson, 1947, p. 1). Undoubtedly there are bounds to the development of such explanations. These bounds result from the relation between surface structure and deep structure in language, and the permissible grammatical transformations between them

2.2.3.4

(Chomsky, 1972, p. 17); " the grammar of a language must contain a system of rules that characterizes deep and surface structures and the transformational relation between them, and . . . that does so over an infinite domain of paired deep and surface structures . . . the speaker makes infinite use of finite means." The significant spoken sentence is apparently only the exposed tip of an enormous iceberg structure of thought relationships available to the speaker as he forms his sentence.

The verbal statement form makes use of classifications, identified and referenced by words that are class names. Because of the extremely large number of relationships that can be developed between classes, enormous variety and selectivity are possible in sentence formation. The juxtaposition of words in the sentence develops a unity powerful in itself. Each sentence is only the articulated part of an elaborate structure of meaning available to the thought processes of the speaker.

REFERENCES

Black, Max, *Models and Metaphors: Studies in Language and Philosophy*, Cornell University Press, Ithaca, N.Y., 1962.

Chomsky, Noam, *Language and Mind,* Harcourt Brace Jovanovich, New York, 1972.

Craik, Kenneth J. W., *The Nature of Explanation,* Cambridge University Press, Cambridge, England, 1943.

Empson, William, *Seven Types of Ambiguity,* New Directions, New York, 1947.

2.2.3.5 Information Based on Authority

Two forms of authority-based information must be dealt with as fact; one is the expert knowledge of a specific field, the other is the expert knowledge of a specific situation.

Pertinent information derived from direct *experience* is different from that derived from *tradition* (what has recently been described in design as typological information). The difference can be illustrated by looking at the difference between two kinds of information equivalent in their derivations, *fact* and *authority.* In a discussion of *argument* as one of the forms of discourse Brooks and Warren (1958, p. 154) define *evidence:*

Either fact or opinions may constitute evidence, and both are applicable in support of propositions of fact or propositions of action. . . ."The facts of the case" are important as evidence, but they are not the only thing that can be used as evidence. Arguers also appeal to the opinions of other people who are supposed to have authority. "Expert testimony" is offered in the courtroom as evidence to support a case. . . .This so-called expert opinion is not the only kind that may appear as evidence. The law also recognizes the "character witness," an ordinary person who offers his opinion as to the character of the defendant.

Brooks and Warren note that authority is based on both experience and success (Brooks and Warren, 1958, p. 158). In applying this principle to design information, if the designer is to know how much faith

ARCHITECTURE, PROBLEMS AND PURPOSES

and credibility to place in such authority, he must develop a scale for rating the experience and success an authority brings to his testimony (i.e., his information).

An article on the development of the School of Architecture at the State University of New York at Buffalo (*Progressive Architecture*, July 1971) contains a helpful five-level rating scale for the degree of authority or expertness. A condensed version of the scale describes five levels of capability in a particular field of knowledge:

1. **Acquaintance.** Knows that it exists and what it is.

2. **Familiarity.** Knows the jargon in the field and how to use consultants.

3. **Proficiency.** Is capable of work in the field under supervision or is informed about the state of the art in the field.

4. **Mastery.** Is skillful in work in the field without supervision or has expert knowledge of the state of the art.

5. **Expertise.** Has extraordinary skill and knowledge in the field with a capacity for innovation in the art.

In design, information derived from authority can be ranked according to this scale, which is derived from demonstrated knowledge or skill and is equivalent in its higher levels to the information provided by an expert witness in a courtroom.

Another kind of authority in problem solving, and especially in design, is that of the client. The client might not have any expert knowledge within a defined discipline, but he has an expert knowledge of the problem under consideration. It is his problem, after all. His is an authority like that of the character witness based on a broad familiarity with a situation, not like the disciplinary depth of the expert.

A final comment on information based on authority is worth quoting. In a *Scientific American* article John Cohen (1957, p. 128) notes that with "increasing age and experience, uncertain situations are structured in closer and closer accord with the objectivity of mathematical expectation." Clearly the more experienced individual, the expert, has been exposed to a larger sample of the entire population of results that ensue from events and actions within his area of expertness.

REFERENCES

Brooks, Cleanth, and R. P. Warren, *Modern Rhetoric,* 2nd ed., Harcourt Brace & World, New York, 1958.

Cohen, John, "Subjective Probability," *Scientific American,* **197**(5), (1957).

2.2.3.6 Information Based on Fact

Fact is information that is of "eyewitness" quality. Single witnesses are fallible, and their testimony is seldom accepted as fact unless it is corroborated. An important related problem is whether a fact is specific only to a single situation or is general to many similar situations.

Whereas information based on authority is secondary, or derived information, that based on fact is primary, or "eyewitness" information. Although factuality seems to be a simple idea, criteria for factuality have been developed over time that suggest it is not really simple in practice.

Brooks and Warren (1958, p. 155) recite several of these criteria that bear upon the legitimacy of factual evidence:

1. Is there opportunity for the witness to observe the event?
2. Is the witness physically capable of observing the event?
3. Is the witness intellectually capable of understanding the event and reporting accurately?
4. Is the witness honest?

Rosenthal (1970, pp. 153-156) describes a broad range of factors that can distort observation in behavioral research. Undoubtedly the same factors can apply to any circumstance where direct observation of events is important in establishing fact. He lists the following effects: observer, interpreter, intentional, biosocial, psychosocial, situational, modeling, and expectancy effects. Each produces its own distortion of the apparently factual observation.

In taking evidence, whether in the courtroom or in the scientific laboratory, a strong reliance is placed on multiple observations that corroborate each other rather than on single, univerified observations. Corroboration can come from several sources:

1. From the independent testimony of several witnesses who report on the same event.

2. From the internal consistency between reports on several events, even when the reports are from the same witness.

3. From the correspondence of the testimony with a generally accepted body of knowledge about a specific subject area.

That the untrained witness is unable to give good factual evidence is notable. Much of what each witness perceives depends on the mental set he brings to his observations; much depends on the availability within his mental organization of categories into which the observed events can be fitted. Julian Hochberg (1968, p. 330) writes:

The perceived structure of an object may consist of two separable components: (a) the features glimpsed in momentary glances, and, (b) the integrative *schematic map* into which these features are fitted.

2.2.3.6

Accurate observation depends then, not only on an adequate set of glimpsed features, but also on the existence of a schematic map bearing a close enough correspondence with the structure of the external event to permit its accurate internal representation.

In an article treating this subject in full detail Jerome Bruner (1968, pp. 634-662) talks about the process of *cue* utilization. He notes several stages in cue utilization that vary from the relatively open identification and searching to the more closed confirmation. The stages are: (1) primitive categorization, (2) cue search, (3) confirmation check, and (4) confirmation completion. According to Bruner the strategies by which cues are used vary in the different stages. The conditions under which the strategies are evoked also vary. Cue searching occurs under relative uncertainty; a more selective search for confirming cues occurs under partial certainty; a sensory "gating" or confirmation completion occurs under certainty. It is evident that fitting the glimpsed features to a mental structure is not a simple process. Bruner describes it as one of fitting a cue or group of cues with a category specification for those cues.

If an instance is to be assigned to a category, it must fit a rule that specifies the following:

1. The properties or criterial attribute values required of an instance. . . .
2. The manner in which . . .attribute values are to be combined in making an inference . . . [about] category membership: whether conjunctively, . . . relationally, . . . or disjunctively . . . .
3. The weight assigned various properties in making an inference. . . .
4. The acceptance limits within which properties must fall to be criterial.

When these several conditions of Bruner's have been satisfied, an instance or event can be assigned to a mental category.

Under most circumstances of perception this process occurs in an automatic, "un-conscious" manner. By contrast when there is a formal engagement in a self-conscious problem-solving process, each part of this categorization procedure must be brought into full awareness if the process is to be most useful.

Another aspect of factual description that bears strongly on problem solving and affects the information available for solution is the degree of generality of the information. Does it apply only to the particular situation? Does it apply to a number of similar situations? Or is it quite general information that can be applied across an extremely wide range of different circumstances? Homans (1950, pp. 43-44) develops descriptions of these different levels of generality as they pertain to descriptions of social behavior. Whereas any description must describe persons, elements of their behavior, and the setting

2.2.3.6

in which they exist, the description must also say whether it consists of:

1. . . . descriptions of individual events.
2. . . .description of the average behavior of a limited number of persons in a limited area over a limited span of time.
3. . . . descriptions of behavior that may . . . apply to many groups, and to persons in many kinds of relations to one another.

To observe an event and report on that observation is not enough. Some sense of the uniqueness of the event, or of its possible repetitiveness and repeatability must be present also, if the event is to be truly useful in problem solution.

Churchman (1961, p. 101) makes a similar point in another context when he discusses characteristics of measurement:

One of the most significant aspects of modern science is the realization that one does not measure unless one also measures the error of measurement. In plainer language, measurement includes the process of control. In less plain language, measurement is an organization of experience in which information is "fed back" concerning the accuracy of the measurement.

Whether the problem solver is dealing with measurement or not, it is important for him to know how accurate his information is and how far it can be generalized.

REFERENCES

Brooks, Cleanth, and R. P. Warren, *Modern Rhetoric,* 2nd ed., Harcourt Brace & World, New York, 1958.

Bruner, Jerome S., "On Perceptual Readiness," in Haber, Ralph N., Ed., *Contemporary Theory and Research in Visual Perception,* Holt Rinehart & Winston, New York, 1968.

Churchman, C. West, *Prediction and Optimal Decision,* Prentice-Hall, Englewood Cliffs, N.J., 1961.

Hochberg, Julian, "In the Mind's Eye," in Haber, Ralph N., Ed., *Contemporary Theory and Research in Visual Perception,* Holt Rinehart & Winston, New York, 1968.

Homans, George C., *The Human Group,* Harcourt Brace, New York, 1950.

Rosenthal, Robert, "The Social Psychology of the Behavioral Scientist: On Self-Fulfilling Prophecies in Behavioral Research and Everyday Life," in Tufte, Edward R., Ed., *The Quantitative Analysis of Social Problems,* Addison-Wesley, Reading, Pa., 1970.

2.3 THE DIFFERENT FORMS OF PROBLEM INFORMATION

As the student begins to undertake different design problems, he finds he must manage information in widely different forms. He must deal with demand information (both client requirements and external

2.3

The information the designer uses can be organized into demand statements (which are negotiable) and supply statements (which are manipulatable). The design process fits supply with demand.

constraints of various enforcement agencies) and with supply information (what present conditions exist and what the client's resources are for bringing change to those conditions). He begins to learn what relations exist between the different kinds of information and to what degree the different information is negotiable or manipulatable.

2.3.1 Client Requirements as Demand Statements

Demand statements include the requirements of the design client and his reference group.

To design a building for a specific client, the designer must know who the client is, what the client wants to achieve, and what activities the client wants to engage in. If the client has already prepared a program (or if a faculty member has prepared a design program), the designer might also have information about the amount of space the client wants allocated to particular activities and about specific equipment that must be provided to assist those activities. Some parts of this information can be given in a highly organized or in a highly structured form, but much of it might be unstructured. Clearly all parts of the information from a client are related. What are those relationships?

2.3.2 Regulatory Agency Requirements as Demands

Demand statements also include the requirements of regulatory or enforcement agencies, for example, zoning boards, building code agencies, and public health departments.

Ordinarily a building must also satisfy the demands of some group of regulatory or enforcement agencies, which can include zoning boards, building code agencies, public health departments, fire marshals, and the like. The student may be furnished information about their existence, mandates, regulations, enforcement procedures, or specific requirements, or he may be required to seek such information for himself.

2.3.3 The Negotiability of Demand Statements

Client requirements are usually complex and can be contradictory. They are often negotiable and will ordinarily be modified as design proposals evoke other requirements.

By comparison with professional practice the student problem often imposes harsh and unvarying design requirements. The faculty often set unvarying requirements to deal with a large group of students in an equivalent manner. (So also do governmental agencies.) Such rigidity can cause the student to have a stronger respect for program requirements than he sometimes should have. One of the best insights into problem solving can occur when the student discovers unreasonable (or even contradictory) program requirements and realizes that it is entirely reasonable to set such requirements aside.

I remember an occasion when a group of students engaged in a project discovered such an inconsistency. The instructor was not available for comment, and the group had to risk one way or the other what was the best approach. A gasp of relief went from the entire group when the instructor announced just before the presentation that he had discovered an inconsistency. Such occurrences prepare the way for the practitioner to say to the client, "How firm is the requirement that you stated about . . . ?" The student has learned a great deal when he has learned that demand statements and, consequently, information about demand, are negotiable.

2.3.4 The Existing Condition as a Supply Statement

Supply statements include the existing condition of the design client, the site he has available, the known systems by which requirements can be met, and the condition of the manufacturing and construction industries.

The student must know what the existing conditions are. He must know, not only what the client's present circumstances are, but also what conditions exist on the site, in the way of climate, transportation to the site, utilities and services to the site, and so on. He must have some sense of what building materials and products are available to use in construction. Some of this information is specific and pertinent to the project, but other information is more global and applicable to any project within a given socio-geographic area. One of the greatest difficulties a designer can face is to design a building outside his own social and geographic milieu; not only is he likely to misinterpret social needs and customs and the quality of the climate; he is also not likely to know what materials and techniques are available for building.

It is not easy to impose limitations on a student project that have to do with construction technology, for the student acquires only gradually an understanding of what is and what is not possible. But what must come through for the student in problem solving is that what is possible and what is available are both considerably less negotiable than demand. Instead, from among all the existing conditions, the designer can choose which ones to manipulate to bring them into accord with the client's required conditions.

2.3.5 The Client's Resources as a Supply Statement

Supply statements also include the client's resources for bringing about change in his condition.

The degree to which a client can afford to manipulate his existing conditions depends on the resources he has. Student problems usually restrict resource considerations to a dollar budget figure translated into a permitted square footage for the building according to some average cost. Attention is seldom given to such things as the borrowing capability of the client, his capital position, his other property holdings, or any of a number of things that affect his resources.

If the designer were truly to examine client resources, he might have to examine a number of things: the quality and skill of the client's personnel, his ability to borrow additional funds, and even his experience and ability to adapt to the new conditions he desires.

2.3.6 The Manipulatability of Supply Statements

Solution of a design problem usually requires the manipulation of supply statements to satisfy demand statements.

Problem solution requires the manipulation of supply conditions to achieve the required conditions the client has specified. Whereas the supply conditions are usually chosen for manipulation, the problem solution process requires the manipulation of both demand and supply *information* to determine what supply conditions to manipulate. The problem-solving literature talks about two processes, *working forward* and *working backward.* It is possible to work forward from the conditions that exist toward a desired condition; it is possible to work backward from a desired condition toward the conditions that exist. Often both processes are used simultaneously; invariably the knowledge of both the existing and the required conditions affects the working process. Whatever the starting point the other condition becomes a goal toward which the work proceeds.

2.3.7 The Spectrum of Demand-Supply Statements

Objects provide *functions* that support *behaviors* that accomplish *purposes* of the *persons* who are the clients of design. These several terms are in an ends-means relationship, and a set of demand statements can be in terms of the *person*, his *purposes*, his desired *behaviors*, his required *functions*, or the preferred *objects* having those functions.

In the paragraphs that discussed client requirements a spectrum of different kinds of problem information was described that included the person (the client) for whom design is to be accomplished, his purposes, his desired behaviors, the supporting functions that his behaviors require, and the objects that can provide those functions. This spectrum is clearly a structured ends-means sequence. It can be read from the other direction thus: *Objects* provide *functions,* which support *behaviors,* which accomplish *purposes* of the *persons* who are the client of design. In the accompanying diagram (Fig. 2.1) the relation between a person and an object is defined by behavior; that between person and behavior, by purpose; and that between object and behavior, by function.

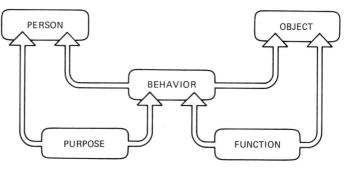

Figure 2.1 An ends-means information spectrum.

2.3.7

The design student learns to deal with this spectrum, even though he might not do so quite as explicitly as this diagram does. In some scholarly literatures the words *purpose* and *function* are used nearly interchangeably; in the design literature *purposes* are associated with persons and *functions* with objects.

The design student soon discovers the implicit relation between these terms that this discussion has made explicit. He uses that implicit understanding to uncover contradictions between statements from different parts of the spectrum. A program might require in one part that a dining room provide seats for fifty persons (behavior) and in another that the area of the room be 250 square feet (function); these two requirements are contradictory by the (behavior-derived) standards that usually hold today and by the kinds of tables and chairs (object) available. The usual institutional dining room would probably require three times that area for that number of persons.

The discovery of such an inconsistency, or the confirmation of the accuracy of information by the comparison of data from different parts of the spectrum, shows the strong relation that holds between the parts of this spectrum in design problem solving.

2.3.8 The Mixture of Problem Statement Forms

The usual problem statement is a mixture of statements at all of these different levels.

The person-object spectrum indicates the different forms in which the client can provide information for the designer. Usually the client provides such information without a careful concern for its form. The design program usually has information from all parts of the spectrum juxtaposed and combined into a total statement. The client can describe who the building users will be, what their purposes are, what things they will be doing, how much space in what location they will need to do it in, and what color the walls should be painted—all within the same statement. The client describes the entire situation he desires, and it is then up to the designer to disentangle the different information and sort the different statements into their logical relationships. To some degree these different forms of statement are interchangeable, and the client, according to his disposition and to how specific and articulate his wishes are, can express those wishes in any of the person-object forms. Although these different forms of expression are not logically equivalent, they are motivationally equivalent; they define the same disposition (of the client) while emphasizing the person, his purposes, his behaviors, a desired function, or an object possessing that function.

2.3.9 Information Inclusion of Different Statements

Statements at these different levels are not equivalent; there is a difference of inclusion at each

The various forms of information are not logically equivalent, because there is a difference of inclusion in the different statement forms. As the form of expression moves from the *person* end of the spectrum toward the *object* end, more and more data are factored out. When a person is faced with some problem, he has a number of different directions to take in seeking its solution; when he decides that some

ARCHITECTURE, PROBLEMS AND PURPOSES

level. As the form of statement moves from the *person* level toward the *object* level, more and more data are factored out of consideration.

change in his physical environment is required, then the direction the factoring process will take is already determined.

All solution requires simplification, but what is more important is to discover what form the simplification takes and what is omitted from further attention as each simplifying step is taken. An examination of the information spectrum from this viewpoint can be helpful: (1) at the *person* level everything is included and nothing is factored out; (2) when *purposes* are defined, nonpurposive orientations of the individual are omitted; (3) when desired *behaviors* are described, there is a tendency to emphasize structured, task-oriented behaviors and to omit the unstructured, socially oriented parts of behavior; (4) when the description is of required *functions,* there is a tendency to emphasize the acquisition of function capability at the expense of allocative considerations (there is also a tendency to emphasize the spatial placement of functions at the expense of temporal scheduling of functions); and (5) when the desired *object* is described, the description usually omits the skill of the person who will be using the object.

The accompanying diagram (Fig. 2.2) shows more clearly than any amount of narrative could how this factoring process occurs at the different levels of description. The diagram indicates the manner in which the *person* end of the spectrum is more inclusive than the *object* end. An *object* description is much less inclusive because so much has been factored out.

2.3.10 Statement Transformation in Design

The design process transforms information from one level to the next until an object statement is achieved. In architectural design conventional names are associated with each transformations: purpose to behavior, *programming*; behavior to function, *planning*; function to object, *design*.

The factoring diagram (Fig. 2.2) also indicates the conventional names used in architectural design for the procedures that convert information from one part of the spectrum into information in the next, less inclusive part of the spectrum. *Programming* converts *purpose* into *behavior* information; *planning* converts *behavior* into *function* information; *design* * converts *function* into *object* information.

Each of the different forms of information just listed is part of a demand-supply relationship. Each form can be seen as a *demand* upon the next form as a *supply.*

If the entire design process is diagramed as a flowchart, each information conversion can be seen as a separate segment in the flowchart (or morphology). A typical segment has the following pattern: input information (demand information) is combined with supply systems information by means of a group of operations; the result of these operations is accepted or rejected; when accepted, that new

*The word *design* is used throughout this book to indicate an overall problem-solving process of a specific kind. The word can also be used to describe a more limited part of that process, which is concerned specifically with visualizing and proposing the articulated shape, dimensions, materials, colors, and finishes of physical objects that are intended to provide a set of defined functions. Here *design* is used in this second sense.

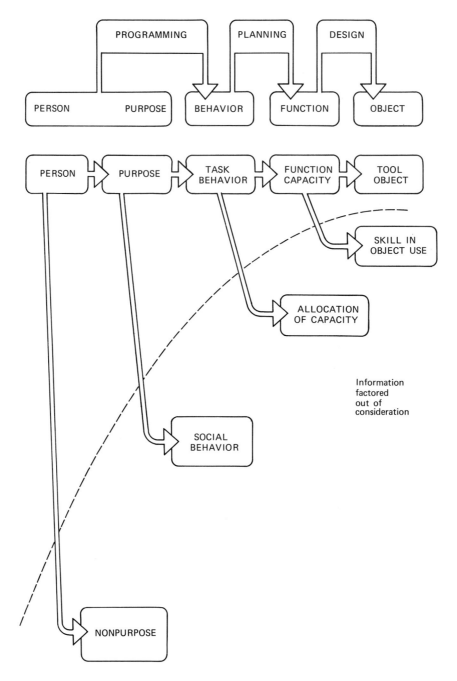

Figure 2.2 Design phases and information factoring.

form is supply information in response to the original demand information. Such a segment within a flowchart is shown in the diagram (Fig. 2.3).

When a supply statement has been produced in response to a demand statement in one segment of the flowchart, that supply state-

54   ARCHITECTURE, PROBLEMS AND PURPOSES

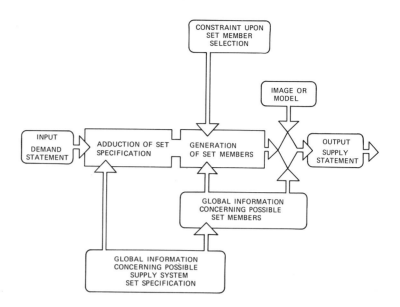

Figure 2.3 A demand-supply segment of a flow chart.

2.3.10

ment then becomes a demand statement on the next segment. Where, for example, *purpose* is a demand, *behavior* is a supply; where *behavior* is a demand, *function* is a supply; where *function* is a demand, *object* is a supply.

When a demand statement is relatively abstract and the supply statement relatively concrete, the operations required to produce the supply statement also include the specification of a set of supply statements and a search for set members that match the specification.

2.3.11 Transformations within a Demand-Supply Diagram

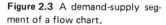

Each such transformation is a segment within a demand-supply chain. The entire series of transformations can be placed in a morphological diagram.

By using the two basic ideas already developed in this section, the information spectrum and the division of information into systems of demand and of supply, it is possible to place the full range of information used in design into a diagrammatic relationship. The diagram is produced by placing the person-object information spectrum as the horizontal dimension of a matrix and the demand-supply information as a vertical dimension of the same matrix. By imposing a diagram of the demand-supply segment of a flowchart onto each part of the matrix between the different parts of the information spectrum, it is possible to show the general direction of information flow in the entire design process. The diagram appears as Fig. 2.4.

The direction of information flow can be shown only as a general direction because of the many different legitimate procedures for undertaking design. Moreover, many different design methods can be used.

If the diagram were used to classify design methods by information input and output, there would be a great many different patterns of information flow through the diagram.

2.3.11

Despite its complex appearance the diagram is relatively simple. The several segments in the person-purpose-behavior-function-object spectrum are shown from left to right. The demand-supply forms of information *within each segment* are shown from top to bottom. The demand-supply dimension, arranged for convenience, includes (1) constraints, (2) requirements, (3) "synthesis," (4) analysis, (5) conditions (existing), and (6) resources.

Although I assume that no sequence through the diagram is required, typical patterns are undoubtedly followed as design is accomplished.

2.3.12 A Diagram of Design Process

Such a morphological diagram can also be used to develop a task list that will assist the design process.

When the same descriptors are used to define a task list in architectural practice, the diagram takes a different form. It must show, not only a specific task to be accomplished, but also the product that results.

The components are grouped in a different way. After a *statement of process,* which combines both *architectural intentions* and client *institutional intentions,* the diagram develops a problem statement and a statement of limits. It proceeds to develop a statement of possibilities.

The *statement of problem* results from a comparison between the client's *present state* and his *required state.* The *statement of limits* is a combination of information about *constraints* and about client *resources.*

The *statement of possibilities* is a sequence of problem solution stages that range through the planning and design phases to produce a series of *proposals*, which are accompanied by *justifications* that provide cost analyses and feasibility studies.

The diagram is shown in Fig. 2.5.

2.3.13 The Technical Discussions

The technical discussions that follow are concerned with causal structure and with means-ends analysis. The discussion of means-ends analysis repeats some of the material already covered above, but it does so to describe more closely the linked relationship between the several terms in the information spectrum and then to define what a means-ends relation is. A third technical discussion elaborates on the relationships in the information spectrum and shows how a number of writers have organized material according to that spectrum. A final discussion provides a more detailed and technical exposition of the processes within a morphological segment.

2.3.13.1 Means-Ends Analysis in Problem Solution

Problem solution is guided by means-ends analysis, which depends on an achieved classification of recurring patterns of events.

Design depends on an understanding by the designer of the overall structure of a situation (Wertheimer, 1959, p. 243). The causal connections that can *possibly* exist between an initial and a terminal state are relatively well understood. In projecting a problem solution, the designer is guided by a means-ends analysis of the situation. This article examines the functioning of a means-ends analysis.

When a person is in a goal-seeking circumstance, his behavior is determined by that goal. He will act in such a way and choose the means that will bring him most quickly to that end or goal (Heider, 1958, pp. 102-103). George A. Kelly (1963, p. 65) assumes that man makes his choice in a fashion to enhance his anticipations. He makes what Kelly calls *"the elaborative choice."* "If he constricts his field of vision, he can turn his attention toward the clear definition of his system of constructs. If he is willing to tolerate some day-by-day uncertainties, he may broaden his field of vision and thus hope to extend the predictive range of his system." Undoubtedly, in a goal-seeking or a problem-solving circumstance, the individual can move from one of the modes (constricting certainty) to the other (broadening understanding); it is likely, however, that the preference for constricting certainty will be the prevailing choice.

To "constrict certainty," the problem solver has a number of guides based on experience. As he perceives components of his problem, he engages in a continuous classifying process, and this provides information. Classification "can give us more information than we have at the moment direct access to—that is, it helps us to extrapolate and to predict." (Abercrombie, 1960, p. 114.) A person anticipates events by noticing recurring patterns of events that are meaningful for him. First he divides the flow of events into recurring segments; then he notices "replicative aspects" within those segments (Kelly, 1963, pp. 50-51). When he has done so, it becomes feasible for him to make predictions. "What is predicted is not that tomorrow will be a duplicate of today but that there are replicative aspects of tomorrow's events which may be safely predicted. Thus man anticipates events by construing their replications." (Kelly, 1963, p. 53.)

When he has construed the events in a formal problem-solving process by a carefully organized procedure of scientific observation, he can begin to say just how sure he is of the replicative aspects. He can do so in a mathematically formal way when the events are quantifiable through the procedures of statistics. When the events are rather more qualitative, he can use any of a series of terms to describe how sure he is of the dependability of the predictive statement. "The terms *speculation, hypothesis, theory,* and *law* form a progression according to the increasing adequacy of the evidence." (Weinland, 1970, p. 30.)

When classification is used to assist prediction, the events are usually unitary and simple. When an attempt is made to understand a more elaborately structured sequence or set of circumstances by reference to a similar known sequence or set of circumstances, the process of comparison is called *analogy*. "The well-recognized danger of using analogies is the tendency to push them too far—to treat the two things as like in respects in which they are in fact unlike." (Abercrombie, 1960, pp. 117-118.) Analogy tends, however, to get used for prediction because the designer does not often have anything better to assist it. By comparison with extrapolation and the use of "if, then" propositions, both based on empirical observation of past events and classification processes, analogy is extremely unsure (Fischer, 1970, p. 258). For an analogy to serve as an explanation or as a prediction of events, the two instances compared must be similar in all important respects, and differences between them must be accounted for as being unimportant (Brooks and Warren, 1958, p. 163). Clearly the effort to classify events as alike when they contain a great many different variables is very difficult to accomplish. The ability to use classification processes for prediction depends on a decomposition of events into elements of as few variables as possible.

REFERENCES

Abercrombie, M. L. Johnson, *The Anatomy of Judgment,* Basic Books, New York, 1960.

Brooks, Cleanth, and R. P. Warren, *Modern Rhetoric*, 2nd ed., Harcourt Brace & World, New York, 1958.

Fischer, David H., *Historian's Fallacies: Toward a Logic of Historical Thought,* Harper & Row, New York, 1970.

Heider, Fritz, *The Psychology of Interpersonal Relations,* Wiley, New York, 1958.

Kelly, George A., *A Theory of Personality: The Psychology of Personal Constructs*, Norton, New York, 1963.

Weinland, James D., *How to Think Straight*, Littlefield Adams, Totowa, N.J., 1970.

Wertheimer, Max, *Productive Thinking*, Harper & Row, New York, 1959.

2.3.13.2 Means-Ends Analysis and Class Specification

The causal conditions for an event are difficult to specify. Still the problem solver, on naming some desired end, must be able to name a *class* of means related to that end. A means-ends relation is the unit formation of an event with a class of causal conditions.

David Fischer has listed various sets of antecedents regarded as pertinent to causal explanation by different persons. He distinguished between a cause that acts to produce an event (the set of antecedents in which he was interested) and a reason (a characteristic that the related events share with other similarly related events), which is obviously not necessarily causal. Fischer (1970, pp. 180-181) makes clear his distinction between a cause, which is pragmatic and probabilistic, and a reason, which is essential by syllogistic argument. Where the one is an empirical, probable, and pertinent cause, the other is a logical inclusion by argument from the characteristics of a

ARCHITECTURE, PROBLEMS AND PURPOSES

class of which the event is a member and that could easily be trivial in a causal discussion. The cause that has force for Fischer is based on what Polya (1957, pp. 186-187) has called the heuristic syllogism, an argument based on implication, empirical observation, and probable cause.

Enormous difficulties are involved in specifying what the necessary and sufficient conditions are for an event to occur—thus Fischer's difficulty with what are appropriate antecendents that must be named in a causal explanation. This difficulty is illustrated in a humorous fashion by Ernest Nagel (1956, pp. 1890-1891) with a quotation from Robert Graves and Alan Hodge. A borough council meeting is trying to phrase an ordinance on the condition of dogs in the borough park. The final satisfactory ordinance is, "All dogs in this Park must be kept on the lead." But before that phrase is achieved, each of a series of unsatisfactory proposals is considered: "No dogs must be brought to this Park except on a lead." (They could be released.) "Dogs are not allowed in this Park without leads." (Ordinance was addressed to dogs.) "Owners of dogs are not allowed in this Park unless they keep them on leads." (Owner would have to bring dog to enter park.) "Nobody without his dog on a lead is allowed in this Park." (A citizen would have to acquire a dog to enter park.) "Dogs must be led in this Park." (Requires everyone to bring his dog to the park.) "All dogs must be kept on leads in this Park." (Requires that dogs be kept in the park rather than elsewhere.) Anyone who has participated in the formulation of legal wording for ordinances, rules, or contracts knows that the humor in the series of proposals is in the representation of the difficulty of such phrasemaking with complete accuracy.

The difficulty of the problem solver is not the same as that of the historian (with whom Fischer is concerned). If the problem solver is to draw on the experience available to him through an appropriate classification of experience, he must be able to use or call for classes of causal acts. If he is to use a means-ends analysis, he must, on naming some desired end, be able to name a class of means that will lead to that end. His cause must be an action that is a logical inclusion within a specified class of means. Allen Newell (1969, pp. 369-370) describes three parts characteristic of any method used in problem solution: (1) problem statement, (2) procedure, and (3) justification. Justification is the argument by which the problem solver demonstrates the necessary connection between the problem statement and the problem solution; it is, in effect, a means-ends analysis. It is "the proof or *justification* that the procedure in fact delivers the solution to the problem (or delivers it within certain specified limits)." (Newell, 1969, p. 371.) It is thus, necessarily, a logical argument.

A means-ends analysis produced a segmented sequence of methods that match demand information as required output (end) with supply information as specified input (means). Such means-ends matching can occur in a long sequence of segments or in a single segment alone.

A means-ends analysis can take a number of different forms, depending on the motivation within the problem situation. Paul Lazarsfeld (1972, pp. 235-236) gives a list of standard structural schemes that have been developed for applied research in standard situations. Each is in a matched means-ends format:

1. *The push-pull scheme*, used in studying reasons for migration from place A to place B, or for shifting one's preference from any item X to any other item Y. The elements in this scheme are: the attributes of X and the attributes of Y [matched or compared with each other and the motives of the respondent].

2. *The attributes-motives-influence scheme*, used in classification of reasons fo· choosing a given item X. The elements of this scheme are: the attributes of X, the motives of the respondent, the channels of influences concerning his choice.

3. *The technical-properties-resulting-gratification scheme*, for studying "What is it about X" that the respondent likes. . . .

4. *The where-is-it, what-barriers-keep-it-there, who-is-to-blame scheme*, for studying respondent's explanation of shortages of anything. . . .

5. *The underlying-reasons-precipitating-cause scheme*, used in classifying answers to the questions, "Why did you do so-and-so?" and "Why did you do it just then?". . . .

Each of these schemes clearly provides a structured relation of cause-effect, supply-demand, or means-ends in its organization of information. The designer is so used to making such means-ends connections that the very process passes unnoticed.

What exactly, then, is a means-ends relation? Within Guilford's scheme showing the *products* of intellect are included *units, classes, relations, systems, transformations,* and *implications.* He defines *relation* as "some kind of connection between two things, a kind of bridge or connecting link having its own character. Prepositions commonly express relation ideas alone or with other terms such as the expressions 'married to,' 'son of,' and 'harder than.' " (Guilford, 1967, p. 64.) He indicates (since his work is primarily concerned with the measurement of intellect) that, "In verbal analogies tests, any of the *standard relations* [my emphasis], including opposites, genus-species, part-whole, action-agent, verb-object, and the reverse of most of these, plus many others, are used." (Guilford, 1967, p. 242.)

In the well-known work by Bruner, Goodnow, and Austin, *A Study of Thinking* (1956), a distinction is made between the different kinds of conceptual categories: conjunctive, where two or more attributes must exist together to define a category; disjunctive, where some attribute or some other attribute is adequate each by itself to define a category; and relational *"The relational concept or category* is one defined by a specifiable relationshp between defining attributes." (Bruner, Goodnow, and Austin, 1956, p. 43.) Unfortunately, except for this mention in a single paragraph, the remainder of the study is devoted to conjunctive and disjunctive categories. Again in a Bruner article (1968, p. 642) reference is made to the same three ways in which attributes can be combined to form categories—but without any discussion of the relational category. Interestingly, in that same article, several relational concepts are noted as being among what are probably the full repertory of "innate" categories. "Causation," as an innate relational category is of special interest in the same way that, in the 1956 study with Goodnow and Austin, among "three broad classes of equivalance categories" (affective, functional, and formal), the functional category is of special interest. Bruner, Goodnow, and Austin say about the functional category, "Rather than an internal state rendering a group of things equivalent, now equivalence is based on an external function. The objects of a functional category fulfill a concrete and specific task requirement—'things large enough and strong enough to plug this hole in the dike.' " (Bruner, Goodnow, and Austin, 1956, p. 5.) Causation and functional categories are clearly among the relational categories that are in our strong interest to understand. A single other Bruner reference pertains to this subject. In a study of the classification process in children (Bruner and Olver, 1965, p. 423) is a form of classification the authors refer to as "edge-matching." Associative links are formed between neighboring items, and the associations then pile up in linked pairs. This is the form that a means-ends analysis finally takes. The links in a means-ends analysis are, however, a specific kind: they are causal or functional links.

What is the character of those relational links? Two concepts apply. First is the notion of *unit formation*, based on the work of the Gestalt psychologists and developed as a body of hypotheses by Fritz Heider (1958). Heider's work is extraordinarily clear in its conceptual structure and can be applied (I believe) to impersonal objects as well as to persons. It depends on relationship as the basis for unit formation. Second is the idea of convergent incorporation as the means by which "Two distinct configurations . . . are bonded by a specific relationship." (Barnett, 1953, p. 196.)

Heider (1958, p. 177) shows that, when two entities are seen as belonging together, they also make up a cognitive unit. Since such units have important consequences for interpersonal relations, a first task is to consider what conditions lead to unit formation. He reviews the work of Wertheimer: "Many of the conditions have been systematically investigated by the Gestalt psychologists who demonstrated that the formation of units is an important feature of cognitive organization. The Gestalt experiments often involved the perception of simple figures in the demonstration of such unit-forming factors as similarity, proximity, common fate, good continuation, set . . ." He continues, "Unit-forming factors particularly relevant to groupings involving persons can be seen in the following: things that are made by a person, or that are his property, belong to him. Changes that are attributed to a person as effects of his actions also belong to him in a certain sense. A person may be seen in a cognitive unit with other persons because of kinship, nationality, or religion." (Heider, 1958,

p. 178.) He comments as well on the tendency to level small differences and to sharpen larger differences (Heider, 1958. p. 182). The importance of Heider's comments is the use of ideas such as ownership and causal actions as unit-forming attributes. Here are perceptually dissimilar elements formed into units by conceptual relators.

Barnett's work (1953), some five years earlier in its publication than Heider's, is concerned with a more complex subject and is therefore not as conceptually simple. It does, however, carry the idea of unit forming by relationship somewhat further. After noting that bonding can occur by such specific relationships as spatiality, temporality, comparativeness, genetic, causal, correlative, incorporative, and attitudinal (Barnett, 1953, pp. 186-187), he says, "The significance of incorporation as a mechanism for identification lies in the fact that it can establish what seems to be an equation between two totally dissimilar wholes—that is, dissimilar when they are considered alone and in themselves." (Barnett, 1953, p. 200.) What Barnett refers to as convergent incorporation is what Heider has referred to as unit formation, the joining of two formerly unrelated and dissimilar elements by some new developed relation between them. The relation that is of most concern to the designer is the causal relation, or the means-ends relation, or the functional relation; each is a different designation for much the same relationship.

To discover that dissimilar elements can be linked together by some functional relationship is not very surprising, but an advantage arises from developing the formal relationship for the problem-solving process—especially for a design problem-solving process. The formal relationship is as follows:

1. A person's behavior is in a means-ends relation to that person. His behavior supplies some function that his person requires or demands. The name ordinarily given to that relationship is motivation, or need, or purpose. If the motive is attached to the person, the person is spoken of as having objectives. If the motive is attached to the behavior, it is spoken of as goal-seeking behavior. In this discussion I refer to the relationship as *purpose.*

2. A person's physical resources, specifically his tools and his physical facilities, are in a means-ends relation to his behavior. His physical tools and facilities supply some function that his behavior demands or requires. The behavior is given some function-performing name. Cooking, dining, writing, and dressing are all examples of behavior that has been functionally labeled. When, by contrast, the function is attached to some tool, object, or other physical facility, that facility is recognized by its function-related name. The object is not named by its geometry but by its function. In this discussion I refer to this

2.3.13.2

specific means-ends relationship between a person's behavior and a person's physical resources as *function.*

The two-part means-ends relationship is shown in the diagram (Fig. 2.6). Pairs of relatively concrete wholes or configurations are connected and formed into units by a relatively abstract relationship. Within the total, three elements are connected by two relationships. This is a skeleton of the entire set of relationships that exist in the design problem-solving process.

3. Once this set of means-ends connections has been formed, it becomes not just three elements connected by two relationships; instead it becomes a continuous chain wherein any two of the elements that are separated by a third element are also linked by that third element. The abstract object *function* is in a means-ends relation to the abstract object purpose; they are placed in relation by *behavior.*

4. The entire ends-means chain is then as follows: *in order for a person to exist, his purposes must provide for that existence; to accomplish his purposes, his behavior must serve those purposes; for his behavior to be carried out, certain function capabilities must often be supplied; for those function capabilities to be provided, some arranged physical object must exist to provide that function.* If this is a simple seeming ends-means chain in its exposition, it is a complex

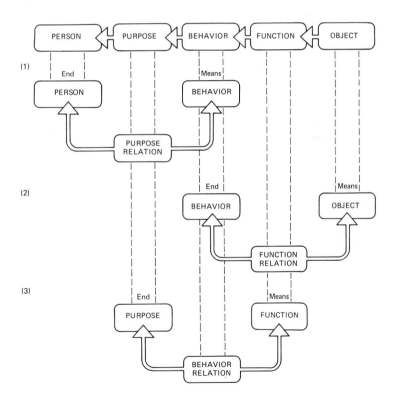

Figure 2.6 An Ends-Means Chain

ends-means chain in its actuality. A number of complications can occur in determining the specific means to achieve a certain end; trade-offs are possible, for example, between such things as function capability and the allocation or scheduling of resources to a function, and between such things as the arrangement of physical objects and skill and knowledge in their use.

In his discussion of the process of innovation Barnett (1953, p. 188) describes by diagram the possible substitutions that can occur when a hybridization of a pair of existing configurations (that possess a pair of equivalent relations between two parts) occurs. If one configuration has part A in an R_1 relation to B, Barnett describes the possible interchanges that can occur with another configuration that has X in an R_2 relation to Y. He notes six possible patterns of substitution. By contrast, if part A is in an R_1 means-ends relation to part B, and if B is determined, then the means-ends relation defines an entire set of components that are in a means relation to that end.

REFERENCES

Barnett, H. G., *Innovation: The Basis of Cultural Change,* McGraw-Hill, New York, 1953.

Bruner, Jerome S., J. J. Goodnow, and G. A. Austin, *A Study of Thinking,* Wiley, New York, 1956.

Bruner, Jerome S., and R. R. Olver, "Development of Equivalence Transformations in Children," in Anderson, Richard C., and D. P. Ausubel, Eds., *Readings in the Psychology of Cognition,* Holt Rinehart & Winston, New York, 1965.

Bruner, Jerome S., "On Perceptual Readiness," in Haber, Ralph N., Ed., *Contemporary Theory and Research in Visual Perception,* Holt Rinehart & Winston, New York, 1968.

Fischer, David H., *Historian's Fallacies: Toward a Logic of Historical Thought,* Harper & Row, New York, 1970.

Guilford, J. P., *The Nature of Human Intelligence,* McGraw-Hill, New York, 1967.

Heider, Fritz, *The Psychology of Interpersonal Relations,* Wiley, New York, 1958.

Lazarsfeld, Paul F., *Qualitative Analysis,* Allyn & Bacon, Boston, 1972.

Nagel, Ernest, "Symbolic Notation, Haddocks' Eyes, and the Dog-Walking Ordinance," in Newman, James R., Ed., *The World of Mathematics,* Vol. 3, Simon & Schuster, New York, 1956.

Newell, Allen, "Heuristic Programming: Ill-Structured Problems," in Aronofsky, Julius S., Ed., *Progress in Operations Research*, Vol. 3, Wiley, New York, 1969.

Polya, George, *How to Solve It,* Doubleday, Garden City, N.Y., 1957.

2.3.13.3 The Spectrum of Means-Ends Relations

Many writers have used information spectra that relate closely to

An event, a situation, or an object can be described in a number of different modes; each can be described in different ways. These various ways range from the more to the less inclusive. If the thing being described is a person and the action situation in which he exists, and

2.3.13.3

the person-purpose-behavior-function-object spectrum. Each pair of terms in this spectrum is means-ends related. The several terms can be connected in a linked sequence.

the spectrum of inclusion levels is related to his decision process, there are five usefully distinct levels of description: (1) at the most inclusive level the person (or within a different context, the institution) and his personality, (2) at a next level a purposive or intentional description, (3) at the next less inclusive level a behavioral description, (4) at a less inclusive level still a function description, and (5) at the least inclusive level an object or tool description. *Objects* provide *functions* that support *behaviors* that accomplish *purposes* that are held by *persons*. It will be helpful to keep these several inclusion levels in mind during the discussion of the schemata described by different writers.*

An organization of information that relates to the last three of these levels is proposed by Ray Studer (1972, p. 280), who compares the sequence followed by the behavioral scientist with that observed by the designer. Whereas the designer moves from a description of required behaviors to a set of simulated functions to a set of proposed object descriptions (environmental stimuli), the behavioral scientist moves in an opposite direction. The scientist moves from object descriptions to functions to behavior descriptions. Studer's relationships are shown in the accompanying diagram (Fig. 2.7). In this particular exposition Studer omitted the person and purpose levels; he has not omitted them in other writing, and they undoubtedly provide the organization and motivation for the behavioral description.

In a theoretical paper on the organization of a problem-solving machine, Walter Jacobs (1970, p. 426) describes the several organization levels that such a machine would require. He proposes: (1) a drive level that would develop an overall plan and make decisions, (2) subordinate to that a submethod level that would recognize situations and make choices, (3) subordinate to that a subtask level that would receive perceptions and express intentions, and (4) a body level that would be interactive with the environment. Although the categories do not correspond exactly, there is a relationship between his drive level and the most inclusive or person level, between his submethod and subtask levels and the purpose and behavior levels, and between his body level and the function level. The diagram (Fig. 2.8) shows the organization of Jacobs' categories and their apparent relationship to the categories of information described above.

Figure 2.7 A behavior-function object relation. (Adapted from a diagram by Studer, 1972, p. 280. Used by permission of the American Psychological Association, Inc., Washington, D.C.)

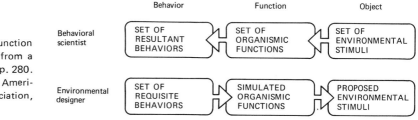

*The person-purpose-behavior-function-object information spectrum is my invention and should be seen as a schema for which I am responsible. Where I have related the writings of different persons to that schema, it is a relation that I have put each writer's words into and not a schema of that writer.

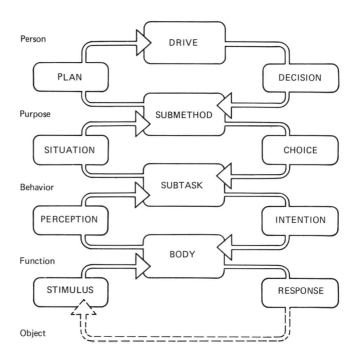

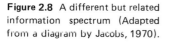

Figure 2.8 A different but related information spectrum (Adapted from a diagram by Jacobs, 1970).

2.3.13.3

Constance Perin (1970, p. 77), drawing on the work by Barker and by Harris, describes a related sequence of description levels: (1) at the most abstract conceptual or purpose level she refers to *behavior streams* or *activities;* (2) at the behavioral level, to *behavior circuits;* and (3) at the function level, to *actions.* The *action* level is the discrete behavior that Marvin Harris refers to as an *actone* and that Barker refers to as a *unit;* it is what the designer understands as an isolated function capability rather than organized behavior serving some purpose. I have undoubtedly distorted Perin's intention by placing her terms into relationship with the terms that I use; her terms were intended only to provide a framework for a hierarchic analysis of behavioral events, but I have placed those terms into a purpose and function context.

In a somewhat different mode Max Black (1962, pp. 220-241), in describing the different means of representing a circumstance by models, identifies a number of different model types from the very abstract or conceptual to the very concrete and specific; he discusses: (1) at the person level the *archetype,* (2) at the purpose level the *root metaphor,* (3) at the behavior level the *theoretical model*, (4) at the function level a *math model* or an *analogue model,* and (5) at the object level a *scale model.*

Finally George Polya (1965, pp. 8-10) agrees substantially with a portion of Black's abstractness levels by defining at the behavioral level a *heuristic description*, at the function level a *mathematical* or *relational description*, and at the object level an *image* description.

These different levels of inclusion and description are summarized and shown in relationship in the accompanying diagram (Fig. 2.9).

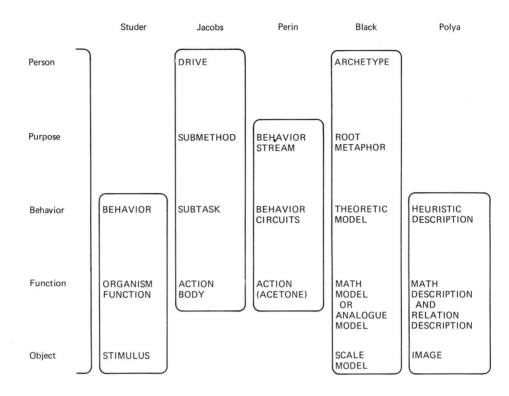

Figure 2.9 The relation between several spectra.

2.3.13.3   Although it is possible to analyze the structure of events, objects, and processes by these different levels of inclusion, the more important insight that can be gained from this review is the understanding that each of these analytic levels is important for any decision process. Miller, Galanter, and Pribram (1960, pp. 13-16) provide an understanding of the method in which these different levels can be linked together in a decision sequence. The TOTE mechanism, which permits a hierarchic linkage of one decision into another (as a component of the information on which that other decision will be based), is basic and essential to an understanding of how these various levels are associated.

Many writers pursuing different points of view have displayed a hierarchic organization of event description that can be associated with the five different levels I have described. Specific kinds of linkage from one level to another are joined together in a decision process by a TOTE sequence (Walter, 1951, pp. 183-184; Bruner, 1972, pp. 124-125.

REFERENCES

Black, Max, *Models and Mataphors: Studies in Language and Philosophy*, Cornell University Press, Ithaca, N.Y., 1962.

Bruner, Jerome S., "Origins of Problem Solving Strategies in Skill Acquisition," in Rudner, Richard, and I. Scheffler, Eds., *Logic and Art: Essays in Honor of Nelson Goodman*, Bobbs-Merrill, Indianapolis, 1972.

REFERENCES

Jacobs, Walter, "Help Stamp Out Programming," in Banerji, R. B., and M. D. Mesarovic, Eds., *Theoretical Approaches to Non-Numerical Problem Solving*, Springer-Verlag, Berlin, 1970.

Miller, George A., E. Galanter, and K. Pribram, *Plans and the Structure of Behavior*, Holt, New York, 1960.

Perin, Constance, *With Man in Mind*, M.I.T. Press, Cambridge, 1970.

Polya, George, *Mathematical Discovery* Vol. 2, Wiley, New York, 1965.

Studer, Raymond G., "The Organization of Spatial Stimuli," in Wohlwill, Jacques, F., and D. H. Carson, Eds., *Environment and the Social Sciences: Perspectives and Applications*, American Psychological Association, Washington, D.C., 1972.

Walter, W. Grey, "Activity Patterns in the Human Brain," in Whyte, Lancelot L., *Aspects of Form*, Indiana University Press, Bloomington, 1951.

2.3.13.4 Demand-Supply in the Morphological Segment

A design flowchart consists of a sequence of similar morphological segments. A segment has demand statement and supply system statement inputs and supply statement outputs. Each supply output is a demand input on the next segment.

In the relatively detailed flowcharts, or morphologies, by Honey (1969, pp. 1389 ff.) or Asimow (1962, p. 19) a typical segment within the morphology has a pattern as follows: (1) data or input information along with external information are modified by some operation or method, (2) a decision (based on an evaluation of the acceptability of the result of the operation) is made, and (3) the result of that decision is treated as output from that morphological segment. The information output, along with other external information, is then treated as input information to a new segment of the process. Thus the *input* of two kinds of information, an *operation* on that information, a *decision*, and an information *output* form a typical segment of a design problem-solving process.

Since the kind of operation performed on the input information is guided by the needs and purposes of the overall process (Nadler, 1967, pp. 2-3), then the first three components of each segment— information, operation, and decision—form an equivalent set with the components of a motivational orientation described by Parsons as *action theory* (Parsons and Shils, 1951, p. 5). Parsons' terms for the components within a motivational orientation are cognition, cathexis, and evaluation.

Honey (1969, pp. 1389 ff.) describes design as consisting of three basic procedures: *layout, design of functional systems,* and *component design.* It seems likely that a reduction of design to only those procedures assumes too much. It takes for granted a prior analysis of objectives, behavior, and functional need on which layout must be based; it is too glib as a description of the basic procedures in design. At a simpler level of analysis, however, these three components are the essential elements in any single process segment; if they are to be applied to any segment other than physical design, the names applied to the components must be made more general. Consider the nature of each component.

ARCHITECTURE, PROBLEMS AND PURPOSES

2.3.13.4

Layout in architectural design is a process used to specify where various behaviors are to be performed and where various functions in support of those behaviors must be provided. Layout is concerned with the spatial relationships (the proximities) that must exist between the different required functions. Layout also specifies the size of area required for each functional area. In essence *layout* in design is the equivalent of a demand statement, and it forms one of the inputs in a morphological segment.

Design of functional systems in architectural design is the selection, preliminary sizing, and rough arrangement of those systems that will be required to provide various functions needed in the building. In essence *design of functional systems* in architectural design is the equivalent of a supply systems statement, and it forms the second input (of external information) to the morphological segment.

Component design in architectural design is the process by which the available and selected functional systems are mated with the layout; in such a mating the functions required in various locations and in whatever quantity are used as the final determiners of the functions to be supplied. The system of supply is matched with the systems of demand. *Component design* is a process of matching specific demand with possible supply to obtain a specific supply; it is a *matching* process. It is the process or operation component within a morphological segment.

When a match is accepted, by comparing the degree of match with some criterion, a selection is made and a decision achieved. Evaluation and selection are the decision component in the morphological segment.

The selection becomes the supply statement in response to the original demand statement. The supply statement is the output from the morphological segment. It is clear, then, that any segment within a morphology (any *method* within an overall *process*) can be thought of in terms of input of both demand and supply systems information, a process that matches supply with demand, and a decision that selects a specific supply. Within such a sequential process, each segment combines supply and demand input to produce a supply output— which becomes a new demand input on the next segment. There is a very clear transformation of two kinds of information into another kind of information. A tabular arrangement (Fig. 2.10) of the terms used by several different writers can help to clarify the relationship. Although the description of design by L. Bruce Archer (1967) has not been incorporated into this present discussion, it is useful to include the terms Archer uses for comparison with those of the other writers. Scant justice is done to Archer by such a brief synopsis of the procedure he describes. The terms placed in parallel with the terms by other writers are only approximately equivalent.

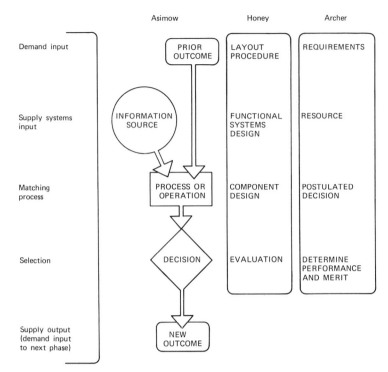

Figure 2.10 Different terminologies for demand-supply segments.

2.3.13.4 In summary when demand information is combined with supply systems information, the operation in the segment transforms that information into supply information; that supply information, in turn, becomes demand information on the next segment. It is interesting to compare this sequence with the sequence in the Hegelian dialectic (Windelband, 1958, pp. 591-592): thesis, antithesis, synthesis (new thesis).

REFERENCES

Archer, L. Bruce, *The Structure of Design Processes,* U.S. Dept. of Commerce, National Bureau of Standards, Gaithersburg, Md., 1967.

Asimow, Morris, *Introduction to Design*, Prentice-Hall, Englewood Cliffs, N.J., 1962.

Honey, C. R., "Information Flow in Architectural Design," *The Architect's Journal*, May 21, 1969.

Nadler, Gerald, *Work Systems Design: The IDEALS Concept*, Richard D. Irwin, Inc., Homewood, Ill., 1967.

Parsons, Talcott, and E. A. Shils, Eds., *Toward a General Theory of Action*, Harvard University Press, Cambridge, Mass., 1951.

Windelband, Wilhelm, *A History of Philosophy*, Vol. 2, Harper & Row, New York, 1958.

2.4 NOTATION SYSTEMS IN DESIGN

Drawing is the dominant notation by which the designer communicates with himself and with others. To understand the most appropriate use of this dominant form of notation, one must place it in a context of other notational systems.

As the student starts his education in architecture, he begins to learn a number of different notation and representation techniques. The usual secondary education has placed a very small emphasis on graphic skills such as photography and drawing, but every student who enters architecture *knows* that it requires an ability to draw; in fact a student often enters architecture *because* he likes to draw. These two things in combination cause drawing to be overemphasized. The student who knows something about drawing wants to exercise his skill, and the student who does not know anything about it is worried that he does not have the required skill and wants to catch up.

Whereas drawing is one of the useful skills in design, drawing that requires talent and high skill is not essential. It can even become a handicap when the person enters practice, for there is a strong tendency to use a person with such skill for delineation and not for design; I have known several persons who suffered by being used in that way.

The most useful drawing is relatively easy to learn; it consists of diagrammatic drawings and sketches that can be used to illustrate relationships. An ability to do quick free-hand representations of building shapes and spatial relationships is important and can usually be acquired with a bit of practice and an acquaintance with a few simple techniques. Architectural drafting (for the production of "blueprints") is so simple to learn as a technique that most schools do not even bother to teach it; by contrast the *content* of drafting is so complex that most schools find it very difficult to teach in any comprehensive way. It is therefore left to the architectural offices to teach and for the graduate to acquire when he enters an office apprenticeship.

To place drawing, then, within a context of other forms of notation and representation, it will be helpful for us to see what things the designer needs to represent and what techniques are available.

2.4.1 The Canon Uses of Notation Systems

Any system of symbols or images by which a person communicates ideas or events is a notation system. A profession or academic discipline tends to formalize its own notation system into a set of canon terms.

Any system of words (whether spoken or written), of symbols, or of images that a person can use to represent some set of conditions to himself or to others is a notation system. The designer can have a need to represent the condition of any part of the information that has been described; he may need to describe the person who is the design client, or he may need to describe the client's purposes, his behaviors, the functions that his behaviors require, and the objects that can supply those functions.

Ordinarily notation is thought of as something more formal than mere representation. The implication is that some set of representations is organized into a system. This is usually true. Because each profession (or each academic discipline) tends to deal with the same material repeatedly, it also tends to organize the method by which it represents that material into a coherent system. The use of a standard vocabulary of notations helps the professional organize the material into familiar categories and determine whether he has considered all the information he usually considers.

It would not seem possible to forget major features of a building, but such things have happened. Legend (i.e., drafting room gossip) tells that one of the early hotels that was built with its lobby on the second floor, giving over valuable ground floor space to shops, was designed without any way to get from the street and the ground floor level to the second floor lobby. Only when the building was in construction was the error discovered. The embarrassed architect had to produce some quick revision to provide the necessary stairs. One way of understanding such an extraordinary error is to understand that the typology of building components (and the notation scheme) did not yet contain a sufficiently strong and habitually used lobby-stair component. I do not insist on this as an explanation; I use this example only to illustrate the interdependent relationship between what can be considered in the real world and what can be represented in the problem-solving process.

The purposes of notation are to record information about the problem in such a manner that the problem solver can manipulate that information to try possible solutions. He uses notation to communicate his solution to others for their consideration and their execution of the solution. The purposes of notation are to record, manipulate, experiment, propose, and communicate.

2.4.2 The Development of Notational Vocabularies

Before a designer can use a notation scheme, he must acquire in that notation a vocabulary that has direct meaning for him.

To use a variety of notation schemes, the student must acquire a vocabulary of various forms of representations and associate each with its real-world counterpart. As the young designer first learns the use of notation in drawing, his tendency is to be more detailed and pictorial than is necessary and helpful. Some students and practitioners never learn that drawings can be relatively abstract and economical just as well as they can be concrete and pictorial. Like words, drawings can range from the completely abstract and general to the concrete and specific. The word *chair* refers to a very broad group of objects; the phrase *Windsor chair* refers to a smaller group of objects, chairs made of wood that have backs composed of spokes in a fan-like formation; finally the specification of a chair by manufacturer's name, catalog number, color, and any other required detail can specify the object completely. In the same way a chair can be represented in a drawing by an appropriately sized square, by a more detailed shape to represent a chair type, or by an exactly drawn shape to represent some specific chair. The level of abstractness chosen depends on the purposes of the notation.

In addition to abstractness a single other quality in a drawing notation scheme that usually is extremely important is the accurate representation of sizes. It is important for the student to have a memorized vocabulary of sizes. I remember that the large studio on the upper floor of Robinson Hall at Harvard was about 145 feet long. I remember that the quadrangle just south of Robinson Hall was very close to an acre in size, and that the entire central part of the campus, known as the Yard, was about 95 acres in extent. Since I can still visualize those places, I can compare the places I represent in drawings with these "standard" places in my memory.

2.4.3 Interchanging Uses of Different Notations

There is some interchangeability between different notations according to the working process and preference of the designer.

Today the use of systematic methods in design is controversial. Some favor the use of verbal and quantitative methods as an aid to the design process; analysis by verbal and quantitative notations can help the designer to see what directions to take and reduce the total effort in the use of drawing notations. And some favor the more traditional methods that rely more strongly on diagrams and drawings.

I once had the experience of working under an architect who relied almost exclusively on a sketching notation. He did comparatively little diagraming and almost no verbal analysis. He produced sketch after sketch of the basic building plan on yellow tracing paper; when he found one he liked, he would ask a junior designer to draw the scheme to scale, to check whether it could provide all the required sizes of rooms. As often as not, when the junior designer returned, the architect had gone on to other schemes that were more interesting to him. He sketched endlessly, repeating schemes that he had already tried and trying schemes that could not possibly have worked because of specific constraints on circulation patterns in the building program. After having several schemes ignored that I had drawn to scale for a dormitory project, I spent some time analyzing just what pattern of relationships a scheme had to have to satisfy the program requirements. This verbal and diagrammatic analysis was of no interest to the architect. He did not solve problems by using that kind of notation; he used a more pictorial notation that suited his problem-solving style, and he was willing to spend the additional time that the pictorial notation required. I do not disparage his approach. He was a good designer and a thoughtful architect. If his design process was not very efficient, that was his choice.

By contrast with his approach other designers use an extreme amount of verbal analysis before moving to diagrams and drawings.

2.4.4 Ambiguity and Clarity in a Notational System

Notations vary in their typical degree of concreteness or abstractness. The more abstract notation is also more ambiguous.

Each form of notation varies from the more abstract to the more concrete. An important characteristic of the more abstract is that it is also more ambiguous. In earlier stages of problem solution the need is for flexibility and changeableness. The more abstract notation is more economical to produce and, for that reason, easier to abandon. Because it is so abstract, it can often suggest schemes other than the one the notation was used to represent. A relatively abstract notation is ambiguous and suggestive and is often the more useful during problem solution. By contrast a more concrete notation is probably more useful when a problem has been solved and the problem solver is trying to communicate his solution to other persons.

2.4.5 Degrees of Abstractness in Notational Systems

Within a specific notation system there are different degrees of abstractness and concreteness that can be related to the person-object information spectrum.

As notation schemes are seen in relation to the information spectrum, several facts emerge. First, the different kinds of information are themselves more or less abstract. Second, the different kinds of notation range in expression from the more concrete to the more abstract. Third, within each notation scheme are degrees of abstractness and concreteness; each has a range of expressive capability.

Within the information spectrum (Fig. 2.1 p. 52) person-related and object-related information tend to be the most concrete. Behavior-related information, although still concrete, is somewhat less so (there are simply no adequate notational systems to represent the concreteness of behavior). Purpose-related and function-related information tend to be more abstract. The relative abstractness is implied by the form of the diagram. The more the information is concerned with a relationship, the more abstract it is.

When reviewing a full spectrum of means for communication and possible notation schemes that can be associated with each, one can rank them from most concrete to most abstract in expression. Starting with the relatively concrete, one can list enactments and performances, television and motion pictures, photographs, drawings, diagrams (with labels), and language and other verbal expression and end with the relatively abstract, quantifications and mathematical expressions.

Within each mode of expression are relatively abstract and relatively concrete notations. I have already described how this is true in drawing; it is equally true for the other modes of expression and communication.

ARCHITECTURE, PROBLEMS AND PURPOSES

2.4.6 A Tabular Array of Notational Systems

The abstractness-concreteness of the various forms of notation can be shown in a tabular array.

Rather than discuss each mode, I can accomplish much the same thing by use of a tabular array. Higher in the array indicates more abstract, and lower, more concrete. This relation holds for the entire array and also for the relative abstractness-concreteness within each mode of expression. The array appears in Fig. 2.11. Examples of a number of different modes of notation appear in Figs. 2.12 through 2.15.

Figure 2.11 The relative abstractness of different notation systems.

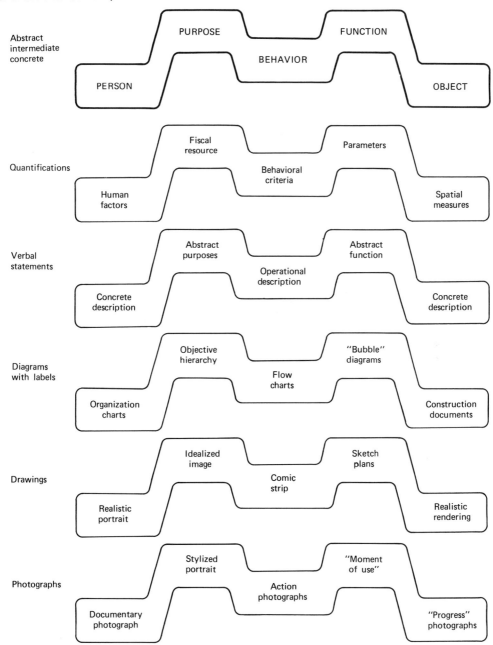

Site
evaluation

"Bubble"
diagram

Function
zoning

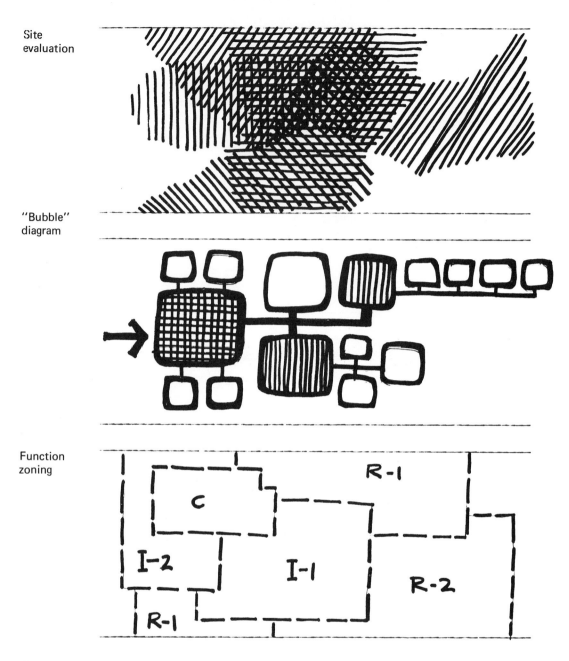

Figure 2.12 Diagrams with labels
("bubble" diagrams).

ARCHITECTURE, PROBLEMS AND PURPOSES

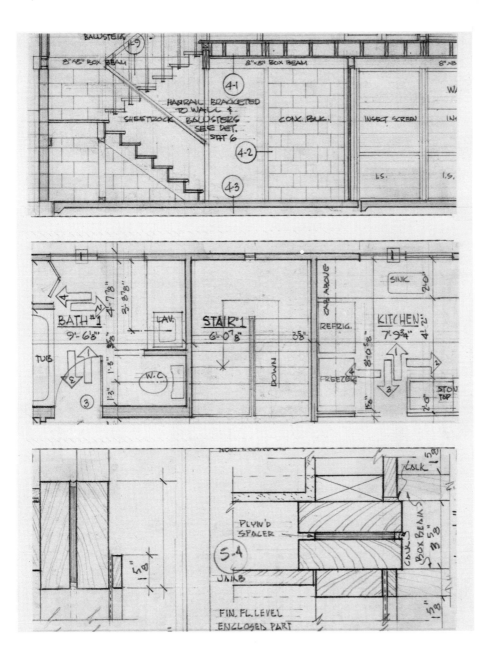

Figure 2.13 Diagrams with labels (construction documents).

Site
plan
notation

Floor
plan
notation

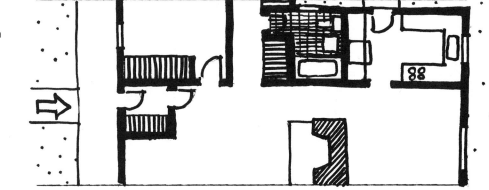

Elevation
notation

Figure 2.14 Drawings (sketch
plans.

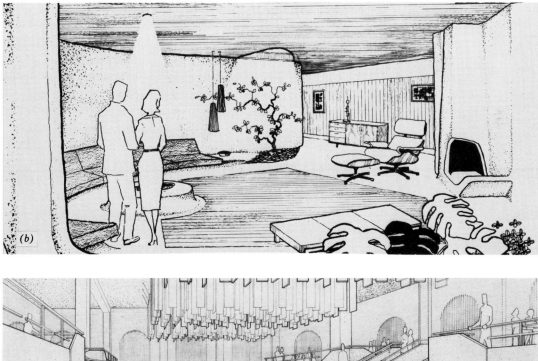

Figure 2.15 Drawings (pictorial renderings).

2.4.7 The Technical Disscussions

The technical discussion that follows is concerned with the existence of *canon* terms in a professional vocabulary, that is, with the very existence of a professional vocabulary. It is this professional vocabulary to which a notation scheme corresponds.

The discussion also deals with the process by which information is *encoded* into such a set of canon terms in order for the professional problem solver to use the information.

2.4.7-1 Equivalent Substitutions

A professional problem solver encodes problem information into canon terms that are typical of and standard for his profession. Each notation scheme in professional use has a formal and precise set of terms.

The information used by the experienced problem solver in a specific field is different from that available to the general public about that same field. This different availability is due in large part to the development of a distinctive "small group" professional vocabulary containing words necessary for the problem solver's solution process. Those words represent concepts and categories essential for the problem solver's thought. When information is encoded for solution, it is translated from a more public and more widely known vocabulary into the more specific and more useful vocabulary of the professional problem solver. When that vocabulary is highly formalized and extremely precise in its terminology, the encoding process is called canonization or converting to canonical terms.

Kenneth H. Craik (1968, pp. 29-37) notes the difference that will exist in the perception of the environment by the general public, by groups formed on the basis of relevant personality measures, by special user-client groups such as the elderly or the young, and by special competence groups. Among special competence groups he includes architects, planners, and designers—"Groups whose members are thought to possess special competence in the comprehension and description of environmental displays." (Craik, 1968, p. 31.) The implication is, no doubt, that a special conceptual structuring is available.

To the degree that a special competence exists and a special conceptual structuring is available, technical and professional methods for the "presentation of environmental displays" and technical components in the "nature and format of judgments [about environmental displays]" also exist.

Agnew and Pyke (1969, pp. 31-32) provide a scale of language from entirely private to "entirely" public. Their scale, which ranges from "Individual Pragmatics" to "Large Group Syntax," is reproduced in Fig. 2.16. Toward the public end of this spectrum are subgroup semantics and subgroup syntax. Encoding would convert language from large-group to subgroup semantics and syntax.

To develop a computer program for the solution of algebra word problems, one of the procedures that Paige and Simon (1966) list is

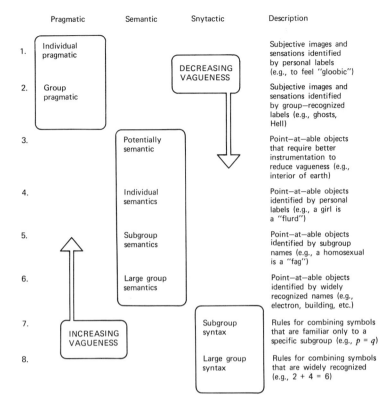

Figure 2.16 Abstractness levels in verbal notation. (Adapted from a diagram by Agnew and Pike, 1969, pp. 31-32. By permission of Prentice-Hall, Inc., Englewood Cliffs, New Jersey.)

2.4.7.1

"make mandatory substitutions." This procedure "reduces certain words and phrases that appear in the text to standard or canonical form, thus reducing the variety of expressions that have to be handled subsequently." In an exactly similar way encoding or canonization is a professional categorization that prepares the material in the problem statement for subsequent manipulation.

Among the characteristics of a canon vocabulary are both precision and succinctness. Both are eloquently illustrated in a cartoon sequence by Hellman (*The Architect's Journal*, April 19, 1972) in which the architect (this time as a layman) takes some sixty-seven words to describe how he would like the brickwork arranged in a building. In turn the foreman (as a professional), using canon terminology, tells the mason precisely what to do by using only nineteen words. The architect himself uses in his longer instruction a different level of canon terminology that is applicable to a broader range of physical geometric elements. One can imagine the client of the architect, without even this level of entry to a technical vocabulary, attempting first to articulate his interests to himself and then to express them to his architect.

The encoding or canonizing process is not for modifying information, although such modification does occur after encoding has taken place. Encoding should convert information only to more precise, *conceptually equivalent* information in a form useful for solu-

2.4.7.1

tion. As this is acccomplished and the problem solver obtains the information he needs for solution, canonization provides another advantage for the problem solver: he is able to determine whether the information he has is complete or whether he will have to supply other information for solution to go forward (Amarel, 1970, p. 182). In the solution of ill-defined problems by closure, canonization is an even more essential part of the solution.

Finally the relation of encoding and decoding as parts of the design process is well displayed in a diagram accompanying an article by Gordon Best (1969, pp. 151-152) that shows information input, encoding, processing, decoding, and output. The processing of the encoded information is affected by other information stored from experience; that information is of enormous importance in problem solution, and it can be applied to a problem only after the problem has been stated in a canon form.

REFERENCES

Agnew, Neil M., and S. W. Pyke, *The Science Game: An Introduction to Research in the Behavioral Sciences*, Prentice-Hall, Englewood Cliffs, N.J., 1969.

Amarel, Saul, "On the Representation of Problems and Goal Directed Procedures for Computers," in Banerjii, R. B., and M. D. Mesarovic, Eds., *Theoretical Approaches to Non-numerical Problem Solving,* Springer-Verlag, Berlin, 1970.

Best, Gordon, "Method and Intention in Architectural Design," in Broadbent, Geoffrey, and A. Ward, Eds., *Design Methods in Architecture*, A. A. Paper No. 4 (Symposium, Portsmouth School of Architecture, 1967). Architect's Association, London, 1969.

Craik, Kenneth H. "The Comprehension of the Everyday Physical Environment." *American Institute of Planners Journal*, **34**(1), January 1968.

Hellman, *The Architect's Journal*, April 19, 1972.

Paige, Jeffry M., and Herbert A. Simon, "Cognitive Processes in Solving Algebra Word Problems," in Kleinmuntz, Benjamin, Ed., *Problem Solving: Research, Method, and Theory*, Wiley, New York, 1966.

2.5 DESIGN AS A DATA TRANSFORMATION PROCESS

Design is a process of data transformation. The designer starts with information about a person and ends with information about an object. Each stage in this trans-

In design the student (as well as the professional designer) starts with information about a client; he ends with information about a building that is in some fitting relationship with the information he had about the client. How does he get from the one form to the other? He has evidently transformed the one kind into the other.

The student comes to understand the process in several different ways. He understands the overall pattern of the transformations he uses. He understands that, for a transformation to occur, he must propose what its result will be; to do this effectively, he learns what the origin of his proposals is. Finally he learns that each proposal, once made, can be tested for its logical relationship with the information on which he based the proposal.

2.5.1 The Pattern of Transformations: Programming, Planning, and Design

In a design process the several stages are programming, planning, and design. Planning is a typical heuristic that solves a less constrained problem as a guide to the solution of the whole more constrained problem.

Early in architectural school the student designer learns a nearly invariable sequence. He begins with what is called *programming;* he engages in a process called *planning;* he completes his work with a related process called *design.* (Note: the entire process is also called design; here design refers to a specific part of that larger process.) In some of his earlier years in school the student is usually given a complete program to work from; in his later years he is usually asked to develop the program himself.

In developing a *program*, the student designer works from a number of different kinds of information, bringing it into an organized form that corresponds to the organized relationship of activities in the proposed building. The program usually names each activity location by a conventional name (kitchen, meeting room, office, etc.); it says, if necessary, what the character of the activity is and how much space each activity requires. The program also says what activities are to be placed together and what relations they share.

As the designer moves into the *planning* phase, he converts the information from the verbal notation of the program into a visual diagrammatic notation that represents the comparative sizes of the different required areas and the relationships between them. This "bubble diagram" is an abstraction from the program, for it uses only two characteristics of the required spaces. (This is a typical heuristic, a problem-solving strategy that uses only part of the constraints, or requirements, to achieve a solution; the abstracted solution is then used as a guide to achieve the entire solution.) It diagrams building functions.

In the design phase the bubble diagram and other information are used to develop a relatively concrete proposal for a building that provides all the characteristics stated in the program. This concrete .description is an *object* description.

These several transformations are related to the information spectrum described above. *Programming* collects information about the *person* (client) and his *purposes* and converts it into information about *behaviors* (activities); *planning* takes information about behaviors and converts it into information about *functions; design* takes information about functions and converts it into information about *objects* (the building).

2.5.1

This can be shown in a modified version of the information spectrum diagram (Fig. 2.17). The relative abstractness and concreteness of the different forms of information bear out what was said about the levels of abstractness in the last section.

2.5.2 Proposal as the Basis for Design Transformations

Design solution deals with the simultaneous resolution of many different unknowns. Since logic cannot deal effectively with multiple unknowns, logic in design is achieved by the proposal (or assumption) of a solution and its analysis in terms of the problem requirements. The statement form $A \Rightarrow B$ (A, initial state; $\Rightarrow$, transformation; B, terminal state) is basic for an understanding of logical analysis.

In describing transformations, only the requirements that exist in the client's program have been considered so far. Clearly other data about typical behavior patterns, the sizes of human beings, the sizes of standard building parts, and the constructability of various building configurations are all part of the information that goes into shaping design proposals. These various kinds of information contribute to the development of proposals, which is the heart of design process and is vital in studio instruction. To know how proposals occur is important.

Imagine an example in structural design. To design a steel beam, the principal information one requires is the length of span, the distribution of the load on the beam, and the equation that develops the relation between that information and the section modulus of the beam. When these things are known, a beam having the required section modulus can be selected from a table. By contrast, to design a concrete beam, one requires information not only about span and loading but also about the beam to be designed. The designer needs to know the size of the beam and the position of the reinforcing bars in the beam before he can design the size of the beam, the position of the reinforcing bars, and the number and size of the bars. The process the designer must use in designing a concrete beam is to assume (to propose) a beam size and bar position; he must do so because there are too many unknowns to handle in an equation directly. Only when he has reduced the number of unknowns by assumption can he then compute the remaining unknown.

Design proposals occur for the same reason. So many different unknowns are involved that there is no way in which a particular unknown can be logically derived. Its logicalness depends on too many other unknowns. But when a comprehensive proposal is made,

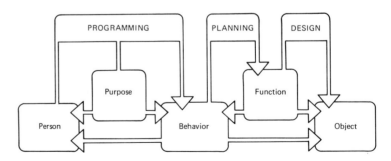

Figure 2.17 Design phases and the information spectrum.

ARCHITECTURE, PROBLEMS AND PURPOSES

then each logical relationship between the components of that proposal and the requirements that led to the proposal can be tested.

The relationships in such an information transformation can be represented by a simple formula. If A represents the initial information (a set of requirements), if B represents the terminal information form (an object to supply those requirements) and if $\Rightarrow$ (pronounced "arrow") represents the logical transformations that convert A into B (or, what is the same thing, the logical relations between A and B), the entire transformation can be shown by the form $A \Rightarrow B$. This is a three-term logical expression.

Logical expressions have been used for centuries, and invariably, the only circumstance in which such an expression can be used to solve a problem is when two of the terms are known and one is unknown. If fewer than two terms are known (when there is, for example, only a set of requirements), solution requires a "closure" of one of the other terms from an unknown to a known term. This closure (of assumption, or of proposal) is an essential technique in dealing with an ill-defined problem.

One way of describing the difference between a well-defined and an ill-defined problem is that closure has to be performed to solve an ill-defined but not a well-defined problem.

Closure (or proposal) is an essential technique in all parts of the design process and at all scales of design. The designer learns to make proposals to himself that he then tests aginst the requirements of the problem he is attempting to solve.

When I was first working as a draftsman-junior designer in an architect's office, I was very confused by the way in which the older draftsmen knew what pieces of wood or metal to use in designing the detailed construction of different parts of the building. No catalogue was available wherein all the different known shapes could be found when needed. It took me some time to realize that many of the shapes were "made up" by the draftsmen. Using a few known available sizes, they then cut and shaped those pieces on paper to fit the design and construction requirements with which they were concerned. The naive beginning designer often has trouble learning how much proposing he must do to design; the more mature and skilled designer who has become extremely familiar with the process forgets how much of it he does.

2.5.3 The Origin of Proposals

Proposals have their origins in canonization, existing solutions,

Proposals have many origins.

1. Canonization. Because the problem is stated for a particular professional designer, the information the designer brings to problem solving is structured according to the usages of his profession.

2. Existing Solutions. The designer draws on the known successful ways of doing things. At times this orientation is hardened into a use of unvarying traditional forms; at other times the designer draws on the latest fashion in successful (built) solutions. Between these extremes the kind of problem the architect has and the kind of building he is attempting to design are influenced by the body of typical work that exists. There are established building types, and there is an established typology of known solutions.

3. Standard Practice. At a somewhat less formal, less self-conscious level usual ways exist for doing particular things. Some of these practices are embodied in rules of thumb, and some are brought into action without having their origin questioned. The rule of thumb can be illustrated by practice in concrete beam design discussed above; if the designer starts with a beam depth of one inch for every foot of span, he will have reasonable success and will not have to do a great number of iterations of his work. The rule of thumb provides a good starting place.

4. Regulations. Some standard practices are considered so essential that they are codified into regulations or ordinances. Such requirements are often a useful beginning for the designer.

5. Variations. Transpositions and modifications from any of the above can sometimes form a useful way for generating proposals. Some good part of design consists of trying such manipulations on an established set of components. As an example of this the architect usually spends considerable time in trying variations in the placement of rooms when he is designing a building.

6. Inventions. The designer's imagination can suggest something that has not been thought of or tried before. It is difficult to say at what point a variation is so great that it becomes an invention; perhaps it occurs at a conceptual level, where the organizing idea of the thing is different from any other organizing idea.

2.5.4 Testing the Proposal by Analysis and Fitting

Problem solution is not by analysis-synthesis; it is by analysis-proposal-analysis-fit.

A proposal (a problem statement closure) cannot stand by itself. It is not enough to propose; design requires proposal and testing of the proposal. The designer tests a proposal by examining the logical relationships between the proposed object and the activity requirements the client has stated. The question that must be answered is whether the building will permit and support an activity in the way the client requires.

The problem solution description that uses the terms *analysis* and *synthesis* is not very helpful; usually the term *synthesis* is not clearly defined. A better description is given by the sequence of terms

ARCHITECTURE, PROBLEMS AND PURPOSES

analysis-proposal-analysis-fit. First the p[...]
problem statement, is *analyzed.* Second[...]
solution. Third, the proposal is *analyzed*[...]
solution proposal are tested for their *fit*[...]
problem statement. Although the fit is r[...]
will be acceptable for solution, and othe[...]
not. The procedure outline proposed her[...]
to the mental process TOTE (Test-Oper[...]
Miller, Galanter, and Pribram.)

The information the designer deals with occurs in a spectrum, and
the forms of information are in an ends-means relationship. The logic
of this relationship is what must be tested.

As the designer tests that logical relationship, he also tests the
causal connection between events that will occur as the result of his
designing. The degree to which that test is accurate depends on several
different relationships. It depends on whether the designer has accurately represented (encoded) the client's requirements, on the degree
to which his notation for building design accurately represents the
qualities of the real physical building it is intended to represent, and
on the degree to which the logical relations the designer uses accurately represent causal processes in the world of events. Fig. 2.18
shows how these several relationships are connected.

2.5.5 The Technical Discussions

The technical discussions that follow go into considerably more detail
about the information encoding (translation) process, the information
transformation process, and the design problem. The section dealing
with design problems discusses what the unique properties of design
problems are in a context permitting description of all kinds of problems.

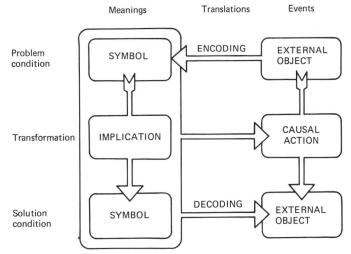

Figure 2.18 Relations between
translation and transformation
processes.

ula $A \Rightarrow B$ is a univer-
applicable problem state-
nt form. For solution to occur,
wo of the terms must be in a
known condition (either given or
assumed) so that the third term
can be adduced.

In the well-known pioneering study of problem-solving processes *Productive Thinking*, Max Wertheimer (1959, pp. 238-243) describes the problem solution process as one in which a situation, S_1, which contains stresses and a lack of structure, is transformed by the problem solver into a situation, S_2, in which the stresses are resolved and where a structure is provided. He indicates that the change of state can occur in a number of different ways.

Depending on how the situation is viewed and on what the motives of the problem solver are, a number of kinds of problem situation transformations are available. Wertheimer notes the following (1959, pp. 241-242):

(1) $S_1 \ldots S_2$ The basic situation change, described above.

(2) $\ldots S_1 \ldots S_2 \ldots$ Where both situations are parts of an ongoing process.

(3) $S_1 \ldots$ Where a concrete goal is not defined, and part of the problem consists in defining that goal.

(4) $\ldots S_2$ Where S_1 does not play a significant part, but there is a well-defined goal or objective.

This conception of the problem solution process, consisting of two separate states or situations, one prior to the other, and connected by some transforming process, would appear to underlie the work by a number of later researchers in problem solution studies. It has been especially important to the work of several investigators in information-processing studies.

The clearest unconfounded description of the state transformation model is in the work of Walter Reitman (1964, pp. 282 ff.). He develops a statement form, $A \Rightarrow B$ (which can also be expressed as a vector $[A, B, \Rightarrow]$), that is universal in its application to problems. A is used to represent some initial state; $\Rightarrow$ (arrow), some transformation process; and B, some terminal state. All three terms can be compound, and in all but the simplest of problems each term *is* compound. The process term can also be a sequential term. The strength of this problem representation is in the requirements it imposes on the problem solver. He must decide very clearly what his known and unknown terms are.

In defining a problem by means of this statement form, each of the three terms has associated with it a list of attributes, so arranged that the list defines a class of possible elements. Using the vector terminology appropriate for the Newell, Shaw, and Simon information-processing language IPL-V, Reitman states, "Any vector $[A, B, \Rightarrow]$ will be said to be a *problem vector* if it has associated with it a *problem requirement*. A problem requirement specifies that another vector

[A', B', $\Rightarrow'$] should be found so that A', B' $\Rightarrow'$ will be elements of A, B, $\Rightarrow$, respectively, and so that the process $\Rightarrow'$ applied to A' will yield B' uniquely, which we write as $A' \Rightarrow' B'$." (Reitman, 1964, p. 288.)

For a problem to be solved, two of the terms in the statement form must be known for the third term to be adduced, so that when applied to A', the process $\Rightarrow'$ will yield B' uniquely. Essentially a problem statement form must be in a two-knowns condition if solution is to be accomplished.

If two known terms already exist, the solution process is fairly clear, but if only one term or none is adequately known, then terms have to be supplied by assumption or even by arbitrary choice for solution to proceed (Amarel, 1970, p. 182).

The statement form also raises another difficulty (and supplies a strength of understanding) for the problem solver; although a third term can be adduced from two known terms, there is no guarantee that a known-world counterpart to the adduced third term is available. Presumably (to use an example by Reitman) the problem solver can deduce what would be required to change ($\Rightarrow'$) a sow's ear (A') into a silk purse (B'); the initial and the terminal state can be adequately known, and he has only to deduce what the process sequence would have to be. That no known sequences are easily available does not harm the *logic* of the solution process.

The problem statement form used by Reitman thus implies several stages of problem solution: (1) placing the problem in a two-knowns form, (2) deducing what the third term must be, and (3) searching for a real-world counterpart to the deduced third term.

Reitman's examples make clear (1964, pp. 284-287) that this statement form can be applied to several kinds of problems. He gives examples of problems that require design or creation and are future oriented, of a research problem that is past oriented, and of one that is process oriented and is essentially a managerial or engineering problem. Design, management, and research problems appear to be distinguished by whether the "present reality" is in the initial, the process, or in the final term.

Finding numerous examples of problem models that use this basic form, $A \Rightarrow B$, to describe the major components of a problem is easy enough. A typical problem-solving model in design uses this format (Best, 1969, pp. 151-152). The three terms are labeled input, process, and output. The input is clearly concerned with the present reality that must be encoded into a form suitable for the manipulation of process. The output is in an information format that must be decoded to have its real-world impact at some future time.

What we know as problem solution, which requires the encoding and decoding described above, relies on external adjuncts to memory and on information manipulation (Shepard, 1964, p. 271). Before the

2.5.5.1

problem solver can tackle a problem of any degree of complexity, he requires at the start pencil and paper; as he moves further into more and more complex solution processes, he undoubteldy requires other, more complex supports. The simplicity of the Reitman format permits its development into whatever complexity of structure is required for complex problem solution.

REFERENCES

Amarel, Saul, "On the Representation of Problems and Goal Directed Procedures for Computers," in Banerjii, R. B., and M. D. Mesarovic, Eds., *Theoretical Approaches to Non-numerical Problem-Solving,* Springer-Verlag, Berlin, 1970.

Best, Gordon, "Method and Intention in Architectural Design," in Broadbent, Geoffrey, and A. Ward, Eds., *Design Methods in Architecture* (Symposium, Portsmount School of Architecture, 1967), Architect's Association, London, 1969.

Reitman, Walter R., "Heuristic Decision Procedures, Open Constraints, and the Structure of Ill-Defined Problems," in Shelly, Maynard W., II, and Glenn L. Bryan, Eds., *Human Judgments and Optimality,* Wiley New York, 1964.

Shepard, Roger N., "On Subjectively Optimum Selection Among Multiattribute Alternatives," in Shelly, Maynard W., II, and Glenn L. Bryan, Eds., *Human Judgments and Optimality,* Wiley, New York, 1964.

Wertheimer, Max, *Productive Thinking,* Harper & Row, New York, 1959.

2.5.5.2 The Total Solution Process: Encoding, Transformation, and Decoding

The entire process of problem solution requires encoding, transformation, and decoding. Whereas encoding and decoding are equivalent substitutions (translations), transformation (described in 2.5.5.1) is a nonequivalent substitution.

Problem solution is often divided into three different steps: encoding, processing, and decoding. Reitman's description (1964, pp. 282 ff.), referred to in Section 2.5.5-1, assumes that information is already encoded and ready to be processed. Some writers speak of the processing step as a *translation;* consider whether that is an appropriate description.

The chapters of this book may be viewed as inquiring into the relations between the statements of a problem in one language and the achievement of a solution or decision in another, or the statement of values or preferences in one language and the achievement of a decision in another, or both. (Shelly and Bryan, 1964, pp. 5-6.)

In essence, a problem statement contains a description of the solution object in one form and a request to find a description of this object in another, specified form. The second form is usually more directly useful to the poser of the problem. In most cases it consists of an explicit specification of the internal structure of the solution object, while the initial form is mainly concerned with the relative position of the object in the overall structure of the problem environment. (Amarel, 1970, pp. 181-182.)

Although neither quotation speaks of problem solving as a translation process, the first talks about establishing a relation between the language in which a problem is stated and that in which its solution is stated, and the second talks about the problem's being stated in one form and its solution's being achieved in another, specified form—with an implication that all that is required in problem solution is a conversion to an appropriate form. It may be unfair to both of these writers to suggest that they are making problem solution into a simple translation process from one language to another, or from one form to another, and yet that is what they appear to suggest.

Two issues are actually at stake in making transformations or substitutions of information in problem solving: (1) when the process is one of encoding or decoding, it is important that the substitutions made be *equivalent* (2) when the process is a conversion from a problem statement to a solution statement, it is important that the substitution be *inequivalent* (although a means can be substituted for an end in problem solution, the two things are not equivalent).

The state transformation Reitman discusses is an inequivalent substitution. A closer look at that process reveals that it is a complex of more basic operations. Three of those are closure, adduction, and search. Other basic operations that can occur in a transformation are abstraction, classification, induction, inference, reference, sequencing, and the like. A number of operations must occur whenever a transformation takes place.

According to K. J. W. Craik (1943, p. 50) the entire problem solution process requires two equivalent substitutions and one set of inequivalent substitutions. He says:

> . . .there are three essential processes:
> 1. "Translation" of external process into words, numbers, or other symbols,
> 2. Arrival at other symbols by a process of "reasoning," deduction, inference, etc., and,
> 3. "Retranslation" of these symbols into external processes (as in building a bridge to a design) or at least recognition of the correspondence between these symbols and external events (as in realizing that a prediction is fulfilled).

It is important that both the translation and the retranslation be equivalent substitutions (Craik, 1943, pp. 62-63):

> . . . meaning . . . appears to be used in two senses—general meaning or meaningfulness, which would be the power of words to symbolize things and events through the neural events which parallel those things and give rise to words and images. Meaning is also used in ordinary language in a particular sense to signify the object referred to by a certain word: this, then, is the particular reference or symbolism involved.
>
> "Implication" would be the power of these neural mechanisms to operate on each other as the real events act causally on each other, so that the words or other symbols arouse each other as the real events produce each other. Implication would thus be a kind of artificial causation in which symbols connected by rules represent events connected by causal interaction.

The important "translation" is *not* from a problem representation to a solution; that can hardly be called a translation, since the two representations are not equivalent. The important translation is between external events and their internal representations in symbols.

2.5.5.2

A distinction can be made between equivalent substitution (or translation) and inequivalent substitution (or transformation) by reference to a diagram, which also shows the relationship that Craik requires between symbols and events and between implications and causal actions. Problem solution depends on the existence of the relations described in the diagram. (Fig. 2.18, p. 87).

Craik notes (1943, p. 82) that "only this internal model of reality—this working model—enables us to predict events which have not yet occurred in the physical world, a process which saves time, expense, and even life."

In contrast, however, Roger Shepard warns that "formal optimization techniques will not generally be optimum in the real world. For the formal optimization is attained only with respect to the abstract model—not with respect to the world itself." (Shepard, 1964, p. 262.)

REFERENCES

Amarel, Saul, "On the Representation of Problems and Goal Directed Procedures for Computers," in Banerjii, R. B., and M. D. Mesarovic, Eds., *Theoretical Approaches to Non-numerical Problem Solving*, Springer-Verlag, Berlin, 1970.

Craik, K. J. W., *The Nature of Explanation*, Cambridge University Press, Cambridge, England, 1943.

Reitman, Walter R., "Heuristic Decision Procedures, Open Constraints, and the Structure of Ill-Defined Problems," in Shelly, Maynard W., II, and Glenn L. Bryan, *Human Judgments and Optimality*, Wiley, New York, 1964.

Shelly, Maynard W., II, and Glenn L. Bryan, *Human Judgments and Optimality*, Wiley, New York, 1964.

Shepard, Roger N, "On Subjectively Optimum Selection Among Multiattribute Alternatives," in Shelly, Maynard W., II, and Glenn L. Bryan, *Human Judgments and Optimality,* Wiley, New York, 1964.

2.5.5.3 Purposes and "Plans" in Problem Solution

Problem solving depends on a "plan," an organized process that controls the order of a sequence of operations. It is a form of "personal causation" characterized by an invariance of ends and a variability of means.

To move from a problem statement in one form to a solution statement in another form, one must take a series of steps (K. J. W. Craik's [1943, p. 50] three essential processes—see p. 000). This section is concerned with the second of these processes, which is neither a translation nor an equivalent substitution. Instead it is a transformation of information and can be thought of as an *in*equivalent substitution.

In attempting to describe how actions are controlled by an organism's internal representations of its universe, Miller, Galanter, and Pribram (1960, p. 13) state that behavior is organized into temporal patterns, and "What we must provide . . . is some way to map the cognitive representation into the appropriate *pattern* of activity." They suggest that the organism has available to itself a series of possible *plans* to effect modifications in its *image* of the world. *"A Plan is any hierarchical process in the organism that can control the order in which a sequence of operations is to be performed."* (Miller, Galanter, and Pribram, 1960, p. 16.)

In a discussion of the development of a particular level of aspiration Kurt Lewin (1964, p. 287) had stated in a 1946 article that "the choosing of a goal of a particular degree of difficulty, presupposes: (1) that a number of goals are seen as subgoals within a larger goal structure, (2) that the action itself is conceived as a part of the goal, and (3) that the child [children were being studied as subjects] understands the meaning of rules and is ready to keep them." Lewin suggests that the very selection of a goal implies some level of understanding of the intermediate steps toward achieving that goal.

By contrast discussions concerned directly with a theory of problem solution are a good deal less positive. Frank Restle (1969, p. 149) describes a portion of the difficulty: "Therefore, to hold a partial solution, the subject must have some concept of what the total solution will look like and be able to fill in that scheme gradually and with a certain confidence. The computer programs, and our verbal description of the problem usually proceed step by step through a schema of the solution to the problem thereby implicitly assuming that the subject has such a schema and can store partial successes. What our theories do not say is how does the subject evaluate and handle partial solutions?"

Charles M. Eastman (1970, p. 138) has a similar comment: "Two issues make decision making in a problem solving situation unique: (1) the necessity of making sequences of decisions where succeeding decisions use the results of prior ones as input; (2) the lack of means to directly evaluate single decisions in the sequence." Eastman notes that *initially* evaluative ability exists for the results of sequences. What he does not say but implies is that with a growth of experience it is possible to learn whether or not a particular decision in a sequence will permit the eventual accomplishment of the entire sequence.

Any action to accomplish a particular imaged result can be described in terms of *personal causation.* The phrase *personal causation* is used by Fritz Heider (1958, p. 103) to describe behavior that moves from an *initial focus* through some *mediation* (or mediating conditions, or actions) to a *terminal focus.* Heider states that there are two essential components of action: capability and motivation. Where motivation is associated with the *terminal focus,* capability is associated with *mediation.* Other, similar terms are used by Wertheimer, Reitman, and others.

Before following Heider's argument a bit further, it is useful to make a distinction between *causal inference,* which attempts to explain what produced a particular event, and the *personal causation* of the action-oriented problem solver. A number of attempts have been made to say which causal antecedents should be included in causal explanation. David Fischer (1970, p. 186) lists eight different positions held by various historians:

2.5.5.3

1. All antecedents
2. Regularistic antecedents
3. Controllable antecedents
4. Rational and/or motivational antecedents
5. Abnormal antecedents
6. Structural antecedents
7. Contingent-series antecedents
8. Precipitant antecedents

Fischer says that "The specific kind of causal explanation that a historian employs must be selected according to the nature of the effect to be explained and the nature of the object of explanation."

Now the differences between explaining why something has occurred and taking actions to make a thing occur are very great. Explanations of occurrence must take a very great number of things into account; by contrast action can center on its own capability. Nonetheless the two are related, since the growth of experience depends on causal explanation. Causal explanation guides personal causation. It is important in developing skill as a problem solver to be aware of which group of actions taken together produces a desired result.

In considering personal causation where some individual P tries to cause X, where X is his goal (Heider, 1958, pp. 100-101), attention must be centered on controllable and on rational and motivational antecedents. All other antecedents outside the problem solver's control must be treated as part of the initial focus or the initial condition to be changed. The decision theorists distinguish between these two classes of antecedents by the names *decision variables* and *context variables*.

A principal characteristic of personal causation is equifinality, the invariance of the end (or terminal focus) and the variablility of the means (or mediation) (Heider, 1958, p. 101). Noticing this characteristic of personal causation, Heider records three characteristics of *mediation* (1958, pp. 103-104):

1. The mediation is "atomistic"—that is, the parts of the mediation in themselves are relatively independent of each other. They do not, in the ideal case, form what may be called internally conditioned units. . . . With action, for instance, the way I move my fingers to shingle the roof is only in small measure determined by my previous finger movements. It is more closely conditioned by my intentions as related to the demands of the task. . . .

2. In spite of atomistic mediation the terminal effect can be described as a unitary entity. When someone builds a wall the many part actions which are independent in themselves are combined by the intention of the person to produce the unitary object. This is what may be called "concerted action," the causal lines of the part action converging toward the outcome of the action. . . .

3. The mediation is vicarious—that is, the same terminal focus may be reached by different paths. With action, for instance, the intention to have the roof fixed (initial focus) and the actual roof in repair (terminal focus) may be bridged by such diverse routes as doing the work oneself, paying to have it done, using wooden shingles or asphalt, and so on.

ARCHITECTURE, PROBLEMS AND PURPOSES

2.5.5.3   Heider's comments on processes of mediation can be summarized:

1. Mediation is atomistic.
2. Mediation is convergent.
3. Mediation is vicarious.

Heider observes that, expressed in a slightly different way, there are two kinds of convergence in personal causality: by different part actions and by different means.

The various conditions that pertain to operations or processes—what I began by calling inequivalent substitutions—require the careful consideration of at least the following three relationships:

1. The causal connection between an initial state and a terminal state.

2. The decomposition of a focus, or state, and the relationship of part actions to parts of the focus.

3. The existence of alternative paths or processes by which the same end can be achieved.

Let us look at each relationship in turn.

1. The Causal Connection. A causal connection can be established by a number of different routes. In fact, enough different means to a particular end are available that Heider does not hesitate to speak of convergence on a terminal focus (or terminal state). He speaks of that terminal focus as being equifinal (I would prefer to speak of it as *tending* to be equifinal). I have observed that a means-ends analysis, which is implied by personal causation, does not have the same complexity as a full causal explanation; given a distinction by the problem solver between context and decision variables, the solver can give primary attention to decision variables.

2. The Decomposition. If the decomposed parts of a focus or state are atomistic, they are not also isolates. Considering that some component of a situation or process is detachable or "independently operative" is what R. M. MacIver and D. H. Fischer refer to as the *fallacy of mechanistic cause* (Fischer, 1970, p. 178), the fact that a component fails to be interactive with other components. It must be assumed that a component requires fitting with other components for it to be an integrated and essential part of a situation or process.

3. Alternate Paths. There is little question that some alternatives and processes are better than others; there is also little question that, within the relatively loose means-ends analysis possible (when the problem solver does not have a multitude of experiences to call upon), some processes will not produce progress in the causal sequence. Some will not work. The problem solver must be able to generate process alternatives at appropriate points in a causal sequence and test whether or not the transformed information or event is at a next causal stage or not.

The problem-solving literature describes a number of different process combinations. Each can be seen to be a version of one or the other of the three relationships just described: causal connection, decomposition, or alternative choices. They are described in parts of the problem literature as *means-ends analysis, decomposition and fitting,* and *generation and matching.*

The different phases of the problem-solving process in design move through a sequence from the more general to the more particular, even though some of them vary in their degree of abstractness. They move from person to purpose statements, to behavior statements, to function statements, and finally to object statements. If we consider any single move from one statement to the next (taking the move from statements of purpose to statements of behavior as an example), the component processes proceed in the following manner:

1. A set of purpose statements is given.

2. *Decompose* compound statements into component statements.
   a. Collect component statements into dependent groups. Examine for contradiction.
   b. Examine groups for complementarity or *fit.*

3. Use *means-ends analysis* to develop specifications for behaviors that will accomplish purposes organized by 1. Components of the means-ends analysis are:
   a. Required purposes (a demand input).
   b. Available behaviors (a supply input).
   c. Behavior specification (a supply output).

4. *Generate* sets of behaviors. (Decompose as necessary.) *Match* against specifications from 2.

5. Select best set of behavioral statements.

A similar process is then iterated through each phase.

REFERENCES

Craik, Kenneth J. W., *The Nature of Explanation,* Cambridge University Press, Cambridge, England, 1943.

Eastman, Charles M., "Problem Solving Strategies in Design," in Sanoff, Henry, and S. Cohn, Eds., *EDRA 1: Proceedings of the first annual Environmental Design Research Association Conference*, no publisher named, 1970.

REFERENCES

Fischer, David H., *Historian's Fallacies: Toward a Logic of Historical Thought,* Harper & Row, New York, 1970.

Heider, Fritz, *The Psychology of Interpersonal Relations,* Wiley, New York, 1958.

Lewin, Kurt, *"Behavior and Development as a Function of the Total Situation,"* in Cartright, Dorwin, Ed., *Kurt Lewin: Field Theory in Social Science,* Harper & Row, New York, 1964.

Miller, George A., E. Galanter, and K. Pribram, *Plans and the Structure of Behavior,* Henry Holt, New York, 1960.

Restle, Frank, "Mathematical Models and Thought," in Voss, James F., Ed., *Approaches to Thought,* Merrill, New York, 1969.

2.5.5.4 Choosing Problem Solution Strategies

The problem statement form $A \Rightarrow B$ can be used for analyzing problems. The disposition of information between the several terms can provide guidance in the selection of solution strategies.

For a change process statement $(A \Rightarrow B)$ to be useful in problem statement, it must have associated with it a way of representing the amount of information that exists in each term of the statement. There must also be a way to show the relationship of the entire statement to the real-world situation and especially to its time state.

A coding for the amount of information associated with each term can be adapted from the measure of information used in decision theory (Ackoff, Gupta, and Minas, 1962, p. 13): certainty, risk, and uncertainty. Since these terms in decision theory are concerned with the sureness that an action will lead to some known outcome, the terms must be modified to represent the adequacy of information. Three levels of information can be defined, as follows:

Code   Term and Term Description

1   *Known*: Full information, adequate for complete description of the state or process. A fully known term can also be referred to as being in a "closed" condition.

2   *Range*: Not fully known, but the possible states in which the term can exist *are* fully known. The term can be "closed" to a known condition by assumption.

3   *Unknown*: The condition of the term is not known, and the possible states of the term are so numerous that not all states can be reviewed. The term can be "closed" to a known condition only by an arbitrary choice.

A series of examples will illustrate how the coding can apply to different kinds of problem statements. Since the statement form, $A \Rightarrow B$, is derived from an article by Walter Reitman (1964, pp. 282 ff.), it is also possible to use two of the prototypical problems that Reitman describes to illustrate the application of the coding to a problem statement:

Code	Problem Description
$A \Rightarrow B$	

1 2 2 How can an AM-FM receiver be redesigned similar to the original, without radical retooling, to meet the lower price of a competitor? (Reitman, 1964, pp. 282 ff.)

1 3 1 How can a sow's ear be converted into a silk purse? (Reitman, 1964, pp. 282 ff.)

2 2 1 The detective's problem. How did the dead person get killed inside a locked room?

2 1 2 How should unused production machinery in a factory be put to use?

As these examples illustrate, the insertion of a code for the amount of information into each term of the change process form defines a specific problem class. It follows that a logical expansion of the number coding (to display every possible combination of the three numbers taken three at a time) develops a comprehensive typology of problem statements.

On the basis of such a classification, problems can be grouped according to the strategies required for their solution. To achieve such a grouping, one must make a single assumption. Since logical processes in problem solution must accurately represent causal processes in the world of events (Craik, 1943, pp. 62-63), a solution procedure requires that two of the terms in a problem statement form be *known* for the third term to be adduced. If two terms are not known, solution requires some tentative conversion of two of the terms to a *known* condition before logical operations can proceed.

This assumption being kept in mind, the use of the problem statement form (which presupposes an encoding of problem information) suggests that there are three essential steps in problem solution:

1. A Preparation Phrase. The problem statement is closed to a form having two known terms.

2. An Adduction Phase. The remaining unknown term is adduced from the "prepared" known terms by logical processes. The logic of problem solution is neither strictly deductive nor inductive but instead consists of adducing answers to specific questions so that an explanatory "fit" is achieved (Fischer, 1970, pp. xv-xvi).

3. A Search Phase. The real-world counterparts of both the closed terms and the adduced term are sought.

These are logical, but not necessarily temporal, phases. Whereas the phases usually proceed in the order shown, any solution process that is at all complex can have the phases occurring simultaneously or out of sequence. The iterative nature of solution, where the simultaneous fitting of many different elements requires the modification and adjustment of previously chosen elements, prevents any commitment to a hard, unvarying sequence in the process.

Having described these problem solution phases, I can now display the following:

1. The range of problem types based on a logical expansion of the information coding.

2. A problem class designation that indicates the amount of information in a problem statement (based on an arithmetic sum of the coding; the lower the number designating the class, the greater the amount of information in the problem statement).

3. A grouping of problem types by the basic strategy required for problem preparation.

These problem types, classes, and groupings appear in Fig. 2.19.

In the problem-solving literature the kind of problem that requires closure is known as ill defined. In such a problem the kind of closure the problem solver makes affects the kind of solution he achieves. Closure often occurs only gradually during an extended solution process (Reitman, 1964, pp. 282 ff.). If a particular closure fails to achieve an adequate solution, then it can be changed. All such closures occur from the problem solver's general fund of information (Amarel,

Figure 2.19 A problem typology based on amounts of information in each term of a problem statement.

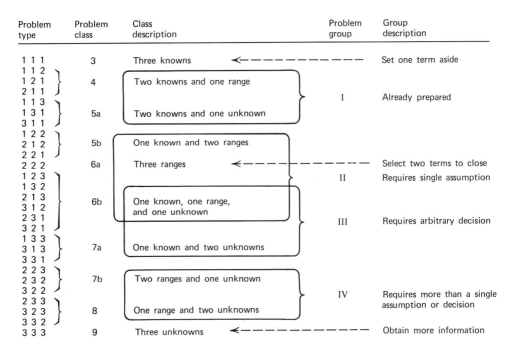

Problem type	Problem class	Class description	Problem group	Group description
1 1 1	3	Three knowns		Set one term aside
1 1 2				
1 2 1	4	Two knowns and one range		
2 1 1			I	Already prepared
1 1 3				
1 3 1	5a	Two knowns and one unknown		
3 1 1				
1 2 2				
2 1 2	5b	One known and two ranges		
2 2 1				
2 2 2	6a	Three ranges	II	Select two terms to close
1 2 3				Requires single assumption
1 3 2				
2 1 3	6b	One known, one range, and one unknown		
3 1 2				
2 3 1			III	Requires arbitrary decision
3 2 1				
1 3 3				
3 1 3	7a	One known and two unknowns		
3 3 1				
2 2 3				
2 3 2	7b	Two ranges and one unknown		
3 2 2			IV	Requires more than a single assumption or decision
2 3 3				
3 2 3	8	One range and two unknowns		
3 3 2				
3 3 3	9	Three unknowns		Obtain more information

1970, p. 182). To solve an ill-defined problem, the solver must deal with vague information (Newell, 1969, pp. 411-412). Evidently he must deal with vagueness by assumption or by arbitrary choice.

To understand the special character of design problems, we must consider another feature of problem statement. It is important to know how the problem statement is related to real-world events and where in its form the *present reality* of the problem solver is located. Whereas the distribution of information in the problem statement defines the internal structuring of information, the placement of the present reality describes the relation of the problem statement to the world of events and defines what actions the problem solver can take in modifying real-world conditions.

A classification of problem types by the location of the present reality in the problem statement appears in Fig. 2.20. Where the present reality is in the terminal state, there is a "research" problem; where it is in the process term, there is a "management" problem; where it is in the initial state, there is an "action" problem. Such a reality placement implies that research problems are concerned with past events, management problems with present events, and action problems with future events. Although this implication is broadly true, the table in Figure 2.20 also indicates that each kind of problem has more variety than such a simple generalization would suggest.

From the foregoing discussion it is possible to state clearly the kind of problem a design problem is. *A design problem is an action problem that is ill defined and that requires closure for its solution. It is*

Kind of problem	Typical questions	Coding $A \Rightarrow B$		
		A	⇒	B
Research problem	What was the former state?	x	1	1
	What process occurred?	1	x	1
	What do the data predict?	1	1	x
		A	⇒	B
Management problem	What can be the input?	x	1	1
	What process is best?	1	x	1
	What will be the output?	1	1	x
		A	⇒	B
Action problem	What can be changed?	x	1	1
	What process will serve?	1	x	1
	What state can be achieved?	1	1	x

Present reality

Figure 2.20 A problem classification according to the location of "present reality" of the problem. A coding of either "2" or "3" is indicated by *x*.

2.5.5.4

especially the kind of problem that requires closure of the terminal state. Based on partial information about the purposes of a client, the design problem is concerned with closure to the level of detail required to describe the desired attributes of physical objects. When such closure has been achieved, adduction of the processes by which the terminal state can be obtained is sometimes a relatively trivial exercise; such processes are often extremely well known.

REFERENCES

Ackoff, Russel L., S. K. Gupta, and J. S. Minas, *Scientific Method*, Wiley, New York, 1962.

Amarel, Saul, "On the Representation of Problems and Goal Directed Procedures for Computers," in Banerjii, R. B., and M. D. Mesarovic, Eds., *Theoretical Approaches to Non-Numerical Problem Solving*, Springer-Verlag, Berlin, 1970.

Craik, Kenneth J. W., *The Nature of Explanation*, Cambridge University Press, Cambridge, England, 1967.

Fischer, David H., *Historian's Fallacies*, Harper & Row, New York, 1970.

Newell, Allen, "Heuristic Programming: III-Structured Problems," in Aronofsky, Julius S., Ed., *Progress in Operations Research*, Vol. 3, Wiley, New York, 1969.

Reitman, Walter R., "Heuristic Decision Procedures, Open Constraints, and the Structure of III-Defined Problems," in Shelly, Maynard W., II, and Glenn L. Bryan, Eds., *Human Judgments and Optimality*, Wiley, New York, 1964.

2.5.5.5 Typological Information as a Basis for Problem Solution

Design solution relies heavily on typological information. It may be that most problem solutions are composed of pieces of old solutions. There is enormous mental economy in such solutions.

Information based on tradition in design is like that based on the authority of a highly qualified individual; furthermore, that based on the building tradition is being resurrected as a legitimate form of design information because of what has been called a typological approach to design. A legitimacy in this approach is worth discussing.

Robert Gutman (1972, p. 394), Alan Colquhoun (1972, p. 400), and Tomas Maldonado (1964, p. 16) have each commented (each quoting the one before) on the importance of *building types* in the design process and of building typologies as a major source of information for design solution. A major part of design solution is accomplished by reference to prior solutions, sometimes in their parts or their components and sometimes in their entirety.

Such an enormous amount of detail is involved in any design process that to make each decision afresh would be to throw away every particle of past experience the designers had acquired. The designer, as Colquhoun has observed, tends to rely on "type" solutions.

Maldonado's comments (1964, p. 16) are slightly different; he suggests the development of a vocabulary of types that can be used in a self-conscious way. His approach appears to be similar to Alexander's in the development of a "pattern language." Maldonado is, however, pessimistic; he worries (quite appropriately in my view) that difficulties will continue to exist so long as type definitions are not precisely stated at a theoretical level. He believes that the several functional classes to which a component can belong must be carefully identified.

Two supporting comments are worth citing. I have already referred in the discussion of heuristic processes (Section 2.1.5-2) to Solomon-off's inductive inference model of solution, that all heuristic processes are combinations of successful past processes. This in itself is strong support for the use of a typology for solution in design. The other comment is by D. E. Broadbent (1958, pp. 62-63), who observes that the device by which the demands on memory capacity are reduced is the memory of a "last state" rather than of all the processes and intermediate states that led to that last state. Presumably, in design, the architect's last building of the type under consideration was a cumulative improvement over his other efforts to design buildings of a similar kind. As such, that last state building would be the best guide to the design of a new building of the same sort.

There are, of course, difficulties with this approach. Use of a last state depends on there having been a growth of experience and a modification of practice, state-by-state as that experience developed ("hill climbing" must be in use as a procedure); a willingness must have been present to produce a modified "next state" from the accumulated experience recorded by the last state record. Use of a last state also depends on the existence of adequate records; unfortunately no useful means for communicating and sharing experience across the design professions have been available. The last state record tends to be a record of the accumulated experience of only the individual practitioner—not of the total profession. Finally a dependence on typological information can constitute for some practitioners an excuse to avoid modification and justify the repeated use of the last state design as being adequate for any new project of the same type. A way is needed to ensure that typologies are not used in that fashion.

REFERENCES

Broadbent, D. E., *Perception and Communication*, Pergamon Press, New York, 1958.

Colquhoun, Alan, "Typology and Design Method," in Gutman, Robert, Ed., *People and Buildings*, Basic Books, New York, 1972.

Gutman, Robert, *People and Buildings*, Basic Books, New York, 1972.

Maldonado, Tomas, and Gul Bonsieppe, Hochschule fur Gestaltung, Ulm, No. 10/11, May 1964.

2.6 THE DECOMPOSITION OF PROBLEM STATEMENTS

Problem solution usually requires the decomposition of a problem into its parts. As the designer moves from an ends statement to a means statement, he usually also moves from a whole statement to a parts statement.

I have talked at length about the person-object spectrum of information that distinguishes between purpose and function statements. I was attempting to illustrate this spectrum to a group of academic linguists, when one of them asked,

.Suppose that I said my purpose was to have you build me a kitchen. Isn't that a purpose statement at what you would call the function level?

All right, but why do you want a kitchen?

Why, to keep my pots and pans in.

But why do you want to keep your pots and pans in it?

I want them to be *next to my* salt and pepper.

Etc. . . .

However I tried, I could not move the linguist through an ends-means spectrum. Instead he was moving me through a whole-part subdivision. Finally, after going through this exercise, my linguist acquaintance recognized that a statement of required functions was weak by itself. He said:

If I don't let you find out what my purposes are, then I would have to be satisfied with any kind of kitchen that you provided so long as it had all of the parts that we had agreed that it should have.

Of course, he was exactly right in his assessment. What we did not say, because the conversation took a different turning, is that an ends-means spectrum often depends on a whole-part decomposition. It is often easier to talk about reasons for parts than about reasons for the whole.

Usually a problem (and the ultimate solution) can be divided into a number of different parts. The problem can usually be seen as part of some larger whole situation, and its solution as part of some larger context or setting. Often the only way to understand a thing is to decompose from its whole into its parts and also to compose it as a part of some larger whole. The diagram (Fig. 2.21) illustrates how a thing can be dealt with as a whole broken into parts and as a part that, taken together with other parts, can make a larger whole.

The student designer usually discovers the need to break a thing into its parts for analysis. In fact a direct relation can be discovered between the extent of movement in the ends-means spectrum toward the means (or object) direction and the amount of whole-part subdivision required in analysis.

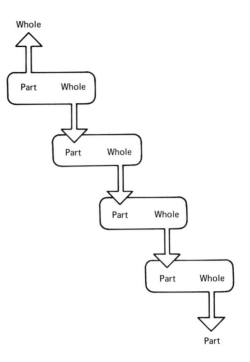

Figure 2.21 Whole-part relationships.

2.6.1 Problem Detail Related to Problem Solution

Clients furnish different amounts of detail in their problem descriptions. The problem with few requirements has many solutions and is therefore more difficult to solve. The problem with many requirements has fewer solutions but is easier to solve.

Design problems have different amounts of detail. The student designer soon discovers that the problem with the greater amount of detail is often easier to solve than the more "open" problem with less detail. The two kinds of problems at either end of a range from much to little detail are very different (Fig. 2.22). Although the problem with more detail is usually more complex, requiring considerable study for its solution, the decision criteria are firm; the number of solutions is limited, and the work can proceed until one is achieved. By contrast the problem with little detail has very weak decision criteria and consequently a great many solutions; to select one, the designer must set additional criteria of his own. The work goes in a halting fashion until he has developed his own set of detail requirements.

If the problem with low detail is a school sketch problem not to be taken too seriously, or if the faculty will accept the student designer's criteria without question, things are not so serious. But if the designer is working for a client who must agree with the criteria the designer adopts, the designer risks a great deal in setting additional criteria of his own. Clients differ enormously in the amount of detail that they are capable of furnishing and willing to furnish. They differ enormously in the amount of detail they wish to consider during the design of a building. Some institutional clients with little experience in building facilities for themselves have little detail information and

ARCHITECTURE, PROBLEMS AND PURPOSES

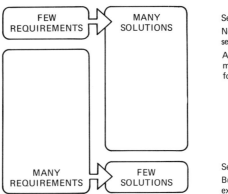

Figure 2.22 The influence of "requirements" on problem solution.

2.6.1

are relatively open. Other institutional clients have highly codified requirements based on a considerable body of experience in constructing facilities for themselves. There may be considerable truth in the statement by C. Northcote Parkinson (in *Parkinson's Law*), "It is now known that a perfection of planned layout is achieved only by institutions on the point of collapse."

One can see a similar variation in clients for residential design. I have dealt with clients who brought enormous scrapbooks of ideas collected over a number of years that were all to be incorporated into a single house. I have had clients who could agree about the design of a house when a sketch plan was scratched into the dirt road adjacent to their lot. I have had clients who were unable to articulate their needs but were enormously concerned over the articulation of the design solution; such a client requires large amounts of time and effort because each effort is a gamble that the designer's criteria are a match with the criteria the client is unable to articulate.

In such circumstances the designer is wise to invest effort only gradually in verbal descriptions, diagrams, and drawings. He should keep his work as spare as possible as he gradually secures the client's understanding and agreement. Early mistakes in programming, if they go undiscovered, are much more costly in time and more costly to repair than mistakes at later stages.

2.6.2 The Relation between Analysis and Decomposition

Demand and supply statements are not meaningful or useful until they have been analyzed into detailed statements.

As the designer converts information in one form to that in the next different form (in the person-object, ends-means spectrum), he must engage in a detail consideration of the information in each form. This can be illustrated by the conversion that takes place when the designer moves from a set of function statements to a set of object statements. The function statements can be thought of as demand statements and the object statements as supply statements in response to the demand.

One architect (see the technical discussions that follow) has

THE BASIC SOLUTION PROCESS

2.6.2

described this transformation in terms of three basic operations, refering to them as (1) layout, (2) functional systems design, and (3) component design. *Layout* identifies those locations where specific functions are required. *Functional systems design* identifies the patterns in which physical components are arranged to supply those functions. *Component design* develops an interaction between the layout and the functional systems that determines a best configuration of components according to both the demand and the supply systems criteria.

Each kind of information transformation can be thought of in these terms. The designer can weigh in detail what demands and what supply systems exist and what interactions occur between them.

2.6.3 Incompatibility between Statement Decompositions

Problem solution is difficult because demand statements do not decompose along the same lines as supply statements.

In design one basic difficulty always exists: supply systems do not decompose along the same lines as demand. Solutions do not compose along the same lines that problems do. This difficulty is not restricted to design problems. In all problem solving neither problems nor solutions can be decomposed into such elementary components that a one-to-one match between problem and solution elements can be achieved. This simple fact can be made clear by an example. By listing all the functions a bathroom must accommodate (hand washing, shaving, shampooing, light laundering, tooth brushing, bathing, showering, exercising, defecating, medicating, ministering, hot soaking, and so forth) and the functional systems available to provide for and assist those activities (lighting, water supply, water containment, water drainage, linen storage, medicine storage, toiletries storage, and so on), it is clear that a one-to-one match does not exist. Instead each activity uses several systems, and each system supports several activities.

2.6.4 Interdependence between Demand Statements

Some demand statements are interrelated; others are independent. Problem solution can be simplified by organizing demand statements into related hierarchic groupings.

Because demands are interrelated, techniques have been developed for grouping interdependent demands. Some demand statements are not related and are completely independent of each other; the need to wash oneself in some privacy might have only a weak interdependence with the need to have an outside walkway visible by guests, but the need to wash oneself would surely have a strong interdependence with a need to dry oneself after washing. Of the interdependent demands some are complementary (like those just mentioned) and some are contradictory (the need to be private in one's house and the need to see who is at one's door).

2.6.5 Interdependence between Supply Statements

Supply systems are sometimes complementary and sometimes contradictory. If their contradiction (or interference) cannot be avoided, the more important system must be given priority.

Systems of structural support, systems of (utility) supply, and the spatial systems through which people move can interfere with each other. A substantial part of physical object design is arranging the object in such a way that its several integral systems do not interfere. Plumbing waste lines must sometimes pierce beams, as well as walls and floors. Air ducts can interfere with both. The vertical dimension of inhabitable space is sometimes controlled by the utility systems concealed above the ceiling.

Spatial interference is the obvious and simple interaction that occurs between systems. Other, less obvious interactions occur. The sizes of the heating and the cooling systems may depend on the brightness (and heat production) of the lighting system. The necessary brightness of the lighting system may depend on the amount of glare and brightness from the windows. The size of the windows and the heat loss from them affect the size of the heating system, and so on.

Usually the people systems (i.e., the spaces intended to serve the needs of the building's occupants) are chosen as most important, and the other serving systems are made to defer to them. There are, of course, exceptions to this general rule. A regional post office, for example, that houses a very large sorting system will be likely to neglect human concerns in favor of the sorting process and the machinery that operates it. Buildings that have to protect their occupants against extremes of climate (or extreme environments) might well neglect human concerns and processes in favor of the protective enclosure systems.

2.6.6 Demand-Supply Interdependencies

Sometimes a demand cannot be met by any existing supply without contradicting another demand.

Some demands cannot be met by the available supply systems. It is not possible for any reasonable cost to manufacture equipment that does not break down or wear out. Just as demand statements consist not only of client requirements but also of external constraints, so also supply statements consist not only of existing conditions (which include available equipment) but also of the client's resources, which permit him to purchase the supply systems.

One of the clearest demand-supply conflicts appears when a client wants more of a building than he can afford to buy. A building (as a purchase) consists of an enormous number of different products and services, all purchased together. It is not unusual for a client to assume that such a complex purchase is also a confused and crudely computed purchase. Because he does not see the procedure by which the contractor computes costs, he assumes that there is considerable softness in any price quoted to him. He treats such costs and prices with suspicion and assumes that they can be manipulated to his interest.

THE BASIC SOLUTION PROCESS

2.6.7 Design Solution and Statement Interdependence

A significant part of design solution consists in discovering the interactions between demand statements, supply statements, and demand-supply statement sets.

The design student learns that a problem must be decomposed for solution. Often the only way it is possible to understand an ends-means analysis is by decomposing a demand statement until it becomes clear what supply systems are required. At the same time the student learns not to expect a one-to-one fit between demand and supply statements. The world does not work so easily as that. A good part of design solution consists in discovering the interactions between demand statements, supply statements, and demand-supply relationships.

The student learns it is possible to consider a part of a design problem at a time. Solving a partial problem does not necessarily form part of the solution to the complete composite problem, but a partial solution can serve as a guide to a whole solution.

2.6.8 The Technical Discussions

The discussions that follow go into more detail about analysis, synthesis, and decomposition.

2.6.8.1 Analysis and Synthesis in Design

Analysis and synthesis are basic problem-solving processes, but they are not simple processes. Terms that recognize the complexity of these two processes may be more useful for the problem solver.

Perhaps the simplest instructions ever given to students to assist their solution processes are "analyze" and "synthesize." Although some difficulty rests with the instruction to synthesize (see Section 2.5.4), it is probably among the most useful simple instructions.

The words used to state problems are usually too general to be helpful. To make these statements useful, one must break them into parts explicit enough to communicate with other persons. Wilson (1952, p. 25) notes of scientific research that, even when a person is dealing with an idealized version of reality (by which he means an isolation of events that are an adequate approximation of the reality under investigation), "it is usually convenient to break the idealization into a number of parts for separate treatment, i.e., to *analyze* the problem. The possibility of doing this rests on the question of whether or not there exist parts approximately independent of one another or mutually interacting in simple ways." Later, he says, "When the *parts* [my emphasis] of a problem have been solved, the application of this knowledge, or perhaps of the consequences of some set of hypotheses, to an observable situation may require that various of the parts be put together. In other words, an approximation to a real situation may be constructed by *synthesis* from relatively simple parts." Wilson has stated the classic process of problem solution. *Analyze* the problem into simple parts, develop simple solution components for those parts, synthesize those components into a whole or total solution. The only difficulty with such an image is that solutions to parts of a problem do not ordinarily compose into a whole, or—which is much the same thing—available solutions cannot be analyzed into components that match those into which problems can be analyzed.

Despite this difficulty, analysis and synthesis are basic and essential processes; they are just not the only ones. Among the writers who have discussed problem solving in such relatively simple terms the better words are the somewhat broader terms that Guilford uses in *The Nature of Human Intelligence* (1965): *divergent production* and convergent production. These words have the advantage of not carrying the stigma of simplism that *analysis* and *synthesis* carry.

As usual Polya (1965, pp. 68-69) brings to his discussion an awareness of the complexity in problem solution. He includes terms for operations that are the equivalent of analysis and synthesis, *isolation* and *regroup.* He places them within a set of terms that describe the full complexity. He lists:

Mobilization
Recognition and remembering
Isolation, prevision, and combination
Regrouping and supplementing
Organization

The accompanying diagram (Fig. 2.23), based on one by Polya, shows the relation of these terms to each other.

Among other writers on design process Leonard Olsen (1972, p. 112) notes the need for "meaningful problem decomposition and reclustering." He had in mind the early efforts of Christopher Alexander in developing mathematical techniques for clustering misfits between a present and a desired condition.

Olsen's insight is accurate; there are not as good ways of decomposing and grouping problem statements as there are of decomposing solution statements. In architectural design and its associated problem-solving processes, demand statements do not decompose in such a way that their components fit with those of decomposed supply statements.

REFERENCES

Guilford, J.P., "Three Faces of Intellect," in Anderson, R.C., and D. P. Ausubel, Eds., *Readings in the Psychology of Cognition,* Holt, New York, 1965.
Olsen, Leonard, Jr., "A Model of Environmental Design," in Preiser, Wolfgang, F. E., Ed., *Environmental Design Perspectives,* Virginia Polytechnic Institue, Blacksburg, 1972.

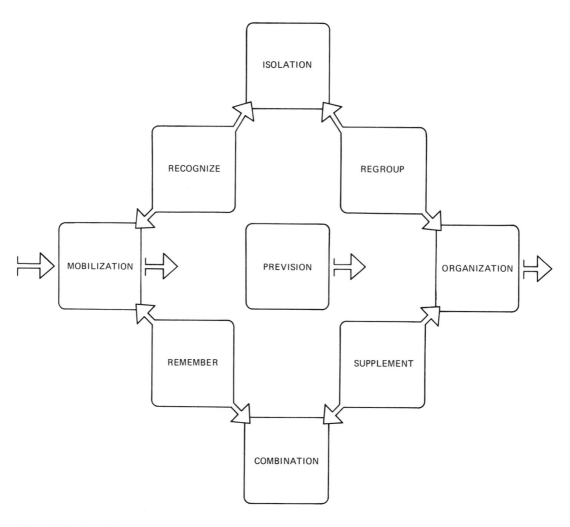

Figure 2.23 A relation between different operations in problem solving. (Adapted from a diagram by Polya. 1965).

REFERENCES

Polya, George, *Mathematical Discovery,* Vol. 2, Wiley, New York, 1965.

Wilson, E. Bright, Jr., *An Introduction to Scientific Research,* McGraw-Hill, New York, 1952.

2.6.8.2 Basic Proceeses: Decomposition and Fitting

Problem solution requires the decomposition both of demand and supply statements to whatever degree is required to achieve a fit

Any list or sequence description can be expanded into enormous detail, depending on how much is required for description. Large amounts are subsumed under single terms. An example using terms from Murtha (1973, p. 37) is shown in Fig. 2.24.

The present discussion of decomposition and complementary fitting is concerned with the breakdown into its components of any

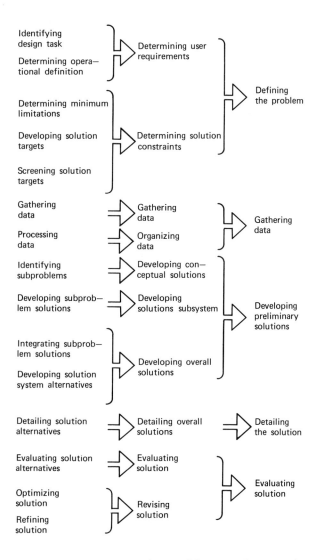

Figure 2.24 Different degrees of
detail in sequence lists. (Adapted
from a Table by Murtha, 1973).

2.6.8.2

between some demand (or set of
demands) and some supply (or
set of supplies).

single term, description, or state. Any problem complex enough to
deserve attention is likely to be composed of a number of disparate
but complementary parts. It will probably require a solution similarly
composed. It is the complementary quality of the separate elements
that permits those separate elements to be treated as a whole problem.
Heider (1958, pp. 186-187) observes that, when dissimilar entities
complement each other, they can be formed into a larger entity. He
gives as an example the complementary relation that can exist
between male and female when when they form a unit designated
marriage.

If a means-ends sequence can be decomposed by symbols thus:

$$A \Rightarrow A' \Rightarrow A'' \Rightarrow B$$

then complementary decomposition of a problem state at any given
point in a solution sequence can be designated thus:

$$
\begin{array}{ccc}
& A'(1) & & B'(1) \\
A \Rightarrow & A'(2) & \text{or} & B'(2) \Rightarrow B \\
& A'(3) & & B'(3)
\end{array}
$$

where $A'(1)$ and its equivalent expressions represent complementary decomposed components of A, the initial state (or the available object), and $B'(1)$ and its equivalents represent complementary components of the terminal state (or the desired object).

In commenting on the manner in which a means-ends analysis reduces the extent of search necessary in a problem space for an acceptable solution, Newell and Simon (1972, p. 428) point out that the degree to which a problem can be decomposed into elementary units able to be transformed by elementary operators strongly affects the simplicity of the search process. "If the difference between any two objects can be factored into a set of elementary differences which do not interact and each of which is associated with an elementary operator that removes it without introducing new differences, then solving problems will be an entirely purposeful activity with no trial and error whatsoever. Interaction among differences, or, what is the same thing, unavailability of operators to handle all the individual differences independently will generally make a certain amount of search necessary."

Leonard Olsen (1972, p. 112) includes as one of the essential features in a "complete paradigm" of a more comprehensive design system "an attempt at a more meaningful problem decomposition and reclustering in physical terms"; he references the efforts of Christopher Alexander (1971, pp. 42-43), which are interesting because they were the first notable effort to form a subsystem and clustering of "misfit variables." These variables are the noted differences between "form" and "context" (in the terms of Newell and Simon, between an available and a desired object?). Alexander's contribution was to observe that many such misfit variables are interlinked into "dependencies" and that to solve one such misfit requires some adjustment in the solution of other dependent misfits. His procedure (unfortunately, for the designer a fairly complex one) leads to a careful clustering of the dependent misfit variables and to their separation from other dependent clusters. Alexander has followed this process a degree further by the development of a "pattern language," a group of diagrammatic form organizations that presumably are based on typically occuring dependent clusters of misfit variables.

Charles Eastman (1970, p. 147) describes Alexander's method of generating problem decompositions as "bottom-up" planning that is in contrast with the "top-down" planning that has occurred traditionally in design. Top-down decomposition is based on the typological orientation that has existed in design for many years. Since the pattern language approach has apparently not been pursued consistently enough for its advantages to be apparent, designers will probably have to rely on a typological approach for some time to come. Whether or not Alexander's approach is so strongly different to warrant being called bottom-up, by contrast with top-down, is open to some question; my suspicion instead is that it is an articulation of the inarticulate processes that produce the typological problem clustering within traditional design. His approach needs to be recognized as that and used when the usual typological structuring fails to assist the problem-solving process.

So far the several writers I have referenced have been commenting on *problem* decomposition. I want to turn now to comments on *solution* decomposition. Before doing so, however, let me insert a caution. Mixture and confusion of language exist among concepts such as initial state, problem state, problem, solution, solution state, and terminal state. Clearly the decomposition of an initial state is not the same as that of a problem, for a problem is the collection of differences between the initial and some desired terminal state. Further confusion arises in speaking of the decomposition of a solution; is a solution a set of operators, the result of their action, or the result of the terminal state produced by their action? Polya finds an "unfortunate ambiguity" in the term *solution* since it can refer to the *object* of the solving process, the *procedure*, the *result* of the work, or the *work* itself (Polya, 1962, pp. 126-127). In most instances a precision of reference is not vital, but sometimes a lack of precision can obscure meaning.

I refer elsewhere to a journal article by C. R. Honey (1969, pp. 1389 ff.) in which he describes three different procedures in design: *layout*, design of *functional systems,* and *component design. Layout* is a demand description, and the schematic design of *functional systems* is a supply systems description. In the same sense, where layout corresponds with problem decomposition, the schematic design of functional systems corresponds with solution decomposition. *Solutions do not decompose along the same lines as problems do.* The Newell and Simon comments make it clear that neither problems nor solutions can be decomposed into such elementary components that a direct one-to-one matching between problem and solution elements can occur. Honey's description of *component design* deals with matching *functional systems* to *layout* and with matching solution to problem subsystems. The important point is that solutions decompose along the line of those available subsystems that furnish specific sets of functions. This is true whatever the level of abstractness or concreteness of the problem statement and the solution process.

The fact that problem and solution decompositions are not equivalent causes incompatibilities to occur between subsolutions and related subproblems. In the present window technology (for example) the designer cannot acquire added view from his building (which he wants) without also incurring the possibility of added heat loss (which he does not want); the functional subsystem, called windows, that he uses as a solution to the problem of acquiring view damages whatever other solution he might have devised for overcoming heat loss from the building. Archer (1965, p. 10) discusses five degrees of compatibility between the solutions of any two related subproblems:

1. Wholly incompatible solutions.

2. Mutually incompatible optima.

3. Unilaterally incompatible optima.

4. Alternate optima.

5. Coincidental optima.

Knowing the degree of compatibility of typical pairs of functional systems is important information for the designer.

Given the existing forms of solution decomposition, it follows that two of the most useful heuristics deal directly with this form of decomposition. Charles Eastman has described "planning" (1970, p. 145) and "buildup" (1972). What he has labeled "planning" is not the same *abstraction procedure* described by Newell and Simon (1972, pp. 433-434). Eastman's planning includes that process, but it also includes the top-down decomposition of problems (Fig. 2.25) and the bottom-up aggregation of "design-units" (Fig. 2.26). When such design units have been aggregated, they are then dealt with as a formed set and can, in turn, be aggregated with other formed sets at a next hierarchic level. Buildup is the process by which an element is added one at a time to a partial arrangement. Evaluations of each placement occur, and "backtracking" takes place when an element placement has proved unsatisfactory.

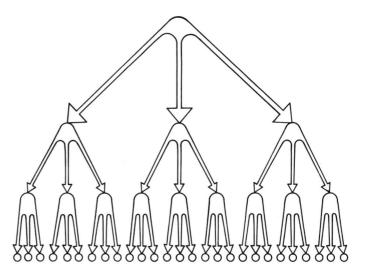

Figure 2.25 Decomposition

ARCHITECTURE, PROBLEMS AND PURPOSES

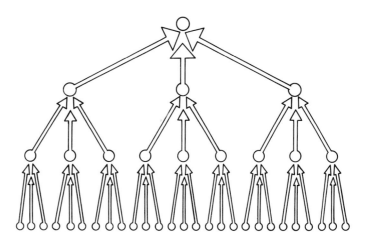

Figure 2.26 Aggregation

2.6.8.2   In the several writers referenced on solution decomposition there
has been either implicit or passing reference to the changing degree of
consideration of detail. Manheim (1964), making explicit reference,
uses such increasing detail consideration to organize the decomposition of solution development; such decomposition tends to be
sequential (although shifting back and forth from one scale of detail
to another), but it is also a different form of solution decomposition
from the simultaneous decompositions at each scaler level discussed to
this point. Both forms of decomposition, scaler decomposition from
general to specific, as discussed by Manheim, and complementary
fitting at any single scale of consideration, as discussed by the other
writers, are essential to problem solving.

REFERENCES

Alexander, Christopher, *Notes on the Synthesis of Form,* Harvard University
Press, Cambridge, Mass., 1971.

Archer, Bruce L., *Systematic Methods for Designers,* Council of Industrial
Design, London, 1965.

Eastman, Charles M., "Problem Solving Strategies in Design," in Sanoff, Henry,
and S. Cohn, Eds., EDRA 1: *Proceedings of the first annual Environmental
Design Research Association Conference,* no publisher named, 1970.

Eastman, Charles M., *DMG-DRS Journal: Design Research and Methods,* 6(3),
July-September 1972.

Heider, Fritz, *The Psychology of Interpersonal Relations,* Wiley, New York,
1958.

Honey, C.R., *The Architect's Journal,* May 1969.

Manheim, Marvin Lee, "Highway Route Location as a Hierarchically Structured
Sequential Decision Process," unpublished doctoral dissertation, M.I.T.,
Cambridge, Mass., May 15, 1964.

Murtha, Donald Michael, "A Comparison of Problem-solving Approaches Used
by Environmental Designers," unpublished doctoral dissertation, University of
Wisconsin, Madison, 1973.

Newell, Allen, and Herbert A. Simon, *Human Problem Solving,* Prentice-Hall,
Englewood Cliffs, N.J., 1972.

REFERENCES

Olsen, Leonard, Jr., "A Model of Environmental Design," in Preiser, Wolfgang F.E., Ed., *Environmental Design Perspectives,* Virginia Polytechnic Institute, Blacksburg, 1972.

Polya, George, *Mathematical Discovery,* Vol. 1, Wiley, New York, 1962.

2.6.8.3 The Experienced Character of Events

Events occur within a spatial (part-whole) and a temporal (causing-caused) context. A person perceives events by relating glimpsed features to an integrative schematic structure.

Each thing experienced occurs at some place and in some time. It has other things next to it and before it and after it. Even in such a simple experience as touching an apple, the apple exists on a table in a room or in some such place, and it had existed earlier as a green, unripe apple, and it will exist afterward as an eaten apple or possibly as a rotted apple. The individual knows all these things when he touches the apple, and they all contribute to his touching experience. A sensory reaction is the result, not only of what is occurring simultaneously, but also of what has gone before and what is likely to come afterward. Various circumstances and "irrelevant concomitant conditions . . . alter a situation profoundly." (Kohler, 1968, p. 494.) All the noticeable conditions are major determiners of sensory experience.

Events occur as whole experiences; because the noticeable parts are all brought together, persons tend to perceive even the most complex situations as wholes. The experience a person has of the apple depends on its components and setting. Not only does he notice its color, shape, texture; its skin, stem, and leaves; its look, fragrance, and feel; he also notices its position, bowl, table, room, building, city, and geography. A person responds to his *entire* situation. Indeed an individual is so sensitive to the entirety of his situation that his needs can change dramatically in response to changes in the situation (Lewin, 1964, p. 280). A social intrusion can modify his hunger; the entrance of an acquaintance can cause him to ignore the apple.

Since behavior responds to the momentary situation, it is interesting to perceive the degree of complexity that can exist in the description of behavior. "We can describe an action as a sequence of muscle twitches, or as a sequence of movements of limbs and other parts, or as a sequence of goal-directed actions, or in even larger units." (Miller, 1960, p. 13.) In reporting that there is no best such level for description, Miller says that "a proper description of behavior must be made on all levels simultaneously." Whether we talk about an event, a circumstance, or behavior, we must talk about the full complexity if we are to do justice to its totality.

Miller's statement implies that the individual perceives the totality of events by means of a structured perception process; he talks about different hierarchic levels of description. (The structuring of perception is, of course, well remarked by many writers.) This implied structuring is pervasive. One writer comments, "The perceived structure of

2.6.8.3

an object may consist of two separable components: (a) the features glimpsed in momentary glances, and (b) the integrative schematic map into which those features are fitted." (Hochberg, 1968, p. 331.) Given sufficient bits and pieces of color usually found associated with an apple in the shape and shading an apple has, the individual will begin to look for a stem and leaves and expect to smell an apple's fragrance. Fragmentary cues begin the structuring of his *apple* expectation.

The perceived event, then, is holistic; perception is sensitive to changes in the situation; description of perception can be arranged in a hierarchic structure; the perceived structure consists of the parts and a scheme into which those parts are placed.

REFERENCES

Hochberg, Julian, "In the Mind's Eye," in Haber, Ralph Norman, Ed., *Contemporary Theory and Research in Visual Perception*, Holt, Rinehard & Winston, New York, 1968.

Kohler, Ivo, "The Formation and Transformation of the Visual World," in Haber, Ralph Norman, Ed., *Contemporary Theory and Research in Visual Perception*, Holt, Rinehart & Winston, New York, 1968.

Lewin, Kurt, "Behavior and Development as a Function of the Total Situation," in Cartright, Dorwin, Ed., *Kurt Lewin: Field Theory in Social Science,* Harper & Row, 1964.

Miller, George A., E. Galanter, and K. Pribram, *Plans and the Structure of Behavior*, Henry Holt, New York, 1960.

2.6.8.4 The Selection of Events for Experience

Whereas each experience is of a total structure, the individual can select an individual component of that experiences for his attention. The individual also notices similarities between experiences.

Although each perceived object is part of a whole experience (the object structure organizes the components that make up the object, and the context structure organizes the object of perception with other perceived objects), it is also true that the individual can actively select a particular object for his attention. If he selects the apple for his attention, he also selects the bowl for its context, and the apple's color, fragrance, skin, leaves, and stem for its components and attributes. If he selects the bowl for his attention, then he also selects the table for its context, and the apple as one of its components or attributes. Downs and Stea (1973, p. 18), commenting on the focusing of attention, state, "What is an object at one spatial scale can become an attribute [of the next larger object] at another. . . .The scale of analysis of the problem at hand defines what is an object and what is attributive and locational information." They illustrate this shifting of focus by listing a sequence of contexts, objects, and attributes. I have shown their sequence in tabular form and have inserted two items for completeness (Fig. 2.27).

When the focus of attention has been centered on an object, another perceptual mechanism permits the maintenance of focus.

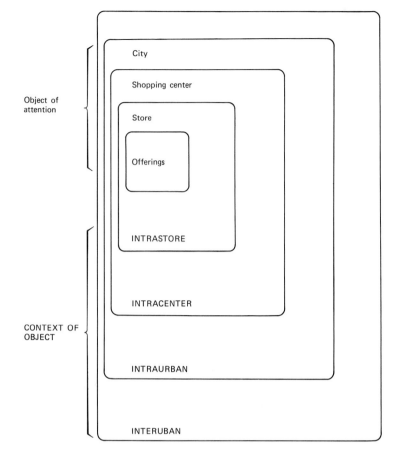

Object of
attention

City

Shopping center

Store

Offerings

INTRASTORE

INTRACENTER

CONTEXT OF
OBJECT

INTRAURBAN

INTERUBAN

Figure 2.27 The shift of focus between objects, contexts, and attributes.

2.6.8.4

A grouping mechanism exists that maintains the identity of objects over temporal and spatial transformations. "...there must be a process capable of conserving a record of the likely transitions and contingencies of the environment. The moment-to-moment programming of perceptual readiness depends on such integrations." (Bruner, 1968, p. 645.) The human being is thus able to form categorizations by noticing the sameness in related events. The unique orange fruit perceived this moment and the last moment and the next moment are grouped together with similar orange fruits perceived in other times and other places to form a class of orange fruits. Human beings have "a strong and early tendency to treat events as non-independent of each other over time." (Bruner, 1968, p. 645.) In this perception of sameness or similarity there are different degrees; the degree of sameness affects the kind of category formed. Kenneth J. W. Craik (1943, p. 69) distinguishes four degrees of similarity of perception:

1. Those in which all the conditions of stimulation are similar.

2. Those in which there are differences in the peripheral stimulation but similarities in central stimulation.

3. Those in which there are differences in central stimulation but where the central stimulation is the same in certain important respects.

4. Those in which the differences extend to all direct sensory qualities but in which the sameness is confined to abstract characteristics such as triangularity, number, or other relations.

The first of these is apparently a description of whole context similarity, the second of object similarity, the third of object aspect similarity, and the fourth of object attribute.

An ability to communicate about these similarities is strongly affected by the degree to which individuals share equivalent categorizations and common terms for those categorizations. (See Figure 2.16, p. 81, which develops a scale of communication effectiveness from public to private.)

Craik discusses the ability of the individual to discriminate relationships more accurately than absolute magnitudes (Craik, 1943, p. 66). Similarity and dissimilarity relationships thus become the basis for a structuring of perceptions. Finally the form and extent of similarity, along with the accessibility of already formed categories of similarity, permit a classification to occur (Bruner, 1968, p. 640). Such an event also permits a word reference for the classification to be evoked.

As the individual focuses on a particular part of the environment, he observes objects that share a similarity with previously experienced classes of objects. The degree of similarity evokes environmental, object, aspect, or attribute classes that permit an accurate word referencing of the perception that occurred.

REFERENCES

Bruner, Jerome S., "On Perceptual Readiness," in Haber, Ralph Norman, Ed., *Contemporary Theory and Research in Visual Perception,* Holt, Rinehard & Winston, 1968.

Craik, K. J. W., *The Nature of Explanation,* Cambridge University Press, 1943.

Downs, Roger M., and David Stea, Eds., *Image and Environment: Cognitive Mapping and Spatial Behavior,* Aldine, Chicago, 1973.

2.7 INFORMATION FACTORING IN DESIGN

As the designer moves across the information spectrum, more and more and more data are factored

Any problem-solving process is one of selection. Depending on the circumstances of the problem, the selection may be toward the best, the acceptable, or something in between. The problem literature talks about selecting for maximal, minimal, and optimal solutions. Searching for the acceptable is known as *satisficing.*

Whatever the particular goal or aspiration of the designer, design out of consideration. The designer assists this process by becoming more selective in the kinds of information he considers.

can be seen as a satisficing process. The acceptable is not necessarily the minimal. Whenever any process of solution must take a great number of factors and possibilities into consideration, it must be seen as satisficing. It is not possible to maximize for every factor.

The design student soon learns that he can achieve a satisfactory design by following the general procedure described, which moves deliberately from the more general to the more specific and ends in a concrete proposal. The process is one that factors more and more possibilities out of consideration until the solution to the design problem is achieved.

As the student learns more and more about design, he also learns what combinations of things produce the results he wants and what do not. As he becomes expert, he learns to omit from consideration those things that do not produce results.

Design seems so complex because any combination of physical elements produces multiple results and effects. Such elements can be seen as *functional,* as *symbolic,* as *affective* (emotion-producing), or as *ordering* elements because of the order they provide. The student designer is made aware of this multiple result of his work, but he has not had adequate techniques for dealing with these results separately. An extension of the factoring process can be used to provide such a technique.

2.7.1 Design as a Factoring Process

The manner of problem definition factors information out. As decisions move from the more general to the more particular, more and more information is omitted. As decisions are made, the solution process moves in a more restricted direction.

Factoring in design occurs, first, because the process is oriented toward producing as a solution some change in the physical environment of the client. Any problem statement factors out a great many possible solutions. It does so by the way it defines the problem and by the focus it gives to th solution effort. The statement of a problem as a *design* problem factors out many possible solutions.

In addition to the influence of problem statement on a solution direction, the process the student learns also influences his solution. The student learns to move from the more general to the more specific; the use of *programming, planning,* and *design* processes in that sequence permits the *search* for a design solution to take place in a reasonably efficient way. Decision at the more general level factors out larger areas of concern and permits the designer to reach decisions more quickly. As he moves through the information spectrum, he uses an orderly factoring process. As he makes decisions, he removes information less vital to his solution process.

The practitioner learns to secure the agreement of his client at each different stage. As agreement is made to adopt a particular direction, work can proceed in a more restricted way that moves closer to the solution. A constant backing up to rewrite the program when work

ARCHITECTURE, PROBLEMS AND PURPOSES

has progressed to the design stage can prevent the designer from ever achieving a solution.

Undoubtedly the client or the designer sometimes discovers an oversight in the earlier stages of the work that must be corrected. Even if no oversight has occurred, circumstances can change in such a way as to require revisions to earlier stages of the work and a consequent revision to the factoring that had been used in the process.

2.7.2 Learning as a Factoring Process

As the designer becomes more experienced, he omits directions that in the past were not successful. Learning is thus a factoring process.

As the student of design learns to develop proposals, he gradually discovers that certain patterns of proposal cannot usually achieve good solutions. He can discover, for example, that "dead-end" rooms are preferable for many activities over rooms that lead to other rooms, because circulation to those other rooms can disrupt the rooms' activity and because space must be allowed for circulation. He may discover that building arrangements with very long, straight hallways seem uncomfortable to many persons and that they are best avoided. As he discovers these negative patterns, he avoids using them and factors out all proposals based on such patterns.

The designer applies the same factoring to information in the design process. As he discovers that certain kinds of information are not helpful, he tends to ignore those (however interesting they might be) and factor them out of his solution.

This factoring poses a difficulty. Certainly this learning is essential in design (or in any learnable profession), but how far should the learning and factoring proceed? One can imagine a designer carrying the process so far that he produces the same building, no matter how varied the requirements of the problem. Had the process gone too far with Mies van der Rohe when he produced only glass-box buildings? In part, learning as a factoring process depends on the designer's aspirations. If he wishes to achieve high skill in design, he learns to use factoring to achieve efficient work, but he holds himself ready to set that learned factoring aside the moment it seems inappropriate. He constantly questions the validity of his factoring.

2.7.3 Factoring across the Information Spectrum

As design moves across the information spectrum, there is an orderly factoring out of information

As the designer moves from the *person* end to the *object* end of the spectrum, very orderly factoring occurs. To understand it, he must also understand some of the different relationships possible between a *person* and an *object*; these provide one of the bases for factoring. He can consider four such relationships:

that is related to the several modes of person-object relationship: function, symbol, order, and affect.

1. Function. The object (the building or its parts) is a tool that actively assists in task *performances*. The building is a *"function" object* defined by the *functions* it provides.

2. Symbol. The object (the building or its parts) forms a setting that passively assists social interaction or *association*. The building and its component parts are *"symbol" objects*. The object is defined by the *meanings* it provides.

3. Order. The object (the building or its parts) is itself an end and provides an "external" *experience* for the person viewing it. The building, its parts, and its setting are interactive *"order" objects*. The object is defined by how it is classified by the person viewing it and by the *image* associated with that classification.

4. Affect. The object (the building or its parts) is itself an end and evokes an "internal" *response* from the person viewing it. The building and its parts are emotion-producing *"affective" objects*. The object is defined by the affect it evokes.

These four person-object relations are summarized in the accompanying diagram (Fig 2.28), which shows a symbolized *person* to *object* relationship and its implications in the *behavior, function,* and *object* parts of the information spectrum. The four relationships defined (function, symbol, order, and affect) are useful to remember. A slight rearrangement of the order in which the object characteristics are named (symbol, order, function, and affect) produces an acronym,

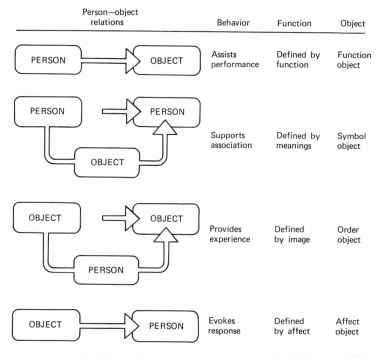

Figure 2.28 Person-object relations in design.

SOFA. In speaking of these, I will refer to the SOFA characteristics of objects.

Invariably every building and most objects of every kind exist simultaneously in all these relationships with persons. All buildings have all the object characteristics I have defined. When a building has a kitchen for food preparation, or an operating room, or any room organized to assist the performance of specific tasks, it exists as a function (or tool) object. When the building or a room in the building is designated as a meeting place, or when a door (or any other building component) communicates by its appearance what it is to be used for, then the building or its part exists as a symbol object. When the building is perceived as an object to be in some size, geometric, and color relationship with its surroundings and with its own parts, then it exists as an order object. Finally when a building evokes some response in an individual, whether positive or negative, it exists as an affective object. All these characteristics exist in every building; they are isolated here for analysis. During design one or the other of these factors is often emphasized more than the others.

Though it is clear how these different relations can exist and what their implications are in the *behavior, function,* and *object* parts of the information spectrum, that relationship should be pursued across the information spectrum in more detail.

Whatever the form of *behavior* under consideration, that behavior does not depend on an integrative *function capability* alone; it also depends on an *allocation* of time and effort, a choice to make use of that specific function capability. Behavior depends both on the existence of a function capability and on a choice to make use of that capability in a certain priority.

In a similar way whatever the *function* capability under consideration, it does not depend on an *object* alone but on the degree of *skill* of the person who will bring that object into use. To move from thinking about allocation (at the function phase of the information spectrum) to asking what composes allocation (at the object phase), there must be a weighing of two things: the situation in which the choice is made and the values of the chooser with respect to the desired behavior. This set of relationships is shown in the accompanying diagram (Fig. 2.29).

A Factoring Chart. If the different *modes* of behavior (defined by the person-object relationships) are expanded across the behavior, function, and object *phases* of the information spectrum, they compose the major part of a factoring chart that permits an explanation of the typical information factoring that occurs in design. There is only one more step to complete the chart.

Two of the behavior modes—the *performance* and the *association* modes—are purposive, since they are essentially means to the accom-

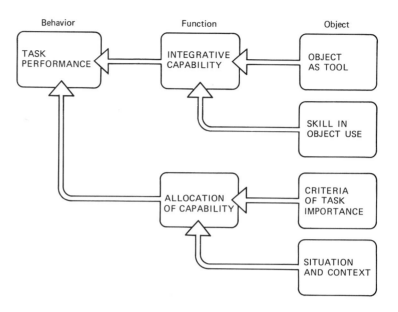

Behavior   Function   Object

TASK PERFORMANCE ← INTEGRATIVE CAPABILITY ← OBJECT AS TOOL

SKILL IN OBJECT USE

ALLOCATION OF CAPABILITY ← CRITERIA OF TASK IMPORTANCE

SITUATION AND CONTEXT

Figure 2.29 Composition of factors across part of the information spectrum.

2.7.3

plishment of some other end. The other two behavior modes—the *experience* and the *response* modes—are essentially nonpurposive ("ludentive," after the Latin word for "play"), since they are ends in themselves. The chart can be completed by grouping behaviors in this manner in the *purpose* phase of the spectrum (Fig. 2.30).

The chart will repay some careful study. The design student discovers, sooner or later, that he is required to deal with these different characteristics in the objects he designs; he must deal with them in relation to the different modes of behavior those objects support. A difficulty occurs when the designer is talking about the design object in terms of one mode, and his critic or client is talking about behavior in terms of a different mode. A study of the chart can help the designer to identify such failures of communication and respond in a way to improve communication.

The Factoring Process. In the simple information spectrum described earlier (person-purpose-behavior-function-object) different kinds of information are ignored at each phase. If a client presents himself *whole* and asks assistance with his problem, then no information is left out except as the architect fails to observe his condition or to ask questions. The architect can move through the entire spectrum, considering all the behavior modes to secure a comprehensive view of what problems are to be solved and what course he might take in solution.

If, instead, a client presents only a statement of specific *purposes* and asks the architect to help him accomplish them, then the entire bottom half of the diagram is omitted. The client has failed to provide information about his nonpurposive behavior modes.

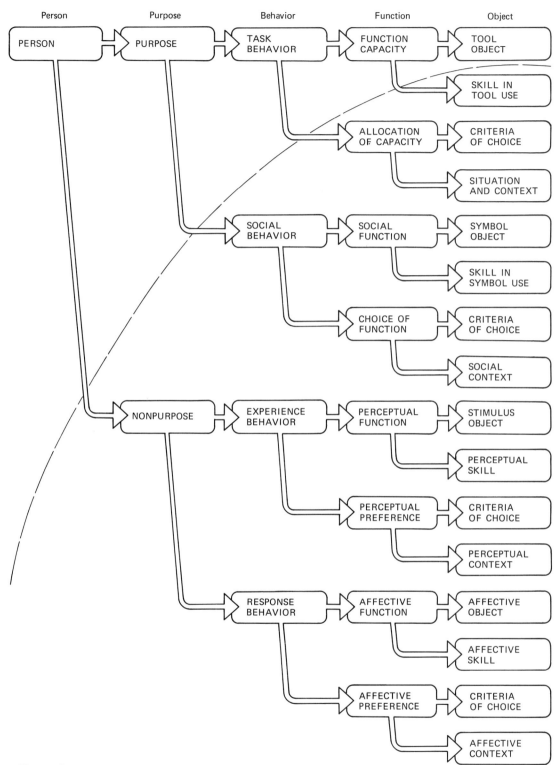

Figure 2.30 An information factoring chart.

If instead of telling the architect about his purposes, he tells him about the performances and *behaviors* in which he wishes to engage, then he leaves out all the possible information relating to the bottom three-quarters of the diagram.

If the client, instead of telling about desired performance behaviors, indicates what performance-related *functions* he wants the building to provide, he omits the relative importance of the various functions and his allocation among various functions. In doing so he omits the possible information in seven-eighths of the total diagram.

Finally if the client describes in detail the *objects* and building forms he requires that will provide those functions, he omits, in addition to his earlier omissions, concern for the skill that users of the building have and fails to take into account the possible information in fifteen-sixteenths of the diagram.

In the statement of most design problems, by contrast with the suppositions I have just reviewed, the information furnished to the designer is a motley mixture of material from all phases of the spectrum and pertains to all or to several of the behavior modes.

Eventually the designer transforms all this into information about the building he is designing. His design moves from the person end of the spectrum at the left toward the object end at the right. As he makes a transformation from one information phase to the next, he factors out information. He might do so in a legitimate way, when he has determined that it will not assist him as he moves into the next phase. He might also factor out information vital to an understanding of the object he is trying to design and to the uses and purposes the object will serve. Without some understanding of the information spectrum and of factoring he is more likely to factor out vital than needless information.

Lest there be some misunderstanding of factoring, let me discuss it in terms of mixtures and trade-offs at each information phase in the spectrum.

No individual is only purposive in his orientation; some part of all behavior is experiential and responsive and nonpurposive. Even the most serious business institution provides coffee breaks and vacations. More important for the individual (and for his institution) than achieving any specific purpose is securing the continuation of his own existence. When purpose runs out, because it has been achieved, the institution and the individual both begin a search for other purposes conducted according to nonpurposive criteria.

If discussion is restricted to purposive activities, then two forms of activity must be reviewed. Performance does not occur in isolation, according to external criteria; it also occurs as associational activity, according to internal group interaction criteria. If the purposive orientation is toward associative behavior (meetings, lectures, conferences, negotiations, etc.), then certain performance behaviors must occur to support the association behavior. Someone must unlock the building, turn on the lights, remove the trash, turn off the lights, and lock the building.

In thinking, for example, about the provision of meeting room or cooking functions, there must also be a discussion of how much func-tion to provide. There must be a weighing of the relative importance of the various component functions and of other "competing" functions. Thought must be given to how to allocate resources and to how the allocation will affect the distribution of time by the building's user. Given some limited amount of a particular function capability, for example, the prior existence of classroom space on a university campus, it is possible to solve the need for additional classroom space entirely by time allocation. The university can schedule classes in its existing space for a longer period of time. There are trade-offs between the provision of function in spatial array and that in temporal array. Decision on function cannot occur without decision on allocation.

In exactly similar fashion function capability is not provided only by the object designed. It also depends on the persons who use and operate the object. Again a trade-off occurs between the complexity of designed objects and the skill of the persons using the object. If a person were always so skillful and careful in climbing and descending stairs that he never risked falling, then the stairs would not require a handrail. If the persons using the stairs fell frequently, even with a conventional handrail in place, then a more complicated and complex system of safeguards might be required. A highly skilled carpenter can drive home a finish nail with an ordinary hammer and a nail-set and not leave a mark on the wood surface; an unskilled workman requires a nailing machine, and even then he can damage the surface.

In summary the accomplishment of purpose requires some combination of performance and association behaviors; performance behavior, some combination of function capability and an allocation of resources to that activity; function capability, some combination of physical object (as tool) and skill. As the designer moves through the information spectrum during his design, he has better control over some parts of this information than over others. He can say more precise things about performance than about association, about function than about allocation, and about the nature of the design object than about the skill of the persons who will use the object. In consequence he finds himself factoring some parts of the information spectrum out of design as he proceeds. Let him only remember that leaving those things out does not also place them out of existence. Whenever the design has had to omit information, it is likely to be that much less successful. Such omission often cannot be avoided, but it is important that the designer know the omission has occurred.

2.7.4 Limiting the Design Vocabulary

Design based on a severely limited vocabulary of objects removes symbol, order, and affect from consideration. With function as the sole remaining consideration, a design strategy based on a limited vocabulary can give the designer a stronger conscious control over the design process.

The preceding discussion has shown how it is possible to bring very complex information pertinent to design into some order. It demonstrated how important it is for the designer to use fully all the available information. It emphasized the factoring that occurs in all problem solving and in design.

Since the discussion was based on the SOFA characteristics of objects and the behavior related to them, it is possible to understand these further by considering another question. When dealing with the function characteristics of an object (in isolation from the others) to support performance behavior, one can usually say whether or not the designed object is adequate to the task but not whether it is more than adequate. How can the designer know when he has done more than needed? The discussion that follows does not provide a way for answering that question in any real problem situation, but the theoretical answer illustrates the complexity and interaction of problem elements.

Suppose the designer has only a severely limited set of elements to build with—one kind of masonry, column, beam, piping, sink, and so on. If he had a vocubulary of that kind to work with, he would have no trouble saying whether he had done more than enough. He could match the desired performance behaviors directly with *function* objects needed to assist those behaviors.

Notice, with such a limited vocabulary, what happens to the other SOFA characteristics. The *symbol* characteristics are so consistent, because they are so familiar, that they are entirely transparent; that is, when a person sees the object, he reads directly through its form to its meaning. The *affective* characteristics of the objects are no longer of any impact; familiarity has dulled their emotion-provoking qualities. Few choices can arbitrarily impose *order* on the building design; such a limited vocabulary is strongly ordered already.

In such a fashion one could argue that a limited vocabulary consistently used could remove from important impact all but the function characteristic of a designed object, and it would be possible to say that the design had been done only in response to the requirements of a performance-oriented behavior.

It is interesting to speculate whether a design strategy that used a limited vocabulary as a heuristic would give the designer greater control over his process. If the designer used an arbitrarily limited vocabulary to achieve a first solution in response to performance behavior requirements, he could then release constraints to deal with each of the other SOFA characteristics one by one in a self-conscious, purposeful fashion.

2.7.5 The Need for Aesthetic Measurement

Such a strategy can permit the designer to achieve a conscious control over symbol, order, and affect. The designer cannot presently control these factors, since he is unable to measure their impact.

A relation exists between information used in design and the process of narrowing the design choice to a final selection. Although I spoke of a limited vocabulary design as being highly ordered, I do not wish to leave the impression that there is any relation between the factoring process and the amount of order in a particular solution. Factoring could lead to a relatively ordered or disordered solution. It does not necessarily achieve a highly ordered solution.

The possible confusion between a design solution and an ordered design reminds me of a very bright student who had a severe handicap. In design ability he was ahead of most of his fellow students. In one of the usual six-week "long" problems he was finished with a usually brilliant solution by the end of three weeks. His difficulty was that he could not leave the solution alone. He refined and refined it for another three weeks and finished his problem by turning in a set of drawings with four walls and a roof. He had achieved a highly refined, very highly ordered design—with almost no content. His fellow students had a high respect for his ability; they swore that if you could take his drawings away from him at the end of three weeks, he would be considered the best student in the school; they also joked that, if he ever had to do an eight-week problem, he would probably turn in a set of blank pages. The successful design is not the most ordered one but an appropriate blend of the several SOFA characteristcs. It is an *appropriately* ordered design.

2.7.6 The Technical Discussions

The first discussion contains an examination of psychological factors affecting problem placement. A second discussion deals at greater length with the limited vocabulary design strategy. A third treats order in relation to motivation.

2.7.6.1 Psychological Criteria in Problems

A problem classification scheme that takes psychological criteria into account must consider whether the problem is internal or external, whether it requires allocative or integrative processes,

On the assumption that the basic processes of problem solution are for maintaining some given state of equilibrium in the individual—in the face of variations in his environment—a psychological model developed by Parsons and Shils (1951, pp. 108-109 and p. 255) recognizes that equilibrium can be reestablished in a number of different ways. Much depends on how the problem of disequilibrium is defined and what processes are required for its solution.

2.7.6.1

and whether its solution requires known processes or the learning of new processes.

Figure 2.31 A problem typology based on a psychological model of problem solving. (Adapted from a Diagram by Parsons and Shils, 1951, p. 255. By permission of Harvard University Press, Cambridge, Massachusetts.)

First, the problem can be defined either as external (where adjustments must be made in the relation of the individual to the external environment) or as internal (where adjustments must be made in the individual's motives or in the priority of his actions).

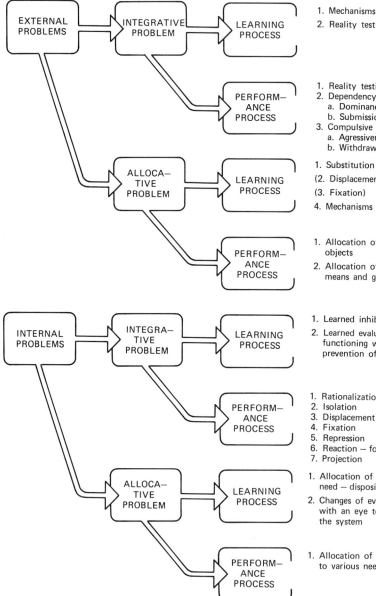

EXTERNAL PROBLEMS → INTEGRATIVE PROBLEM → LEARNING PROCESS
1. Mechanisms of congnitive learning
2. Reality testing

PERFORM—ANCE PROCESS
1. Reality testing
2. Dependency
   a. Dominance
   b. Submission
3. Compulsive independence
   a. Agressiveness
   b. Withdrawal

ALLOCA—TIVE PROBLEM → LEARNING PROCESS
1. Substitution
(2. Displacement)
(3. Fixation)
4. Mechanisms of cathectic learning

PERFORM—ANCE PROCESS
1. Allocation of attention to different objects
2. Allocation of cathexes to different means and goals

INTERNAL PROBLEMS → INTEGRA—TIVE PROBLEM → LEARNING PROCESS
1. Learned inhibition
2. Learned evaluation patterns of functioning with an eye to prevention of conflicts

PERFORM—ANCE PROCESS
1. Rationalization
2. Isolation
3. Displacement
4. Fixation
5. Repression
6. Reaction — formation
7. Projection

ALLOCA—TIVE PROBLEM → LEARNING PROCESS
1. Allocation of functions to various need — dispositions
2. Changes of evaluation patterns with an eye to maintaining the system

PERFORM—ANCE PROCESS
1. Allocation of "action time" to various need dispositions

2.7.6.1

Second, the problem can be defined as allocative (where the individual must make decisions between the allocation of time, attention, or other resources) or integrative (where the individual responds to changes in the environment by appropriate adjustments).

Finally the problem can be defined as requiring for its solution either known performance processes or new processes developed by the problem solver.

The diagram in Fig. 2.31 (Parsons and Shils, 1951, p. 255) tabulates problems categorized by these three different defining attributes. Although the designer should be aware of the full range of possible problems, it is fairly clear that, for the environmental problem solver, several problems are of relatively less interest.

Undoubtedly the individual must sometimes change his motives or motivational priorities; a professional problem solver may need to point out such a condition to a client. But it is also clear that the process by which the individual makes those changes is no business of the problem solver. It should also be clear that allocative problems are of deep concern to the professional problem solver, but these tend to be ones of management that are more the exclusive concern of the client rather than of the designer or environmental problem solver (Parsons and Shils, 1951, pp. 108-109).

The primary interest for designers is in external problems requiring integrative efforts. Within this area both those problems that can be dealt with by performance and those that require learning are of interest. It should be possible to equate the former with those that use canonical terminology and typological information and the latter with problems requiring creative effort and achieving invention.

Within external integrative problems the comments by Parsons and Shils on *reality testing* and on the performance processes based on *dependency* and *compulsive independence* provide some useful insight for general solution processes. (I omit any mention of cognitive learning.)

Whether reality testing is concerned with "adjudicating" conflicts between two factual propositions or between a factual and a need disposition, the basic process used is effect analysis, or as Parsons and Shils express it, "allowing the law of effect to operate." It is essentially a process for projecting circumstances into the future to see "which actually serves to guide action." The reality testing they describe is nothing more nor less than a form of means-ends analysis. When a comparison is made between a factual proposition and a need disposition, the difference is between what Newell and Simon describe as "the available object" and "the desired object" (Newell and Simon, 1972, p. 416).

The discussion (Parsons and Shils, 1951, pp. 140-141) of *dependency* and *compulsive independence* as performance processes is of much greater interest. Although Parsons and Shils apply these

2.7.6.1

processes only to social objects, "alters"—that is, other persons—it is possible to recast the entire discussion so that it applies equally to impersonal objects or to an entire environment with which "ego" is in relationship.

When a person is in some preferrred relationship with an object or environment, and some threat arises to the continuation of that relationship, he can take one of two possible courses of action: (1) he can cope with the threat by maintaining and striving to retain the relationship at all costs, though in doing so he develops and maintains a *dependency* between himself and the object, or (2) he can determine to relinquish the relationship in reaction to the formation of dependency needs; in doing so he develops a *compulsive independence.* Within a dependency relationship there are two alternative courses: either the person is able to *dominate* the environment, overcoming the lack of accord between himself and the object (or environment) and causing it to serve his purposes, or he ends by *submitting* to the lack of accord and modifying or foregoing those purposes that are not in accord. When the person has elected compulsive independence as a mode of coping with his lack of accord with an object or the environment, he can choose an aggressive mode of behavior in which he modifies the environment to this purposes, or he can choose a *withdrawal* mode in which he leaves the object (or environment) with which he is no longer in accord to seek some other object (or environment) where such an accord can be reestablished. Because the analysis by Parsons and Shils (1951, pp. 140-141) deals only with actions by "ego" and not with any actions or response by "alter," the analysis can be adapted to impersonal objects and environments as well as to a social object or person.

REFERENCES

Parsons, Talcott, and Edward A. Shils, Eds., *Toward a General Theory of Action,* Harvard University Press, Cambridge, Mass., 1951.

Newell, Allen, and H. A. Simon, *Human Problem Solving,* Prentice-Hall, Englewood Cliffs, N.J., 1972.

2.7.6.2 The Use of Limited-Vocabulary Design

A limited vocabulary used in design imposes a very strong order, establishes a transparent symbolism, and drains away any affective qualities. The use of a limited vocabulary can permit the designer

How can the several SOFA design characteristics (symbol, order, function, affect) be isolated to develop design precision?

I propose to isolate function to show I am dealing with object function as a design characteristic instead of with one of the other SOFA characteristics. I propose the following strategy.

From the entire range of physical objects I select a limited vocabulary of components or elements that are most common in the design

2.7.6.2

to gauge whether he has done
more than his design program
requires.

tradition of the culture in which I work. I then undertake design in response to function requirements, using only elements within the restricted vocabulary I have established.

A very interesting series of results follows from such a strategy.

1. Limiting the number of choices in this manner imposes a very strong order on the design. Whatever I do within the limited vocabulary is highly ordered, and I am not tempted to sacrifice component function for other considerations of artificially imposed order.

2. As I become extremely familiar with the limited vocabulary, any affective qualities formerly attached to shapes, sizes, or colors in the elements of the limited vocabulary are drained away. Familiarity and uniformity will have removed any emotional affect the elements could have.

3. Finally as I work within the limited vocabulary, any symbolism that exists (the only likelihood is self-symbolism), because of its pervasiveness and high recognition value, becomes transparent, so that meaning is read directly and symbolic qualities are neutralized insofar as they ever can be.

As I become familiar with such a limited vocabulary of design elements, I find that situations repeat themselves, and I can respond to functional requirements by object function characteristics rapidly and efficiently.

The process does not, of course, stop here. I have not so far been talking about anything more than a design strategy that isolates the separate function characteristic and deals with it separately and consciously.

Once I have dealt with object function, I can then turn to symbol and affect. I can begin gradually to release constraints of the limited vocabulary and make conscious choices to develop any symbolism I had programmed for the design. I would release constraints further to substitute forms, sizes, colors, or textures that produced affects or different degrees of order called for by the program.

Let me note directly that the strategy I proposed is a speculation. I can see the beginnings of an orderly procedure, but to establish it requires many trials; I need to invent a limited vocabulary and work with it in experiment. Finally I have to develop orderly checks on affective and symbolic usages.

Although limited-vocabulary design is proposed here as a design strategy, the knowledgeable reader recognizes that it has existed in fact. Any consistent vernacular architecture, as exemplified by the Italian hill town or the New England Village, is, indeed, limited-vocabulary design. The design of such a community has on its long-term resident (not on a visitor) exactly the effect that I described limited-vocabulary design as having on the designer: a strong system of order, little or no affective quality, and transparant symbolic uses.

Limited-vocabulary design indicates a method by which design can be undertaken with some precision. Once the techniques on which that precision depends have been developed, it is possible to measure the least required effort in design. It is possible to specify functions to be supplied by objects that will support behaviors of the users.

Clearly one of the difficulties in design decision is knowing whether the designer has supplied only what was needed and not more. The strategy of using limited vocabulary design to isolate the several SOFA characteristics can help ensure that the designer's proposal deals with the least required action to supply the stated purposes.

This precision in design methodology having been achieved, the following benefits can accrue from the use of limited-vocabulary design:

1. **Architectectural Problem Solving.** Undoubtedly precision in design methodology is of benefit in the design of buildings. The architect can know he is dealing separately with function, order, symbol, and affect. He now deals with them simultaneously and without any control over the process. Although many architects are skillful in deal-with these simultaneous factors, there is a low level of predictability in the process except for that provided by conventional usage. The technique of limited-vocabulary design can develop predictability, can ensure that function is provided for in a controlled way, and can permit the architect to control whatever degree of departure from a neutral "vernacular" style is warranted by programmatic considerations calling for symbolic and affective qualities in design.

2. **Architectural Education.** Limited-vocabulary design can be an enormous aid in education— not for the beginner but for the advanced student. What better way can exist for the student to experiment with and begin to develop control over the quality of the environment than to learn this technique?

3. **Design Automation.** Clearly limited-vocabulary design makes design more amenable to automation. Such isolation of the several design characteristics is an essential step if the design profession is to develop mechanical aids that will make its process even more effective.

2.7.6.3 A Measure of Order*

The level of order required in a designed object is not constant. It is related to the function of the object and the purposes of the user.

The design literature concerned with order appears to be founded on a basic fallacy—the notion that there is a level of order that can be applied uniformly to achieve successful design. Much of the literature, instead of speaking of different levels of order, speaks instead of order in opposition to disorder (or chaos). This difficulty exists in part because measurements have not been devised that could distinguish different degrees of order.

*From *Man-Environment Systems,* January 1976. Used with permission.

2.7.6.3   The neglect of a concern with different degrees of order would indeed be curious if there were not also a substantial neglect of interest in the need for different levels of stimulation in the individual. Kurt Lewin (1964, p. 280) has described the changeable character of need, and indeed the variation in need and preference is well remarked. But when explorations of environmental preference are undertaken (Hershberger, 1969, pp. 86 ff.; Lowenthal and Riel, 1972, p. 189), the transitory nature of specific preference and its relation to purpose and disposition are ignored. That statistical treatment can factor out such variation is of importance only if the researcher is trying to determine how to design a completely uniform environment in the least objectionable way. This typical omission of a concern with variation in need can also be illustrated by the research orientation in a direction-finding study by Gordon Best (1970, p. 73). "The feeling of 'lostness' varied widely from one town hall user to the next . . . it became necessary to define the state of 'lostness' in an operational way." The study direction exhibited little interest in differences of feeling of "lostness" and why such variation might have occurred.

Studies of stress-seeking behavior (Klausner, 1968, pp. 137 ff.) have described the different preferences between individuals for different levels of stress but have only touched in passing on the moment-to-moment change in stress preference in the same individual. Even when an individual seeks out the extreme stress associated with skydiving, he does not seek it every moment of his waking life. Klausner's language suggests the existence of cyclic preferences for extremes of stress, but the subject is not pursued.

The design-related literature also follows this pattern, and it may be that Helson's notion of an adaptation level (an optimal level of stimulation) for the individual may have so influenced the treatment of the subject (Wohlwill, 1966, pp. 33 ff.; Rapoport and Kantor, 1967, p. 210)* that the far more useful investigation of the change in a need for stimulation has been neglected. If there is an optimal perception rate that avoids, on either extreme, monotony and chaos, then it is one that undergoes considerable change as the motivation of the individual changes.

Finding this neglect is not especially surprising. The design orientation must, after all, take into account the "duration" and permanence of works of plastic art (Huizinga, 1970, p. 166). Ray Studer (1969, p. 70) points out the paradox that exists when designers try to solve dynamic human problems by means of static, formal solutions. The building does not typically adapt itself to the user; instead the user brings a richness and variety of behavior to the static setting (Goffman, 1963, p. 22).

*Later papers by Rapoport (Rapoport and Hawkes, 1970; Rapoport, 1971) note that a variation in motivation is an influence on the individual's response to the environment; they seem, however, to fail in relating such variation to a need for different levels of environmental order.

2.7.6.3

Although the building does not adapt as a work of art, it develops a system of relations that is an interpretation of some structure to which it is pertinent (Gauss, 1957, pp. 34 ff.); the order within building design can reflect the structure of institutional organization, of user behavior, or of building function. No matter what set of forms the designer selects, the skilled and experienced user orders (internalizes) his environment to reflect the conceptual structuring of the institution that occupies and controls the environment (Sommer, 1966, pp. 70 ff.). Invariably a relationship exists between the physical form and the organization of activity related to it (Steinitz, 1968, p. 233). Whereas the *designer* initiates, the *user* completes the relationship between the order of physical form and the structure of behavior and of institutional organization.

It is also true that, where the ordering related to a specific institution is limited in its spatial extent, the sensory reaction of users is not so limited; it is a product of that ordering and of the accompanying sequential and adjacent stimuli, whether similarly ordered or not. Each event is experienced within a context of other events. The individual building thus cannot be experienced in isolation (Kohler, 1968; Huxtable, 1973). Despite this, individual building designers have typically not placed their buildings in accord. Indeed no scheme has been available by which designers could communicate with each other about design intention and level of ordering.

Robert Venturi (Venturi and Brown, 1968, p. 36) describes the different urban order produced by the lack of consistent order between individual buildings; he rejoices in the nearness of chaos. Certainly a high level of stimulus and a relatively low level or order is an appropriate form of organization for the entertainment world of a boisterous resort such as Las Vegas. What Venturi fails to discuss is whether such near chaos is not good in itself and whether or not such a vivid manner of ordering could or could not be universally applied; he thus leaves the impression that it could. Venturi has his exact counterpart in Richard Sennet (1971), who would apparently trade social order for disorder in the expectation of also trading anomie for vivid social presence. Both give the impression of preferring wholesale assault where measured and purposeful action might suffice.

But indeed, the design professions do not have any valid response to such proposals. Their basic difficulty is that they have nearly no criterion for homogeneity or heterogeneity (Gans, 1961, p. 504). The only thing that can be said with certainty is that standards for order cannot be based on any inherited prescription for "good" order. Instead the criteria for homogeneity and heterogeneity can be derived only from the purposes of the persons who will use the environment. Specific criteria (e.g., Fox Point, Wisconsin, Village Ordinance No. 227: Buildings are not to be too like nor too different from neighboring buildings in order to protect property values) can be based only on

136

ARCHITECTURE, PROBLEMS AND PURPOSES

2.7.6.3

the meanings and implications of that order and of a departure from that order.

Neither order nor chaos is absolute, and to act as if either was and to turn from a preference for order to one for chaos or complexity would be to deal with a comparatively permanent plastic object, the building, as if it were a relatively transitory object of fashion (Hein, 1967, p. 64). Order at any larger scale requires cooperative action, and designers do not yet have the tools for understanding what actions are possible and what are required. Because of diverse wants, diverse lifestyles, and fluctuatingly diverse transitory desires, a corresponding diversity of environmental ordering is needed (Stretton, 1972, p. 136). Different kinds of cities are needed, and in them, different kinds of precincts pertinent in their differences to the purposes of the persons who will use them. An acceptance of chaos, however interesting, will not organize or provide such pertinent differences. Instead a method of measuring the level of order that exists must be developed.

REFERENCES

Best, Gordon, "Direction-finding in Large Buildings," in Canter, David, Ed., *Architectural Psychology,* RIBA, London, 1970.

Gans, Herbert, "Planning and Social Life: Friendship and Neighborhood Relations in Suburban Communities," *Journal of the American Institute of Planners,* **28**(7), 1961.

Gauss, Charles E., "Order and Structure in Science and Art," *Student Publications of the School of Design,* **7**(1), 1957.

Goffman, Erving, *Behavior in Public Places,* Free Press, New York, 1963.

Hein, Piet, "Of Order and Disorder, Science and Art, and the Solving of Problems," *Architectural Forum,* **127**(5), December 1967.

Hershberger, Robert G., "A Study of Meaning and Architecture," in Sanoff, Henry, and Sidney Cohn, Eds., *EDRA 1: Proceedings of the first annual Environmental Design Research Association Conference,* no publisher named, 1970.

Huizinga, Johan, *Homo Ludens: A Study of the Play Element in Culture,* Beacon Press, Boston, 1970.

Huxtable, Ada Louise, "Architecture: Anti-Street, Anti-People," *The New York Times,* June 10, 1973.

Klausner, Samuel Z., "The Intermingling of Pain and Pleasure: the Stress-Seeking Personality in its Social Context," in Klausner, Samuel Z., Ed., *Why Man Takes Chances,* Doubleday, Garden City, N.Y., 1968.

Kohler, Ivo, "The Formation and Transformation of the Visual World," in Haber, Ralph Norman, Ed., *Contemporary Theory and Research in Visual Perception,* Holt, Rinehart & Winston, New York, 1968.

Lewin, Kurt, "Behavior and Development as a Function of the Total Situation," in Cartright, Dorwin, Ed., *Kurt Lewin: Field Theory in Social Science,* Harper & Row, New York 1964.

Lowenthal, David, and Marquita Riel, "The Nature of Perceived and Imagined Environments, *Environment and Behavior,* **4**(2), June 1972.

Rapoport, Amos, "Designing for Complexity," *Architectural Association Quarterly,* **3**(1), Winter 1971.

Rapoport, Amos, and Ron Hawkes, "The Perception of Urban Complexity," *Journal of the American Institute of Planners,* **36**(2), March 1970.

REFERENCES

Rapoport, Amos, and Robert E. Kantor, "Complexity and Ambiguity in Environmental Design," *Journal of the American Institute of Planners,* 33(4), July 1967.

Sennett, Richard, *The Uses of Disorder: Personal Identity and City Life,* Random House, New York, 1971.

Sommer, Robert, "Alien Buildings," *Arts and Architecture,* 83(3), April 1966.

Steinitz, Carl, "Meaning and the Congruence of Urban Form and Activity," *Journal of the American Institute of Planners,* 34(4), July 1968.

Stretton, Hugh, "Planning to Break the Rules," *Royal Australian Planning Institute Journal,* October 1972.

Studer, Raymond G., "The Dynamics of Behavior-Contingent Physical Systems," in Broadbent, Geoffrey, and Anthony Ward, Eds., *Design Methods in Architecture,* Wittenborn, New York, 1969.

Venturi, Robert, and Denise Scott Brown, "A *Significance* for A&P Parking Lots or Learning From Las Vegas," *Architectural Forum,* 128(2), March 1968.

Wohlwill, Joachim F., "The Physical Environment: A Problem for a Psychology of Stimulation," *Journal of Social Issues,* 22(4), 1966.

2.8 THE USE OF IMAGES IN DESIGN

The designer uses an imaging process to achieve an integration of his design effort. The successful designer knows how to get information into his process and how to make his image explicit for use.

No one knows how design ideas are achieved. What is known is that different persons are not equal in their ability to imagine some spatially organized arrangement. Some are able to visualize an imaginary spatial arrangement in considerable detail; others can only structure gross relationships in their minds and must then use graphic representations to work out the detail. How those images are achieved and whether they are achieved by prior internal visualization or with the assistance of pencil and paper diagrams are unimportant; the image must eventually be converted into some public, objective form before it can be assessed. The image and the information associated with it are not useful until objectively available. If a person claims to have gloriously vivid internal images that he cannot get onto paper, we may congratulate him on having such enjoyable experiences, but they are of no use to him or to anyone else for problem solution.

If some discussion is proceeding today about whether the design process or the design product is more important, then it is a waste of everyone's time. No process, however elegant, that fails to lead to a *product* is of any use. No product that is not justifiable by an orderly and reasonable *process* is of much help. If designers and design methodologists are today worried over imposing a product on an unsuspecting public, one can respect their concern, but one can also suspect that it is overinflated. The designer almost never produces the completed environment. He produces the bare structure and enclosure—the *potential* environment, which the environment's users make *actual.*

2.8.1 Modeling Reality with Images

The mind uses images to model real-world conditions. By operating its image model faster than reality, the mind uses images to predict how reality will proceed.

One of the basic notions about problem solution has to do with the use of images, by which the mind is able to model some part of the real world. The mind can then operate its model of reality faster than reality operates and use the model to predict how reality will proceed. Clearly, if it is able to do that, it can try a number of different possible organizations of reality to see how much it likes each one.

The design student must learn how to make the mind produce this model or series of models. One thing he soon learns is that reading over the program for a problem and daydreaming about the problem does not accomplish much. He discovers that his mind will not use information it does not really possess and that it does not possess information it has not in some fashion processed. He discovers that one of the real reasons for doing area layouts of different proposed spaces in the building is to permit his mind to acquire the information about the relative sizes of required spaces. He discovers that one of the reasons for doing bubble diagrams is so that his mind can acquire the information about required relations between spaces.

Much comment about the "incubation" phenomenon has occurred in the literature on creativity. The mind does not always solve complex problems immediately; on occasion, when the conscious parts of the mind have fully absorbed the information associated with a problem and a solution does not come immediately, the mind sometimes solves the problem unconsciously; the solution pops into the mind unexpectedly.

When the design student receives such a solution, when he has thought of such a basic scheme, or *parti,* then he still has a great deal of work.

2.8.2 Control over the Imaging Process

The mind's production of insightful and creative images of problem solutions is not under conscious control; instead there is conscious control over the preparation of the mind for image production and over the verification of solutions that images contain.

Idea attainment is described as occurring in four noticeable stages: *preparation, incubation, illumination,* and *verification.* The greatest attention and interest appear to have been focused on *incubation* and *illumination,* those parts over which the creator seems to have no conscious control. Relatively little attention is given to the more important phases of *preparation* and *verification,* those parts over which he does have control. It would seem likely that an organized approach to preparation and a pondering of the most productive forms of verification might assist problem solving enormously.

The development of theory is not far enough along to offer more than speculation at this time, but I have little doubt that the experienced designer has learned useful preparation methods and appropriate ways of verifying the ideas and insights he has.

2.8.3 Developing a Sensitivity to Image Solutions

Achievement of a solution through imaging is sometimes a fugitive process. The designer must become sensitive to occurrence of the solution.

All designers have lost ideas. Sometimes an insight is achieved that is so tenuous that a too hasty examination or a too-long-delayed development will destroy it and make it unavailable for use. I have sat on occasion with a basic idea for a building scheme that seemed so good that I was frightened to examine it closely. I wanted to let it develop before attempting to commit it to paper. I suspect that I usually waited longer than I need have done. Unfortunately little help can be offered except to suggest that the student designer become aware of his own processes and try to discover how he works best with himself. The phenomenon of idea occurrence has not been investigated in an orderly way so that it is useful for the designer—not, at least, in my knowledge.

2.8.4 Unequal Abilities in Imaging

Different persons have differing abilities in image production. Some persons simply do not have visual images.

Some persons simply do not have visual images. Instead they may be able to hear entire symphonies in their heads or to conjure up entire odor settings and sequences. However capable such a person, he will be severely handicapped in design. It is essential for the designer that he be able to visualize objects.

What is required in visualization can be stated further. To be able only to see a picture of something in the mind is not enough. To be able to see two different pictures of the same object and place them in accurate relationship is essential. The designer must be able to depict objects from imaginary points of view (as in a section drawing, or in a reflected ceiling plan, or in a developed drawing in which related surfaces are unfolded). An inability to perceive and imagine such relationships will handicap him severely.

When the designer must deal with a client who is unable to visualize, he is almost equally handicapped. His drawings will not communicate very much to such a client. He must work with models, and it is best that the models be as large as possible. Unless the designer is sensitive to the client's ability to visualize, he may spend endless time and much effort in a fruitless attempt to communicate.

2.8.5 Displaying Images with Drawings

A solution image is of no use unless it can be externalized for

Diagrams and drawings are the designer's chief tools for communication. They are not without their limitations, as I have just indicated, but nothing yet is more useful in most circumstances.

The first use of a designer's drawings is not in communicating with

examination and analysis. The
designer's principal use of drawing
is in communicating with himself
about his images.

other persons but in communicating with himself. Only when he has
brought the idea from his imagination onto paper (in however crude a
form) can he begin to discover whether the idea will suffice to solve
the problem.

2.8.6 The Technical Discussions

The discussions that follow go into more detail about imaging in
problem solving. There are also more detailed discussions of processes
of idea attainment.

2.8.6.1 The Structure of Problem Situations

Problem solution moves from a
relatively unstructured to a relatively structured situation. Because the usual problem-solving
process requires a long sequence of
steps, there is no strong method
of selecting the first steps.

In addition to his recognition that a solution process involves a
change of state Wertheimer (1959, pp. 238-243) defines a specific
group of forces that move the problem solver from a problem to a
solution situation. He notes that the problem situation, S_1, contains
structural strains and stresses and that these are resolved in the solution
situation, S_2. He defines a problem situation as one that has structural
troubles; he defines a solution as a situation in which those structural
troubles are straightened out. He describes the process in these terms
(Wertheimer, 1945, p. 239):

> . . . when one grasps a problem situation, its structural features and requirements
> set up certain strains, stresses, tensions, in the thinker. What happens in real
> thinking is that these strains and stresses are followed up, yield vectors in the
> direction of improvement of the situation, and change it accordingly. S_2 is a
> state of affairs that is held together by inner forces as a good structure in which
> there is harmony in the mutual requirements, and in which the parts are deter-
> mined by the structure of the whole, as the whole is by the parts.

Wertheimer thus makes the structure of the whole problem situation
the essential key to an understanding of the solution process.

In describing the components in this process, he lists (Wertheimer,
1945, pp. 234-236):

1. Genuine, direct, *productive processes.*

2. Factors and *operations* at work—essential to thinking.

3. The features and operations determined by *structural requirements*
   (and they are related to whole characteristics).

4. That traditional operations exist but in this whole relationship.

5. That thought processes show a consistency of development.

6. That in their development they lead to sensible expectations,
   assumptions.

In summary a solution process evokes a series of basic operations that move in a consistent developmental way toward a solution; they are controlled by the *structure* of the entire problem situation. If these insights do not appear surprising to us now, it is possibly because Wertheimer's work permits us to treat them as commonplace thirty years after their first publication.

Wertheimer's insight was that problem situations are structured. By contrast Gordon Best comments on the particular structuring the solver brings to the problem. When the solver has discovered a relationship in the problem information, he has then interpreted the problem. In his interpretation he has invented concepts that bring unrelated ideas together, and in doing so, he brings a *structure* to the problem based on his experience (Best, 1969, p. 158).

Whereas Wertheimer had assumed that the *structure* existed in the situation, Best, after twenty-five years' development in the psychology of perception, is certain that the *structure* is provided by the problem solver.

Although both writers recognize the existence of the structure of a situation, and one of them is sure where it comes from, neither has said what structure is. A useful, concise definition is given by Michael Lane (1970, p. 24): "A structure is a set of any elements between which, or between certain sub-sets of which, relations are defined." This is a relatively precise definition that is very close to the much looser definition that Guilford (1967, p. 242) provides for the term *system*. For Guilford "system" is nearly interchangeable with "structure." In his discussion he quotes a definition of structure by Helen Peak, "'systems of relationships between identifiable parts.'"

Lane makes it very clear that the structure he describes is derived from the experience of the problem solver. Beyond this it is difficult to go. Wolf (1962, pp. 174-175), for example, in a discussion of the relevance of information, states that the problem solver is dependent on past experience, and then goes on to say, "Another factor . . . is a very real influence. I mean just the vague feeling or intuition that certain things are relevant, while others are not." It is apparent that the structure of a situation to which information must relate is sometimes not highly articulated. Similarly, in a discussion of the suitability of a system of classification, Abercrombie (1960, p. 118) presumes that it is "based on the perception . . . of a pattern of correlated features, and seems to involve . . . aesthetic judgment. One may be able, sooner or later, to justify logically the preferment of one arrangement above another, but the stage of formulation is often preceded by a general vague feeling of unease, a notion that there is something wrong somehow with one arrangment." Again there is a failure of the articulation of structure but with never a doubt that the structure can eventually be articulated.

Polanyi (1958, pp. 115-116) is able to establish three such levels of articulateness:

1. the readily specifiable properties which a class of things are known to share apart from their common key-feature. . . .
2. the known but not readily specifiable properties which these things share. . . .
3. the indeterminate range of anticipations expressed by designating something.

For Polanyi the common experience is that thought moves from the more articulate structuring of thought into the less articulate, anticipating that the future will confirm the rightness of the conception that has structured the thought.

As he moves into a discussion of thought sequences, Polanyi is aware that the important element in such a sequence is not its detail but the outline by which one thought is connected to the next, and so on, to the completion of the thought chain. A grasp of a general procedure *is important where the details of that procedure* are not. Again such a sequence is undoubtedly based on the experience of other related or similar sequences; it is also based on the components that can fairly compose it; the sequence is rooted in an understanding of the structure or system on which it is itself based (Polanyi, 1958, pp. 118-119).

Finally Frank Restle (1969, p. 149) raises the basic question for solution processes that can be answered only in terms of understood or known systems or structures; he says:

Therefore to hold a partial solution [when a problem requires the correct response to five separate searches and a fit between them] , the subject must have some concept of what the total solution will look like and be able to fill in that scheme gradually and with a certain confidence . . . . What our theories do not say is how does the subject handle and evaluate partial solutions.

The term *scheme* is equivalent with *structure, system,* and *outline.* Since no other source is known, the individual must base his intimation of the overall scheme on those he has experienced that are somehow similar.

REFERENCES

Abercrombie, M. L. Johnson, *The Anatomy of Judgment,* Basic Books, New York, 1960.

Best, Gordon, "Method and Intention in Architectural Design," in Broadbent, Geoffrey and A. Ward, *Design Methods in Architecture,* A. A. Paper No. 4, Symposium, Portsmouth School of Architecture, Architect's Association, London, 1969.

Guilford, J. P., *The Nature of Human Intelligence,* McGraw-Hill, New York, 1967.

REFERENCES

Lane, Michael, Ed., *Introduction to Structuralism,* Basic Books, New York, 1970.

Polanyi, Michael, *Personal Knowledge,* University of Chicago Press, Chicago, 1958.

Restle, Frank, "Mathematical Models and Thought," in Voss, James F., Ed., *Approaches to Thought,* Merrill, Columbus, Ohio, 1969.

Wertheimer, Max, *Productive Thinking,* Harper & Row, New York, 1945.

Wolf, A., *Textbook of Logic,* Crowell-Collier, New York, 1962.

2.8.6.2 Intuitive Solution Processes

Successful problem solution requires extended and intensive preparation. Given such a preparation, the mind seems to have a "natural adaptation to imagining correct theories."

The often-repeated formula that describes the stages in the process leading to original insight was stated succinctly by Wallas (1970, pp. 91-92) in 1926; the stages are (1) preparation, (2) incubation, (3) illumination, and (4) verification. Although this formulation has been confirmed repeatedly by a number of writers, it is descriptive without being explanatory. The descriptions confirm that the event of *illumination* is not able to be forced and occurs without any pattern of time relationship with the *preparation* stage-except that it ordinarily comes after that stage. The *incubation* stage is descriptively empty, since it is merely that time between the preparation stage and the time when illumination occurs. *Verification* occurs as an "afterthought" that follows as a matter of course and convenience.

If this description ever had any value, it is in the confirmation that a conclusion or solution can be achieved without the necessity for a conscious sequence of logical steps between it and the initiating problem. The steps can be supplied as connectors in confirmation of the relation between the two events. Its value is in noticing that a solution can occur "spontaneously."

It is unfortunate that the emphasis in Wallas's writing has been placed on incubation, an area about which little can presently be determined; this places creative work and problem solution into the area of intuition or mysticism, saying in effect that there is no accounting for creativity.

In point of fact what led to the creative act was the hard work that had gone into preparation before the insight was achieved, and the hard work that went into the confirming verification, and the efforts, often long and strenuous, that permitted an effectuation of the insight. Brewster Ghiselin (1963, p. 28) states:

A great deal of the work necessary to equip and activate the mind for the spontaneous part of invention must be done consciously and with an effort of will. Mastering accumulated knowledge, gathering new facts, observing, exploring, experimenting, developing technique and skill, sensibility, and discrimination, are all more or less conscious and voluntary activities. The sheer labor of preparing technically for creative work, consciously acquiring the requisite knowledge of a medium and skill in its use, is extensive and arduous enough to repel many from achievement.

ARCHITECTURE, PROBLEMS AND PURPOSES

Ghiselin might have spent an equal discussion on the effort that comes in some fields of creative work after the insight has occurred. In architectural design an idea for a solution can come and be sketched quickly within minutes; discovering whether it is workable in all its parts can take days or even weeks.

C. S. Peirce makes interesting comparable comments, stating that "Man's mind has a natural adaptation to imagining correct theories of some kinds." Peirce was apparently impressed, not that the mind produced insights, but that it produced so relatively few false or inappropriate insights. Peirce phrases the impression he has of the mind's power to select appropriate hypotheses in the following manner:

...we shall do better to abandon the whole attempt to learn the truth... unless we can trust to the human mind's having such a power of guessing right that before very many hypothese shall have been tried, intelligent guessing may be expected to lead us to the one which will support all tests, leaving the vast majority of possible hypotheses unexamined. Of course, it will be understood that in the testing process itself there need be no such assumption of mysterious guessing powers. It is only in selecting hypothesis to be tested that we are to be guided by that assumption. (Tomas, 1957, pp. 249-250.)

Peirce then held the position in 1901 that man's mental structure places severe limitations on the kinds of concepts he can entertain, that there are in fact only certain kinds admissible to thought. He held that this is true because there has been in man's long history of development an equally long history of successful induction permitting man's survival—to the extent that his induction processes accurately and efficiently reflected reality.

Such comments do not explain how "correct" theories are achieved, nor do they assist the problem solver by saying what he might do to assist the process by which theories are even generated. At best the statements suggest that the problem solver might examine even his casual ideas for possible solutions to his problem. At worst the comments are encouraging, for they suggest that problems are often more easily solvable than a dispassionate view of the problem situation might suggest.

If the designer is to understand problem-solving processes, he can do better than depend on incubation. Bruner claims (1956, p. 243) that, if a person is to understand intelligent or adaptive behavior, he must work with units larger than a single response, that he must work with sequences of response, and that these sequences and the steps in them must be externalized for him to get at them. He states that "so-called 'eureka' problems in which the subject is given all the elements out of which a solution must be fashioned are peculiarly unsuited to the requirements of getting behavior observably externalized, unless the problem is such that successive, attempted solutions can be observed." When Wallas described the preparation, incubation, illumination, and verification sequence, he did little more than note that the "eureka" problem exists.

REFERENCES

Bruner, Jerome S., J. J. Goodnow, and G. A. Austin, *A Study of Thinking,* Wiley, New York, 1956.

Ghiselin, Brewster, Ed., *The Creative Process,* New American Library, New York, 1963.

Tomas, Vincent, Ed., *Charles S. Peirce: Essays in the Philosophy of Science,* Liberal Arts Press, New York, 1957.

Wallas, G., "The Art of Thought," in Vernon, P. E., Ed., *Creativity,* Penguin, Harmondsworth, England, 1970.

2.8.6.3 The Image as a Model of Reality

The mind uses images to anticipate and control future events. The usefulness of an image depends on its accuracy as a model of reality. That accuracy is related to the degree of correspondence between the mind's experience of statistical occurrences and the totality of statistical occurrence of the events being modeled.

In the literature on thought process references have been made to a structure of thought, to an outline of thought sequence, and to images that assist the thought process. Some part of this variation in descriptions is undoubtedly due to the varying ability of individuals to form images of events and to the individual's ability to be in different mental modes; sometimes the individual forms images and sometimes he does not.

A pioneering study by Sir Francis Galton in 1883 first disclosed evidence of the enormous variation in imaging ability (Hunter, 1957, pp. 140-141). Work since that time, reported by W. Grey Walter (1951, pp. 184-185), has disclosed a relationship between imaging ability and the brain's alpha rhythm; apparently persons without alpha rhythm activity think consistently by means of images, those with persistent alpha rhythm activity never use images, and those with varying alpha activity sometimes use images and sometimes do not.

Those who have imaging ability are able to use it to model situations in the environment. Undoubtedly persons who do not have the image-forming ability have an ability to model complex situations in some other fashion—for example, by a structured sequence of events remembered in a temporal manner or else by a verbal, descriptive structure organized to review the salient features of the situation. Although each of these several means of representation is best suited to different conditions, it seems to be unarguable that each can be substituted for another to carry on the everyday business of living.

Once, when I was delivering a friend from the downtown area to his residence, he commented he was glad to learn a new way to get home. Since the route we were taking was extremely direct and involved only three thoroughfares and two right-angle turns between them, I was startled and asked how he usually went home. He replied by describing the route that carried him three times the direct distance out of his way. He took the route because it was the one he had learned when he had first arrived in the city two years earlier. He had not been able, apparently, to organize the spatial relationships and had found his way by a remembered sequence of events and landmarks.

In the discussion that follows, remember that the imaging process is not universally available for problem solution, that there are forms of imaging other than the visual, and that there are methods of modeling reality other than imaging (Hunter, 1957, pp. 141-142; Gibson, 1966, p. 277).

Eugene J. Meehan defines purpose in terms of "two fundamental human needs or requirements"; he delineates them: ". . . first, [there is] the need to *anticipate* future events so that behavior can be adapted to them; second, [there is] the need to be able to *control* future events (the past is beyond control) so that man can become something more than a servile prisoner of natural forces." (Meehan, 1968, pp. 19-20.)

In developing a theory of personality, George A. Kelly goes considerably further with such thoughts, for his theoretic development starts with the process by which the person anticipates events. The basic postulate and the first two corollaries in his theory are as follows (Kelly, 1963, pp. 103-104):

1. Fundamental Postulate. "A person's processes are psychologically channelized by the ways in which he anticipates events."

2. Construction Corollary. "A person anticipates events by construing their replications."

3. Individuality Corollary. "Persons differ from each other in their constructions of events."

Galanter and Gerstenhaber, writing in 1956, had said [referring to the operations of the environment as a "machine" or "mechanism"], ". . . we say that an organism is faced with a problem if it is motivated to *predict the behavior* of the machine. The process by which the mechanism is predicted is called 'thinking' and adequate (in the sense of achieving the reward) prediction is called a 'solution.' " They state that the first step in the solution of a problem consists in the construction of a model of the pertinent features of the environment "machine." They observe that "Imagal thinking is neither more nor less than constructing an image or model of the environment, running the model faster than the environment, and predicting that the environment will behave as the model does."

In more detail they point out that a model can be manipulated according to various hypothetical conditions and constrains so that one can see how the environment might behave. The individual is then able to observe these imagal outcomes and project them onto his environment (Galanter and Gerstenhaber, 1956, pp. 127-128).

There are, of course, basic difficulties in achieving an accurate correspondence between the behavior of the model and that of the environment. The accuracy of the model can often be expressed only in statistical terms that depend on the experience of the individual operating the model; each perception he has is what Ames has called "an involuntary bet" based on his past experiences; but even if his perceptions are accurate, his prediction that they will operate in certain ways is accurate only according to the degree that his statistical experiences have corresponded with the totality of the statistical occurrence of events of that kind.

Galanter and Gerstenhaber imply that the image or model is more subject to the manipulation of the individual than the environment is from which the model is derived. Kurt Lewin, in a 1946 paper, comments directly on this manipulatability: "Levels of irreality, being more fluid than the level of reality, are, consequently more easily influenced by both wishes and fears. This is why dreams and daydreams mirror the needs of the child." He says further, "Needs affect the cognitive structure not only of the psychological present, but, even more, of the psychological future and past. This is particularly important for the level of aspiration." (Lewin, 1964, pp. 274-280.)

The idea of the nervous system as a model of reality is not particularly new; K.J.W.Craik (1943, pp. 120-121) had explored that idea in 1943, but considerable analysis of models since that time has brought an increased understanding of the advantage a model has. Max Black (1962, pp. 236-237) comments, "Those who see a model as a mere crutch are like those who consider metaphor a mere decoration or ornament." He observes that the advantage in using a model is not in its picturability but in the fact that its properties are well-known so that it can be used in representation from the modeling system to the system being modeled. "To make good use of a model, we usually need intuitive grasp ('Gestalt knowledge') of its capacities, but so long as we can freely *draw inferences* from the model, its picturability is of no importance." (Black, 1962, pp. 232-233.)

John Raser (1971, pp. 8-9) speaks of a model as a specific form of theory that "allows us, in a sense, to 'play' with the theory in a rather concrete, physical way." If Raser means the word *play* in its full implications (which he might well do), then Huizinga's comments on play (1955, pp. 8-11) are useful. Play permits a person to deal with the modeled situation:

1. In a freer or more voluntary way.

2. In a nonordinary, or a fun way.

3. In a way that creates order.

4. In a way secluded in time and place, that is, especially set aside.

5. In a tension-producing and tension-releasing way.

6. In a way that abides carefully by a set of rules.

I might well have stretched Raser's intention too far by this application of Huizinga's comments, but at the same time, it appears right that all the characteristics Huizinga attributes to play activity are also ones that can be applied to the use of models and especially to the use of images as models of reality.

REFERENCES

Black, Max, *Models and Metaphors: Studies in Language and Philosophy,* Cornell University Press, Ithaca, N.Y., 1962.

Craik, K. J. W., *The Nature of Explanation,* Cambridge University Press, Cambridge, England, 1943.

Galanter, Eugene, and Murray Gerstenhaber, "On Thought: The Extrinsic Theory," *Psychological Review,* **63** (4), 1956.

Gibson, James J., *The Senses Considered as Perceptual Systems,* Houghton-Mifflin, Boston, 1966.

Huizinga, Johan, *Homo Ludens: A Study of the Play Element in Culture,* Beacon Press, Boston, 1955.

Hunter, Ian M. L., *Memory: Facts and Fallacies,* Penguin, Harmondsworth, England, 1957.

Kelly, George A., *A Theory of Personality,* Norton, New York, 1963.

Lewin, Kurt, "Behavior and Development as a Function of the Total Situation," in Cartwright, Dorwin, Ed., *Kurt Lewin: Field Theory in Social Science,* Harper & Row, New York, 1964.

Meehan, Eugene J., *Explanation in Social Science,* Dorsey, Homewood, Ill., 1968.

Raser, John R., *Simulation and Society: An Exploration of Scientific Gaming,* Allyn & Bacon, Boston, 1971.

Walter, W. Grey, "Activity Pattern in the Human Brain," in Whyte, Lancelot Law, *Aspects of Form,* Indiana University Press, Bloomington, 1951.

3. Influences on Problem Solution

Design depends on closure (or assumption) for solution. The kind of assumption made affects the kind of solution achieved. The kind of assumption is *affected by* a number of different things, ranging from the kind of problem the designer considers to the experience and tools he brings to his solution process.

The solution of design problems is subject to a number of different influences. Because these problems are ill defined and require assumptions for their solution, the kind of assumption made affects the kind of solution achieved, and is, in turn, affected by a number of different things, ranging from the degree of problem severity to the kinds of tools the designer uses.

One of the strongest influences on the solution is the nature of the problem, whether it is an emergency requiring a quick and (if necessary) makeshift solution, or whether it is a chronic problem requiring eventual and deliberate solution. The amount of available time affects the quality of solution achieved. The designer begins to understand relatively early how he must adjust his assumptions and the depth of his study to the available time. He learns to modify the amount of detail in his solution according to the available time.

A second very strong influence on solution is the designer's image of the problem in relation to his total image structure. His prior experience and the manner in which his view of the world has developed both have an emphatic and powerful influence on his solutions. Each person develops a view of the world that is value structured in ways unique to him. Whenever a problem occurs, the designer imposes his already-established values on it. The stronger the designer's internal value structure, the weaker his response to the totality of the problem. All persons distort events by the way they perceive them; such distortion affects the assumptions they make and the solutions they achieve.

Ancillary motivations also affect the solution. The designer might want to achieve a solution with the least amount of effort (because he has other, more important matters in hand); by contrast he might want to be very sure that *some* solution is achieved, whatever its kind; by further contrast he might want desperately to avoid any possibility of the slightest error in the process by which a solution is achieved. In school the design student can have other courses that require his attention, he can often be under extreme pressure to complete his work for the sake of a grade, or he might wish to avoid mistakes to save face with his fellow students. In professional practice the designer must work against a deadline imposed sometimes by office budgets and sometimes by the client. He might wish to avoid errors in his solution that could badly damage both his profit and his reputation.

The process the designer uses strongly affects his solution. Is he willing to rely on and to adapt an already tried solution, or does he insist on inventing a totally new one? Does he put his greatest effort into the earlier parts of the process (into programming) that can narrow and reduce the time spent on later parts, or does he put his greatest effort into later parts (into design)?

The methods the designer selects and the tools he uses also affect the solution. How early does the designer invest work in a detailed consideration of a particular scheme, and how much solution effort does he invest? The most skilled designer can sometimes become committed to a bad solution because he has invested too much work in its development. The designer can easily mistake work on a drawing for work on the design that the drawing represents; he can value a particular drawing so much that he chooses the design for the sake of the drawing. The designer must learn early to keep means as means and not let them become ends.

The method which the designer evaluates his proposals has an immense effect on the solution. One of the beliefs (myths?) of the design profession is that its holistic response to the holistically presented totality of a design proposal provides a superior method of evaluation. The designer believes he can evaluate a number of different attributes simultaneously, but contrary evidence also indicates that such an evaluation process only lets one or a few attributes become dominant, overruling the others. Does the designer use only such a visually based evaluation, or does he also keep checklists or rating schemes by which he evaluates the detail of a project as well as its totality?

In addition to all these topics, the single strongest influence on design solution is the social nature of the design process; design might even be called a social version of imagination (getting the image onto paper to be considered by several persons). This topic is important enought to defer to a separate chapter.

3.1 PROBLEM SEVERITY AND PROBLEM GENERALITY

A strong influences on solution is the character of the problem being considered. How *severe* is the problem and how *general* is the problem's occurrence?

A world with nothing but terrible problems and a few solutions would be difficult to bear, but one with no problems might be equally unbearable. Most people need some problems for stimulation and some solutions for reward and relief. Although solutions are a life need, necessary for existence and well-being, the problem-solving activity is just as necessary.

It is not possible, of course, to talk equally about relatively simple problems and extremely difficult problems, but to say how bad a problem is, one must develop some careful definitions. There are two ways to describe how bad problems are: in terms of their severity and of their generality.

A definition of problem severity can be based on a distinction drawn earlier between the initial and the terminal state of a problem. These can also be thought of respectively as a problem state and a goal state. The distance between them can be used as a measure of severity.

ARCHITECTURE, PROBLEMS AND PURPOSES

Problem generality can be defined in terms of the pervasiveness of a particular problem and the need to commit resources to its continuing solution.

After a full discussion of these definitions it will be possible to describe one of the very strong influences on problem solution, the investment decision. The problem solver must decide how much he is willing to spend to solve a problem once and for all by changing the physical environment, instead of solving it over and over again by a series of repeated actions.

3.1.1 Individual Variations in Stress Preference

Although an individual varies from time to time in his preference for stress increase or decrease, he varies less in his preference for a typical level of stress. Some persons tend to be action avoiding and others action seeking.

When the designer has achieved a solution to his current problem, and while he is still engaged in some of the more mechanical chores associated with presenting his solution, he begins to wonder what the next problem will be. If he has acquired any skill in drafting, he can do the mechanical tasks without much attention, and his mind can be free to consider other matters. When all problems are solved, the mind usually begins to seek new ones.

It is easy to describe this in the school experience because of the artificial structure of the problem-solving sequence. Although it would be more difficult to describe this sequence in a person's life, still the same events occur. When problems overlap, the individual usually undertakes the simultaneous and overlapping solution of as many different problems as he is comfortable in handling. Undoubtedly different levels of problem tolerance are related to the individual's motivation at different times in his life. I can remember that one time in my college career I had some twenty-five major events (examinations, term papers, design problems, etc.) all falling due within a three-week period; I was just able to handle that level of involvement, but I could not have borne that intense an involvement in problem solving for a much longer period of time.

The strain on the individual that results from problem stress seems to depend on two things: First, how severe is the problem? Second, how pervasive is it? Pervasiveness can appear in more than one form; there can be many different problems of different degrees of severity, and there can be many of the same or similar problems. Undoubtedly, different tolerance levels exist in the same individual for different mixtures of problems.

Different individuals have different tolerance levels for problems.

Part of the literature talks about individuals who are action seeking and about others who are action avoiding. Undoubtedly individuals could be ranged along a scale according to their willingness to deal with, and their preference for, different levels of stress. Some individuals are very conservative and prefer to experience as little change as possible. Others are bored by a lack of change and seek the stimulation change provides. Individuals differ remarkably in their ability to handle stress, ambiguity, and problems. Whatever their action preference they also differ at different times. Even the person who likes the stimulation of parachuting out of airplanes does not wish to do so continuously.

3.1.2 Defining Problem Severity

Problem severity is the degree of difference between an existing condition and a preferred goal condition. Since neither condition is static, the severity of a problem condition can change for the better of the worse.

Problems can be described by talking about an existing *problem condition* or about a desired *goal condition*. Whichever is emphasized, the one implies the existence of the other. Whatever kind of problem the design student is asked to think about, there is always some present condition that is unsatisfactory and some nonpresent (future) condition that is preferred.

The difference between these conditons can be small or great. A person can want only a new carpet in one room, or can want a different house in a different location that will provide a number of very different functions for him. The distance between the two conditions depends on the quality of the exisiting condition and on the aspirations of the person describing his preferences.

Both conditions are dynamic. The present condition might be improving or deteriorating; the individual's aspirations can be increasing or decreasing.

If *problem severity* is defined as the difference or the "distance" between these conditions, it must also take into account their dynamic nature and the way in which their movement affects the severity of a problem. The accompanying diagram (Fig. 3.1) shows this relation.

When the designer understands this relationsnip, he can also understand how the placement of his problem within the diagram can indicate what his solution strategy should be. A problem placed in the lower right part of the diagram requires action as soon as possible; one placed in the upper left might not require action at all.

3.1.3 Defining Problem Generality

Problem generality is the freq-quency of repetitive problem

As a particular problem occurs repeatedly, it becomes possible to plan for its occurrence. The designer begins to provide for the time that the problem's solution will require and begins to set aside the resources required. In such a circumstance a measure of the problem's severity is not enough; the designer also needs a measure of its general-

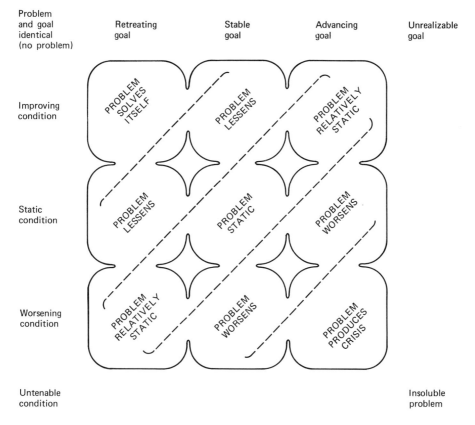

| Problem and goal identical (no problem) | Retreating goal | Stable goal | Advancing goal | Unrealizable goal |

Improving condition

PROBLEM SOLVES ITSELF · PROBLEM LESSENS · PROBLEM RELATIVELY STATIC

Static condition

PROBLEM LESSENS · PROBLEM STATIC · PROBLEM WORSENS

Worsening condition

PROBLEM RELATIVELY STATIC · PROBLEM WORSENS · PROBLEM PRODUCES CRISIS

Untenable condition   Insoluble problem

Figure 3.1 Problem severity.

3.1.3

occurrence. The infrequently occurring problem can be solved by an *allocation* of attention and existing resources. The frequently occurring problem might be solved by an *integrative* solution that modifies the circumstance of problem occurrence.

ity. He needs to be able to say something about how many people are affected, how widespread the problem is, and how frequently it occurs. Even when a problem is not very severe, if it occurs regularly enough, it will become a source of major irritation and can require a substantial resource commitment.

An *allocative* solution to a frequently occurring problem is one achieved within the existing framework of skills, tools, and time availability. Suppose a person is working in a large room that has one pencil sharpener mounted some distance from his desk. He can solve the problem of dull or broken pencil points by walking to the sharpener each time. If his usage of the sharpener becomes frequent enough to create a substantial irritation and interruption of his work, he can begin to sharpen a number of pencils on each trip. If he uses different kinds of pencils requiring an investment in a large number of pencils of each kind to reduce his trips to the sharpener, then he might decide that a strictly allocative solution is not adequate. He might favor an *integrative* solution that changes the situation.

When he can next afford to, he buys a pencil sharpener and mounts it on his desk. He has traded some of his resources in money for the time and energy he devoted to walking to a remote sharpener. He must still sharpen pencils, but he has saved the walking interruption.

Although this problem is trivial, it is a model of the problem that occurs in building construction: When allocation by itself does not reduce a problem sufficiently, an integrative solution may be required. When a problem becomes general enough in its occurrence, first an allocative solution alone might be adequate; if the problem is so general that the allocation of attention (time), effort, and resource is very great, the problem solver might consider an integrative solution.

The integrative solution attempts to solve the problem once and for all in order to replace the repetition of solution under allocation. Most integrative solutions do not avoid some form of allocation, but for an integrative solution to be worth considering, it must reduce substantially the allocation of attention and effort for each problem occurrence.

In the diagrams that follow, the first shows an increasing level of allocative response; the second shows an increasing level of integrative response. Both are related to the generality of problem occurrence. It is easy to see that there is a trade-off from one diagram to the other according to the attention, effort, and cost associated with a primarily allocative solution by contrast with the attention, effort, and cost associated with a primarily integrative solution. The first diagram (Fig. 3.2) shows a range of allocative responses; the second (Fig. 3.3) shows a range of integrative responses.

3.1.4 The Influence of Available Resources

The designer's response is strongly affected by the kinds of resources available to him.

Problem-solving efforts depend on the resources of the solver. The student in school is not so aware of this influence, but the young designer considering a move from employment in an established office to his own independent practice becomes intensely aware of all the resources in the established office he has taken for granted. Each office develops its own library of product information and begins to develop preferences for the use of some products and not for others—as a result of good and bad experiences with those products. Each office develops standard practices including preferred construction details and specifications, an organization of skilled persons and the typical responsibility assignments for each, and procedures by which it manages the day-to-day supportive activities that preserve it as a problem-solving institution.

The ability to exist as an entity, the access to persons who have the required skills, and the access to money resources required for operation all affect the ability of a solver to attack problems. The individual can undertake only a limited kind of problem by himself; larger ones require a design institution that can respond appropriately to the requirements.

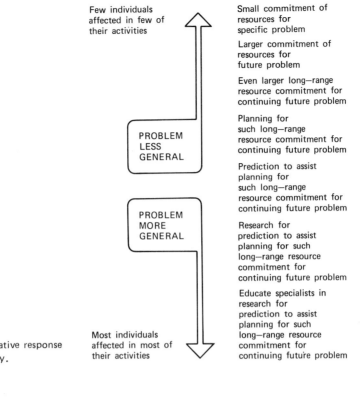

Few individuals
affected in few of
their activities

Small commitment of
resources for
specific problem

Larger commitment of
resources for
future problem

Even larger long–range
resource commitment for
continuing future problem

PROBLEM
LESS
GENERAL

Planning for
such long–range
resource commitment for
continuing future problem

Prediction to assist
planning for
such long–range
resource commitment for
continuing future problem

PROBLEM
MORE
GENERAL

Research for
prediction to assist
planning for such
long–range resource
commitment for
continuing future problem

Educate specialists in
research for
prediction to assist
planning for such
long–range resource
commitment for
continuing future problem

Figure 3.2 An allocative response
to problem generality.

Most individuals
affected in most of
their activities

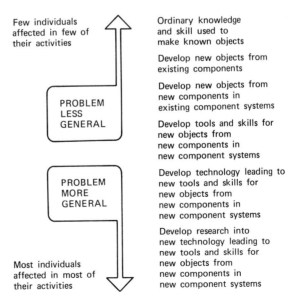

Few individuals
affected in few of
their activities

Ordinary knowledge
and skill used to
make known objects

Develop new objects from
existing components

Develop new objects from
new components in
existing component systems

PROBLEM
LESS
GENERAL

Develop tools and skills for
new objects from
new components in
new component systems

PROBLEM
MORE
GENERAL

Develop technology leading to
new tools and skills for
new objects from
new components in
new component systems

Develop research into
new technology leading to
new tools and skills for
new objects from
new components in
new component systems

Figure 3.3 An integrative response
to problem generality.

Most individuals
affected in most of
their activities

3.1.5 The Technical Discussions

The discussions that follow go into more detail about the difference between allocative and integrative solutions and about the criteria for choosing one or the other. The first discussion is concerned with the nature of integrative and allocative processes within a larger context of problem description. The second is concerned with an exchange theory that says why choices are made between alternative courses of action.

3.1.5.1 Conflicts in Object Attraction

The problem solver deals with complex forces. He can, for example, be attracted and repulsed by the same object. His action results from a balance of such forces.

The usual problem models assume that some basic need or desire of the problem solver is unfulfilled. They speak of an objective the problem solver has or of some failure of accord between a person and an object in his environment and his attempt to reestablish accord. In addition to seeing the problem solver's need to convert some existing condition into some other preferred condition, the usual problem model treats that condition as if it were unitary and simple. The model presented here deals with a nonunitary problem condition with complicating motives and multiple objectives.

Kurt Lewin (1964, pp. 258 ff.) describes the different forces acting on an individual as he attempts to obtain or achieve some desired object or goal. He shows that, where an individual is attracted by a desired object, he is also repulsed by a feared or disaffected object. When a problem contains both attractive and repulsive features, the behavior of the individual results from a summation of the attractive and repellent forces acting on him.

Several different combinations of placement of the repellent and attractive forces can occur:

1. Both an attractive and a repellent force can be imbedded in the same object.

2. Two attractive forces can be imbedded in different incompatible objects; that is, both cannot be attained. (Note: Balaam's Ass is a special case of this combination wherein the two forces are exactly equal.)

3. Two repellent forces can be imbedded in different objects in such a way that they tend to drive the individual in opposite directions from them.

4. One object can be attractive and another repellent; other things being equal, this would not be a conflict situation.

5. Each of two different objects could contain both attractive and repellent forces.

3.1.5.1

Clearly the examples cited are only the simpler kinds of situations that might exist; it is easy enough to imagine more complex circumstances.

As a result of the summation of the combination of forces the individual tends to *approach* or to *avoid* a particular defined object in the environment. Lewin expands on this basic model by listing the kinds of conflict that can exist for the individual under different approach-avoidance circumstances.

Where a problem condition is compound or complex, it is possible for an approach-avoidance conflict to arise. Where problem solving requires the resolution of such a conflict, the thoughts Lewin puts forward can be taken into account and can assist the solution process.

REFERENCES

Lewin, Kurt, "Behavior and Development as a Function of the Total Situation," in Cartwright, Dorwin, Ed., *Kurt Lewin: Field Theory in Social Science,* Harper & Row, New York, 1964.

3.1.5.2 The Costs and Benefits of Actions

In evaluating choices the problem solver weights alternative actions in terms of their costs and benefits. This is as true for implicit intuitive choices as for explicit economic choices.

It is common experience that each person balances costs against benefits in even his most ordinary activities, and given the kinds of choice addressed in the conflict model described above, there is an inclination on the part of the individual to maximize benefits and minimize costs (Homans, 1961, pp. 96-97). As Homans observes elsewhere, individuals use just such intuitive (and, no doubt, imprecise) computations to decide whether a trip to the water cooler is justified, taking into account the distance to the water cooler, the effort required to get there, and the loss of time from other activity, by comparison with the level of thirst, the satisfaction to be obtained by quenching that thirst, and the satisfaction from engaging in a brief change from routine.

Such cost-benefit computations are not simple or simplistic and take into account a number of different factors associated with the proposed activity. Homans (1961. pp. 53 ff.) reviews five of these factors:

1. The degree to which the activity has been rewarded in the past.

2. The degree to which the activity is similar to previously rewarded activity.

3. The degree of value of the reward associated with the activity.

4. The degree to which one has been recently rewarded in that fashion.

5. The degree to which a failure of justice in reward will evoke anger.

3.1.5.2

Although the phrasing Homans uses , paraphrased above, is strictly concerned with exchanges between persons and particularly and explicitly with the social costs and benefits of actions taken by persons, his principles are capable of a broader interpretation. Denton (1973, pp. 20-21), for example, states, "It is clear that Homans viewed these five propositions as applicable to explaining exchange between humans and non-human environments." It is also clear that Homans was aware that exchange propositions had been applied to physical objects and services and to their evaluation long before he applied such propositions to the social worth of exchanged activities.

There is, in fact, no doubt that a broader application can be made of Homans's proposition; my paraphrasing has even done so. It is possible to apply the propositions to environmental objects, just as though they were social objects and from that to gain new insight into the relations possible between a person and his environment.

The Homans propositions are more useful than similar propositions in economics (from which they were probably derived) could be, because they take into account valuations based on affective and perceptual responses, which are incapable of an exact accounting or balancing.

REFERENCES

Denton, Trevor, "Social Relations and Physical Environment—A Critical Bibliographical Review," Department of Sociology and Urban Studies Institute, Brock University, St. Catherines, Ontario, Canada, 1973.

Homans, George Caspar, *Social Behavior: Its Elementary Forms,* Harcourt Brace & World, New York, 1961.

3.2 THE DESIGNER AND HIS IMAGES

The designer's attempt at problem solution is affected by the kind of image the designer produces, by the strength of internal relationship between the parts of his image, and by the strength of relation between components of his image and components of external reality.

Each attempt at solution is strongly influenced (1) by the kind of image the designer produces, (2) by the internal relationships between the parts of his image, and (3) by the relationship between his image and external reality. Each designer's images have some degree of spatial, temporal, and relational structuring and some typical level of emotional and value content (a preference for some kinds of images over others), and they stand in some degree of accurate relationship to reality. It may be that the worst dilemma in the use of images is the conflict between a strong internal structure between the image parts and a strong external structure between the image and the problem reality with which the image deals.

ARCHITECTURE, PROBLEMS AND PURPOSES

3.2.1 The Character of Images

Whereas every image has some spatial and some temporal component, the designer's images tend to emphasize the static spatial quality of objects or environments. The designer prefers to work "in plan" as if all parts of the building were simultaneously perceivable.

The designer has tended to work with spatial more than with temporal images. Any image at all has both a spatial and temporal component, but the designer emphasizes the spatial rather than the temporal aspect. The building plan is a device to assist him in doing so; it is similar to a map, which is a device for dealing with larger scale spatial relationships. To use a plan, the designer imagines himself at some very great height above the building with a powerful telescope. He imagines that he is looking straight down, that the building has been sliced horizontally, and that the top part has been removed. The designer is therefore able to see spatial relationships simultaneously that in reality he could experience only sequentially. Because he learns to use a plan automatically to show spatial relationships in a proposed building, he is often oriented to design a good plan instead of a good building. The design critic talks about a plan relationship that would not be perceivable in the real building; if the student designer has let such a relationship dominate his design, to the detriment of other, more directly perceivable relationships, he can justifiably be criticized.

At the same time persons, who use a building organize their impressions of it into some kind of image structure. Some tend to use a spatial (and visual) structuring, others, a sequential structuring. To find their ways through the building, the spatially oriented can examine their mental "plan" of the building, but the more temporally oriented seem to remember a series of turnings or directions. It may be that for those who visualize a mental "plan" to find their way, a structured plan relationship can be as useful as the reality of the building.

If images have both temporal and spatial qualities, they do so in relation to the person whose mind has generated the image. If there is an image, there is also some implied place and time from which the image is "seen." The usefulness of imaging is that the designer can change that point of view at will to examine the effect of what he has designed. Some young designers develop the bad habit of "viewing" their designs only from above, as though they were examining a model of the building. The designer needs to get in the habit of moving his mental point of view; he must move inside his building, or he must move "around the corner" of a detail to see if things are connected in the way he has imagined. The designer soon learns to do so; his mistakes in imagining and representing building relations eventually force him to do so.

The usefulness of a plan (or a section, or elevation) drawing is the manner in which it displays simultaneously everything that occurs in the plane being considered, so that all these things appear undistorted in shape and dimension. They can be measured. By contrast, the difficulty with a plan drawing is that it does not show the three-dimensional connections to things not in the plane of the drawing in the way that a perspective or isometric drawing does.

Because the plan depends on a well-established set of conventions, it can badly distort unusual conditions like curving or sloping walls. The student designer soon learns what the limits of these conventional representations are. The drawings below (Fig. 3.4) show how the conventional plan representation of a wall and a water closet can mislead the designer if he is not aware of the drawing's limitations. The designer learns to use different kinds of drawings and different points of view to prevent himself from being misled.

3.2.2 The Internal Structure of the Image

Every image is based on the designer's experience and its categorization. The internal relation between those categorizations dominates his image.

Images are structured internally. They occur in some coherent and logical relationship based on the past experience of the designer. That they are structured in very different ways is evident from the kind and variety of work produced by different design students. There are two components of this different structuring.

In the first place different designers *generate* different kinds of images. An example of this difference that is simple enough to describe in words is that between a "baroque" and a "classic" orientation. Some persons produce very complex interconnected images that are rich in detail and elaborated in their relationships as far as time and skill will permit. By contrast some persons produce relatively simple images and work to simplify them even further.

In the second place different designers are affected by value and *prefer* different kinds of images. There is, no doubt, a close relationship between *generating* and *preferring*, but there is also a difference; it is possible to value and prefer a kind of image that one is not able to generate.

I remember an event that can illustrate the different abilities and preferences designers have. In my first year of design studies one student was having difficulty because of his tendency to overcomplicate his buildings; he had a strong design ability, but the faculty favored simplicity and clarity. Things went badly for him, since, even if he might have preferred to develop simple building plans, he could produce only complex ones. His real abilities showed only once during that year when we were given a frivolous one-day sketch problem as relief from a serious long problem. During the winter an owl had moved into the single tall pine tree on campus and was making a good living from the pigeons and squirrels who were the usual campus occupants. In a moment of whimsy the faculty asked us to design a monument to the "Year of the Owl." The only student who was really able to deal with such a subject matter was the student with a "baroque" orientation. He designed a fountain with a sculptured owl perched triumphantly on a twenty-foot-high pile of sculptured pigeon and

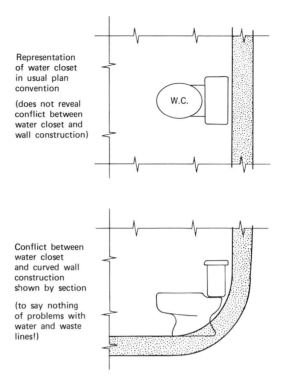

Representation
of water closet
in usual plan
convention

(does not reveal
conflict between
water closet and
wall construction)

W.C.

Conflict between
water closet
and curved wall
construction
shown by section

(to say nothing
of problems with
water and waste
lines!)

Figure 3.4 Limits of conventions
in representation.

3.2.2

squirrel bodies and bones. He had given a farcical "baroque" response
to a farcical subject. None of the rest of us could have designed such
an elaborate monument, and we all admired and preferred his design.

There is not yet a good way to talk about the internal structure
images have. The old fine arts language that referred to *unity, harmony, balance, beauty,* and the like was never very helpful. Although
there was not much doubt that these words referred to some quality
of coherence or structure in an image, there was a great deal of doubt
about what it was and about whether any two individuals meant the
same thing when they used those words.

No doubt designers are concerned with the quality of internal structure and relationship that their images have, but they also have to be
concerned with how those images are related to the external demands
placed on their designs. There is undoubtedly a conflict between a
strength of internal structuring and a closeness of external structuring.

3.2.3 The External Structure of Image Relationships

Every image is a simplification of
external reality. The useful image

All images are simplifications of reality. Any representation invariably leaves out some parts of the real world. The amount of detail in
the real world is beyond the individual's ability to perceive or understand. He can always obtain more detail than he now has, and he
ordinarily has more detail than he can possibly use in design.

3.2.3

often omits detail that cannot
bear upon problem solution; it
never omits detail that does.

It is important for the designer to be able to simplify his image enough to leave out detail that could not possibly bear upon his design decisions. It is equally important that he include detail that will. Consider the following example. As the designer is working out the arrangement of various components in his design, he must consider the plumbing system. It is *crucial* for him to know that he has a direct and continuous path for a major drain line to follow within the enclosed spaces of his building allocated to utilities; it may be *helpful* if he knows what the outer dimensions of the drain pipe are; it is probably *not necessary* for him to know the configuration of the hub and spigot joints used to connect one piece of pipe to the next; it would be *ridiculous* under most circumstances for him to represent the color and texture of the pipe in his drawings. The designer must concern himself with the amount of external structuring of his image that is essential for his purpose.

Design begins from a list of purposes and desired behaviors. It moves into a relatively abstract expression of these behaviors in terms of required functional areas. Such an abstract expression can have a very high internal structuring only remotely connected with the realities of behavior or of object construction; it is an idealization. As the designer then moves from such an idealization into the design of the physical object that would provide those idealized functions, he finds that the clarity of internal structure the idealization had is gradually reduced to fit with the actualities of need and of construction practice. A great part of the skill in design consists in maintaining the internal structure of image that had been achieved while achieving as strong an external structure as possible. If there is inevitably some conflict between an idealized internal structure and an achieved external structure, the designer hopes to keep it to a minimum. Every designer learns to bear the disappointment associated with the reduction of internal order as his design is converted into a specific and concrete proposal. Most of us have had the experience of seeing a good strong design lost to the exigencies of cost and construction.

Whereas the main body of this book is concerned with achieving a strong external structure at the expense of arbitrary, idealized internal design structure, I can still say this because there are degrees. Le me illustrate.

A home builder once said to me, "I would much rather work from a plan that I had drawn on butcher-paper with the owner that only showed overall room sizes. That kind of plan is much easier than working from the plans that you architects draw with all of their precise dimensions." When I asked why, I was told, "When the plumber puts his pipe in the wrong place, I can move the wall to where his pipe is. I don't have to make him take his pipe out and move it to where the wall is going to be."

ARCHITECTURE, PROBLEMS AND PURPOSES

3.2.3

In such an instance the external structuring has become all-important. Any plan for a building shows some level of internal structuring, some basis by which the proposed building is organized. If the building is then redesigned according to the plumber's mistakes, then the internal structuring is very unimportant. Undoubtedly the builder, whatever he might have said, would have his own limits in accommodating the mistakes of a willful or mischievous plumber. That is the point. What is the best balance between an internal image structure and an external structure?

3.2.4 The Technical Discussions

The discussions that follow go into considerable detail about various aspects of the image: the image proper, the internal image structure, and the external structure.

3.2.4.1 The Relation between Internal and External Image Structure

Every image has some degree of internal structure (the relation between image parts) and of external structure (the correspondence of image parts with reality). There is an inverse relationship between them.

Kenneth Boulding's book *The Image* describes in detail the way in which individuals use images as internal representations of the exterior world they inhabit. I use the components of his description to develop a somewhat more organized view of the image pertinent to a discussion of solution processes (Boulding, 1966, pp. 47-48).

In Boulding's list of image components there appear to be three different kinds of elements: (1) elements of the image proper, (2) elements that have to do with the internal structure of the image, and (3) elements concerned with the external structure of the image. Although no firm and hard line separates one group from the other, such a grouping will serve fairly well for discussion. Boulding's components can be grouped as follows:

1. Elements of the image proper
   The spatial image
   The temporal image
   The relational image
   The personal image

2. Elements of internal image structure
   The value image
   The affectional image
   The conscious image

3. Elements of external image structure
   The certainty image

The reality image
The public image

It is useful to divide Boulding's components in this fashion, since there is now a somewhat extended literature that discusses the content of thought, the internal constraint upon that thought, and the external constraint that correlates thought with reality.

Downs and Stea (1973, pp. 14-15) describe Fishbein's replacement of "the holistic concept of an attitude with a formulation containing three components: *cognitions* or beliefs, *affect* or attitude, and *conations* or behavioral intentions." There would appear to be a correspondence between these three components and the grouping I have devised for Boulding's image elements:

Cognitions	Elements of image proper
Affect	Elements of internal image structure
Conations	Elements of external image structure

Wendell R. Garner discusses internal and external constrain extensively (1962, pp. 173-74):". . .it is quite clear that external constraint is primarily identifiable with perceptual discrimination [the learning of one-to-one correspondences], and internal constraint is primarily identifiable with free recall type of learning [list completion learning]." External constraint describes the correlation between the learned or cognized material and external reality. Internal constraint describes the internal mental structure that defines whether a particlar category of learned or cognized material is complete, or in what other relationship it exists with other mental material.

In understanding the character of internal and external constraint, it is useful to make a comparison with the equivalent ideas applied to the verification of a testing or experimental procedure—reliability and validity. Reliability is analogous to internal constraint, for it is concerned with the internal consistency of the testing procedure and with whether that procedure is repeatable in such a manner as to produce equivalent results. Validity is analogous to external constraint, for its concern is with the correlation of the test with the reality it is testing. As Norman Denzin summarizes the point, "The question of validity of an instrument asks to what extent the event being measured corresponds to what is intended to be measured." (Denzin, 1973, pp. 103-104; see also Bruyn, p. 255.)

A substantial part of Garner's inquiry deals with the interrelationship of internal and external constraint. I pursue this in other parts of this study but for now the pertinent point can be summarized in Garner's words, ". . .the form of internal and external constraint cannot be manipulated independently, since a given selection of stimuli completely determines the form of both types of constraint. Thus, it

ARCHITECTURE, PROBLEMS AND PURPOSES

3.2.4.1

is impossible to have forms of constrint which are optimum for both discrimination and free recall simultaneously." (Garner, 1962, pp. 173-174.)

Internal and external constraint have had a place in psychological writing for a considerable time whether couched in those terms or not. William James comments on the conflict between external events and internal consistency, "Objects which violate our established habits of apperception are simply not taken into account of at all. . . .On the other hand, nothing is more congenial. . .than to be able to assimilate the new to the old, to meet each threatening violator. . .and ticket it off as an old friend in disguise." (James, 1961, p. 195.) According to

James internal constraint on the content of thought is more powerful and must be taken more into account than external constraint. The individual prefers to maintain his consistent mental structure rather than accept a reality that is inconsistent with that structure.

REFERENCES

Boulding, Kenneth, E., *The Image: Knowledge in Life and Society,* The University of Michigan Press, Ann Arbor, 1966.

Bruyn, Severyn T., *The Human Perspective in Sociology: The Methodology of Paritcipant Observation,* Prentice-Hall, Englewood Cliffs, N.J., 1966.

Denzin, Norman K., *The Research Act: A Theoretical Introduction to Socio-logical Methods,* Aldine, Chicago, 1973.

Downs, Roger M., and David Stea, Eds., *Image and Environment: Cognitive Mapping and Spatial Behavior,* Aldine, Chicago, 1973.

Fishbein, M., "A Consideration of Beliefs and Their Role in Attitude Measure-ment," in M. Fishbein, Ed., *Readings in Attitude Theory and Measurement,* Wiley, New York, 1967.

Garner, Wendell R., *Uncertainty and Structure as Psychological Concepts,* Wiley, New York, 1962.

James, William, *Psychology: The Briefer Course,* Harper & Row, New York, 1961.

3.2.4.2 Elements of the Image Proper

Every image has a spatial compo-nent, a temporal component, rela-tional components, and personal components.

Roger Downs and David Stea (1973, pp. 13-14) draw a careful dis-tinction between perception, which is concerned with direct sensory experience, and cognition, which includes thinking, problem solving, and organization of information and ideas as well as perception:

". . . cognition occurs in a spatial context when the spaces of interest are so extensive that they cannot be perceived or apprehended either at once or in a series of brief glances. These large-scale spaces must be cognitively organized and committed to memory, and contain objects and events which are outside of the immediate sensory field of the individual."

By such a definition of cognition Downs and Stea have listed just those elements of Boulding's that I have included under the subhead elements of the image proper: the spatial, temporal, relational, and personal image. They posit a spatial context that cannot be perceived except temporally, that is outside the immediate sensory field of the individual, and that must be relationally organized and committed to memory.

Although the perception of events by both spatial and temporal modes is pervasive, the distinction between them is one of the most commonly made. For example, W. Grey Walter comments; ". . . the whole pattern of the perceived world is extended both in space and in time, but there is reason to believe that the methods of perception are different for the two classes. . . . The obvious radical difference between space-patterns and time-patterns is that the latter are projected upon a uni-directional parameter." (1951, p. 181.)

By contrast, though arguing for the recognition of both spatiality and temporality, James J. Gibson suggests that we *not* treat them as discrete material handled by different mental operations: "A natural stimulus for proprioception or perception has the following characteristics. First, it always has some degree of adjacent order. Second, it always has some degree of successive order. And third, it always therefore has some component of non-change and some component of change." (1966, pp. 39-40.) Gibson, too, in these short sentences, appears to be dealing with the spatial, the temporal, the relational, and the personal.

It is undoubtedly true that Boulding's list has dealt with some of the basic categories of thought, but as with all list making, it is possible to find variation from one category to another according to the personal priorities of the list maker, his purposes, and the level of abstractness of the terms. It is possible to go even further afield in drawing comparisons with Boulding's list of image elements; Aristotle's list of categories of judgments (Ross, 1955, p. 8), for example, contains, among other related items, place, time, relation, and location. As a group these correlate closely with the first four of Boulding's list. Unfortunately the remaining categories on Aristotle's list correlate badly with Boulding's elements, and so there will not be occasion to refer to them at greater length.

Finally as a tie into the next group of image elements that deal with the internal image structure, notice a classification of concepts by Jerome Bruner that has an interesting correspondence with three of the "image-proper elements": spatial, temporal, and relational. Bruner's classification (1956, pp. 41-43) includes conjunctive, disjunctive, and relational concepts. There is, I believe, a correspondence between a conjunctive concept (which is the simultaneous and therefore the spatially adjacent existence of two events) and spatiality. There is correspondence between a disjunctive concept (which is the nonsimultaneous existence of one or another event) and temporality. Finally there is an obvious correspondence between the relational image and a relational concept.

REFERENCES

Bruner, Jerome, Jaqueline J. Goodnow, and George A. Austin, *A Study of Thinking*, Wiley, New York, 1956.

Downs, Roger M., and David Stea, Eds., *Image and Environment: Cognitive Mapping and Spatial Behavior*, Aldine, Chicago, 1973.

Gibson, James J., *The Senses Considered as Perceptual Systems*, Houghton Mifflin, Boston, 1966.

Ross, W. D., *Aristotle Selections*, Charles Scribner's Sons, New York, 1955.

Walter, W. Grey, "Activity Patterns in the Human Brain," in Whyte, Lancelot Law, *Aspects of Form*, Indiana University Press, Bloomington, 1951.

3.2.4.3 Internal Image Elements

The internal structuring of an image influences the problem solver's evaluation, consciousness, and affectional response. Evaluation is in structured relation with other evaluations. Conscious consideration is in a structured relation with out-of-consciousness events. A strong internal structure "produces" high moments of affections, but weak internal structure "produces" lower moments.

In this discussion of internal image structure it will be useful to remember the distinction between internal and external structure. Garner (1962) discusses external constraint as the correspondence between elements in two different systems, and in the discussion here, between the external stimuli (or the objects that produce them) and the internal image of those stimuli. He discusses internal constraint as the organization within one such system, and for the discussion here, the organization of the mental image that causes its various parts to be in an expected and understood relationship.

An interesting commentary upon the differences that result when one or the other of these sets of constraints is given priority can be seen in a statement by Sir Arthur Quiller-Couch in *The Art of Writing*. Quiller-Couch says (speaking in 1916):

> . . .while the capital difficulty of verse consists in saying ordinary things, the capital difficulty of prose consists in saying extraordinary things; that while with verse, keyed for high moments, the trouble is to manage the intervals, with prose the trouble is to manage the high moments. (1961, pp. 89 ff.)

Evidently the more emotional high moments are emphasized and managed by the higher degree of internal constraint that the forms of verse impose; by contrast the ordinary things are managed in their complexity and tedium by the higher level of external constraint.

I have defined the three image areas—affective, value, and conscious image—as belonging within the area of internal image structure. Each is a complex subject in its own right, and I must limit a discussion to the very brief review pertinent to a discussion of image structure. It is a bare introduction.

There appears to be some general agreement that cognitions carry with them *affective* qualities. Krathwohl, for example, in discussing the organization of educational objectives, emphasizes the importance of relating cognitive objectives to their affective counterparts (Krathwohl, 1964). He is able to develop an extended typology relating comparable elements within both the cognitive and the affective domains. Such a typology is not, however, very helpful in establishing what relationship might exist between the two domains.

A more interesting and useful set of comments is made by John Dewey:

> Moments and places, despite physical limitation and narrow localization, are charged with accumulations of long gathering energy. . . . To see, to perceive is more than to recognize . . . . The past is carried into the present so as to expand and deepen the content of the latter. (1934, p. 24.)

He says also:

> . . . the live creature adopts its past; it can make friends with even its stupidities, using them as warnings that increase present wariness . . . it uses past successes to inform the present. . . . Only when the past ceases to trouble and anticipations of the future are not perturbing is a being wholly united with his environment and therefore fully alive. (1934, p. 18.)

Dewey points out that the moment of passage "from disturbance into harmony" is the moment of intensest life; finally he states that emotion is evidence of the achievement of that harmony (1934, p. 19).

In a less ecstatic manner Stephen C. Pepper discusses several forms that emotion can take in relation to art (and I believe it possible to assume, in relation to image). He describes mood as nonextraordinary emotion that colors ordinary events along two different scales: strength-to-delicacy and excitement-to-calm (1949, pp. 119-123). [When grouped with a good-to-bad valuation, these fit very closely with Osgood's (1952, p. 228) three main clusters by semantic differential: strong-weak, active-passive, and good-bad.] Pepper describes the named emotions associated with drive and drive frustration: love, anger, hate, and so on. He suffests that the James-Lange theory of sensory fusion applies to the coloring of external events as well as of internal events like needs, drives, and the like. Pepper's book seems curiously dated when it talks about drives as instinctive; despite the apparent accuracy of its other comments, there seems to be only a modest usefulness in trying to explain emotion in terms of its content.

Langner and Michael (1963, p. 400) describe the increasing maladaptation of individuals in the face of an accumulation of life stresses. Their work is not concerned with emotion as such but with mental health at the epidemiologic level; they therefore touch on emotion only in passing, quoting Menninger on the symptomatology of maladaptation. An increased emotional level is apparently associated with even the first level of maladaptation that Menninger describes.

In the comments above concerning emotion, there is a range from the positive and ecstatic, through relatively neutral mood, to intense emotion associated with stress and the maladaptation associated with that stress. Two additional observations will help to tie these disparate comments together.

James Gibson observes that concentrated perception is economical, centered on its focus of interest and ignoring all else (1966, p. 286). Sherif, Sherif, and Nebergall (1965, pp. 238-239) propose as one of

3.2.4.3

their hypotheses that, the more highly involved an individual is in his stand, the fewer the categories he will use and the more his judgments will be at extreme bimodal positions. It is apparent that under stress the individual increases his emotional level and that this emotion is associated with an external and an internal focusing. His judgment process turns from multivariate to bivariate. This is in extreme contrast to Dewey's description of the openness of the individual who is moving toward equilibrium with his environment. Apparently disequilibrium produces a narrowing and a closing of the individual.

These several comments can be summarized by making a single modification of Dewey's description and substituting for his notion of harmony a notion of an appropriate level of stimulation or stress (there can, after all, be a level of stress that is too low):

Into Harmony	Out of Harmony
Appropriate stress level	Inappropriate stress level
Open, expansive	Closed, centering
Positive emotions	Negative emotions
Multivariate decision	Bivariate decision
Less involved	More involved

There is comment then that emotion is the inevitable accompaniment to a change in the relation between the internal image (and the structure of that image) and the external environment on which that image is based. Emotion accompanies the developing union between the image and its environmental counterpart; it also accompanies a developing separation between the environment and its correlative image.

In discussing the value image, there is a need to review briefly:

1. The range of evaluative dispositions that can exist.

2. The relationship between classification and evaluation.

3. Cognitive consistency in evaluation.

4. The basis of evaluation in group norms.

5. The relation of evaluation to the action or decision situation.

6. The structuring of evaluations into a hierarchy of goals.

7. The use of a goal image in arriving at evaluations.

1. There are differences of scope, of dynamics, and of time frame in evaluative dispositions. Paul Lazarsfeld (1972, pp. 241-242) develops a full array of such dispositions from the relatively fleeting *preference* to the relatively enduring *trait*. He includes in his typology preference, trait, need, directional traits (e.g., aggressiveness), expectations,

tendencies, intentions, and motivation. As Downs and Stea note, the more global of these dispositions can be directed toward entire classes of objects, and the less global can be directed toward single objects (1973, pp. 15-16).

2. There is little question that evaluation is closely related to classification processes. Whether or not something is evaluated as good depends on what kind of thing it is; at the same time being classified by kind depends on being a good enough thing of that kind to merit such a classification. This is an ancient problem (Peltz, 1971, pp. 69-78) that is typically dealt with today by separating the two activities into identification and evaluation. The systems-analytic view defines the first as "satisficing" behavior and the second as "optimizing." behavior. Even within such classification processes, however, there are individual differences, and the *symbolic interaction* view is that human beings act on the basis of object meanings that they hold individually.

3. Whatever the variation in preference (for example) that can occur from moment to moment, evaluative mechanisms require a consistency in their responses to objects. Objects of perception can be linked with other objects of perception; when they are so linked (by proximity, interaction, ownership, etc.), then either both linked objects must hold the same evaluative valence or else the perceptual linkage must be broken (Heider, 1958, pp. 177-182).

4. Evaluative dispostions can be determined by group-derived anchoring norms and by ideology or by principle (Lewin, 1964, pp. 288-289)

5. Kurt Lewin (1964, pp. 238-303) develops a careful description of the relation between a task in an immediate situation, the entire evaluative disposition, and the longer range objective as it organizes action into a hierarchy of goals and subgoals. He shows that the immediate situation is invariably influenced by the situation in which it exists.

6. Lewin claims that needs are organized into hierarchies but that their positions within these hierarchies undergo continuous long-range and short-range change. Behavior is thus organized by needs; a group of needs becomes the equivalent of a specific intention. The choice of a goal that results depends on an understanding of the entire required logical relationship between that goal, subgoals, and the actions required to achieve them.

7. Finally Lewin holds that a person makes a decision about such goal structures by alternately seeing himself in one or the other of the future situations that correspond with the possibilities that exist. Evaluation depends then in part on the ability to image a future condition that can result from a course of action.

3.2.4.3   I shall not venture much concerning the conscious image; a brief comment on levels of image content and of image structure must suffice.

Without even attempting to outline the burden of subconcious content that Freud and his followers have disclosed, it is useful to look again at Dewey's comment about those out-of-awareness attachments from the past that images carry. They also carry out-of-awareness aspirations for the future. Each new experience and each desired experience in relation to an image object adds content to that image. Added associational links are built between that object and other image objects.

A person's conscious image appears to be only the trunk of an enormous branching structure of possible interpenetrating meanings. Just as the association of words in metaphor generates a set of interactions that produce new meanings, so the association of images produces new meaning combinations.

Finally the structure of meaning that exists in relation to the image is elaborately complex, with multiple levels of concreteness and abstractness.

REFERENCES

Denton Trevor, "Social Relations and Physical Environent—A Critical Bibliographic Review," Department of Sociology and Urban Studies Institute, Brock University, St. Catherines, Ontario, Canada, 1973.

Dewey, John, *Art as Experience,* Minton Balch, New York, 1934.

Downs, Roger M., and David Stea, Eds., *Image and Environment: Cognitive Mapping and Spatial Behavior,* Aldine, Chicago, 1973.

Garner, Wendell R., *Uncertainty and Structure as Psychological Concepts, Wiley, New York, 1962.*

Gibson, James J., *The Senses Considered as Perceptual Systems,* Houghton-Mifflin, Boston, 1966.

Heider, Fritz, *The Psychology of Interpersonal Relations,* Wiley, New York, 1958.

Krathwohl, David R., Ed., *Taxonomy of Educational Objectives, Handbook II: Affective Domain,* David McKay, New York, 1964.

Langner, Thomas S., and Stanley T. Michael, *Life Stress and Mental Health,* Crowell-Collier, New York, 1963.

Lazarsfeld, Paul F., *Qualitative Analysis,* Allyn and Bacon, Boston, 1972.

Lewin, Kurt, "Behavior and Development as a Function of the Total Situation," in Cartwright, Dorwin, Ed., *Kurt Lewin: Field Theory in Social Science,* Harper & Row, New York, 1964.

Osgood, Charles E., "The Nature and Measurement of Meaning," *Psychological Bulletin,* **49**(3), May, 1952.

Peltz, Richard, *Journal of Aesthetics and Art Criticism,* **30**(1) Fall, 1971.

Pepper, Stephen C., *Principles of Art Appreciation,* Harcourt Brace, New York, 1949.

Quiller-Couch, Sir Arthur, *The Art of Writing,* Capricorn Books, New York, 1961.

Sherif, Carolyn, Mauzafer Sherif, and E. Roger Nebergall, *Attitude and Attitude Change,* W. B. Saunders, Phildelphia, 1965.

3.2.4.4 External Image Elements

The external structuring of an image can be considered in terms of its reality, its certainty, and its objectiveness. The reality of an image is related to its intractability; its certainty, to confirming evidence; and its objectiveness, to confirming evidence shared with other individuals.

External image structure is concerned with the correspondence between the image and events in the external world that the image represents. Boulding identifies three dimensions of such a representation: certainty, reality, and objectiveness. There are differences in the degree of certainty a person feels about different parts of his image; parts are sharp and clear, and he is *certain* about them; other parts are vague and he is uncertain about them. He typically has a sense of which parts of his image are about the *real* world and which are dreams or imaginings. Since he receives information in many different forms, the structure of the reality image is extremely complex and related to the source of his information. *Objectiveness,* the degree to which his images are public images shared with some exactitude by other persons, is one of the more difficult areas in the investigation of images; images are inherently private, and there is great difficulty in knowing whether or not a person has succeeded in communicating his image in a substantial fashion to some other persons.

Reality and certainty are closely related and can be discussed together. A comment by Kurt Lewin (1964, p. 274) that irreality is more fluid than reality and more easily influenced defines the basic method by which reality is tested. If perceptions can be manipulated by thinking about them, they are probably unreal; reality is not usually so tractable.

Reality is intractable; it is consistent and, because of those features, it is also predictable within the limits of a person's knowledge. If consistency is used as a test of reality, it is equally a test of certainty. "One of the main assumptions governing [the use of] induction is that all the facts in the universe are related. Every fact is assumed to be consistent with every other fact in an orderly system to which they all belong." (Weinland, 1970, p. 19.) The senses of reality and of certainty, however, depend on more than just the casual once-in-a-while check to see whether observed events are consistent with each other; they also depend on a continuous interplay between a verbal and a nonverbal world. In *Living with Change,* Wendell Johnson comments:

The process of abstracting involves a verbal world and a nonverbal world, that is, a world of words-but-not-things and a world of things-but-not-words...the process, therefore, involves movement back and forth between these two worlds to accomodate the checking necessary to maintain this relationship. (1972, pp. 82-83.)

3.2.4.4   Certainty becomes a major issue in discussions of cognitive mapping. Downs and Stea comment on the degree to which cognitive maps are incomplete, distorted, and schematized (1973, pp. 9-21). They describe how the individual depends on his cognitive map for the location and attributes of objects in his environment; the individual, in fact, depends on his cognitive map of the spatial environment in making decisions and judgments about his behavior. Such direct dependence provides another test of reality and certainty; if the individual's behavior based on his cognitive map of the environment leads him to accurate judgments and successful actions executed within the environment, then the individual can be secure in the reality and certainty of his cognitive map and his image. If his judgments are faulty or his actions unsuccessful, then he must attempt to discover where the fault lies; one fault can be in the unreality or the uncertainty of his image.

An enormous amount of information is obtained through indirect sources. The certainty of an image may be very severely affected by the veracity of the information supplied indirectly. Weinland (1963, pp. 20-21) suggests a great many different ways of checking on the accuracy of reports by other persons; although they depend on such things as the immediacy of the report, description of observation method, and the authority of the person making the report, most of his comments reduce to a process of confirmation by several observers. A consensus report by as many observers as possible is as close as a person can come to certainty when indirect sources of information are used.

To save time and effort, we have a tendency to accept the reliability of indirect reports based on criteria as follows:

1. The report is by an individual who has credentials in the appropriate discipline, and he describes the methods by which he collected data, made inductions, and drew inferences from those inductions.

2. The report is by an expert, one who has had a substantial history of having his reports accepted by his disciplinary peers.

3. The report is not by a recognized expert, but in giving the report he compares his information with other reports by experts in the field and sees where there are agreements and differences.

We have a tendency to accept such reports so long as their substance is in accord with personal observations or with other, accepted reports. Only when the report is not in accord with existing information and opinion, and the substance is important, is there a detailed examination of the rigor with which observations and deductions from those observations were made.

Objectiveness of image is the degree to which an image is shared with other persons. Objectiveness is especially important in design, for a significant part of design is centered in a social imaging process; in other words, whereas an *individual* is able by himself to image a situation and decide on a course of action, by contrast a *group* must find a way of making that image objective to agree that the image fits each person's idea and to agree on a course of action congruent with that image.

It is not always easy to make an image objective. Drawings have their own vocabulary, and although that vocabulary is usually more concrete and less subject to different interpretation than a verbal vocabulary, still, the existence of Thematic Apperception Tests is evidence in itself of the multiple interpretations that can be placed on drawings. (Thematic Apperception Tests are used in psychological testing; drawings subject to multiple interpretation are used to evoke projections of the test subject's attitudes, motives, and fears as he describes the imagined circumstances surrounding the drawings.)

Such a test is ambiguous because it does not provide enough detail. Typically the view shown is of an individual caught with a neutral expression in surroundings so murky that the viewer is forced to provide his own detail if he is to achieve an image closure. A view that shows only an instant of existence does not provide enough detail for the understanding of a situation, but because that view seems "concrete" it is treated as if it were, and the viewer unwittingly provides his own mental detail. He treats as factual what is only inferential.

After hearing a person speak before a group, one can make the accurate (and shared) judgment that the person delivered a well-organized and skillfully presented speech. There is not, of course, a very great change in language to say that the person is a *skillful speaker*, but there is a substantial difference in factuality. The former statement is relatively factual; the latter is relatively inferential. According to Irving J. Lee (1962, pp. 29-40):

A rich source of misunderstanding was the belief of many of the participants in the factuality of their assertions. It was rarely sufficiently realized that a statement of fact can be made only *after* someone observes some thing or relation. Any utterance made prior to observation or when observation is not possible involves an inference or guess.

To describe a person as a skillful speaker implies a degree of familiarity with his speaking ability greater than the one instance described.

A similar source of misunderstanding in language occurs when a class of objects has applied to it a characteristic that only a member of the class can have; again, observers are deceived because there is just enough detail supplied by the class description to be suggestive of completeness, and without awareness the observer supplies by projection the detail needed to provide closure. Consider an example:

thirteen-year-old boys are awkward.* Then add other, more detailed phrases or clauses: for example, who are sons of ambassadors, who are rich, widely traveled, sickly, tall, redheaded. In each instance the additional phrase increases or decreases the credibility of the original statement to some small degree. Once such a closure process is started, however, it is possible to become aware of how little detail exists. Only then is it clear that *awkward* can be applied accurately only to *individuals* who are, in fact, awkward.

Again Lee (1962, pp. 29-40) has a useful comment:

> . . .so pervasive is the unexamined notion that words can have exact meanings compounded in and of themselves in the way a tree has branches, that it is often difficult to persuade a listener that in discussion the other fellow may be assigning a value to his variables which is not at all the one the listener would assign if he were speaking.

The strength and weakness of the word as a class designation are its ability to reference entirely different populations of concrete or specific objects.

Objectivity in concept and in image can exist only when verbal or graphic representations communicate exactly what they were intended to communicate. Lee (1962, pp. 29-40) provides a useful group of tests intended to apply to communications via language; it can be seen, however, that appropriate modifications can permit these same tests to apply to graphic communications. Lee's tests for verbal understanding are:

1. The following of directions.

2. The making of predictions.

3. The giving of verbal equivalents.

4. The agreeing on programs.

5. The solving or problems.

6. The making of appropriate responses.

7. The making of proper evaluations.

In each instance the person attempting to communicate, and wanting to test whether his communication has been successful, must require a response from his receiver that modifies the response while maintaining the meaning. A rote response is not evidence of understanding, only of hearing.

The problem of checking on the graphic communication of understanding, is somewhat more severe. Very few persons have the ability to respond graphically to graphic communication. The designer must

*Awkward in the sense of awkward physical behavior.

3.2.4.4

be willing to accept a verbal response or else subject his receiver to a set of test drawings. "Which of these elevations," he might ask, "do you perceive as corresponding with the plan that we have just seen?" When the receiver had responded accurately, the designer might then be reasonably sure that he was engaged in successful communication. By such means can images be made objective (Black, 1962, p. 120).

REFERENCES

Black, Max, *Models and Metaphors: Studies in Language and Philosophy*, Cornell University Press, Ithaca, N.Y., 1962.

Downs, Roger M., and David Stea, Eds., *Image and Environment: Cognitive Mapping and Spatial Behavior*, Aldine, Chicago, 1973.

Johnson, Wendell, *Living with Change*, Harper & Row, New York, 1972.

Lee, Irving J., "Why Discussions Go Astray," in Hayakawa, S. I., *The Use and Misuse of Language*, Fawcett, Greenwich, Conn., 1962.

Lewin, Kurt, "Behavior and Development as a Function of the Total Situation," in Cartright, Dorwin, Ed., *Kurt Lewin: Field Theory in Social Science,* Harper and Row, New York, 1964.

Weinland, James D., *How to Think Straight*, Littlefield Adams, Totowa, N.J., 1970.

3.3. MOTIVES IN PROBLEM SOLVING

Problem solution always occurs within a context of other problems that compete for the problem solver's attention. Various constraints on the problem solver cause him to solve a problem that is a simplification of the real-world problem. Various motives affect his choice of strategy for problem solution.

Problem solving does not occur in a vacuum but in a context of other problems that compete for attention. Problem solvers are not concerned out of some purity of intellectual interest; they wish to achieve some other end. If they are the problem client, they might want to achieve a less dangerous, less irritating, more convenient, or more fulfilling life circumstance. If they are professional problem solvers, they might want to earn the fee associated with the solution.

Problem solving, however specific it might be to the problem of concern (and disinterested in other matters like fees), is still unquestionably bound by economic fact. Unless the problem solver can earn his keep and the keep of the institution of which he is a member, then he will not be able to continue solving problems in that institutional circumstance. Even where the solution process is not economically constrained, where the problem solver is, for example, a student in school, there is some other form of constraint on the process. At least some form of time constraint is always present. Constraints because of limits on the amount and kind of information available may also be present. There are usually conflicting and competing concerns; the problem solver has to eat, sleep, attend other courses, take examinations, and attend to all the other matters of a student's life. He might have some drastic personal problem, a financial crisis, or a family difficulty that would compete for time and attention with his problem-solving and design efforts. He thus has external motives that affect his design process.

ARCHITECTURE, PROBLEMS AND PURPOSES

3.3.1 Tendencies toward Problem Simplification

Time and cost constraints cause a problem solver to simplify the problem statement. In an ill-defined problem the problem solver adopts two complementary strategies: hill climbing (improving the quality of his proposed solution) and hill leveling (reducing the solution's requirements).

Since a problem can never be pursued into its possibly endless ramifications, a powerful force acts on the problem solver and on the designer to simplify the problem (in addition to the simplifications that occur because of problem definition described earlier). The time limits, the cost limits, and the conflicting demands for time and attention all impose restrictions on what can be considered. Necessity imposes simplifications.

Seeing how this process works in design is useful; more than anything else an understanding of the impulse toward simplification can reveal the true character of an ill-defined problem.

The designer starts with a set of requirements, perhaps supplied by the client (or faculty) and perhaps in part by himself. In addition to a set of specifically stated requirements, the designer has usually internalized an additional set that guide his solution. As he considers the list of requirements or demands, he develops some form of ranking. Indeed some requirements are critical and others are only incidental.

Having moved through the usual program analysis, the designer develops a solution proposal and begins to check it against the list of requirements. If he has an adequate amount of time, he can usually find a solution that will satisfy all the requirements. If his time is limited, he may have to accept a solution that satisfies only a part. He may begin by dropping the least essential criteria; he may then have to omit relatively more important criteria.

The effect of releasing criteria or requirements is to increase the number of possible solutions. An earlier diagram (Fig. 2.22 p. 105) shows the inverse relationship between the number of requirements and the number of solutions (referred to as *demands* and *supplies*). The effect of a gradual requirement release is a gradual increase in solutions (Fig. 3.5).

The solution under time limitations then becomes a composite process: reduce requirements, improve solution, reduce requirements, improve solution, and so on, until there is a match between the requirements and the solution. By releasing enough requirements, the designer increases the number of solutions until it includes one he has in hand.

None of the discussion here is intended to disparge such a process. The ill-defined problem is susceptible to this form of procedure. The procedure assumes, and the designer acts in the belief that a holistic response to the total solution is usually more important than satisfying each one of some original set of requirements. The experienced designer knows that program requirements are very often arbitrary and that the client will accept reasonable modifications of a set of requirements. If he is wrong in what modifications are acceptable, then his solution will be inadequate, and he will have to revise according to the client's direction.

Parts of the problem-solving literature refer to a solution improve-

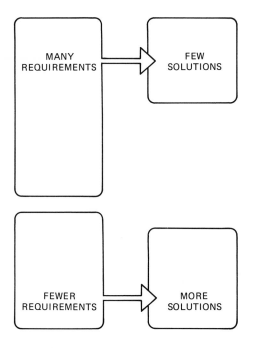

MANY
REQUIREMENTS → FEW
SOLUTIONS

FEWER
REQUIREMENTS → MORE
SOLUTIONS

Figure 3.5 Effects of reduced requirements on problem solution.

3.3.1

ment procedure as "hill climbing." The summit of the hill is the desired solution state, and it is achieved by pushing the proposed solution closer and closer to the summit. The modifications that improve the proposed solution are kept, and those that worsen it are dropped. What has just been described is somewhat different. This process might be referred to as a combination of hill climbing and "hill leveling." There is an attempt not only to improve the solution but also to reduce the difficulty of the problem.

I should insert a caution! There are circumstances when it is inappropriate for the designer to engage in hill-leveling strategies. In competitions, in some school problems, in design examinations, a modification of a set of requirements could disqualify the design from consideration. The designer must know his circumstance, the quality of consideration the requirements have received, and the degree to which those requirements are negotiable.

3.3.2 The Simplification of Decision Criteria

The designer has believed that his visual and intuitive processes permit him to deal simultaneously with many different variables. There is some evidence that he

I have noted already that the designer relies on an intuitive process for achieving a solution and that he thinks that the Gestalt is more important than the elements of which it is composed. He believes the mix to be more important than the ingredients. He argues, and the argument is widely believed across the design profession, that a visual response can deal simultaneously and efficiently with a number of different variables (and criteria).

tends to collapse his decision onto only one or only a few of these variables.

The designer is not alone in making this argument. He is accompanied by any number of persons in the humanities who rely on intuitive (though not necessarily on visual) processes.

There is some difficulty, whatever he might wish to believe, in demonstrating that intuitive (and in his circumstance, visual) processes do take a multitude of variables into account.

Some experimental evidence even indicates that intuitive processes reduce and simplify decisions onto one or a very few variables. It would be very surprising, given the designer's form orientation, if he failed to give priority to the form relationships in design at some disadvantage to other decision criteria.

The curiosity about this claim of the designer is that there is no need for him to make the claim. No one cares very much just what procedure (whether visual or otherwise) helps him generate a proposal or achieve a solution. If he is a legitimate problem-solving designer, he checks the qualities of that proposal in an orderly fashion against the client's program requirements to see which ones he has satisfied and which he has not. This checking has little need for any esoteric visual process but can use simple language statement comparisons. If the designer uses some integrating visual insight to let him know quickly whether a proposal is likely to satisfy a program, that is his own business and should not matter to anyone else.

3.3.3 The Effect of External Motivation

Several forms of external motivation affect the problem solver's choice of solution strategy.

The next four sections discuss specific external motives that can affect the problem-solving approach. First, the problem solver may wish to reduce the amount of stress in the problem situation and the consequent strain to which he is subject. Second, he may wish to reduce the effort required and improve his efficiency in solution. Third, he might wish to avoid making errors in his solution process. Fourth, he might wish to make extremely sure that he will achieve an acceptable solution.

3.3.4 Strain Reduction Motives

The designer might wish to reduce the degree of mental strain required in problem solution.

There are a number of reasons why a problem solver might wish to avoid strain. He might have conflicting demands on his attention and be able to concentrate on his solution during only a limited part of his time. He might be overstrained already. Under such a circumstance he might need to follow a very orderly, low-risk procedure. He might rely heavily on known accepted solutions. I have seen students who were overcommitted in other courses follow this strategy "to get it over with."

3.3.4

There are other reasons. Personal conflicts sometimes make the work process very difficult in a design office. At such times a relatively nonstressful strategy can be essential to keep the office personnel together.

When the solution process must be distributed among a number of people in a large office to accomplish the work in time, it needs to be simpler to permit the work to flow through the office organization. One must also distinguish the simpler task from the more difficult to make assignments to persons with appropriate skill levels.

3.3.5 Effort Reduction Motives

The designer might wish to reduce the degree of effort required in problem solution.

The designer must always work efficiently to keep his costs within his job budget, but there are also times when efficiency is especially important. Costs may be high in other parts of the office, or the budget for a particular job might be unusually low. At such times there is an extreme need for efficiency in design.

Efficiency is demanded on other occasions, too. A client might have a severe time deadline for work completion. His fiscal considerations might impose time constraints on him, and he passes these onto the architect.

Finally when the designer is able to perform efficiently, he is able to consider more different possibilities and might be able to achieve a better solution.

3.3.6 Error Reduction Motives

The designer might wish to reduce the possibility of error in problem solution.

The cost of errors in design work is extremely high. The earlier they occur and the later discovered, the more they cost. Because problem solving in design is sequential, one decision is based on the decisions that have gone before it. If an error goes undiscovered, it means that a great deal of work that was sound but based on faulty information or assumptions must also be discarded. For these reasons, the designer must proceed relatively cautiously in his early stages, not committing himself to a specific direction until necessary.

Aside from these basic cost considerations, there are other personal factors. Most design students hate to commit substantial errors, because they enjoy having the approval of their student peers. Because of his need for respect the student designer is sometimes more cautious in his work than he need be. School is a time for making mistakes and exploring, even if the explorations go wrong.

Still his caution is understandable. The need for respect by one's professional peers extends into the work experience as well. When I was first an independent practitioner, I remember vividly how worried I was

3.3.6

whether the first draftsman I employed would think well of my abilities. I was self-conscious while I worked in the same room with him. I even concealed my sketches until I was sure I had his complete respect.

3.3.7 Failure Reduction Motives

The designer might wish to reduce the possibility of failing to achieve a solution.

Sometimes strain is acceptable, as when efficiency is not a principal consideration and the occurrence of error does not matter, and being extremely sure that a complete solution is achieved is the only important concern. Such occasions are rare; more usually there is some combination of motives (e.g., an adequate solution and effiency in its achievement) that affect the solution strategy.

3.3.8 The Technical Discussions

One of the technical discussions that follow is concerned with motives in concept attainment and the strategies used in accordance with those motives. The other is concerned with simplification.

3.3.8.1 External Motivation and Solution Strategies

Persons undertaking specific forms of concept achievement (a kind of problem solution) adopt strategies influenced by subsidiary motives such as the reduction of strain, of effort, of error, or of failure.

Although many studies have been made of the learning process, the work by Jerome Bruner and his colleagues (Bruner, Goodnow, and Austin, 1956) is among the most definitive. *A Study of Thinking* asks how people achieve the information necessary for isolating and learning a concept, how they retain for later use the information they obtain from encounters with possible data, and how such information is transformed so that it can be used for testing hypotheses. After stating that there are three kinds of concepts requiring different treatment (conjunctive, disjunctive, and relational), the investigators describe a number of studies of the strategies individuals use to attain such concepts. They discovered that different strategies were being used that were related directly to the motives of the subjects being tested.

The investigators were able to infer the following group of motives that in various combinations influenced the selection of a particular concept attainment strategy. The motives were (Bruner et al., p. 54, pp. 82-83):

1. A reduction of the number of encounters with the material from which the concept is to be derived.

2. Certainty in the accomplishment of the concept.

3. A reduction in the amount of strain associated with the attainment process.

4. A reduction in the number of wrong categorizations before the sure attainment of the concept.

In studying the attainment of conjunctive concepts, subjects are presented with an array of cards that display patterns having four variables, each variable having three different values. They are arranged as shown in Table 3.1. It is clear that the full range of variation is 3^4, or 81. There are thus eighty-one cards presented for examination. To begin each experiment, the subject is presented with a card that is a positive instance of some conjunctive concept. Once a positive instance is presented, the subject then has to discover which one of fifteen possible conjunctive concepts the card represents. The total of possibilities is shown in Table 3.2. To attain the concept, the subject follows a controlled procedure; he selects from the array, one card at a time; after each selection, the experimenter says whether the selected card is a positive or a negative instance of the concept.

Table 3.1*

The Different Variables	Possible Values
Figure	Cross, circle, square
Color	Green, red, black
Number of figures	One, two, three
Number of border	None, one, two

*Total range of variation: $3^4 = 81$.

Table 3.2

Number of Variables in Concept	Possible Concepts
One	4
Two	6
Three	4
Four	1
Total	15

During these attempts to discover a concept, the experimenters noticed that their subjects tended to follow one or the other of four different strategies (Bruner et al., 1956, pp. 82 ff.):

1. Simultaneous Scanning. The person uses each instance encountered as an occasion for deducing which hypotheses are tenable and which are not. This strategy is highly exacting, requiring that the subject carry in his head a relatively large number of hypotheses and the state of confirming and infirming instances.

2. Successive Scanning. The person tests a single hypothesis at a time; he limits his choices to those instances that provide a direct test of his hypothesis. This process provides a relief of cognitive strain.

3. Conservative Focusing. Acting on a positive instance, the person modifies one variable at a time, to determine when a variable change is or is not significant. If a single variable is changed, and the new card is still a positive instance, then that variable is not part of the concept. Every choice is safe in that it guarantees an information gain from the choice.

4. Focus Gambling. The person uses a positive instance as a focus but then modifies more than one variable at a time. With luck he achieves a faster information gain; without luck he can achieve no information from a choice.

Bruner and his colleagues discovered other strategies and considerations pertinent to disjunctive concepts, but the example here illustrates the method and the order of information developed.

Although the strategies noticed during these experiments pertain most directly to concept attainment, they also have strong relationships with decision criteria used in utility theory and game theory. They relate also to the variety of techniques described in the information-processing theories and in the design methods area. *Successive scanning*, for example, has its counterpart in *heuristic search*; *conservative focusing*, in *hill climbing*; and *simultaneous scanning*, in various intuitive procedures. There is little question that concept attainment is an important element in problem solution processes; there is also no doubt that *A Study of Thinking* is one of the important studies that must not be neglected by any serious student of problem-solving processes.

REFERENCE

Bruner, Jerome, J. J. Goodnow, and G. A. Austin, *A Study of Thinking,* Wiley, New York, 1956.

3.3.8.2 Problem Simplifications

Problems cannot be stated in their full real-world complexity. Every problem statement is thus a simplification. In an action situation,

An individual understands the world, not by the confusion and complexity of detail it contains, but by the simplifications he has made from that complexity and by the order he has imposed on that multitude of impressions. This need for simplification and order exists whether a person is dealing with some segment of the perceived physical world or with abstracted data useful for some solution process.

problem statements ought to be simplified; the problem solver should demonstrate the need for an increased complexity of problem statement.

In talking about the perception of the physical environment, Kevin Lynch observes (Lynch and Rivkin, 1959, pp. 24-34):

> ...the individual must perceive his environment as an ordered pattern, and is constantly trying to inject order into his surroundings, so that all the relevant perceptions are jointed one to the other.

In talking about scientific research E. Bright Wilson (I have reported his comments on *analysis* and *synthesis* elsewhere) remarks (1952, p. 24):

> Even the most restricted portions of the real world are too complex to be comprehended in complete and exact detail by human effort . . . . As a consequence it is necessary to ignore most of the actual features of an event under study and abstract from the real situation certain aspects which together make up an idealized version of the real event.

Even in such a free activity as play, where presumably a person can choose to deal with as much or as little detail as he desires, he chooses to order and simplify. Into an inperfect world and into the confusion of life play brings a temporary and limited perfection. In *Homo Ludens* Johan Huizinga (1955, p. 10) states the matter emphatically:

> Play demands order absolute and supreme. The least deviation from it "spoils the game," robs it of its character and makes it worthless. The profound affinity between play and order is perhaps the reason why play, as we noted in passing, seems to lie to such a large extent in the field of aesthetics.

If a person is often prevented from achieving simplicity and order in the workaday world, he makes every effort to achieve it when he is not so constrained and has freedom to choose the simplicity or complexity of his experience and objectives.

After reporting the need for dealing with *idealized* events during the research process, Wilson also points out the need to *simplify* those events (1952, p. 25):

> ...also certain aspects of these idealized events are then often altered so as to produce *simplified idealized events* [my emphasis].

One process in constant use in this idealization and simplification is *classification*, with its processes of leveling, sharpening, assimilation, and contrast (Heider, 1958, p. 182).

In a brilliant working paper from 1958 Abraham Kaplan (pp. 12-13) shows that the only method of handling the many factors that must be taken into account in social planning is simplification. He insists that the burden of proof is on complexity of approach, not on simplicity, and that a modernization of Occam's razor might be in order: "variables are not to be multiplied beyond necessity."

3.3.8.2   In the specific strategy for planning, *disjointed incrementalism*, proposed by Braybrooke and Lindblom (1963, p. 114), there is a specific recognition that simplification is required:

The most obvious group of specific adaptations to limited capacities, limited information, and the high costs of analysis are the simplifying omissions to which both the specifically incremental character and the restricted scope of the strategy [of disjointed incrementalism] lead. The practitioner of disjointed incrementalism simply omits from his analysis:

(a) nonincremental policies,
(b) many important consequences of a given policy,
(c) objectives that are not attainable by present or potential means, and,
(d) all those aspects of alternative policies and consequences that do not represent the increments of difference among them.

Here then are four adaptations by omission, each reducing the demand for intellectual capacity and information.

They warn that, if the omission of "important consequences" appears alarming, it is important to remember that they are describing a serial policy-making process and "what one analyst neglects at any one step . . . would be attended to in a later step or by another analyst.

Even within formal optimization techniques the same considerations apply. The formal process requires a model that is an abstraction from the real world; in turn the optimization derived from that model is of the model only. It is not one with respect to the real world from which the model is drawn (Shepard, 1964, pp. 261-262).

Not only is there a need to simplify the amounts and kind of information handled to keep the amount within intellectual capacity, there is also a need to reduce the number of objectives to decrease cognitive strain. The weighting or valuing of multiple objectives appears to be beyond most person's capacities. Russell Ackoff has observed:

The scientific disinclination to deal with what people "ought to value" . . . is manifested in applied research by a tendency to consider only one—generally the most important—objective in seeking solutions to problems. . . . The important point about such "simplification" is that it does not obviate the evaluation problem.

Ackoff has recognized that, if a simplification is not taken with care, it can lead to a substantial distortion that would be something other than a simplification (1962, p. 82).

There is, nonetheless, an inclination, even in quite simple choice situations, where multiple attributes are in some conflict, to let a single one govern the choice. Roger N. Shepard (1964, pp. 265 ff.) discusses this tendency to reduce and simplify decisions theoretically dependent on a number of attributes to one governed by a single attribute. He points out that many persons have believed the intuitive method was appropriate for taking into account a number of different factors but that, unfortunately, the evidence appears to provide them little encouragement. Experiments by a number of investigators have shown that, as the stimuli from a number of variable attributes increase, there are an accompanying marked rise in response error and a marked tendency to rely far too heavily on one or two variables. At the same time the subjective weights reported were distributed over the entire set of attributes; the subjects believed they were taking account of all factors. (Shepard, 1964, p. 266). He comments:

> Possibly . . . our feeling that we can take account of a host of different factors comes about because although we remember that at some time or other we have attended to each of the different factors, we fail to notice that it is seldom more than one or two that we consider at any time . . . the confidence that we have tended to invest in our rational ability to weight and combine many subjective factors appears to have been somewhat misplaced.

According to Shepard a person simplifies his decision processes whether he wishes to do so or not and whether he is aware of doing so or not.

At the same time, even if a person simplifies when he thinks he does not, or if his manipulations in problem solution are confined to solutions of the simplified representations he makes of real-world problems, those solutions must still be applied in the complexity of the real-world situation. Gordon Best has argued effectively against a methodology thought of as definitive:

> . . . a great deal of [abstract and analytic] design methodology is an attempt to explore and explain design definitively. The outcome has been a general inapplicability of these methods in practice.

Best puts the argument in the following way (1969, p. 147):

> . . . design problems encountered in practice are different from those that we conceive in our heads. Practical problems are more variable; they arise in space and time; they have no precise boundaries and each one is different from every other. Yet to tackle these problems we have to interpret them and this interpretation is always a simplification that we can comprehend. It is a definitive simplification and it is from this that we develop our methods for designing. Our methods are appropriate to the problem simplifications we hold in our heads while being of little use involving the problems we face in practice.

> . . . my intention . . . is to illustrate that practical design problems are incredibly variable and not describable in a definitive sense.

Although Best recognizes that a simplification of a design problem is essential for the professional to begin dealing with it in the complexity of the real-world situation, he is unwilling to simplify *the simplifications* and thus provide a definitive procedure. He realizes and argues that such a procedure will break down under the complexity of application in practice.

3.3.8.2

In any effort to understand the design and problem-solving process there must be a clear distinction between an overall process that is a guide with specific methods applicable where appropriate and a rigid or definitive process that reduces the complexity of real-world events to the bounds of a single procedure.

I recommend a careful reading of Best's comments in the original article, for his arguments are important to an understanding of some of the more basic issues in design (Best, 1969, p. 149).

REFERENCES

Ackoff, Russell L., Shiv K. Gupta, and J. Sayer Minas, *Scientific Method: Optimizing Applied Research Decisions*, Wiley, New York, 1962.

Best, Gordon, "Method and Intention in Architectural Design," in Broadbent, Geoffrey, and A. Ward, *Design Methods in Architecture*, A. A. Paper No. 4, Symposium, Portsmouth School of Architecture, Architect's Association, London, 1969.

Braybrooke, D., and C. Lindblom, *A Strategy of Decision*, Free Press, New York, 1963.

Heider, Fritz, *The Psychology of Interpersonal Relations*, Wiley, New York, 1958.

Huizinga, Johan, *Homo Ludens: A Study of the Play Element in Culture,* Beacon Press, Boston, 1955.

Kaplan, Abraham, "On the Strategy of Social Planning," working paper, a report submitted to the Social Planning Group of the Planning Board of Puerto Rico, September 10, 1958.

Lynch, Kevin, and Malcolm Rivkin, "A Walk Around the Block," *Landscape*, **8** , 1959.

Shepard, Roger N., "On Subjectively Optimum Selection Among Multiattribute Alternatives," in Shelly, Maynard W., II, and Glenn L. Bryan, *Human Judgments and Optimality*, Wiley, New York, 1964.

Wilson, E. Bright, Jr., *An Introduction to Scientific Research*, McGraw-Hill, New York, 1952.

3.4 THE INFLUENCE OF SOLUTION PROCESSES

Although there is an overall pattern that any design process must follow, each designer's process varies from that pattern according to the skills and interests of the designer and the needs of his clients.

There are strong tendencies toward simplification of design problems—one that results from problem statement, one that results from reducing requirements of ill-defined problems, and a suspected simplification of decision criteria that occurs in an intuitive process.

Alongside these simplifications are external motivations that affect the solution—a preference for strain-reducing, effort-reducing error-reducing, or solution-certainty strategies.

Each imposes some form of further simplification on design. It is extremely useful to see what form each takes. To do so requires a detailed examination of the overall design process and what occurs within each segment.

Because the usefulness of systematic methods in design has been discussed so much during the past few years, by contrast with what has been conceived as the more traditional method, it is appropriate to relate the range of different strategies to that discussion. Relating these strategies to each other and to the different motivations might reduce the controversy, which, I believe, results from a misunderstanding of what systematic methods can achieve in design. My suspicion is that their impact on the traditional design process has been exaggerated.

3.4.1 Diagraming the Design Process

The design process moves consecutively through statements of purpose, behavior, function, and object. The several processes that convert a statement of one kind to one of the next kind are known as programming, planning, and design.

Design moves through three basic steps: programming, planning, and design. *Programming* converts goal statements into behavioral (or operational) statements and organizes the behavioral statements. *Planning* converts behavioral into function statements and develops relationships between the function statements. *Design* converts function into object statements and organizes the relationship between object statements.

The accompanying diagram (Fig. 3.6) shows the overall sequence, but it is possible to undertake design by some modification in this sequence. For example, the designer could so completely internalize the client's goal statements that he is able to undertake object design directly, omitting the two intervening steps.

In this process the earlier statements are more ends-like (goal-like) and the later more means-like. The process I have described is the most orderly sequential procedure, but the logical sequence is not harmed if a step is omitted. The ends-means relationship is still preserved.

3.4.2 Demand and Supply in a Process Segment

Each of these process segments follows a similar pattern. A demand statement together with a

Each step, though using different statement forms and notations, is organized in the same pattern. To have the sequence applicable and understandable for each step, I refer to initial statements in each step, as demand statements (since they describe the ends for which means must be supplied). I refer to the terminal statements as supply statements.

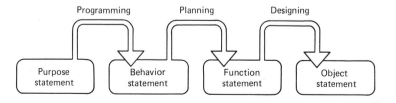

Figure 3.6 Steps in the design process.

ARCHITECTURE, PROBLEMS AND PURPOSES

3.4.2

supply systems statement are converted into a supply statement. The supply statement becomes a demand statement on the next process.

Each step then proceeds in the following manner. The demand statement is decomposed into its parts. Supply systems are then reviewed (from the designer's global information base), a possible supply system is selected, and it is then decomposed into its parts. As the decomposed demand and supply statements are matched with each other, a supply statement is proposed that corresponds with the demand statement. If it matches adequately, it is then selected as the appropriate supply statement, which then becomes a demand statement upon the next step. This process is diagramed in Fig. 3.7.

3.4.3 Abstract and Concrete Segments

A supply statement can be more or less concrete than the demand statement that preceded it. When it is more concrete, it cannot be obtained by logic. The authority of the client must be consulted.

Except for a single variation this pattern of operations occurs (whatever the notation used) in each step. An earlier discussion noted that some of the statement forms are more abstract and some more concrete. A variation occurs in the kind of step that moves from the more concrete to the more abstract and in the kind that moves from the more abstract to the more concrete.

In moving from the particular and concrete to the general and abstract, one can develop a formal and logical induction and can generalize with accuracy.

One cannot, in moving from the general to the particular, do the same. The process is logically doubtful. Because many particulars fit with the general statement, with no criteria for choice among them, the designer must have recourse to the authority of the client.

A basic difficulty with any form of design instruction that has no client as a participant in the process is that the designer does not have this kind of access or recourse. He cannot say to the client, "Is this the kind of thing you meant?" In moving from some general demand statement to some more particular supply statement, the designer in school is on his own. He gets into the habit of being on his own with such decisions, and sometimes when he is in practice he has difficulty in consulting the client.

3.4.4 Pattern Repetition in a Process Segment

Whereas each process segment is similar, a single segment might consist of an ordered sequence of operations. Any single segment might consist of a parallel group of operations.

Despite this difference between the general-particular and the particular-general step, the diagram for each is similar.

Each step is not, however, singular; indeed each consists of a multitude of steps of this kind performed on the decomposed statement. A diagram of the enrire process consists of a great number of such operations within each step and of repetitions of the same step, since securing a fit between different statement forms requires trial after trial. The process is iterative.

The young designer soon learns this. Whether he is involved in pro-

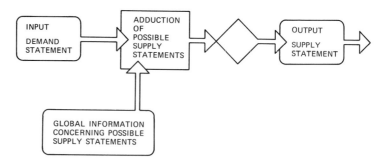

Figure 3.7 A demand-supply segment in the design process.

gramming, planning, or design, he finds himself repeating a step many times. There is undoubtedly more repetition near the end of the process as the designer gets into a more and more detailed consideration of building design. The entire design sequence forms a very complicated diagram indeed. The diagram here (Fig. 3.8) only suggests the level of complexity and does not try to represent the process in full detail.

The diagram is very general. The designer's motivation causes him to adopt different strategies, which have the effect of modifying his process.

3.4.5 Different Degrees of Effort in Design

Design might take a great deal of effort when an original product is required and very little effort when an existing design is satisfactory. The amount of effort is related to the degree of detail in the client's program statement.

Design can entail a very great amount of effort or comparatively little (a level of supporting resources being assumed). The amount of effort is directly related to the degree of decomposition of demand and supply statements in each step. Let me illustrate by describing two extremes.

An architect is hired by a school board to design an elementary school. "How many rooms per grade?" asks the architect. "Three!" says the school board president. "What square-foot cost limit?" asks the architect. "Why, thirty dollars [or forty, or fifty, or whatever inflation level is current]," replies the school board president.

"Well," says the architect, "I believe that I have a plan right here that will suit very well." "Excellent!" says the school board president.

With such a very little decomposition of program and none of plan or of design object, very little effort is required to achieve a building design.

By contrast, when a school board gives detailed thought to the height and color of chalk boards, the size of desks and chairs, and the selection and placement of every material and product in the building, then a considerable design effort is required indeed.

When very specific performance criteria are developed for each of the various systems to be used in the building, even more effort is required.

3.4.6 Differences in Effort Placement

The designer can place his greatest effort in different process segments. Early placement seems to relate to verbal ability and analytic processes. Later placement seems to relate to visual abilities.

Early in their design careers students develop preferences for placing their major efforts into the early programming phases or into the later object design phase of the total process. The preference is probably related to abilities and personality traits. Early placement is probably related to stronger verbal abilities, and later placement, to visual abilities. Early placement may be related to a preference for more orderly analytic procedures, and later placement, to more random search processes. Early placement relates to both analytic procedures and partial or "planning" procedures (a scheme is developed using only parts of the criteria), but late placement relates to holistic orientations in design.

3.4.7 Different Kinds of Design Effort

In each segment the designer can use more subjective or more objective procedures.

Designers with different abilities are willing to engage in different forms of activity. Some prefer very explicit objective procedures and like to check their progress in every stage of their work; others are willing to have a relatively subjective and formless process if it results finally in a building proposal.

Clearly the first sort will prefer harder algorithmic (strong) methods, and the second sort, softer heuristic (weak) methods.

Undoubtedly some advantage resides in the more objective procedure when the work is performed within an institutional framework.

Figure 3.8 An example of the complexity that can exist in just one segment of a design process.

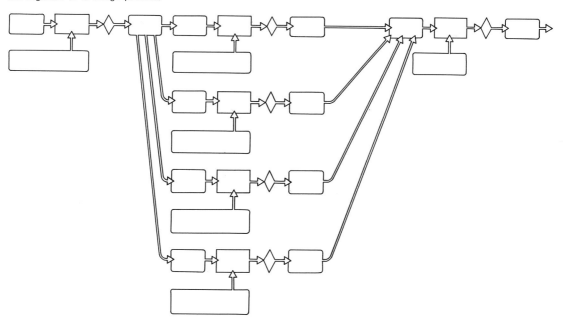

Other persons who share the work can understand how the work is accomplished. The person who can accomplish design by the more subjective method is still valuable, but he must find ways to organize and explain his work.

3.4.8 A Spectrum of Design Strategies

The variations in effort and effort placement produce different design strategies related to the different motivations of the designer. These strategies vary from the use of systematic methods in programming to the use of an already prepared plan.

The variations in amount of effort, in effort placement, and in the kind of effort produce in combination various design strategies, which are related to the different motives discussed in earlier sections (3.3.3 through 3.3.7).

The simple procedure of pulling a plan from a drawer is low in effort and not secure in achieving a solution. Such a simple procedure has a high possibility of error. It has associated with it a high strain level.

A strategy that emphasizes the programming end of the design process and uses systematic, objective methods insofar as possible has an opposite set of characteristics. There is a considerable increase in effort, more security in achieving a solution, a sizable reduction in the possibility of error, and a decrease in strain.

Two ends of a spectrum of strategies with quite different characteristics having been established, it is possible to place other strategies that gradually shift from one end to the other between these two.

A basic group of strategies and their characteristics are shown in the associated diagram (Fig. 3.9).

I have no intention of saying that one strategy is better than another. All share some of the same operations. The strategy that emphasizes programming and systematic methods must still provide a visual design proposal. The one that pulls a previously drawn plan out of a drawer must still check that plan against a set of program requirements.

Different strategies will undoubtedly be preferable in different circumstances.

3.4.9 The Usefulness of Systematic Methods

Systematic methods are more useful in programming than in design.

Systematic methods are more applicable in the programming and planning phases of the process than in the design phase. Systematic methods useful in the design phase are not as useful in developing proposals as they are in analyzing proposals already made.

The methods developed to generate plans by computer, unassisted by the designer, are relatively crude and are not very successful. Although they appear as design procedures that produce building plans, they are, in fact, planning procedures based on partial information only. They are not design procedures that accumulate and synthesize all the pertinent information that needs to go into the design of the building.

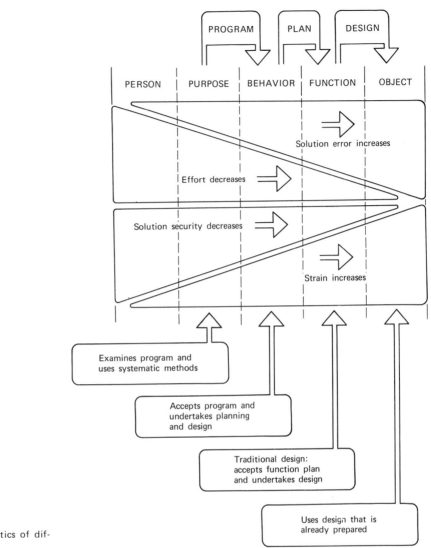

Figure 3.9 Characteristics of different design strategies.

3.4.10 The Technical Discussions

The technical discussions go into more detail concerning the morphologies of the design and problem-solving processes. They discuss the demand-supply interaction fully and the procedures by which proposals occur.

3.4.10.1 Overall Processes in Design

The problem solver can use any of a number of different strategies

When one can say whether a particular method has algorithmic properties or describe the heuristic power of a particular method, it is similar to saying what degree of *control* the problem solver has over the problem-solving process. A method strong in its heuristic power is

3.4.10.1

that are a combination of strong or weak control over process and strong or weak visualization of a goal to be achieved. Since the different stages of design are well defined, it is possible to classify a design method by the progress it provides from one stage to another.

one wherein the problem solver has strong control over his process. To show the full impact of the degree of control over the process on problem-solving strategies, it is also necessary to consider how strong the *goals* of problem solving are.

In a later section (4.1) I review in more detail a categorization of process models based on comments by Lynch and by Braybrook and Lindblom. The models, shown in Fig. 3.10, are categorized according to whether there are strong *goals* and whether there is strong *control* over the solution.

These several models can be related to specific design process descriptions; before doing so, however, I should clarify my use of the terminology. Talking about an action that is a strong *method* is different from talking about a strong overall *process*. A strong *method* is one that has algorithmic properties. By contrast a strong *process* (over which the designer has strong control) might use some weak and some strong methods. The important point in a strong process is that the general sequence is well established and, if followed (even if there are dead ends, and halts and starts), will produce a solution to the posed problem. In a strong process the problem solver knows what method to use next.

In *Design Methods* Jones (1970, endpaper) organizes a review of a number of different design methods and overall processes. Moreover, the different forms that design strategy can take are treated separately. The volume is an excellent review of a broad range of methods; if it suffers from any fault, it is its failure to provide an adequate classification of strategies and to relate overall processes and methods to those strategies. It is worthwhile if the discussion here can remedy some part of that fault. I limit the discussion to strategies and overall processes, since an adequate base has not yet been laid to discuss the variety of individual methods. The strategies and processes that Jones (1970) defines can be related to the categorization of process models described above (Fig. 3.11).

Of some thirty-five methods and processes that Jones identifies and describes, seven (listed in Fig. 3.11 as process descriptions) can

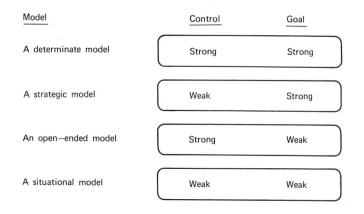

Model	Control	Goal
A determinate model	Strong	Strong
A strategic model	Weak	Strong
An open—ended model	Strong	Weak
A situational model	Weak	Weak

Figure 3.10 A categorization of different problem solving models.

198   **ARCHITECTURE, PROBLEMS AND PURPOSES**

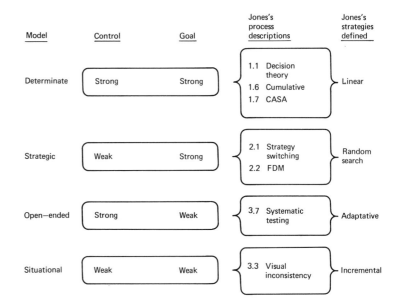

Model	Control	Goal	Jones's process descriptions	Jones's strategies defined
Determinate	Strong	Strong	1.1 Decision theory 1.6 Cumulative 1.7 CASA	Linear
Strategic	Weak	Strong	2.1 Strategy switching 2.2 FDM	Random search
Open—ended	Strong	Weak	3.7 Systematic testing	Adaptative
Situational	Weak	Weak	3.3 Visual inconsistency	Incremental

Figure 3.11 Problem solving models related to specific design methods.

3.4.10.1

be thought of as overall processes, ranging from the early identification of objectives to the final development of solutions. Each is described below:

1.1 Systematic Search (The Decision Theory Approach):
"To solve design problems with logical certainty." [Uses mathematical decision criteria.]

1.6 Page's Cumulative Strategy.
"To increase the amount of design effort that is spent on analysis and evaluation." [Requires identification of *critical* objectives and requires that judgements be limited to quantifiable measures; also requires manufactured components system.]

1.7 CASA (Collaborative Strategy for Adaptable Architecture.)
[Seeks approvals of multiple schematics, multiple systems choices, and so on. Apparently a version of performance specifying.]

2.1 Strategy Switching.
"To permit spontaneous thinking to influence planned thinking, and vice versa." [Not a process so much as a criterion for judging whether a strategy fits the goals of the design organization.]

2.2 Matchett's Fundamental Design Method (FDM).
"To permit a designer to perceive and control the pattern of his thoughts." [Apparently attempts to bring to bear every possible conceptual scheme upon the design process, a grab bag. Provides checklists.]

3.7 Systematic Testing

"To identify actions that are capable of bringing about desired changes in situations that are too complicated to understand." [Appears to be a version of *disjointed incrementalism.*]

3.3 Searching for Visual Inconsistancies.

"To find directions in which to search for design improvements." [Not a process so much as an attitude; opportunistic in its basic approach.]

This group of process descriptions should not be taken as an exhaustive list; it is only a sample useful for our discussion here, since they range across the combinations of *control* types and *objective* types noted above.

Jones develops several strong organizing approaches to design method; he attempts, for example,to characterize methods by the degree to which they move the design process only a single step or several steps forward. That is extremely useful and well worth adopting as a way of characterizing method. Unfortunately the basic model that has guided his organization is based on divergence, transformation, and convergence as three basic phases in design. Although the existence of other dimensions in design is briefly recognized, the categorization of methods and processes seems not to take those other dimensions into account. As a result the categorization system seems particularly flat in that it gives no method for recording sequential transformations from behavioral, to functional, to object descriptions, or from one scale to the next in succession, or in any other of the different manipulations essential to several parts of the design process, whatever the criterion being used for evaluation, or whatever the attitude of the designer.

Although the Jones (1970) list of processes is diverse when stated in terms of the strength of control and of objectives, it is far from comprehensive. A very large number of writers have described, with varying degrees of detail and sophistication, both problem-solving and design processes. One of the most extensive lists I have encountered appears in a Ph.D. dissertation by D. Michael Murtha (1973, pp. 125-130). In an appendix Murtha records the solution sequences listed by some forty different writers (which I have not been able to review in their original publications). These writers are categorized by their concern with listing basic steps, operations, problem-solving procedures, or design procedures; under design procedures Murtha subdivides those writers by their disciplines of concern: systems design, engineering design, machine design, environmental design, or planning.

Murtha (1973) develops his own synoptic list (at several levels of

3.4.10.1

detail) for experimentation; it can serve here in its simplest form as a prototype of the design process in its linear determinate form:

1. Defining the problem.
2. Gathering data.
3. Developing preliminary solution.
4. Detailing the solution.
5. Evaluating the solution.

Note that all such process lists appear to be determinate in form whether that is their author's intent or not. Other means are typically used to show degrees of ambiguity, process iterations, or other characteristics of the process that cause it to be less than determinate.

On occasion a writer attempts to incorporate into a process description some of those other factors that cause the design process to be more ambiguous than the basic elements would imply. A list by Wehrli (1968, p. 107) is an example:

1. Orient
2. Program
3. Analyze
4. Hypothesize
5. Approach
6. Synthesize
7. Evaluate

A closer look at some of the detail under these headings indicates clearly that steps 1 and 5, *Orient* and *Approach,* are not pure process steps. *Orient* includes organizing resources and undertaking the problem, and *Approach* lists characteristics of problem processes.

Clearly design problem solution, like all solutions, requires the identification of unresolved tensions within the problem situation; a mustering of elements, or system of elements, or processes by which those tensions can be resolved; and a resolution of those tensions by an appropriate matching of tension-producing circumstances with tension-reducing elements. Matching is accomplished by evaluation.

REFERENCES

Jones, J. Christopher. *Design Methods: Seeds of Human Futures,* Wiley, New York, 1972.

Murtha, Donald Michael, "A Comparison of Problem-Solving Approaches Used by Environmental Designers," unpublished doctoral dissertation, University fo Wisconsin, Madison, Wisconsin, 1973.

Wehrli, Robert, "Open-ended Problem Solving in Design," unpublished doctoral dissertation, University of Utah, Department of Psychology, 1968.

3.4.10.2 Design Morphologies

Various morphological charts of design process are helpful in understanding the variations that occur in design.

Although a clear relationship exists between the unresolved tension of the problem statement at the beginning of the problem-solving process and the resolved tension at its end (Wertheimer, 1959, pp. 248-253), each solution process includes intermediate steps that connect the beginning with the end, and the relationship between these intermediate steps is not so clear. Charles Eastman comments on this relationship, (1970, p. 138):

Two issues make decision making in a problem solving situation unique: (1) the necessity of making sequences of decisions where succeeding decision use the results or prior ones as input; (2) the lack of means to directly evaluate single decisions in the sequence.

Eastman points out that such a sequence of decision (with the full set of alternate choices) at each decision point generates a decision tree of a magnitude exponentially related to the number of decisions.

Several writers have reported that design moves typically from the more abstract to the more concrete or from the more general to the more specific. Marvin Manheim (1964, p. 16), for example indicates that "each succeeding operation results in increasing detail and precision of specification."

Korobkin (1974), in a short unpublished paper discussing several vantages from which design must be understood, defines:

The increasing specificity model: the overall genesis in design from holistic notions to specific solutions, from large scale general decisions to small scale particular ones.

Since design is not simply a determinate linear model, it cannot be precisely true that every part of the process moves from the general to the specific or from the abstract to the concrete—but there is little question that this is its overall direction. This direction can be seen by examining several design morphologies.

Morphologies are derived, whether by independent observers engaged in social research or by practitioners attempting to formalize their own procedures, by the taking of behavior protocols—by observing what the solver of a design-problem does first, then what he does next, and so on. In taking such a protocol, Eastman (1970, p. 26) describes the kind of information essential for an initial observation:

(1) physical elements which are manipulated (design units,) (2) desired relationships between elements and the desired attributes of elements (we call these constraints), and (3) the manipulations made on a design to fulfill the relationships or attributes. Clues to the source of each piece of information are also looked for.

ARCHITECTURE, PROBLEMS AND PURPOSES

3.4.10.2　This information is then translated into a morphological representation. Although the symbols used in various charts differ slightly from one investigator to another, all such morphologies use symbols to represent events in the process and arrow symbols to represent the sequence or connection between the different kinds of events. The events represented are of three kinds: The supply of data (some charts distinguish between input and output data), operations on the data, and decisions.

Apparently a sequence of events can occur in three different ways: a strictly linear sequence wherein each event occurs before and as a means to the next, a loop or recycle of events wherein the information that results from a linear sequence is fed back to an earlier point in the same sequence to reprocess that portion of the information, and a simultaneous event or multiple-thread sequence wherein several "simultaneous" events are essential for and necessarily prior to a succeeding event.

Illustrations of the representations of different events and the different forms of flow that can occur between events appear in Honey (1969, pp. 1389 ff.) and Gregory (1969).

Various morphologies by Eastman (1970, p. 31); Honey (1969, pp. 1389 ff.); Metz, Train, Olsen, and Youngren, Architects (1974); and Asimow (1964, p. 19) will repay close scrutiny. They appear as Figs. 3.12 through 3.15. The morphology by Asimow, since its first publication in 1962, is undoubtedly the most frequently reproduced illustration in the entire field of *design methods;* it represents compactly and with graphic eloquence some of the complexity of a full range of design decisions. That it is not always pertinent to every design decision does not detract from its power as a diagram.

By examining these morphologies, it is easy to see that each is dealing with a different process. Eastman's appears to begin with physical constraints on the placement of design elements and end with their successful or unsuccessful placement. Honey's morphology begins with objectives but then jumps immediately to layout design based on functional requirements, design of functional systems, and detail design. The Metz, Train, Olsen, and Youngren chart begins with program review and ends with construction. Asimow, who is more directly concerned with industrial processes, begins with the feasibility study and ends with planning for retirement of the product. But whatever the concern or scope of the morphologies, their importance is that they provide a logical connection between a series of information transformations that begin with some form of objectives statement or set of requirements and usually terminate with the specification of a physical product.

Even if the general trend is from the more general to the more specific, not every step moves in that direction. A logical sequence of steps, for example, might be:

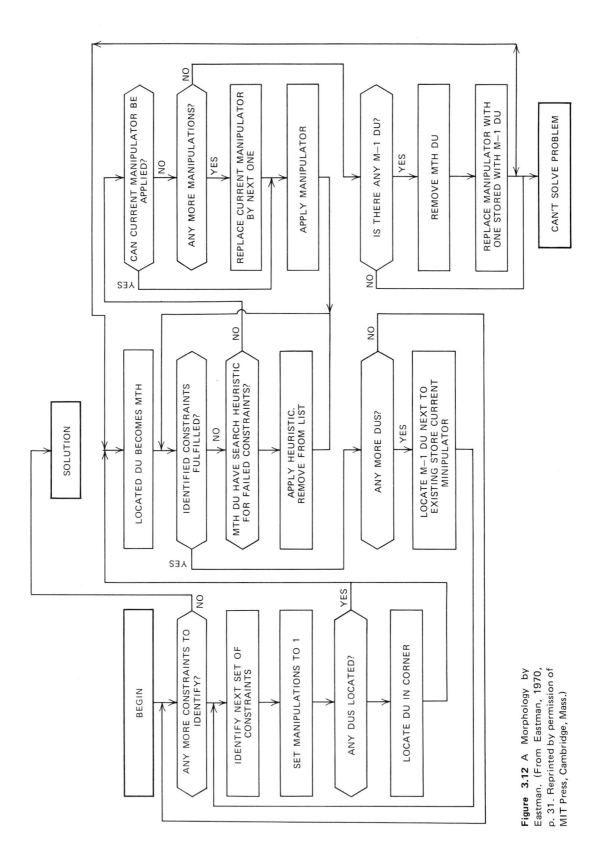

Figure 3.12 A Morphology by Eastman. (From Eastman, 1970, p. 31. Reprinted by permission of MIT Press, Cambridge, Mass.)

ARCHITECTURE, PROBLEMS AND PURPOSES

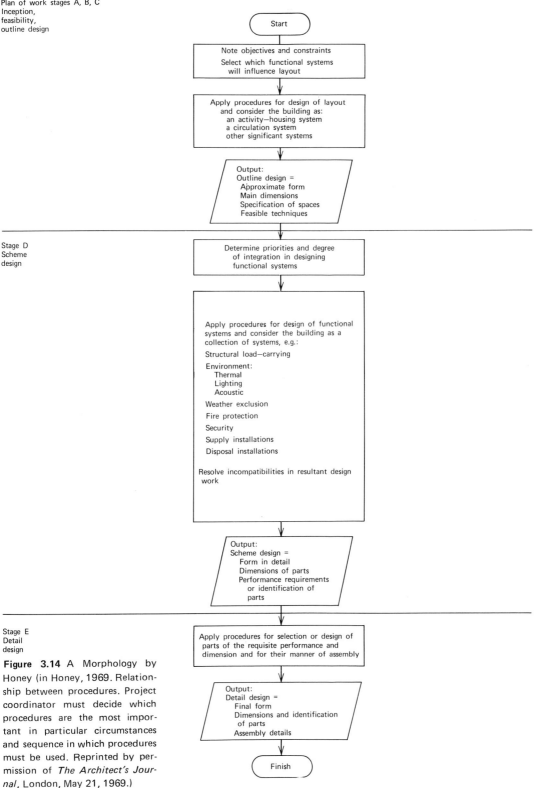

Plan of work stages A, B, C
Inception,
feasibility,
outline design

Start

Note objectives and constraints

Select which functional systems
will influence layout

Apply procedures for design of layout
and consider the building as:
an activity—housing system
a circulation system
other significant systems

Output:
Outline design =
Approximate form
Main dimensions
Specification of spaces
Feasible techniques

Stage D
Scheme
design

Determine priorities and degree
of integration in designing
functional systems

Apply procedures for design of functional
systems and consider the building as a
collection of systems, e.g.:

Structural load—carrying

Environment:
Thermal
Lighting
Acoustic

Weather exclusion

Fire protection

Security

Supply installations

Disposal installations

Resolve incompatibilities in resultant design
work

Output:
Scheme design =
Form in detail
Dimensions of parts
Performance requirements
or identification of
parts

Stage E
Detail
design

Apply procedures for selection or design of
parts of the requisite performance and
dimension and for their manner of assembly

Output:
Detail design =
Final form
Dimensions and identification
of parts
Assembly details

Finish

Figure 3.14 A Morphology by Honey (in Honey, 1969. Relationship between procedures. Project coordinator must decide which procedures are the most important in particular circumstances and sequence in which procedures must be used. Reprinted by permission of *The Architect's Journal*, London, May 21, 1969.)

INFLUENCES ON PROBLEM SOLUTION

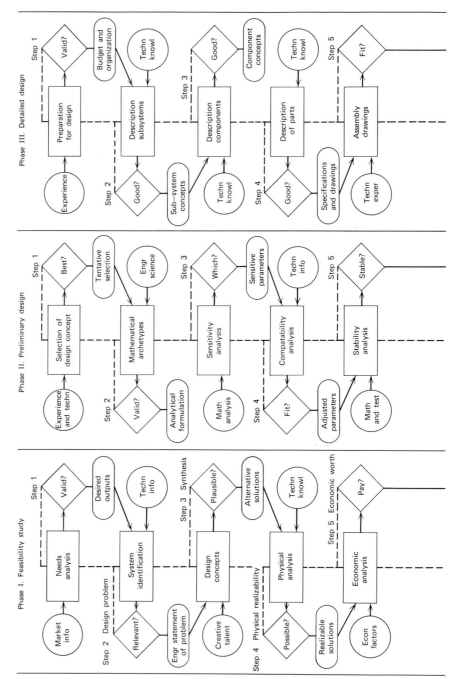

Figure 3.15 A Morphology by Asimow. (From Asimow, 1964, p. 19. Reprinted by permission of Prentice-Hall, Inc. Englewood Cliffs, N.J.)

ARCHITECTURE, PROBLEMS AND PURPOSES

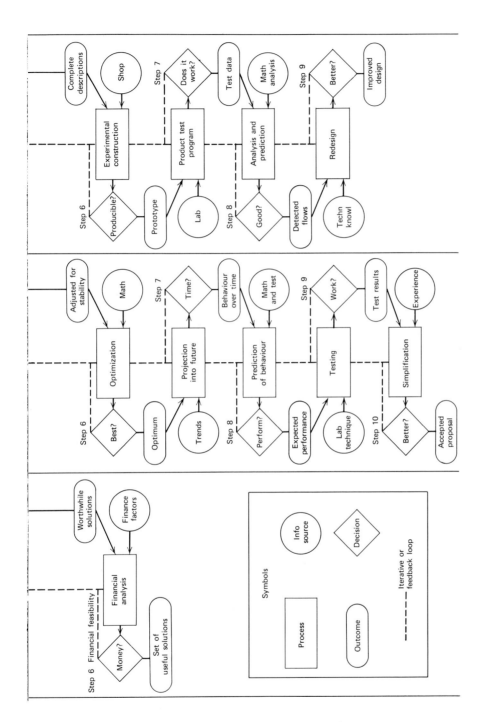

Symbols

Info source (Info source)

Decision (Decision)

Process (Process)

Outcome (Outcome)

Iterative or feedback loop

Step 6 Financial feasibility

Worthwhile solutions → Financial analysis ← Finance factors

Financial analysis → Money? → Set of useful solutions

Step 6 — Optimization — Adjusted for stability, Math
Best? — Optimum

Step 7 — Projection into future — Time?, Behaviour over time
Trends

Step 8 — Prediction of behaviour — Math and test
Perform? — Expected performance

Step 9 — Testing — Work?, Test results
Lab technique

Step 10 — Simplification — Experience
Better? — Accepted proposal

Step 6 — Experimental construction — Complete descriptions, Shop
Producible? — Prototype

Step 7 — Product test program — Does it work?
Lab

Step 8 — Analysis and prediction — Test data, Math analysis
Good? — Detected flows

Step 9 — Redesign — Better?, Improved design
Techn knowl

1. Statement of objectives.
2. Statement of related behaviors (to accomplish those objectives).
3. Statement of required functions (to assist those behaviors)
4. Description of objects, tools, or facilities (to provide those functions).

This sequence moves from an abstract to a more concrete statement (of behaviors), to a more abstract statement (of function), and finally to a concrete description (of physical objects). What is important is not that each step is more concrete but that it is more specific and that the general direction is toward the concrete; it is also important that each step be logically related to the one before and the one after. This relationship can be realized even more forcefully when it is recognized that a program for design might have included in it statements that would not bear on decision until an appropriate one of the separate steps above had been undertaken. It is the rare design client who can stay at the level of abstractness implied by a statement of objectives; a client might define a relatively abstract objective (improving the neighborhood quality), but he might also require that yellow walls be specified, a concrete requirement indeed.

In discussing the relation between steps in the design process, it will be helpful to adapt remarks by James Weinland (1970, pp. 31-32) in listing four attributes of a good hypothesis. Four descriptions of a good design transformation are:

1. It should be in a form that will permit it to be tested (against the constraints) by observation.

2. It should move the process significantly forward.

3. It should lead to other useful transformations.

4. It should be simple in its application and in its methods.

Finally it is worth remarking that response in a design situation can take the several forms that D. E. Broadbent (1958, pp. 43-44) discusses in his book. The individual can respond to a series of stimuli element by element, accumulatively by groups, or totally by a whole sequence. Different parts of the design sequence require these different levels of response.

REFERENCES

Asimow, Morris, *Introduction to Design,* Prentice-Hall, Englewood Cliffs, N.J., 1964.

Broadbent, D. E., *Perception and Communication,* Pergamom Press, New York, 1958.

Eastman, Charles M., "On the Analysis of Intuitive Design Processes," In Moore, Gary T., Ed., *Emerging Methods in Environmental Design and Planning,* M.I.T. Press, Cambridge, Mass., 1970.

Gregory, S. A., "Morphological Analysis: Some Simple Explorations," in Broadbent, Geoffrey, and Anthony Ward, Eds., *Design Methods in Architecture,* A. A. Paper No. 4, Architects Association, London, 1969

Honey, C. R., "Information Flow in Architectural Design," *The Architect's Journal,* London, May 21, 1969.

Korobkin, Barry, unpublished interim report, A.I.A. Communications Fellowship HGSD, February 5, 1974.

Manheim, Marvin Lee, "Highway Route Location as a Hierarchically Structured Sequential Decision Process," unpublished doctoral dissertation, Department of Civil Engineering, M.I.T., May 15, 1964.

Metz, Train, Olsen, and Youngren, Architects, unpublished chart, Chicago, Ill., 1974.

Weinland, James D., *How to Think Straight,* Littlefield Adams, Totowa, N.J., 1970.

Wertheimer, Max, *Productive Thinking,* Harper & Row, New York, 1959.

3.4.10.3 A formal Means-Ends Organization

If a problem can be formulated in terms of *objects* and *operators*, then for each object stage it is possible to specify what operator will move the problem state toward a solution. Such a list of objects and the appropriate operators can be assembled into a *table of connections.*

A means-ends analysis is such a strong heuristic that Newell and Simon make it a principal feature of GPS (General Problem Solver), their computer program to replicate human problem-solving processes 1972, p. 416):

This kind of [means-ends] analysis—classifying things in terms of the functions they serve, and oscillating among ends, functions required, and means that perform them—forms the basic system of heuristic of GPS.

They make the following assumptions:

1. Differences can be detected between an available object and a desired object.

2. Operators can be characterized by changes they produce and can be used to try to eliminate differences between the available and the desired object.

3. If an operator is not applicable, a changed input may permit it to be applicable.

4. It is profitable to try to eliminate "difficult" differences, even at the cost of introducing other differences of lesser difficulty.

As they say (1972, p. 414):

GPS operates on problems that can be formulated in terms of *objects* and *operators.* An operator is something that can be applied to certain objects to produce different objects (as a saw applied to logs produces boards). The objects can be characterized by the *features* they possess, and by the *differences* that can be observed between pairs of objects.

3.4.10.3

Clearly the objects so described need not be physical. GPS is a so-called working-forward program; changes are permitted in the *available object* but not in the *desired object*. A means-ends analysis, they point out, is a powerful guide to what changes to make in the available object; it does not make changes in the desired object.

Using means-ends as a guide, the executive program considers a goal, evaluates, selects a method, and applies the method toward achieving that goal. The executive program can consider three types of goals (Newell and Simon, 1972, pp. 414-417):

1. **Transform.** Find a way to transform the available object into the desired object (pp. 415-418).

2. **Apply.** Apply an operator to the available object or to some object into which the available object has been transformed (pp. 415-418).

3. **Reduce.** Reduce the difference between the available object and the desired object by modifying the available object (pp. 416-418).

Each goal has a specific method associated with it that uses one of the other goals as a subgoal. The entire program is thus recursive.

For such a program to work, it must have available to it a *table of connections* (Newell and Simon, 1972, p. 149; Eastman, 1970, p. 143) that links specific notable differences with the range of possible operators that can be applied to those differences. Notice that the table of connections links the *difference* between an available object and a desired object with a set of operators. It could not be a means-ends guide if it linked only the *state* of the available object with a set of operators; such information could be useful in problem solution, but it would not have the specific directing ability that a means-ends heuristic has.

In design an extremely important consideration is the degree to which the desired state is known. If GPS is to work, there must be available a full knowledge of the desired state; often, in design, more detailed information must be supplied than was originally available; closure from a partial to a full information state must be made—sometimes by assumption and sometimes by arbitrary choice.

Another heuristic used in GPS is called *planning* (Newell and Simon, 1972, pp. 428-429). This heuristic develops an alternate and simpler table of connections by taking out of existence—by ignoring—some of the kinds of differences that can exist between the available and the desired object. As some differences are ignored, some operators become inessential, so that the entire process is reduced to one with fewer variables. Typically the process produces from an "abstracted" available object an "abstracted" desired object. The aim

ARCHITECTURE, PROBLEMS AND PURPOSES

in doing so is to provide a process plan for the accomplishment of the full detailed transformation on the fully detailed available object. The abstracted process provides a plan for accomplishing the detailed process (Newell and Simon, 1972, pp. 443-434). Such planning heuristics are used in design as well; for example, a designer can use a bubble diagram to develop a scheme for spatial connection between various parts of a building; when he does so, he ignores all the other aspects of shape and required height of space, and the like, to deal only with connections. A similar process is used in the *planning* heuristic.

Consideration of the *abstracting* process in *planning* is similar to the concerns addressed earlier in a discussion of problem *decomposition* and fitting. In the discussion of means-ends analysis, I remarked that certain components had been *factored out* of the process description for simplicity. It is worth making a careful distinction between these several related processes:

1. Abstracting (in GPS, Planning). Omitting selected details or detail differences to carry through to completion a skeleton problem solution as a guide to the more detailed solution required by the original problem.

2. Factoring Out. Omitting selected details as manipulatable parts of problem objects. In the language of decision theory these would be thought of as context variables instead of decision variables. The existence and condition of the omitted details would not be manipulated directly, but their state would influence the manipulation of the remaining details.

3. Decomposing. Separating and isolating selected details of the problem state to have that isolated part compatible with available operators. The decomposed part is not left in isolation but is then fitted with other such isolated parts to recombine into an entire modified problem condition.

The kind of *factoring out* that occurs in a physical design problem was discussed in Sections 2.3 and 2.7; Decomposing was discussed in Section 2.6.

REFERENCES

Eastman, Charles M., "Problem Solving Strategies in Design," in Sanoff, Henry, and Sidney Cohn, Eds., *EDRA 1: Proceedings of the 1st annual Environmental Design Research Association Conference,* no publisher named, 1970.

Newell, Allen, and Herbert A. Simon, *Human Problem Solving,* Prentice-Hall, Englewood Cliffs, N.J., 1972.

3.4.10.4 Generation and Matching

To solve a problem, there must be a way to *generate* candidates that are possible solutions to the problem. There must also be a way to *test* whether a candidate is in fact a solution. When these criteria are separate, the process is systematic and objective. When the criteria are combined, the process is intuitive and subjective.

A clear distinction in the problem-solving literature between the terms *search* and *generate* is lacking. Although both are concerned with finding solutions to problems, there is an interesting semantic difference between them; *search* implies that the solution exists within some defined search space and if the problem solver is clever enough, he will find it; *generate* suggests that the solution might not exist apart from the problem solver's ability to produce a created solution. Some correlation in use occurs with this semantic distinction, but generally the terms are used in a compound form to refer to different levels of solution. *Search and select* is a compound term used to describe the entire procedure by which (often) a rather complex solution is discovered, but *generate and test* is a compound term usually limited in use to the production, by whatever means, of some *alternative* that will satisfy a particular specified condition within a solution sequence. I use them in this fashion (except for terminology such as *heuristic search*, which is the name for a specific heuristic procedure). In this discussion I am concerned with the latter process, but before proceeding, I must point out some other distinctions in terminology.

A specific heuristic called generate-and-test has close resemblances with the process I am describing. It is, however, comparatively specific or confined in its procedure, and therefore rigorous in its meaning—more so than I wish to be in the present description. I quote descriptions of this heuristic procedure and then extend the discussion to the description of a broader process, parts of which are not contained within generate-and-test.

Newell (1969, p. 377) notes that generate-and-test

is the weak method par excellence. All that must be given is a way to generate possible candidates for solution plus a way to test whether they are indeed solutions. . . . A generator is a process that takes information specifying a set and produces elements of that set one by one. . . . Test is a process that determines whether some condition or some predicate is true of its input and behaves differently as a result. Two different outputs are possible: satisfied (+) and unsatisfied (−)

Charles Eastman (1970, p. 141) says of this same method,

The simplest (and most naive) search strategy is named in the problem solving literature as generate-and-test. Essentially, generate-and-test involves trying every possible alternative until one is found that is satisfactory.

He claims that generate-and-test is different from simple trial and error because it is structured to produce sequentially the total set of alternatives. It is a naive procedure because there is no feedback from the test phase to the generate phase.

I have used the generate-and-test heuristic to begin this article because it contains within it the two essential components in a process for supplying elements for a specified class of objects. There must be

3.4.10.4

some way to propose candidates and some way to determine whether or not a candidate is a member of the desired class—whether it has the required characteristics or attributes. There are various methods for proposing candidates, of which the weakest and most tedious is the one in the generate-and-test heuristic. If other methods are examined, it is useful to consider what occurs in the problem solver's thought processes when he recognizes a potential candidate in a generation (or in a searching) process.

Notice two kinds of criteria: one defines membership in a specified set—the criteria by which a candidate is proposed for testing; the other defines membership in another set—the criteria for acceptable candidates—which form the testing criteria for the candidates generated. The weakness or strength (in terms of ability to produce successful candidates) of a particular method depends on the degree to which testing criteria are used to modify the generation criteria. There are three such combinations of use:

1. The generation criteria are used alone (as in generate-and-test); typically, such a usage then depends on a comprehensive generation of candidates.

2. The generation criteria are modified by the testing criteria as the generation of candidates proceeds. This method has a learning process incorporated in its procedures.

3. The testing criteria become part of the generation criteria, and no orderly procedure is discernible.

When the generation criteria are used alone, there are several methods for assuring a "comprehensive" generation of candidates:

1. **Hierarchical Partitioning.** This is the best known of the comprehensive methods and the one used in heuristic search.

2. **Matrix Display.** A variation on hierarchical partitioning that is useful when there are few branching points (and thus few dimensions to the matrix) but a relatively large number of different branches attached to each branching point (and thus a number of different states for each dimension that then produce a large number of cells for each pair of dimensions).

3. **One-by-One Extraction.** This method has only a spurious comprehensiveness, since in a one-by-one extraction from a universe of discourse, the last term in the list must be a remainder, or miscellaneous term that includes all the other elements not yet extracted.

4. **Sociocultural Accretion.** A half-humorous designation for a serious method of generating a list of candidates; it is based on the known typological structuring in a professional or disciplinary area.

The list is based on the conventional knowledge of the discipline and grows or shrinks over time as better experience is gained. Where the other methods are logical in their generation, this method is practical and pragmatic.

When the generation criteria are modified by feedback from the testing criteria, the comprehensiveness of candidate generation is modified by strategic considerations. In the heuristic search of a search "tree" there are pruning strategies known as "depth-first" and "breadth-first" strategies (Newell, 1969, pp. 386-387). The basic assumption in a feedback on the search process is that good candidates do not occur randomly in the search space but instead are grouped together. With that as an assumption, a generated candidate with some of the testing criteria positive could be assumed to be a guide to where to look or how to generate other candidates with even better qualities (Miller, Galanter, and Pribram, 1960, p. 190).

When the testing criteria are made part of the generation criteria, there is not an orderly process in the same sense as in the procedures above. When generation and testing criteria are simultaneous, the process is essentially intuitive, since the problem solver does not know what part of the procedure generated the candidate. Despite this a number of recorded heuristic procedures can assist in such a generation. Perhaps the most nearly comprehensive list is that by Abraham Moles (1957, pp. 53-130), concerned with the heuristics of scientific discovery. Moles groups twenty-one methods under three headings: theory-related, structural, and ideal methods. He includes methods of discovery (which he has drawn from the history of science) such as the method of mixing two theories, that of transference (applying a theory where it was not intended to be applied), that of recodification, that of different representations, and that of aesthetic judgment.* An equivalent development of heuristic discovery methods for problem solving in design would probably be of major service in the development of design.

Examination of the *insights* that result from an intuitive generation-testing procedure was among the earliest investigations in problem solving by the Gestalt psychologists. The work by Karl Duncker, first published in 1935 (Duncker, 1972), demonstrated the relationship between functional fixity and the ability to adapt an object to a required (other) function. Before the object could be used for a new function, it had first to be disassociated from its original function. This work has been confirmed and extended several times over. Lewin (1964, p. 278 and p. 280) makes a similar observation about the plasticity of meaning that is a requisite for the substitution of one activity for another.

*The titles of these methods are a free translation from Moles's titles in the French.

3.4.10.4   Bruner (1968) has probably developed the most careful explanation of this process of recognition. He discusses a group of mechanisms that mediate perceptual readiness—that affect directly the ability individuals have in perceiving objects for which they are "searching" and for which they have "testing" criteria. I put quotes around these words because this is a more formal language than was used in Bruner's article; I do so also to indicate the relation to our own subject. There are four mechanisms (Bruner, 1968, p. 45): (1) grouping and integrating, (2) access ordering, (3) match-mismatch signaling, and (4) gating.

It is possible to interpret Bruner's discussion of each as though they were responses to the following four questions:

1. *How are perception processes affected by the individual's learned expectations concerning typical object "behavior?"*

Bruner points out (1968, pp. 645-646) that a person acts with an expectation of "identity conservation or object constancy" (Bruner, 1968, p. 145). He holds that the individual has a learned record of the likely transitions and contingencies of the environment. He has so learned to treat events as nonindependent over time that he is strongly inclined to interpret random sequences of events as governed by dependent probabilities. Finally he biases his estimates of event likelihood in terms of his desires and fears, despite what an unbiased view might cause him to expect.

2. *How does the strength of a person's motivation in searching for an object and his estimate of the likelihood of finding that object affect his ability to perceive that object?*

Bruner notes (1968, p. 646),

the threshold of recognition for stimuli presented by visual, auditory, or other means is not only a function of the time, intensity, or "fittingness" of the stimulus input, but also varies massively as a function of the number of alternatives for which the perceiver is set. The size of the expected array . . . increases the identification threshold for any item in the array.

In other words the more a person expects to see an object, the more likely he is to identify the object when he sees it. Bruner says further (1968, p. 646),

where one and only one hypothesis is operative with no competing alternatives, it tends to be more readily confirmable.

A person's perception capability for any single category of object is reduced according to the increased number of different categories he is trying to recognize.

3. *How does the precision required in matching an object to a set of specifications affect a person's perception process?*

A person can be set in his perception processes for an all-or-none matching or for a graded matching. In a graded matching he can measure how closely a given input fulfills the specification (Bruner, 1968, p. 648),

> . . . either by indicating how many attributes the object has in common with the specification, or by indicating how far off the mark on any given attribute dimension a given input is.

On the basis of such a first view it is possible for him to increase his sensitivity if an object is within a given distance of specification or to decrease sensitivity if the object is beyond a certain distance from specification. In sequence (Bruner, 1968, p. 648) a person is open and registers on as many cues as possible, then he limits his search to confirming cues, finally with a definite placement he suspends search and even normalizes deviations from specification. A person engages in what Heider (1958) has called "leveling" or "sharpening."

4. *How do automatic filtering processes within the senses themselves affect perception?*

Bruner reports (1968, p. 649) a growing body of evidence that there are "gating" mechanisms within the sensory receptors that are strongly affected by such things as attention and set, so that a person does not, indeed, see a thing when his attention is strongly directed to other important matters within the visual field.

Evidently, in a generation and testing procedure, testing consists of matching a candidate with a set of specifications. In a description of the *match* heuristic Newell (1969, pp. 380-382) confirms in operational terms the material I have presented above from Bruner. Newell states that, for a match procedure to occur, the objects or expressions generated have to be able to be compared part by part. He says (Newell, 1969, p. 382):

> . . . generation occurs on the parts of the expressions, and when parts fail to correspond it is possible to make a local decision on what modifying operation is necessary (though perhaps not sufficient) for the two expressions to become equal.

In the *match* heuristic Newell is concerned with matching two equivalent expressions; presumably one such expression could be a specification and the other a potential member of the specified set.

If a problem solver has been able to derive a set of specifications for a problem solution component at whatever level, he should not forget that the component is also a part of a larger whole; it is the

3.4.10.4

supply output of the stage under consideration and the demand input of the next stage; it is part of the total information state at that stage of solution. Because it is part of a larger whole, there are possibilities for cross-checking and comparison.

A statement by K. J. W. Craik (1943, p. 113) on the ability to use facts in research applies equally well to problem solution. He remarks;

> . . . a small group of known facts gives rise to an enormous number of hypothetical and actual combinations, by whose agreement with each other the first observations of the facts and the hypothesis may be checked. Thus relations breed relations, as it were, and the further consistency of the system and its agreement with experiment gives a magnified view of the truth or falsity of the theory.

The generation of components must survive not only the particular specification by which they were tested but also their placement within the larger context of the total problem state or solution. I deal with that subject in the discussion of the solution search and selection process that follows.

REFERENCES

Bruner, Jerome S., "On Perceptual Readiness," in Haber, Ralph Norman, Ed., *Contemporary Theory and Research in Visual Perception,* Holt, Rinehart & Winston, New York, 1968.

Craik, K. J. W., *The Nature of Explanation,* Cambridge University Press, Cambridge, England, 1943.

Duncker, Karl, *On Problem Solving,* Greenwood Press, Westport, Conn., 1972.

Eastman, Charles M., "Problem Solving Strategies in Design," in Sanoff, Henry, and Sidney Cohn, Eds., *EDRA 1: Proceedings of the 1st annual Environmental Design Research Association Conference,* no publisher named, 1970.

Heider, Fritz, *The Psychology of Interpersonal Relations,* Wiley, New York, 1958.

Lewin, Kurt, "Behavior and Development as a Function of the Total Situation," in Cartwright, Dorwin, Ed., *Kurt Lewin: Field Theory in Social Science,* Harper & Row, New York, 1964.

Miller, George A., E. Galanter, and K. Pribram, *Plans and the Structure of Behavior,* Henry Holt, New York, 1960.

Moles, Abraham A., *La Creation Scientifique,* Rene Kister, Geneva, 1957.

Newell, Allen, "Heuristic Programming: Ill-Formed Problems," in Aronofsky, Julius, Ed., *Progress in Operations Research,* Vol. 3, Wiley, New York, 1969.

3.4.10.5 Search and Selection

Whereas there are a number of *search* strategies, there are two kinds of criteria by which the problem solver can *select* a solution. He can *satisfice*, choosing

I have not attempted to record throughout this discussion the manner in which the *image* that the problem solver has of both the desired object (or solution state) and of the available object (or problem state) has guided his overall process through problem solution; instead, in the present discussions, I have attempted to focus on the logical sequences and decompositions that occur as the problem is

the first solution to satisfy all criteria, or he can *optimize*, choosing the best of several adequate
solutions. In optimizing, the problem solver might use a hill-climb-
ing or a parallel-development
strategy.

solved. Selection depends, of course, not only on an image of both of
those states, but also on the self-image of the problem solver; choice
involves, to some degree, an identification between the person making
the choice and the thing being chosen (see discussion in Section 3.6).

Rather than expand on that subject here, I wish only to acknowl-
edge that the subject exists and to mention its relation to the derived
demand statement that governs a significant part of selection. I wish
also to mention briefly what some components of the demand statement are.

Depending on the broad motives of the problem solver (and of any
client he might have) and on the needs that generated the problem
statement, the demand statement can be extremely narrow, limited
(for example) to some mathematical quantity, or extremely broad,
encompassing the description of an entire environment and affecting
the future life-style of the problem solver and his client. In dealing
with an entire set of environmental objects and actions affected by
those objects, it is impossible to escape making decisions: (1) that
produce certain *functional* capabilities, (2) that place objects in some
kind of perceived *order* with each other, (3) that select objects producing particular emotional *affects* in persons perceiving them, and
(4) that select object forms having specific *symbolic* and referential
powers. Whether the designer thinks about each of these matters consciously or not, his decisions produce objects having values definable
under each of these four categories: symbol, order, function, and
affect. Although he tends to center his efforts in the functional area,
he is also making decisions along those other conceptual dimensions
as well. Mayall (1966, pp. 39 ff.) has commented on the necessarily
broad scope of consideration in design, using approximately similar
categories.

Without my going into further detail about the content of demand
statements, how does the logical organization of selection proceed? I
have been describing a solution process moving through a number of
phases that are more and more specific and connected with each other
by a means-ends logic. In speaking of an overall *design* process involving different sequential steps, Marvin Manheim (1964, p. 15) says:

. . . in each of these operations two basically different kinds of activities take
place. The first kind of activity is the generating of alternative actions. We will
call this generation activity SEARCH. The second kind of activity is the choosing of one from among the alternatives that were generated previously. We will
call this choosing activity SELECTION.

Manheim observes (1964, p. 16) that, although the two activities are
similar in each step or operation, they are also different; as the designer
proceeds through the steps, his concern is with greater precision of
specification and detail. Where the designer is concerned only with a
single step in a sequential process, he is concerned with the total

design or decision at that step. By contrast with generation and testing, which was concerned with the generation of an element within a larger context, search and selection is concerned with the total interrelated statement or solution of which that element is part (Manheim, 1964, p. 15).

All that has been said about generation can also be said about searching; it can follow an orderly, comprehensive process like *heuristic search* or an intuitive procedure. Any differences are due to the integrative or assembled character of the object of search. Several techniques have been reported in the literature: *buildup* is an element-by-element addition to a partly assembled solution object (Eastman, 1972, pp. 79-87); "*planning*" is a preliminary assembly of a group of compatible elements—afterward dealt with as an element-like sub-assembly (Eastman, 1970, p. 145); "backtracking" occurs with both of these processes.

Whereas the testing procedure applied to a potential solution element was a relatively simple matching with a set of specifications, the selection procedure applied to a potential solution complex made up of a number of elements is more complex. A number of matters must be examined. The questions that follow are based on part of a query list by Honey (1969, p. 1390):

1. Are all the requirements listed in the demand statement satisfied? This is the closest to the matching process described in the previous section. But where matching was concerned with the characteristics of a single element, this selection is concerned with whether all such characteristics are supplied. Where the testing of a single element by matching was concerned with whether the necessary characteristics exist for each element, selection is also concerned with whether there are sufficient characteristics supplied across all the elements. These various characteristics are generated by a means-ends procedure.

2. Are all the subsolutions (devised according to available supply systems) compatible and complementary? From the discussion of problem and solution decomposition it is clear that the two forms of decomposition are not in a one-to-one relationship; for that reason, even if the problem is decomposed into subproblems, there is no guarantee, even when all the adduced criteria are satisfied, that the subsolutions are compatible with each other; the subsolutions are decomposed along different lines from the subproblems.

3. Are the subsolutions and the total solution compatible with the elements of the problem that were factored out? I indicated that not all components of a problem and its potential solution are within the sphere of control of the problem solver (there are context variables as well as decision variables); these components do

not, however, simply disappear; instead they must influence the solution finally selected. Do they do so, and is the proposed solution compatible with the state of those variable that were factored out? If a proposed solution passes these several selection procedures, then it can be seen to be a solution to the stated problem. The question remains about how good a solution it is. Let me address that question briefly.

A simple but useful contribution made by decision theory is the establishment of a relation between the quality of a solution and the cost in obtaining it. A rule usefully followed is to stop effort to improve a solution when the cost of making an improvement equals or exceeds the savings of the improvement (this on the assumption that all such costs and savings can be measured). One example of such a measurement appears in Chernoff and Moses (1967, p. 235); they discuss the question of the quality of data that an experimenter should have:

A good choice must balance the cost of acquiring additional data against the utility of having the extra information.

Procedures of problem solving must balance the quality of solution against the cost of improving a solution already obtained. Simon suggests (1957, p. 261) that most problem solvers engage in *satisficing* behavior rather than in *optimizing* behavior. This must undoubtedly be more true where the problem solver cannot demonstrate the value of cost savings in a solution improvement and knows all too well what his costs are in making the solution improvement. Where *optimization* is the effort to achieve a "best" solution that maximizes or minimizes specific variables, *satisficing* is accepting the first solution that satisfies all the problem requirements.

Where a problem solution requires optimization, the problem solver has two major strategies open. He can generate a series of alternate solutions that can be compared as total configurations; the costs in developing such complete alternatives are undoubtedly high, but in certain circumstances there are advantages in being able to start from a completely new set of solution generations. By contrast the problem solver can engage in a solution process called "hill climbing;" this process holds the best total solution so far achieved until some modification of a solution component produces an improvement; that modification then becomes part of the revised total solution (Newell, 1969, pp. 382-383). The advantage of this process is its relatively lower cost; its disadvantage is that the problem solver often has no way to retrieve an earlier state for comparison with a later state—individual improvements in components might not improve a total solution mix. The fact is that transitivity often does not hold across multiple comparisons of total solutions. In addition to these difficulties the problem solver does not have a criterion for when hill climbing should stop.

3.4.10.5
An additional complexity is introduced for both of these methods by the thought that a solution conceived at a more specific or concrete level than its problem statement cannot by any organized process develop a "determinate" solution. Even though the problem solver develops an extremely well-articulated specification of the attributes of a subsolution class, if there is more than one member of the class, he does not have a criterion of choice. He might choose arbitrarily, or he might appeal to "client authority" by a question phrased in the following manner, "Is this solution an example of what you meant when you said. . . ?"

REFERENCES

Chernoff, Herman, and L. E. Moses, *Elementary Decision Theory,* Wiley, New York, 1967.

Eastman, Charles M., "Problem Solving Strategies in Design," in Sanoff, Henry, and S. Cohn, Eds., *EDRA 1: Proceedings of the 1st annual Environmental Design Research Association Conference,* no publisher named, 1970.

Eastman, Charles M., "Logical Methods of Building Design: A Synthesis and Review," *DMG-DRS Journal: Design Research and Methods,* **6**(3), July-September 1972.

Honey, C. R., "Information Flow in Architectural Design," *The Architect's Journal,* London, May 21, 1969.

Mayall, W. H., "Design and Human Satisfaction," in Gregory, S. A., Ed., *The Design Method,* Butterworths, London, 1966.

Manheim, Marvin Lee, "Highway Route Location as a Hierarchically Structured Sequential Decision Process," unupublished doctoral dissertation, Department of Civil Engineering, M.I.T., May 15, 1964.

Newell, Allen, "Heuristic Programming: Ill-Formed Problems," in Aronofsky, Julius, Ed., *Progress in Operations Research,* Vol. 3, Wiley, New York, 1969.

Simon, Herbert A., *Models of Man: Social and Rational,* Wiley, New York, 1957.

3.5 THE INFLUENCE OF METHODS AND SEQUENCE

Because design is a sequential process, and because design solution is always bound by a time limit, what the designer does in what sequence becomes very important.

Because problem solving in design is sequential, and because the achievement of a design solution is invariably bound by time limits, what the designer does in what sequence becomes very important. The professional designer (and the student designer also) must choose his process with care. He cannot always back up for another try; the time at his disposal might not permit it.

Although most solution processes are bound either by time or by the cost of time, the design process seems to be especially so bound. It may be because the process is so strongly sequential, because the process develops so much and such specific detail, or because the product of design is so concrete that time appears to be so influential. Undoubtedly, when other persons and their money investments wait upon the designer's decision, there are strong reasons why the designer must execute his decisions with time as a major concern.

Throughout the remembered history of architectural education, severe time limits have had to be put on execution of the design problem. One reason is fairly obvious. The student designer could study a particular architectural problem for a longer time than would be useful. He could alternate and waver in his decision between several nearly equal solutions. He could elaborate the detail in which he studied his design and executed his presentation without reasonable limit. Placing time limits on his study forces his decisions and forces his learning of speedy decisions.

The deadline for the delivery of a complete presentation has been in architectural education for many years, and the last-minute completion of work by the designer has existed just as long. The nineteenth and early twentieth century *Ecole de beaux arts* gave architectural education a term for describing this event.

Students of the *Ecole de beaux arts* worked in studios under independent master architects all over the city of Paris (and indeed all over France). But their design projects were all brought together in a central gallery for judging. The drawings were in ink and were extremely elaborate. Washes in Chinese ink or water color were used to add tonal value. The legend is that students often had to complete these large and elaborate drawings as they were being wheeled across Paris on the carts used to collect the drawings. *En charette* (i.e., on the cart) thus came to be used as a term for the time just before a problem is due, when the student spends sleepless nights finishing his presentation. A *charette* is involvement in "overtime" work to finish according to schedule. To *charette* is to work long and late to finish.

The architectural student has been trained by this process in the importance of time in problem solution. The effect of time limits on problem solving should be remembered as an all-important factor in discussing the influence of methods and tools on the problem-solving process. Lost time is lost opportunity, and the matters I discuss next are concerned with the loss of opportunity.

3.5.1 The Sequence from General to Specific

Because design moves toward the description of a specific object, it is popularly said that design moves from the general to the specific. It is more accurate to say that design moves from an ends statement to a means statement.

A great temptation occurs in design to move very quickly into sketches that visualize the form of the building. I believe this is not particularly harmful, and it may even be greatly helpful, so long as the designer does not commit himself to any of the early sketches. It does not hurt to have some image of what he might end with, provided the image is tentative and not binding.

Harm may, however, result if the designer overcommits himself in dealing with concrete physical detail before he has made an adequate study of the program. He might waste considerable time in visual studies of building form that are useless, since they have little to do with the actual building program. A cursory review of the program will not usually produce a good plan or a good building.

A popular saying is that design moves from the general to the specific, but the information spectrum in design moves from considerations of the specific *person* or institution to the more general *purpose,* the less general *behavior,* the more general *function,* and then only to the specific *building.* Certainly as the designer moves through the spectrum, he gets closer and closer to specific building design. Moreover, as the designer moves from the words of the program, through the diagrams of the planning process, and finally into the sketches and drawings of the design process, he moves closer and closer toward the visual and the concrete. In considering only the quality of the implied solution, the earlier phases are more general than the later, but the designer should not think there are no specifics of behavior in the program statement.

The reason for the progression through the information spectrum from the person end generally toward the building (object) end is that this is the ends-means direction, and not that it is the general-specific direction. The experienced designer knows the movement is not one-directional. Instead there is movement back and forth, fitting the various means and the various ends with each other.

3.5.2 Overinvestment during the Design Process

Much design work goes awry because the designer has overinvested in the concrete detail of a proposal, in a particular proposal direction, in the process of drawing a particular proposal, or in the presentation of a particular scheme.

After a student has gained some skill in design and in the various problem-solving procedures, the greatest hazard he faces in his work may be overinvestment. He can become overinvolved in some phase or other of his work. Design, because it is based on imagining, is sometimes a very seductive process. It is similar to daydreaming. It is sometimes hard to disrupt—hard to break out of.

The designer can become overinvolved in the concrete and specific detail of his proposal. He can become intrigued by the manner in which the design would be executed in detail—working out the structure and the structural connections, when these are of no importance for the stage of the work. He may find that, for problem solution, he has overinvested his time in specific details of a part of the required design.

The designer can also become intrigued with some particular spatial phenomenon or visual experience that a particular scheme produces. For any of a number of reasons the young designer can become over-committed to one particular scheme at some expense to other possible schemes, which then do not receive equal or appropriate attention. A designer, strangely enough, can ill afford to have favorite colors, shapes, or textures, since having them can interfere with his good judgment. When the designer has overinvested time in a single scheme, he often finds himself going through elaborate contortions to *make* the scheme work. If a scheme does not work out easily and naturally, then he should probably try another scheme, whatever the advantages the first might have.

In an exactly similar fashion the designer can find that he has over-invested in the drawings he has used to develop a scheme. If he has spent a great amount of time drawing the scheme in more detail than was required before he had tried out all things in a simpler fashion, he might not have remaining time for a similar degree of development in a revised scheme. The typical error occurs when the young designer develops a plan and fails to draw the corresponding sections and elevations of the building that the plans represent. Sometimes the designer has failed to imagine major difficulties that will occur. Another typical error occurs when the designer has failed to move up and down in scale to investigate the context of his design and its components. Unless he has had considerable prior experience, it is not easy to foresee the problems that occur in the detail of the rooms in a building without some cursory development of those rooms. In a similar fashion the designer must try how the building works on its site. He must do both of these things quickly, just to assure himself that things *can* work before continuing the development of an overall plan. If he gets trapped in developing room detail, that is just as bad as failing to investigate room detail at all.

These overinvestments can occur in a great many forms. He can become intrigued with the quality of a drawing or with the manner of its delineation. He can even worry about wasting the paper the drawings are on. It is probably correct that, the more experienced the designer, the more likely he is to use a great amount of paper in trying out schemes—that he abandons. The skilled designer learns to use the relatively inexpensive rolls of tissue-thin yellow tracing paper for trial sketches. Only after he has tried a number of schemes and developed one scheme in depth, but with crude drawings, is he likely to move from the inexpensive yellow paper to a better quality paper on which hard line drawings can be done. I can remember, in my own student days, having great difficulty in learning to treat the yellow sketch paper as a material to be used up, to be wasted or abandoned if the scheme did not work out. I spent too much time trying to erase and save crude sketches that were made on paper not intended to be used in that way. Interestingly enough, the same difficulty can occur in computer use. The cost of computer time can seem so relatively high that the designer can be intimidated by it. He hates to waste a resource and is unwilling to use the computer to try things until he knows clearly that they will work.

Finally the designer can overinvest in a presentation. The degree of finish of a presentation implies a great deal about how firmly committed the designer is to the scheme he is presenting. If the scheme is presented freehand in pencil, the persons viewing the drawings can judge that not a lot of time was spent in the drawings and that the designer considers them subject to change and discard. If the drawings are in ink, with a careful execution of colors and textures, and if scale trees and persons are drawn, the viewers are likely to judge that the designer is strongly committed to the finality of what he has presented. The student designer has often not learned to make his drawings imply the degree of commitment he feels for a particular scheme he is presenting. He must learn to do so.

3.5.3 The Postponement of Design Decision

Because design processes depend on a wide variety of information. design decision is usually postponed for as long as possible. More information might be found; better ideas might occur. Postponement is limited by the cost of engaging in a design decision process.

All things taken into account, putting off any decision for *as long as possible* is probably best. In any kind of important decision making, procrastination is useful. Circumstances can change. New information can appear. The person making the decision might get a new idea for a different course of action. (What is said here should be connected with what was said in 3.1 about problem severity and generality.)

If this is true then, the next important task is determining how long "as long as possible" is. Two different circumstances can be considered; they can be illustrated by the school problem and by the office circumstance. In the school problem usually a set time is allowed, and the student designer has to schedule time to work out building detail and to execute drawings; the total time allowed is arbitrary, and no costs are assigned to the time required for a solution. In the office there is not usually a direct and arbitrarily assigned deadline, but the time required for solution is important in terms of cost. One writer on decision theory suggests that the solver imagine himself solving a problem while he is sitting in a taxi with the meter running. The longer he takes, the more his solution will cost. If he can know what fee he will receive for his solution, he can compute (taking overhead and profit into account) how much time he can economically devote to it. An office does not have to make a profit from each project, but it had better function in such a way that the average performance across all its projects is profitable—and the designer must know how much time he has available for solution.

Clearly then the time spent on solution is bound on one side by an arbitrarily set or economically determined deadline and on the other by the quality of solution the designer is willing to accept. Theoretically the longer the time spent on solution, the better its quality. Practically the designer can grow stale in his work and fail to improve his solution, despite additional effort.

3.5.4 How Many Solutions?

Satisficing behavior is difficult to apply explicitly to an ill-defined problem. In design a useful alternative to satisficing is the investigation of *typical* solutions. When appropriate limits have been set, it is possible to conduct an exhaustive study of typical (or typological) possibilities.

In any complex problem-solving process it is not unusual for the solver to be satisfied with only a single solution. The phenomenon is so relatively common that it has been given a name—*satisficing*. When the solver accepts the first solution that satisfies *all his criteria*, then he has *satisficed* the problem; his behavior is known as *satisficing* behavior.

Applying this term to an ill-defined problem poses some difficulty, since "all his criteria" cannot be known in advance. The design problem, of course, has that difficulty. Nonetheless, some form of satisficing behavior occurs in design. Even though the solution criteria are often neither firm nor explicit, the designer often accepts the first solution whose mix of qualities satisfies both his explicit and implicit criteria. The designer's response to a Gestalt is undoubtedly part of his implicit criteria.

Working in direct solution then, the designer might tend to accept the satisficing solution. But also he might take other solution approaches. If he follows a typological approach, he might investigate with some care each of the "typical" solutions. If he takes an analytic approach, he might investigate each possible arrangement of the major building elements in a logically exhaustive fashion. A typological approach might cause the designer to review three or four of the most popular schemes for the kind of building he is designing. The logically exhaustive approach might require an investigation of several times that number, depending on the number of major solution variables and the number of possibilities for each variable.

At each stage in his design the designer makes a decision about the number of possibilities to weigh. Working in a preliminary stage, he might investigate a number of overall schemes but only one each at the next part breakdown. In such an early stage he might be interested only in knowing whether there is *some* workable solution at that part breakdown. Later, when an overall scheme has been determined, he might explore a number of schemes for each part. In every part the designer adjusts the character of his work to the quality of information available. In operations research there is an interesting theoretical answer to the question "How many trials?" The answer assumes that the problem solver has one solution and that by reworking the problem he can improve the solution by some amount. It assumes that compatible ways exist for measuring the cost of achieving an improved solution and of measuring the worth of the improvement. If all this holds, then the problem solver should stop work when the worth of his improvement falls below the cost of achieving the new solution that provides that improvement.

In design hardly any conditions are so exact that the necessary costs can be computed. At the same time the designer probably does make crude calculations of the sort just described, when he decides whether to accept the solution he already has or to try improving what he has by additional effort. When the designer, on finishing a floor plan, discovers a way to provide a few extra square feet of closet space, he finds himself asking whether the effort of redrawing the plan is worth the amount of improvement in the plan.

3.6 THE INFLUENCE OF EVALUATION METHODS

In design there are two components to every evaluation: a holistic evaluation on which choice is based and a confirming analytic and rational evaluation that examines qualities and performances.

As the young designer begins to learn how design works, he begins to realize that a great many different persons can put some kind of design idea onto paper but that not all are successful or even good designers. He sees other students doing the same work he is doing, and there is an attitude in every action of the faculty that some of the work is quite good and some quite bad, with others ranged between. What the student realizes is that evaluation of design is just as important as design development. Not only must he be able to develop building plans, but he must also acquire a fine judgment about which plans are better and which worse.

An ambivalence resides in design evaluation: on the one hand a rational weighing of the different qualities and performances of a design, on the other a selection of a scheme on the basis of its totality. The young designer learns very soon that the totality is not a simple sum of qualities and performances. After a while he is not surprised when a building scheme he had done that satisfies every stated requirement and that is functionally well organized, functionally sound, and reasonably economical fails to receive a high grade. He is not surprised when another scheme with fewer good qualities receives a higher grade because he agrees; although worse analytically, its total impact is better. Good apples, good flour, and good butter do not always make good Apple Brown Betty.

He thus learns two parts to evaluation: a holistic evaluation on which choice is based and a confirming analytic and rational evaluation that examines qualities and performances. He learns that the two should not contradict, but he also learns they are not the same.

As he engages in this kind of evaluation, he also learns that the evaluations he makes and the preferences he has developed are professional. As he discusses buildings with students from other areas of study, he discovers they do not like the same things he likes in a building. If he thinks much about this difference, he finds it troublesome.

If he is to design buildings for people who are not architects, should not he and his clients like similar things in a building? Why do others not have the values and preferences he has? Is it that he is more progressive, and that he must educate his clients to his own tastes? Just what is the difference?

3.6.1 Holistic Evaluation in Design

Choice is the result of a holistic process. It is not rational. Instead it recognizes and affirms that an identification exists between the person making the choice and the object chosen.

Holistic evaluation is more than the designer's response to Gestalt; all persons respond holistically to situations. Whenever a person is in a situation where he must choose, he responds holistically. He cannot both keep his cake and eat it.

Holistic evaluation is the kind of evaluation a person makes when he has to say "yes" or "no." It is not a rational choice; it is a recognition choice. Either that thing fits with him and with the way he sees himself, or it does not. I once had a client say, "I know that the building has everything that I asked for, and it works well—but it just isn't *me*." The recognition of "me" in the building proposal, whether it is a personal or an institutional "me" is vitally important for choice.

Such evaluation depends on a well-formed view of what "me" is. That, in turn, might depend on rational analyses of needs and requirements. But rational and analytic processes are not decision processes; they only contribute to an ability to make decisions. Holistic evaluation is not rational.

If measurable criteria are available ("everything I asked for"), then they can be used to confirm or deny the holistic decision, but they are not a substitute for it.

Holistic evaluation is used in many different areas of choice; it is not restricted to design. In such a different choice situation as employee selection, for example, test scores are not considered conclusive; there must be judgmental factors as well as rational weighting processes.

3.6.2 Rational Factors in Evaluation

Rational evaluation is useful as a check on holistic choice. The difficulty in rational evaluation is that there is no test for factor exhaustiveness. There is also no criterion for the importance of one factor in comparison with another.

Nothing that has been said about the importance of a holistic response should be thought to deny the importance of systematic rational methods. The point is that they are not the same.

One of the most useful practices in design is the development and maintenance of checklists of design questions. What must a building of this kind have? What past difficulties have occurred? What has worked well in the past? How big should this kind of room be? What furnishings should be used? What wall and floor finishes will stand the wear and abuse the building will generate? A record of such matters can be an invaluable aid for the designer.

Such a record can be organized in an orderly fashion to be useful to the designer in the different stages of his design and according to the different parts of the building with which he is concerned. As the designer's experience grows, and as the experience of his design firm expands, such a checklist can grow and become an essential aid to design and a major asset of the firm.

However carefully organized, and however faithfully compiled, such a list has two deficiencies. No test is available for the completeness of such a list, and no criteria have been set for the importance of each item in comparison with others. The only criterion for completeness is the experience of those who have compiled the list, and they might discover a new item for the list tomorrow. The relative importance of different items shifts according to circumstance and to the requirements of each different design project.

It is precisely because there is no test for list completeness or for the internal structuring of the list that such a rational and orderly checklist of qualities and performances is not adequate for decision. If there were a box that had in it originally every possible item of concern about a building, whether explicitly stated or not, and if a checklist were composed of the items that had been recognized and drawn out of the box, holistic evaluation would regard the remaining unrecognized reservoir of items as well as the recognized list. Holistic response is an essential part of decision because there is always an unrecognized reservoir of items.

Explicit evaluative criteria can be confirmed or denied because they are objective. Because the designer is able to articulate the criteria, he can evaluate explicitly by whether or not those criteria are satisfied. By contrast a holistic response is a subjective, nonarticulated evaluation. In the subjectivity rests a major difficulty. A subjective evaluation can also be a biased evaluation, biased in ways the designer does not recognize and cannot explain.

3.6.3 The Relation between Evaluation and Prediction

As the designer evaluates his proposal, he assumes that the client will react to the real building as he (the designer) has reacted to his proposal for the building. His assumption is probably false.

Since the architect is working for a client, he is presumed to be acting in the client's best interest and to be making evaluations and taking decisions for the client. All of his evaluation is based on the assumption (and the prediction) that the client will respond to the real building in the ways that the architect responds to his representations of the building, whether the architect is acting for an identifiable client or for some group of anonymous users.

This assumption is probably false. The architect responds differently because he has been trained and educated to respond differently.

At one level the architect knows this and is aware of the difference in his educated reactions to building form. He has been made aware of it from early in his school career. But at another level he is not aware of the difference; he assumes that his educated responses to building form have not changed his earlier "noneducated" responses but have only made them more sensitive.

Much evidence indicates that this assumption is not accurate. Instead it is very likely that his professional education has not only made his response more sensitive but also has changed the quality of his response.

3.6.4 How the Designer and His Client Are Different

To become a designer, the designer has become different from his client. He tends to perceive form rather than meaning; he tends to prefer environmental change instead of stability; he prefers an environment that *is becoming* rather than one that *has become*.

If the designer's response is different, then he should become very aware of that difference if he is to design buildings for persons not educated as designers. Examining the more obvious differences is useful.

First, the designer's training has caused him to be sensitive to form for its own sake. He learns to separate form from the meanings conventionally associated with it. Design instructors do not intentionally attempt to accomplish this separation; it is the effect of making the student sensitive to form in isolation. Where the designer sees form, the lay person typically sees past form to meaning. People do not like Colonial style or Ranch style homes for their shapes but for their meanings and associations.

Second, because the designer is not tied to the existing meanings in the environment, and because he is oriented to causing environmental change (his education teaches him to solve problems by changing the environment), he tends to be action seeking. By contrast the lay person in relation to the environment tends, on the whole, to be action avoiding. For the most part the lay person does not think naturally of solving a problem by changing the form of the environment.

Third, because of this orientation the designer is likely to take a strong interest in the process of modifying the environment. He is willing to live in an environment that is *becoming*, rather than in one that has already *become*. He tends to deal in environmental potentiality and not so much in environmental actuality. Lay persons, by contrast, are concerned with the actualized environment. In a sense it is entirely correct to say that the designer never deals (when he is working for others) with the actualized but only with the potential environment. The user (who is ordinarily a lay person) makes his own environment actual by the way he inhabits and arranges it.

Comparisons of environment preference between architects and lay persons have indicated substantial differences. Although it is difficult to know how the designer can compensate for these differences (and there are some who will argue that he should not), it is important for him to know that the differences exist and that his choices are probably not the choices a lay person would make.

I do not suggest he should not make designer kinds of choices. I do suggest that he know he is probably not choosing for his client and his building user when he does so.

3.6.5 The Technical Discussions

The technical discussions that follow are concerned with the relation between selection and prediction and between selection and personal identification with the object selected.

3.6.5.1 Selection and Prediction

When the problem solver selects a solution, he predicts that the world state of his solution will correspond with the assumptions in his solution process; that the actions he proposes will bring the outcomes he expects; and that those outcomes will have the values on which his selection is based. Accurate prediction is essential for selection.

When a solution has been developed, whether in terms of alternatives or as the result of a buildup or hill climbing process (even here there is an implicit comparison with an archetypical "alternative"), but before the solution has been decoded from the problem-solving languages or formulations of the problem solver, the selection still depends on the solution's modeling characteristics. Until a solution is selected and an action taken to effect it in the real world, the problem solver depends on prediction. What are his predictions like and how do they affect his selection?

In examining this, we can turn for help to the work in decision theory. It would be inappropriate to enter into any detail of mathematical decision theory or utility theory; there are a number of excellent works that cover that field, from the more elementary and introductory (e.g., Bross, 1965), to the more advanced and comprehensive (e.g., Ackoff, 1962; Chernoff and Moses, 1967), to the relatively abstract and theoretical (e.g., Churchman, 1961). At the same time I would neglect important aspects of selection if I failed to mention the relation that some of the basic thoughts of decision theory have to any selection process.

Decision theory regards the effect of the various actions available to the decision maker. For a list of possible actions another list is made of the possible outcomes from each action. A probability is associated with each of the outcomes and a value or desirability assigned to each. After a decision criterion is adopted, the decision maker can develop a mathematical evaluation of each outcome, and from there, of each action producing a set of outcomes (Bross, 1965, pp. 22-28). Although a number of difficulties are clearly associated with applying this procedure to any very complex solution process, comparing decision with selection will help in understanding what is implied by selection. As selection occurs, the problem solver makes a number of predictions:

1. He predicts that the context within which his solution will be developed and applied or in which his selection is made will be within a range of states assumed by his solution and by his several alternate solution.

2. He predicts that the action proposed by each of his solutions will bring certain specific changes or outcomes in that context that will vary only according to the variance in state of the context.

3. He predicts that those several outcomes will have the values on which his selection is based.

The first prediction is concerned with the accuracy of his understanding of the context variables; the second, with the accuracy of the modeling process he has used, with whether the real world of his solution execution will behave as his model world has behaved (Craik, 1943, p. 51); and the third, with the accuracy of his assessment of his own (or his client's) future needs (Kelly, 1963, pp. 103-104). The selection places these several predictions into conjunction: given a certain condition of the environment and the application of this particular solution, will that solution, at that time, best satisfy the needs he will then have?

The phrase "best satisfy" is, of course, crucial in its manner of definition; how it can be defined returns to the same question raised in decision theory by the phrase "decision criteria." A number of different decision criteria are available, and selection from among them is a problem in itself—it is, unfortunately, a regress problem that seems to have no rational solution at present. It is possible only to note that certain of the criteria are more conservative or cautious than others. The kind of criteria that exist depends on an ability to assess probabilities of outcome, and they might not be useful to the problem solver—but again, the ideas on which they are based can be useful. The basic criteria listed by Bross (1965) are:

1. Selection of the action whose most probable outcome has the highest desirability (p. 104).

2. Selection of the action that could lead to the most desirable outcome (p. 105).

3. Selection of the action that leads to the best of the least desirable outcomes (pp. 105-106).

4. Selection of the action that has the highest mathematical expectation (p. 108).

5. Selection of the action leading to the largest of the least favorable expectations (p. 109).

A *rough* correlation exists between some of these decision criteria and some of the "objectives of a strategy" for concept attainment observed by Bruner (1956, p. 54) among his experimental subjects. The objectives he describes *(numbered to correspond with the decision criteria above)* are:

1. To minimize the amount of strain on inference and memory capacity.

2. [Not pertinent here.]

3. To minimize the number of wrong categorizations.

4. To ensure the minimum number of encounters with relevant instances.

5. To ensure that a concept will be attained with certainty.

If the problem solver cannot always depend on having mathematical statements of probability to assist with his decision or selection, he clearly does need to depend on some form of prediction, since "A person's processes are psychologically channeled by the ways in which he anticipated events" (Kelly, 1963, p. 103). Again Bross is helpful. In a discussion of prediction processes he lists three methods of extrapolation:

1. Persistence prediction (Bross, 1965, p. 34).

2. Trajectory prediction (p. 35).

3. Cyclic prediction (p. 35).

He also lists two methods based on correlation:

4. Associative prediction (p. 36).

5. Analogue prediction (p. 37).

All these prediction methods are based on experience from the past. The most hazardous is the one based on analogy; it can also be seen to have the weakest base in past experience.

If extrapolation processes indicate what the more likely circumstances will be, then a conditional reasoning (If . . . ,then . . .), also based on experience, indicates what can occur in conjunction with each possible circumstance (Fischer, 1970, p. 258). Just such a conditional-reasoning posture is what describes the range of possible outcomes and their desirability in the decision theory procedure. Even if the problem solver is not able to develop probabilities of occurrence, he should be able to reason by implication from conditional statements. If he is also able to develop the range of possible conditions by some orderly process, he will have the best chance of including and dealing with the condition that actually does occur. In discussing the usefulness of various forms of hypothesis, Broadbent (1959, p. 309) suggests that, unless a person has a very high ability to guess accurately, then the most useful hypotheses are those that divide the remaining unknowns into two mutually exclusive groups. A successive procedure (like the best strategy in twenty questions) that repeats this

3.6.5.1

process through different variables will cover the various possibilities most efficiently (p. 310).

Sorokin is also helpful in discussing prediction (Sorokin, 1939, pp. 170-172); he claims that error in prediction depends on several factors and tends to be greater when the prediction is:

1. Further in the future.

2. About less universal activities.

3. About less regular activity patterns.

4. About less stable individuals.

5. About less well-known individuals.

For the regularity of activities (3) to occur, stable social and physical environments are required.

Sorokin's comment that events further in the future are more difficult to predict is the basis for the usual administrative behavior that defers decision until the last possible moment. George Kubler (1971, p. 54) says why this is so with great precision in his statement of *"The Rule of Series"*:

> Every succession may be stated in the following propositions: 1. in the course of an irreversible finite series the use of any position reduces the number of remaining positions; 2. each position in a series affords only a limited number of possibilities of action; 3. the choice of an action commits the corresponding position; 4. taking a position both defines and reduces the range of possibilities in the succeeding position.

In other terms, as a sequence of decisions is taken (or as a sequence of events occurs), the branching tree that represents the full range of possibilities (the heuristic search tree) is automatically pruned from its trunk upward in succession. As alternate possibilities become some one specific reality, fewer successive possibilities remain at each specified future time.

Despite the care a problem solver takes in selection, it is not always possible for him to foresee the result of the occurrence together of a number of less likely events. Heider indicates (1958, p. 91) that a correspondence usually holds between the capability of an individual, the difficulty of a task, and the success or failure in accomplishment of the task. When there is a departure from the typical performance within the individual's known limits, a strong tendency arises to explain that departure by "opportunity" or "luck." The problem solver is always subject to the more unlikely chance.

Prediction terminates, of course, as the solution is converted from the model, or the representations by the problem solver, into the reality engendered by action. As representations are decoded by enactment, the selection of a solution is finally placed in process of

3.6.5.1

confirmation. At this point, and unfolding throughout the action process, the three predictions, of the state of the environment, of the validity of the problem solver's model, and of his estimate of his needs, are all either confirmed or denied.

REFERENCES

Ackoff, Russell L., S. K. Gupta, and J. S. Minas, *Scientific Method: Optimizing Applied Research Decisions*, Wiley, New York, 1962.

Broadbent, D. E., *Perception and Communication*, Pergamon Press, New York, 1959.

Bross, Irwin D. J., *Design for Decision*, Free Press, New York, 1965.

Bruner, Jerome S., J. J. Goodnow, and G. A. Austin, *A Study of Thinking*, Wiley, New York, 1956.

Chernoff, Herman, and L. E. Moses, *Elementary Decision Theory*, Wiley, New York, 1967.

Churchman, C. West, *Prediction and Optimal Decision: Philosophical Issues of a Science of Values*, Prentice-Hall, Englewood Cliffs, N.J., 1961.

Craik, K. J. W., *The Nature of Explanation*, University Press, Cambridge, England, 1943.

Fischer, David Hackett, *Historian's Fallacies: Toward a Logic of Historical Thought*, Harper & Row, New York, 1970.

Heider, Fritz, *The Psychology of Interpersonal Relations*, Wiley, New York, 1958.

Kelly, George A., *A Theory of Personality*, Norton, New York, 1963.

Kubler, George, *The Shape of Time*, Yale University Press, New Haven, Conn., 1971.

Sorokin, Pitrim A., and Clarence Q. Berger, *Time-Budgets of Human Behavior*, Harvard University Press, Cambridge, Mass., 1939.

3.6.5.2 Selection as Identification

During selection a person "tries out" the different possible solutions. He selects that solution with which he can most closely identify. Identification is a *unit formation* between the person and the selected object or circumstance.

Selection, or choice, is an identification process. When the problem solver has gone carefully through his entire analytic procedure and has generated one or more solutions, the selection of one for effectuation is an identification of himself and his interests with it. This identification must take place for selection to occur, even when there has been an affirmative check that the proposed solution meets all the rational criteria noted above: (1) whether all the requirements in the demand statement are met, (2) whether all the subsolutions are compatible, and (3) whether the solution and subsolutions are compatible with those elements in the problem statement that have been factored out. Analytic selection is not the same as affirmation or choice.

For selection to occur, a person alternates between seeing himself in each one of the several future situations that correspond with the several possibilities open to him (Lewin, 1964, p. 271). Clearly the process is not essentially logical or rational. "Surely," writes Roger N. Shepard (1964, p. 277):

3.6.5.2

any optimal decision procedure should entail transitivity [A > B and B > C ⇒ A > C] of preferential choices; but it has long been recognized that just such fluctuations of weights as we have been considering in the case of multiattribute alternatives can easily lead to violations of transitivity.

Selection, according to Shepard (p. 277), is a "try out" procedure. He suggests that:

one device people use to resolve the conflict [of weighting the advantages and disadvantages of different alternatives] and to consummate the decision is to "try out" various frames of mind until they find one whose associated subjective weights give one alternative the clearest advantage over its competitors . . . the change of [attitudinal] state precedes the decision and serves to render the decision possible.

The try out of a situation implies an identification with it.

Let us look at Heider's (1958, p. 178) comments on the unit formation process. He says:

Unit forming factors particularly relevant to groupings involving persons can be seen in the following: things that are made by a person, or that are his property, belong to him. *Changes that are attributed to a person as effects of his actions also belong to him in a certain sense* [emphasis mine].

There is a tendency to associate and identify a person with his actions, with his belongings—in effect, to identify a person with his choice of actions and his selection of alternatives. By the processes of *assimilation* and *contrast* (Heider, 1958, p. 182):

we tend to have an over-all like or dislike of a person . . . the unit of the person tends to be uniformly positive or negative. This is known as the halo phenomenon.

If a tendency exists to form a view of other individuals as a unit with their persons, belongings, and actions (Heider, 1958, p. 183), the problem solver undoubtedly also forms a unit view of himself in the same manner. Selection, then, is based not only on the logical and rational analysis of the merits of an alternative, but an emotionally charged process of identification with the alternative being selected. This is so because, in selecting an action or an object, the individual incorporates it into his self-image; it becomes part of the unit that he is. In Heider's terminology he forms a unit with that selected action or that selected thing.

REFERENCES

Heider, Fritz, *The Psychology of Interpersonal Relations*, Wiley, New York, 1958.

Lewin, Kurt, "Behavior and Development as a Function of the Total Situation," in Cartwright, Dorwin, Ed., *Kurt Lewin: Field Theory in Social Science*, Harper & Row, New York, 1964.

Shepard, Roger N., "On Subjectively Optimum Selection Among Multiattribute Alternatives," in Shelly, Maynard, II, and Glenn L. Bryan, *Human Judgments and Optimality*, Wiley, New York, 1964.

4. Cooperative Problem Solving

Design is a social process. The usual design client is an institution. Design problems are so relatively complex that design can rarely be accomplished by an individual designer. The design process is a social version of the individual person's ability to visualize problem solutions.

Design is a social activity. Ordinarily design occurs in an institutional setting. It is done in collaboration with other people, for other people, and for execution by other people. The designer who works in isolation is so unusual that there is not much need for this book to be concerned with his problem.

Despite the social quality of the process, the individual designer is still important. Individuals originate design ideas, institutions do not. It is when the individual with the design idea attempts to share that idea with another person that his difficulties occur. He must find a way to communicate that idea accurately and completely.

If design is based on the use of images, and if images by themselves are private occurrences, then design is undoubtedly a socialization of the image. Design is a social version of imagination. It is a way of sharing images to agree about them.

The individual designer has his own image difficulties. He cannot be sure of what he has imagined until he has externalized his image by drawing. From this point of view the primary importance of drawings is in self-communication; from any other point of view the only importance of drawings is in communicating images to others. Clearly this is what a considerable part of design is about.

Since design is so strongly social, it is not surprising that design education is also strongly social. Although imagination on which design is based is personal and private, design is learned in a social setting, it is performed in a social setting, and its proposals are socially executed.

The typical design client is not an individual but an institution; the effective designer is a service institution.

With all these thoughts in view it becomes extremely important for the designer to be able to work in an institutional setting. He must know how to work in collaboration with other persons, in a consensual situation, and in a hierarchic setting. He must learn how to communicate his design ideas to others and how to understand their responding communications to him. He must know whether or not he has communicated accurately and whether the persons receiving his communications agree and approve. He must know how to secure their approval.

It is not unusual—in fact it is typical—for the young designer to have a high ego involvement in his work. His design ideas are precious to him, simply because they are his own. This attitude is fostered in the architectural profession by the emphasis on the architect as artist and on the designer as creative intellect. If in architecture the inclination is to give high praise to the creative designer, the same inclination in the scientific disciplines gives high praise to the intellectual "genius." Individual ability is undoubtedly of the greatest importance in many fields, but that importance must not be so emphasized that the creative designer is prevented from working capably with other persons.

The isolated, individualistic designer, with the very rare exception, does not get his work executed.

To understand how design can function in a social setting, this chapter examines it as a series of action decisions. It investigates the dependence of such decisions on the clarity of goal and the sureness of control associated with each decision. It examines the variation in decision style related to goal and control variations.

It proceeds to a review of design as a social interaction process. Design can be seen as a conflict, an advocacy, and a control process.

It then examines team efforts and individual responsibility in both a school setting and in practice. Finally it reviews the process of interaction between the architect and his client.

4.1 DESIGN AS AN ACTION DECISION

Design is concerned with decisions about future actions. Each such decision has two essential components: a goal component and a control component.

There are two components to any design decision, a goal and a control component. The designer must know what he wants to achieve and be able to accomplish the actions that will permit him to achieve it. He must be able to articulate a *goal,* to *control* events to reach that goal, to visualize and design a building (the goal), and to persuade the client, the client's bank, and interested regulatory agencies that he should execute (control) that design. As goal and control circumstances vary, the designer is forced into different styles of decision.

These requirements apply in any "action" problem, that is, whenever the problem is concerned with future events and actions that can affect those events. Design can be examined as an action problem and as a series of action decisions.

4.1.1 Action Decisions and Future Events

All action problems are about future events. They can be contrasted with management problems, which are about present events, and research problems, which are about past events.

Any action decision is future oriented; it is concerned with bringing change that will alter some future condition of the environment.

An action decision can be contrasted with management decisions, which are concerned with present circumstances and their manipulation, and with a research decision, which is concerned with understanding past circumstances.

If each of these kinds of decisions is based on a problem statement, and if the problem statement is represented by the form $A \Rightarrow B$, discussed earlier, then the three kinds of decisions and their related problems can be distinguished by the location of the present reality in the problem statement form. The research problem has its present reality in the terminal state; the management problem, in the process term; and the action problem, in the initial state. The accompanying diagram (Fig. 4.1) displays this relationship.

The design student becomes intensely aware of the distinction between action problems and other kinds. He does not continue in

ARCHITECTURE, PROBLEMS AND PURPOSES

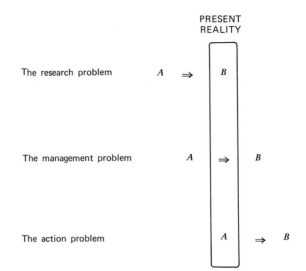

PRESENT
REALITY

The research problem A $\Rightarrow$ B

The management problem A $\Rightarrow$ B

The action problem A $\Rightarrow$ B

Figure 4.1 The placement of "present reality" in research, management, and action problems.

4.1.1

design as an interested but detached spectator of events in the way that the scientific disciplines encourage; he does not attempt to provide computable answers to familiar questions in the way that the management and engineering sciences provide; instead he is aware that he must be actively involved in determining what the future environment will be like.

Action decisions are not limited to formal problem-solving situations that require careful examination of the present condition, careful projection of need, and evaluation of ways to supply that need. Action decisions also include the most casual decisions an individual can take that are concerned with any purposive action. The simplest of such actions has the same components: awareness of the present, the existence of need or desire, and evaluation of alternative actions. These are the three terms in the problem statement form seen in a new way. Awareness of the existing external world condition is the initial state. Awareness of desired internal condition (which is a future world condition) is the terminal state. Evaluation of alternative courses of action that will convert one to the other is the process term.

The existing condition is constant. The initial state is not a variable term in a problem statement (as indicated in 2.3.6, the supply term in a design problem is manipulatable, but it includes both the existing condition and the resources that permit manipulation). By contrast the terminal state is variable, and so is the process term. The variation in these terms determines the kind of decision style available to the designer.

In an action problem the person determining the action, in our present concern the designer, must select a specific goal and must exercise control over alternative courses of action to achieve it. The variations that determine decision style are variations in the goal and in the degree of control by the designer.

4.1.2 Variation in Action Goals

Design is an action problem that is concerned with the closure of a goal. In an action problem it is important whether the goal is an end or a means to some other end. It is important whether the goal is simple or complex. These determine whether the goal is strong or weak.

Design particularizes goals. In different action settings goals are visualized with different degrees of specificity. Design is concerned with making the visualization of goals highly specific and concrete.

Although design problems can be stated in many forms, and the information used for the statement can be from any part of the information spectrum (person-purpose-behavior-function-object), the orientation in design is to convert all of that information into an object form.

In doing so, two different, basic orientations can be taken toward an action goal. First, is the goal to be sought for its own sake as an end or for the sake of something else as a means; second, is the goal to be approached according to only a few relatively simple criteria or according to multiple criteria?

In some ways the first question is artificial. The sharp distinctions that language draws are not always possible between ends and means. Any goal object might at the same time be an end itself and also a means to some other end. The question is, however, taken very seriously in design. Because design has its strong art orientation, there is some tendency to want to treat each goal as an end. Thus the strange difference might occur between the designer's seeing the goal as an end and his client's seeing it simply as a means to the achievement of other purposes.

In a similar fashion the designer might often be at variance with his client and others in his response to the second question. Because the designer is concerned with taking action to effectuate his design, he is liable to tend toward simplification (section 3.3 discussed this tendency at some length), while others with a different orientation and understanding might tend toward complication and elaboration. Interesting conflicts can sometimes occur between the designer, who requires information on which to base a decision, and the social or behavioral scientist, who is strongly aware of how little truth can exist in simple statements. The scientist dislikes simple statements because they cannot be accurate, but the designer dislikes complex statements because they provide a poor basis for decision. If the two are to work together, they have to find some way to compromise their different needs for complexity and simplicity.

With this discusssion as background it is possible to identify different levels of goal strength. If a goal is nonspecific and relatively abstract, the goal is undoubtedly weak. If, instead, the goal is specific and concrete, it could be either strong or weak. If a goal is specific but also complex, it might still be relatively weak. If specific and simple, it is more likely to be strong, but if it is also a means instead of an end, it could still be relatively weak. If specific, simple, and an end it itself, it is likely to be a very strong goal indeed.

4.1.2

A strong goal is one that is articulated in a specific way, simple enough to be easily communicated to other persons, and an end that can be sought for its own sake. By contrast a weak goal is vague and nonspecific, or if it is specific, it is so complex that it is not readily communicable, or if it is communicable, the purposes for which it is sought are so remote that they cannot be easily understood. Fig. 4.2 shows this set of relationships.

4.1.3 Variation in Action Controls

Whereas the goal is the more important consideration in design, control over the process for achieving the goal is also important. Control can be strong or weak according to who exercises the control and what criteria are used for decision.

Whereas concern with the goal of action is important in design, since design is concerned with a goal as a product, control over the actions by which that goal is achieved is also important. The concern over controls takes a somewhat different form.

The designer's control over his process might be strong or weak. His client's control also might be strong or weak. The strength of control is determined by two criteria. First, who is the action (the design decision) for? Second, according to what criteria is the action being taken?

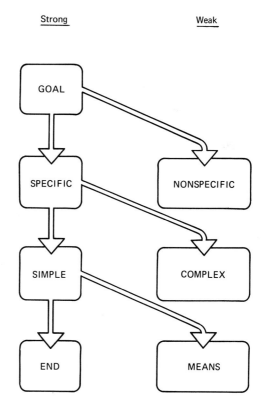

Figure 4.2 The strength of problem goals.

Every action by an individual can be seen as individually or collectively oriented. The person can be acting for himself or for some group he represents or whose values he shares. The designer almost never acts directly for himself as a person, but if the client is seen as the reference person, then the decision in design can be taken for the client individually or for some group to whom the client must respond. More usually he must respond to several groups: a board of directors, a group of stockholders, a municipality, a group of building users, and so on. Design decisions must often choose between one or more of these reference groups and the individual who has the client decision responsibility. In this sense the control decision is between the individual and the social.

Every action by an individual is also taken according to some criterion. Is that criterion a personal, subjective criterion that is not able to be communicated, or is it related to some objective criterion that can be communicated readily? The designer must face this question continuously. Because design has relied on intuitive procedures, the designer has accepted the need to act according to subjective criteria that could not easily be communicated. As he faces stronger and stronger demands for objective criteria, he must find ways to communicate what those criteria are. When he has done so, he will have begun to act according to objective criteria. It is likely that there will always be both subjective and objective criteria in design, but it is also likely that the criteria will shift more and more to favor the objective. In this sense also the control decision is between the individual and the social, and the trend appears to be favoring the social.

With this discussion as background we can define different levels of control. Strong control over process can occur, when decision is oriented toward a single individual. If it is oriented toward one or more collectives, there can still be strong control if decisions are based on objective criteria, but if the decision is oriented toward a collective, and subjective criteria are the only ones available, then control over the process will very likely be weak. Present-day design, which is oriented more and more toward a collective orientation, must be based more and more on objective criteria. Fig. 4.3 shows this group of relationships.

4.1.4 The Different Decision Styles

There are several different decision styles that are combinations of a strong or weak goal and a strong or weak control. They are determinate, strategic, open ended, and situational.

If these two variables, the *goal* and the *control*, are taken together in every combination of strength and weakness, four different decision styles are defined. These four styles, *determinate, strategic, open-ended,* and *situational* (plus a fifth—variations of them), are described below.

1. The Determinate Style. The determinate style is characterized by a strong goal and by strong control over the decision process. It is a

ARCHITECTURE, PROBLEMS AND PURPOSES

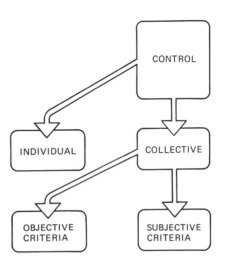

Figure 4.3 The strength of problem control.

4.1.4

style of decision for dealing with relatively simple problems wherein most of the events are predictable. It is a style for dealing with well-defined problems. As such it is useful in design only when the problem is relatively simple and highly familiar and has known answers. It is a style for dealing with a client with centralized decision authority.

2. The Strategic Style. The strategic style deals with a strong and clear goal and with a weak control. The designer has agreed with his client about what is to be achieved but not about how to accomplish it. Under a condition of weak control, there may easily be competing interests; the designer might have to meet new objections to his proposed course of actions at each new turn of events. The style is called strategic because it is the style of decision required by military action; the goal is known, but its achievement depends on an hour-by-hour response to opposing actions by the enemy. Often the designer (or the client) who has a very strong compelling idea, a "grande" design, will adopt this decision style, mustering new arguments, using new persuasive tactics to persuade those who oppose him of the importance of his idea.

3. The Open-Ended Style. This style is characterized by a strong control and capability but by a weak goal. It is a goal-seeking style. It is a style characteristic of the entrepreneurial designer. It is a style that is more interested in the process than in the product. It is also a style appropriate for long-range work dealing with large environmental change, where the decision about objectives fluctuates according to political and economic circumstance.

4. The Situational Style. This style is characterized by weak control and also by weak goals. As such it is strongly influenced by the associated attitudes toward change, which can be actively pursued or passively accepted. Change can be regarded as good or as bad. Several combinations of these attitudes can identify more detailed styles.

5. Variations in Style. Each of these styles describes the designer's style of decision as modified by his social circumstances. None of the styles is defined in a hard way. The circumstances of a problem can change, and that kind of change can modify the required decision style.

The pressures of time and of economics often produce such change. The ineffectiveness of a decision style invariably brings change. It is not at all unusual for work on a project to begin under a weak control; it is also not unusual for a weak control to be converted to a strong control to accomplish the work. The pressures of circumstance often convert a strategic to a determinate decision style and can also convert a situational to an open-ended style.

A story is told about the difficulties that occurred in efforts to situate the (then) new Treasury building during Andrew Jackson's presidency. Committees had engaged in endless discussion without coming to a decision. After months of indecision President Jackson jabbed his walking stick into the ground and said, "Put it there!"

A weak-control decision style was converted into a strong-control decision style. It is not important to the point here that Jackson's decision was probably not a good one, since the corner of the building interferes with the vista between the White House and the Capitol along Pennsylvania Avenue; what is important is the style by which the decision was made.

4.1.5 The Technical Discussions

The discussions that follow develop considerably more detail about the action decision and the various decision styles.

4.1.5.1 The Components of Action Decisions

Every action decision requires an awareness of the decision's circumstance, a motivation related to that circumstance, and an evaluation of different possible actions. Evaluation involves consideration of whom to act for, what standard to act by, and what the action is for in terms both of instrumentality and specificity.

The simplest and most general model that describes problem solving is one based on the description of the conditions requisite for taking any kind of action, however simple. According to Parsons, Shils, and others (1951, p. 5, p. 58), these conditions can be grouped broadly under three categories: cognition, cathexis, and evaluation. The actor in an action situation: (1) must have some awareness and knowledge, (2) must have some desire or other motivation, and (3) must engage in some evaluation of the alternatives open to him. It is possible, of course, for any of these three conditions to occur in a fleeting manner or to be glossed over by the actor in the urgency of his action.

These conditions are expanded by the information-processing theorists (as well as by other writers on problem solving), but the general groupings are similar, or else they can be subsumed under those three categories. Allen Newell (1969, p. 407), for example, lists recognition, information acquisition, evaluation, presentation, method identification, executive construction, and the like, as components in achieving a problem solution. Other sections have provided a more detailed description of the formal problem sequence, and I mention that sequence here only as an example and an extension of the more general *action theory.*

Although cognition, cathexis, and evaluation are the basic elements leading to an expression in action, each category is complex in itself (Parsons and Shils, 1951, p. 58). Each mode of orientation has its equivalent value mode: cognitive, appreciative, and moral (p. 59). Finally they have associated with them three kinds, or modes, of actions: instrumental, expressive, and moral action (p. 165).

Factors within the area of *evaluation* are especially important, for they deal with the *control* of action and the *goals* toward which action moves.

In an action situation, when dealing with complex problems that have some great distance between the present condition and the desired, or preferred, condition, the problem solver must consider a number of different factors that enter into a solution. There are two essential groups of factors: control and goal factors.

Control factors deal with the actor's (i. e., the problem solver's) cognition and evaluation of the problem situation, with the evaluation standards he adopts for application in the situation, and with his choice of a reference group for whom to act (Parsons and Shils, 1951, p. 248). Are his motives so strong that he has not the capacity to evaluate before he acts? Does he have to justify his actions by a set of objective standards? Does he have a constituency for whom he must act and to whom he must report?

Heider (1958, p. 126) states the problem of control, in not so concise a manner but in more detail. He gives some examples of commonly encountered motivating behavior:

1. The most obvious reason for *0* trying to do *X* is his own wish. He likes to do it; the goal in itself is attractive to him.

2. He may do *X* for the sake of some ulterior goal. Then *X,* a means to reach this goal, may be neutral or even disagreeable.

3. He may have been asked to do *X* by a friend.

4. He may do it for somebody he likes without having been asked.

5. He may do it because somebody in authority told him to do it.

6. He may do it because he thinks he ought to do it, because he feels obliged to do it.

7. He may do it because he wishes to establish or maintain a certain reputation, being helpful or courageous for example.

Heider admits that these examples are neither exhaustive nor mutually exclusive. It would appear, however, that the reasons could be sorted into the three reasons concerned with control factors that are recited by Parsons and Shils:

1. Whether to act without evaluating, out of urgency, or whether to act according to an evaluation process.

2. Whether to act by some universal (and objective) standard or by some particular (and possibly subjective) standard.

3. Whether to act by some self-orientation, or by some collective orientation (i. e., by the standards or in the interest of some reference group).

Goal factors deal with the actor's goal orientation: whether the actor is oriented toward a goal perceived as a set of qualities or toward the result of some set of achievements associated with that object, and whether the object of his orientation is seen as specific or as diffuse. Does the actor have an objective, or is he more interested in the experience of the inter-action process and the performances associated with it? Does he focus on some limited aspect of his objective, or does he respond to all of its aspects?

Polya, discussing problem solution (1962, pp. 126-127), points out that "solution" is ambiguous and that it can have several meanings. A problem solution can be: (1) the *object* of the solving process, (2) the *procedure* used in solution, (3) the *result* of the work of the solving process, or (4) the *work* itself. Polya defines clearly the difference between an object with its attributes and a group of performances by that object. He is not so clear in noting the degree of specificity of diffuseness, though *object* and *procedure* are indeed more specific than *result* and *work.*

Again the goal-related reasons cited by Parsons and Shils (although intended by them to be concerned exclusively with persons or social objects) are much clearer in their statement and help in organizing the statement by Polya:

4. Whether to act toward the object as a complex of qualities (ascription) or as a complex of performances (achievement).

5. Whether to act toward an object only in terms of some specific defined relation between them (specificity) or whether to act toward that object without reference to such a definition (diffuseness).

Only when both control and goal factors have been defined is the actor fully aware of the full implications of his actions. Whether he wants to make this set of decisions or not, he makes them, perforce, whenever he takes an action.

REFERENCES

Heider, Fritz, *The Psychology of Interpersonal Relations,* Wiley, New York, 1958.

Newell, Allen, "Heuristic Programming: Ill-Structured Problems," in Aronofsky, Julius, Ed., *Progress in Operations Research,* Vol. 3, Wiley, New York, 1969.

Parsons, Talcott, and Edward A. Shils, Eds., *Toward a General Theory of Action,* Harvard University Press, Cambridge, Mass., 1951.

Polya, George, Mathematical Discovery, Vol. 1, Wiley, New York, 1962.

4.1.5.2 Different Action Orientations

The existence of a strong goal or a strong control determines the decision style. If both control and goal are weak, the decision style is determined by attitudes toward change, whether active or passive and whether positive or negative. Combinations of these attitudes lead to additional decision styles: homeostatic, opportunistic, conservative, or revolutionary.

Problems can be described according to the main abilities the problem solver has in dealing with them. He can have varying degrees of *control* over the process and varying degrees of orientation toward a specific *goal.* Kevin Lynch has described a number of different orientations toward problem solution (Lynch, 1972, pp. 207-213).

Lynch discusses these various orientations in some detail; to assist the discussion, I supply names for the several different decision and management styles he describes.

1. Determinate:

The decision maker's perception of change will be reflected in his style of management. He may regard change as a completely controllable process, a problem to be solved, whose terminus is more important than its becoming. The variables with which he deals are few, the total course foreseen, and the objectives fixed. The process itself can be scheduled in detail or neglected as trivial. (Lynch, 1972, p. 207.)

2. Strategic:

A similar focus on the final aim, but without such a sense of control, is typical of the military model: hold steadily to a grand objective (strategy), but act today as opportunity indicates (tactics). (Lynch, 1972, p. 209.)

3. Open-ended:

There is another conceivable style that admits and enjoys change, adapts [on occasion] to poor control and prediction and to a fluidity of conditions and objectives but is also active and goal-*seeking.* Aims are set and actions devised to achieve those aims, . . .This open-ended style of management is perhaps the one most often appropriate to the dynamics, scale, cost, and long-range implications of large environmental change, where changes are complex, endless, and difficult to foresee [my emphasis] . (Lynch, 1972, P. 212.)

4. Situational:

Alternatively, there may be no final aim other than survival. The manager is a *homeostatic* device reacting to exterior change in order to restore the equilibrium or the previous state. Or he may be less conservative but equally passive: he lets major events happen and acts to seize whatever *opportunity* at the moment appears interesting and desirable, enjoying the benefits of chance. Or equally *conservative* but less passive: he exerts force to keep the world as it is, applying standard solutions and suppressing deviance. Quite in opposition, others desire change itself as an end: the *"perpetual revolution"* [my emphasis] (Lynch, 1972, p. 209.);

By careful thought on these several approaches, they can be organized into a typology along dimensions of strong or weak control and of strong or weak emphasis on objectives. When the several possible combinations between these two dimensions are developed, four dif-

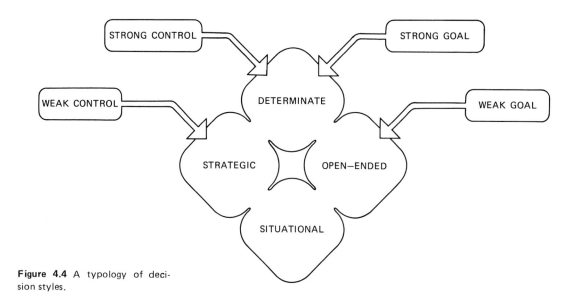

Figure 4.4 A typology of decision styles.

4.1.5.2

ferent problem-solving models are defined, each with a different set of assumptions. The models that correspond with the groupings arranged above in the quotations from Lynch have the following combinations of goal factors and control factors:

1. The *determinate* model, with strong control and strong objectives.

2. The *strategic* model, with weak control and strong objectives.

3. The *open-ended* model, with strong control and weak objectives.

4. The *situational* model, with weak control and weak objectives.

Diagrams are shown (Fig. 4.4 and 4.5) that organize these several styles along the dimensions noted. Fig. 4.4 owes some debt to a diagram used by Braybrooke and Lindblom that organizes decision by the two dimensions high or low understanding and large or incremental change (Braybrooke and Lindblom, 1963, pp. 66-67). Both diagrams also owe some debt to the importance attributed by Osgood (and referenced in Berelson and Steiner) to the dimensions strong-weak, active-passive, and good-bad (Berleson and Steiner, 1964, p. 200).

REFERENCES

Braybrooke, D., and C. Lindblom, *A Strategy of Decision,* Free Press, New York, 1963.

Berelson, Bernard, and Gary A. Steiner, *Human Behavior: An Inventory of Scientific Findings,* Harcourt Brace & World, New York, 1964.

Lynch, Kevin, *What Time is This Place?* M.I.T. Press, Cambridge, Mass., 1972.

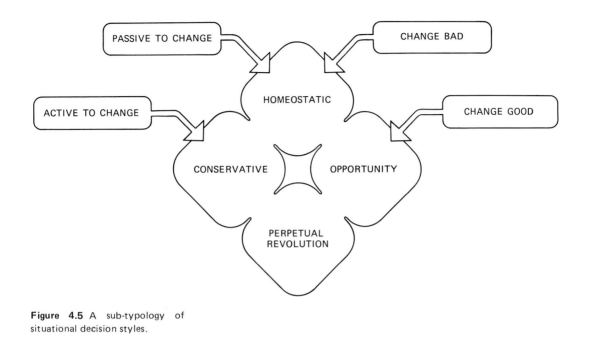

Figure 4.5 A sub-typology of situational decision styles.

4.2 SOCIAL INTERACTION IN PROBLEM SOLUTION

Because design is a social process, the different motives and assumptions that different persons bring to the process can produce conflict. Part of the design process is the resolution of that conflict.

Individuals do not have simple motives, and when they interact with other individuals having related motives, their interactions become very complicated. Each individual brings to such an interaction his own different point of view based on his own set of assumptions. Because his assumptions are different from those of the others, there is usually conflict in understanding, in motives, and in goals. A very clear model (in fact a formalized model) of this conflict is the criminal trial. The prosecution, the defense, the judge, and the jury all base their actions and arguments on different assumptions and motives. The client, the designer, and the contractor also have different motives and act on the basis of different assumptions.

The interaction that occurs in such a circumstance can be understood by reference to a description of the control process in cybernetics. The environment (or a representation of the environment) becomes a part of each individual's feedback loop. The way in which the different individuals respond to the environmental representation communicates their understanding of the situation to each other.

4.2.1 Conflict in the Problem Situation

Every choice in design is the result of balancing the attractions and repulsions of different alter-

Very few things on which a person's preferences fix are free. Each thing a person can desire probably has some cost attached to it. Any selection a designer makes, then, is made by balancing the benefits against the costs.

The idea of choice implies there is more than one thing that can be

COOPERATIVE PROBLEM SOLVING

251

4.2.2

natives. The different parties to a design decision bring views to each choice and often make the choice more difficult.

seen as attractive or repulsive. It appears that any choice is the result of balancing the attractions and repulsions of different alternatives. The simplest form a designer's choice can take is a relatively simple selection among similar building materials; in such a selection positive qualities such as durability, strength, repairability, and functional fit are balanced against negative qualities like cost, poor availability, and bad reputation of supplier. There are multiple attractants and repellants in any decision situation.

A social choice situation poses even greater difficulties. Choice comes to be affected, not just by its content, but by its circumstance as well. As individuals interact, an alternative might be attractive or repulsive, not only for itself, but also because of who favors or opposes that alternative and because of the motives attributable to him. When the designer's position is affected in this way, it might be from pettiness, but it might also be that sound judgement causes him to respond to the way that some other person is affected. Some individuals have such consistently bad motives that their favoring an alternative is reason enough for most wise persons to oppose it.

That each choice situation consists of attractants and repellants does not imply that each *social* choice is automatically a conflict situation. At the same time, given a large enough social group, some disagreement and some level of conflict are likely to exist. Human beings differ enough in their assumptions and their motives that a large group of persons is very likely to contain a person with assumptions different enough to produce some conflict. Some people have made their reputations by disagreeing in every circumstance.

4.2.2 Decomposable Problem Logics

The different formal roles that different individuals have in a design cause them to take consistently different views of each decision.

Any conflict within a situation can be seen as the application of different logical forms to the situation. These forms and the different assumptions on which they are based are most evident in situations where the forms have been institutionalized. An example is the criminal court, where different logical forms are pursued by the prosecution, the defense, the judge, and the jury. This degree of institutionalization assigns roles to different individuals and requires that they argue on the basis of different assumptions. The same information presented in a trial is then interpreted differently according to the assumptions held by the persons taking different roles.

In a similar fashion the roles of architect, owner (client), and contractor require different assumptions. The owner's assumptions are based on his needs and on the belief that no one can understand those needs better than himself. The architect's assumption is that he knows how to fit those needs with physical forms. The contractor's assumption is that he understands how physical components interact and how they can be assembled.

ARCHITECTURE, PROBLEMS AND PURPOSES

4.2.2

Sometimes other assumptions are directed at the other persons engaged in the interaction. The owner, for example, might believe that the architect does not understand him and is careless of costs; he might believe that the contractor intends to cheat him. The architect might believe that the owner does not adequately value his services and is withholding information about his true budget intention. The architect might also believe that the contractor is insensitive to his concern for the quality of the building. The contractor might see the owner as avaricious and grasping, trying to get more from him than he is willing to pay for. The contractor might see the architect as an idealistic, non-practical person who unfortunately must be humored to get the job completed. If these assumptions seem stereotypical, it is because assumptions about persons known only by their roles usually are.

The result of these different assumptions is usually some conflict. Depending on the circumstance, it might be centered in the assumptions, in the perceived motives, or in the persons who fill the different roles.

4.2.3 Social Interaction Processes

The designer communicates his intentions by different forms of notation or representation, which permit a feedback process to occur between the several parties to a decision and assist a resolution of their differences.

If these different assumptions and the different logics to which they lead are to be resolved, there must be some way in which these logics are made explicit so that the several persons who must agree can communicate readily about their differences. This communication is usually achieved by some manipualtion of the environment to which all the interacting persons can respond.

Such manipulation of the environment, or of some representation of the environment, permits the beginning of a number of feedback loops. First, the person making the representation reacts to his own message, to see whether it has taken the form he intended, Next, other persons perceiving the message react to it, expressing their satisfaction or distress, Then, what is most important, the person who made the representation is able to judge whether the reactions of the other person fulfills his expectations. Such a judgment goes beyond a positive or negative response; the quality of a response is less important than its appropriateness, which is sometimes hard to judge, but only after it is known to be appropriate is it important whether a response is positive or negative.

One way to evaluate appropriateness is by multiple participation in the environmental communication process. It is not helpful only to know that a person disagrees, but if the designer can know what the person would do instead, or if he can know why he disagrees, then both can find ways to modify the representation to overcome the disagreement. In this way the environmental representation can be a medium for overlapping feedback loops that can secure a consensual understanding.

Sometimes a communication difficulty occurs because an inappropriate notation is being used. I remember a time when I was engaged on a team problem with five other students. It seems difficult to believe, but we were able to spend an entire week arguing about the shape that an artificial lake should have—without once proposing a shape by a drawing, We were arguing with words. When a faculty member suggested that we argue with drawings rather than with words, we settled our differences within an hour or so.

Just as words were an inappropriate notation for discussing shape, drawings or diagrams would probably be inappropriate for a discussion of meanings and purposes.

4.2.4 Communication and Understanding

A person proposing a design cannot know whether his proposal is understood unless the other persons considering his proposal have restated the proposal accurately or have proposed some logical alternative to it.

Basic to any communication process is knowing whether or not communication has occurred and whether it was accurate. But even more important is knowing whether or not the understanding of the person receiving the communication corresponds with that of the person sending it.

The reproduction of a communication ensures that it was accurately received but not that it was understood. To check on understanding, the person receiving the communication must be asked to interpret, that is, to communicate a different but equivalent thing. Only when the receiver has used his own mental processes to modify it can the sender know whether his message is understood.

The person who wants an exact repetition of a message instead of an interpretation is not so much interested in understanding as in affirmation or belief. Affirmation or belief may be all that is required in a hierarchic setting, but in any other setting belief forms a poor basis for social interaction.

4.2.5 Proposals and Different Assumptions

Any proposal put forward is a hypothesis about the assumptions held by the other participants in the interaction.

Any proposal put forward in a social interaction is a hypothesis concerning the assumptions held by the other participants in the interaction. Since each proposal is a hypothesis, the proposer should expect to make a number of modifications in his proposal until the hypothesis fits with the assumptions of all the parties to the interaction.

Of the many kinds of communication failure in design, perhaps the commonest is to expect that a proposal can be immediately successful and not require modification. Many an architectural presentation has been based on a belief that clarity, specificity, and finality of representation will be persuasive in gaining full acceptance of a proposal.

Part of such belief is based on a mistaken notion of how the design process works. The designer supposes he can discover what the client's goals are and then design a building to correspond . In actuality, goals cannot be discovered, they must be proposed. Goals are too specific to be determined by any process other than proposal.

Purposes can be discovered, but generally, they are so abstract that goals cannot be directly derived from them. Any movement from the more abstract to the more concrete requires a proposal.

4.2.6 The Technical Discussions

The technical discussions go into more detail about the decomposability of logics. They also consider how a control process is a useful way to describe the communication that occurs in design between the designer and the user of an environment.

4.2.6.1 Advocacy Processes in Decision

The unitary logic within a judgmental process can be decomposed into sublogics according to a number of different assumptions.

Although Lewin discusses the complexities of multiple issues that can be in conflict in a problem situation, and his insights can be applied to methods for dealing with such conflict, this present article is based on the proposition by Churchman and Eisenberg (1964, p. 50) that the unitary logic in a judgmental process (and therefore in a problem solution process) is decomposable into sublogics. Whereas Lewin discusses the conflict that can arise in a real problem situation because of the different valence of differently desired or disaffected objects, Churchman and Eisenberg discuss the formal conflict of the courtroom, where the same established "facts" are interpreted from points of view that are different because of the different motivations of the participants.

Churchman and Eisenberg observe:

> The entire process of reaching a verdict can be described in terms of the inputs, the whole logic of the court, and the desired output. The whole logic of the court can be decomposed into the logic of the prosecution, the logic of the defense attorney, the logic of the judge, and the logic of the jury. The last may or may not be further decomposed, depending on the interests of the observer.

In terms of their proposition a case can be made in favor of a course of action, and a similar case can be mustered against it. Careful notice can be taken of what is permitted by the legal constraints on the situation, and decision can be made by weighing the case for, the case against, and the constraints on that course of action. The courtroom, with its prosecutor, defense attorney, judge, and jury, is an accurate model of many aspects of the judgmental process, and, by that, an accurate model of many aspects of the problem-solving process.

A judgment process that uses such a decomposable logic is probably superior to purely subjective opinion (Churchman and Eisenberg, 1964, p. 51). It cures many of the following deficiencies of subjective opinion: (1) ignoring possible alternatives, (2) preweighting of considered alternatives, (3) inadequate gathering of information, and (4) ignoring the full range of possible goals.

The debate "cures" the personal logic of the jury of one or more of these deficiencies. Each side of the debate makes the jury aware of the data for the pro and the data for con; each overweights the alternative it argues for; each displays the goals that support its contention.

The advocacy process of the courtroom is advantageous because there are advocates for opposing positions. Where there is an advocate for only one position, the decision, the judgmental, and the problem-solving processes all suffer.

REFERENCES

Churchman, C. West, and Herbert R. Eisenberg, "Deliberation and Judgment," in Shelly, Maynard W., II, and Glenn L. Bryan, Eds., *Human Judgments and Optimality*, Wiley, New York, 1964.

4.2.6.2 Design as a Control Process

Design can be understood in terms of a control and communication link between the designer and the user of an environment. The designer produces a potential environment; within the limits established by the designer, the user produces an effective environment.

In the introduction of their well-known paper "Elements of a Theory of Human Problem Solving," Newell, Shaw, and Simon (1958, p. 151) state what a satisfactory theory should include:

It should show how changes in the attendant conditions—both changes "inside" the problem solver and changes in the task confronting him—alter problem solving behavior.

As they begin the description of their own theory, they reinforce the concern stated above by saying:

The theory to be described here explains problem solving behavior in terms of what we shall call *information processes*. If one considers the organism to consist of effectors, receptors, and a control system for joining these, then this theory is mostly a theory of the control system.

The rest of the paper would indicate that there was no particular intent to deal with problem solving as a dynamic process (despite the comment quoted above); their task, to deal with the process even for a static situation, was formidable enough, let alone deal with any changes that might occur during the process. It was also clear, however, that for them control was the vital process.

4.2.6.2   The control system that does deal with a dynamic process is based on a feedback system. Feedback compares a signal from the the output of the organism (or system) with a standard signal generated specifically for comparison. The result of that comparison generates a signal that then modifies or maintains the output action of the organism (or system). James G. Miller (1971, pp. 293-294) explains:

> When the signals are fed back over the feedback channel in such a manner that they increase the deviation of the output from a steady state, *positive feedback* exists. When the signals are reversed, so that they decrease the deviation of the output from a steady state, it is *negative feedback.* Positive feedback alters variables and destroys their steady states. Thus it can initiate system changes.

Presumably what affects the manner in which the signals are fed back is the state of the comparison signal input, that signal generated by the organism for comparison. With this context the idea of a standard signal for comparison is not unlike Clark Hull's description (1930, p. 519) of a purposive system: *". . . the purpose mechanism shall be understood as a persisting core of sameness in the stimulus complexes throughout the successive phases of the reaction."* Stimulus-response theory in such a manner dealt with both external and internal stimuli as evoking response. It would seem that the standard signal in a feedback system is purposive.

Because of a need to provide for dynamic characteristics of behavior, and because many features of the design problem function as problem constraints, Leonard Olson (1972, p. 113) suggests that a *control process* is an appropriate model for problem-solving processes in design. He states:

> Such a model is explicitly dynamic, since the process is modeled in stages; it makes explicit feedback to the controller, or designer, concerning results of his action; and in some cases offers partial optimization of the process with respect to known objectives. Formulation of a control process model, however, requires considerable knowledge of the behavior of the total system and in particular its response over time to various values of control variables. . . . Since the complete response of the user-environment system is not known in advance, we will require a stochastic, or adaptive control process model. In other words, a static structure should be coupled with some strategy of dealing with the stochastic, dynamic response of the system.

Olson indicates that the interaction would be between the designer and the user, with the designed environment as a control and communication link between them. He thinks of the designer as producing an environmental setting that the user then manipulates within the range permitted him by the designer. This is much the same conception introduced by Herbert Gans in *People and Plans* (Gans, 1968, p. 6):

> The park proposed by the planner is only a *potential environment*; the social system and culture of the people who will use it determine to what extent the park becomes an *effective environment.*

4.2.6.2

But Olson also sees the user and his behavior as affecting the designer in an interactive control process. This interaction is illustrated by a diagram (Fig. 4.6) derived from Olson.

Clearly, if an interactive control process is to function, not only must there be feedback from the organism's own output (in comparison with the standard signal), but there must also be feedback from actual behavior in the effective environment (in comparison with the anticipated behavior in the potential environment) that affects the standard signal (and thus, the control process), maintaining a negative feedback or engendering a positive feedback. In Olson's conception, the process would be acting in the user of the environment in a similar fashion.

In commenting on such interaction, Geoffrey Vickers (1973, p. 242) reports that the behavior of human beings is subject to a number of different controls that are often in open conflict. He points out further that an understanding of control processes can contribute to theories of human motivation by providing the following insights:

1. Regularities within social systems are created, and not merely recognized, by the mutual expectations they engender.

2. These expectations create common standards; they are also maintained by the same common standards.

3. The discrimination and regulation of relationships by such standards involve the management of conflict at several levels.

4. Match signals are significant as a source of satisfaction and assurance.

The significant fact for a theory of problem solving is the circularity evident in a control process. Feedback is a loop process. Olson comments on that circularity in a designer-user context; Vickers comments on it as a broadly seen social process. Morphologies that represent design processes contain iterative loops that require the comparison of an output from the process with some standard or expected output. The result of such a comparison determines whether or not the process

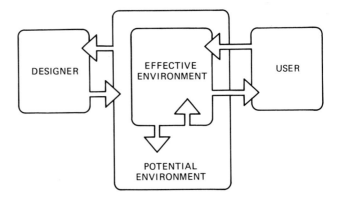

Figure 4.6 An interactive control process model of design decision. The designer-controlled variables determine the range of the user-controlled variables. (Adapted from a diagram by Olsen, 1972.

ARCHITECTURE, PROBLEMS AND PURPOSES

4.2.6.2

must be repeated to obtain a better comparison. This iteration has some elements of the control process in it.

REFERENCES

Gans, Herbert J., *People and Plans: Essays on Urban Problems and Solutions,* Basic Books, New York, 1968.

Hull Clark L., "Knowledge and Purpose as Habit Mechanisms," *Psychological Review,* **37,** 1930.

Miller, James G., "The Nature of Living Systems," *Behavioral Science,* **16**(4), July 1971.

Newell, Allen, J. C. Shaw, and H. A. Simon, "Elements of a Theory of Problem Solving," *The Psychological Review,* **65,** 1958.

Olson, Leonard, Jr., "A Model of Environmental Design," in Preiser, Wolfgang F. E., Ed., *Environmental Design Prespectives,* V.P.I., Blacksburg, Va., 1972.

Vickers, Geoffrey, "Motivation Theory: A Cybernetic Contribution," *Behavioral Science,* **18**(4), July 1973.

4.3 PROBLEM SOLUTION BY TEAMS

Design can be undertaken as a team effort. In such an effort the members of a team are usually generalists, and each can usually undertake any task that any other team member can undertake.

Walter Gropius was convinced in his later years that work in teams is essential in architectural design. He made the point repeatedly that design is too complex and requires too much information to permit an individual to work in isolation. He was so emphatic on this subject that something of a *mystique* developed about team effort. The team was thought of as simply a larger version of the generalist; it was not to contain specialists. Specialists so partitioned the work that the integration of effort that characterized architecture was lost.

The *mystique* that Gropius generated was lost many years ago. If designers work together now in teams, it is because they find it convenient and not because there is some special multiplier effect from teamwork.

At the same time it is worthwhile to consider what techniques are required for work in a design team. Teamwork does occur, often with several persons participating from different disciplines or professions, but work among these professionals does not always go well.

What is required if the members of teams are to understand each other and not duplicate each other's efforts?

4.3.1 How Teams Work

For teamwork in design to succeed, it is important for the team to work together and for it to make decisions by consensus.

For designers to work in teams, they must be in each other's physical presence. This is so because each person on the team must be aware of the work being pursued by each of the other members. It is very difficult for any member to take work away to do independently and then bring it back with the expectation that it will fit with the work by other members. In the interim the direction of the work might have changed.

The decisions taken in team design must be taken by the agreement of the entire team. Voting on decisions scarcely ever works. The difficulty is that decisions must interlock with each other, and a process that depends on voting for decision will be sure to end with decisions in contradiction.

If decisions cannot be taken by vote, the only other procedure by which the group can make a decision (without a leader or other hierarchical device) is by consensus. Unfortunately consensus is notable for the amount of time sometimes required to achieve an agreement. In view of these facts it seems likely that the only teams that work well together do so because they share a system of values and a very strong experience background. The longer a team works together, the better it is at it.

4.3.2 A concern with Both Product and Process

Successful teamwork is based, not only on the production of a product, but also on a concern with the process by which the product is achieved. Team processes are sometimes slow, but they are also usually sure.

To achieve a consensual agreement, there must be a meticulous concern with the process of achieving it. The consensual process might very likely be badly injured by the pressures of business. A strong product orientation occasionally does injustice to process.

A concern for process and for a full participation by all team members is often not compatible with a product orientation. If teamwork is to succeed, there must be persons on the team who have a continuing and careful concern for the proprieties of consensual agreement. These persons must be willing to rank the work process above production.

If teamwork is slow and its decisions unsure what are its advantages? Why is it a useful way of practicing design? It has several significant advantages:

First, the several members of the team can replace each other. Since every person on the team is supposedly familiar with the whole project, the enforced absence of one member does not seriously harm the team effort.

Second, because all the team members have had a voice in decisions, everybody on the team "owns" the project and has a stronger work motivation than he would under a hierarchical organization.

Third, the entire team has the assurance of an agreement by other professionals that the several judgments and decisions have all been sound. Several heads are not always better than one when it comes to creative effort, but they are invariably better when it comes to checking the quality of work against some established set of standards.

4.3.3 Common Difficulties in Teamwork

Difficulty can occur in teamwork when a team member tries to impose his individually achieved solution on the team. Difficulty can also occur when a team member rejects a proposal without explanation and without proposing an alternative.

Both in school and in practice some of my most vivid memories are of times when team efforts failed to work. Those memories are vivid because they were of occasions that were highly charged with emotion. It will be very worthwhile to describe two.

1. An Individual's Solution. A new student joined a team of three advanced students on a project. Program discussion was well started, but design had not begun. The new student was a brilliant and experienced designer and on the second day brought in a complete scheme for the team's consideration. The team had not yet agreed on an approach and were not ready to consider any design, much less a completely detailed one, and so they rejected the scheme with considerable criticism; they tore it apart. The original group continued their discussion, and the new student went home and prepared another scheme. The next day he presented an entirely new original scheme—and the team again tore it to pieces. Again and again the new student prepared whole schemes only to have them rejected. Gradually the original three developed their own point of view, worked out an overall approach, developed diagrams and sketches, obtained each other's agreement at each step, and proceeded to develop a complete scheme that all of them owned.

In his frustration the new student had finally removed himself from the group and had developed his own scheme, which he presented separately. He had not known how to work in an incremental way, sharing his thoughts as they developed with the other team members. The three original team members had rejected his work, in part because he was a stranger, but also in part because he had presented the work whole in a take-it-or-leave-it fashion. To have accepted one of his schemes would have been to make them his subordinates rather than his teammates.

2. How Not to Say "No!". When I was first licensed as a practitioner, I shared office space with another young architect. We were considering the possibility of a partnership and tried working together on a motel design. Since he was committed on another project, I began work on the program and then on design sketches. Whatever I tried was not acceptable to my incipient partner. When I asked why, there was no reason. He just did not like it. Would he propose something instead, so that I would have some sense of what he might like? He did not have time for that, but he did not like what I had done. After this situation had continued for a week or so, we gave up. We decided we could not work together.

If a designer is to be successful in working with other designers, if he says "No!", he must also find a way to say why.

In each of these instances the collaborative effort failed because there was not an equal participation in the design effort. In the first example one member was trying to do too much. His efforts were threatening to the other team members and they rejected his efforts. In the second example one member was unable to do anything but object. His objections were frustrating to the other member and prevented any work from being achieved.

If any one member in either of these efforts had understood the social interaction taking place, a change in that interaction might have been achieved and the collaborations made successful.

4.3.4 Team Organization

In any loosely organized non-hierarchical design effort each individual must be able to contribute to the total effort. Each participant must have access to every other participant. Responsibility must be by a focus of effort rather than by a partition of effort.

Designers are often required to work in relatively unstructured situations. An understanding of what is essential for successful collaboration can be helpful.

First, in any loosely organized, nonhierarchical design effort, each participant must be able to contribute to the total effort in each phase of development. If a group has worked together for a long enough time to develop a group identity, a strong effort by one member might not be threatening to the group. Where a group identity is not strong, then a strong individual effort can threaten. Every person in the group must have an "ownership" in the group's effort.

Each participant must have access to every other participant, and each person must be free to contribute to an area of work tentatively undertaken by another. There cannot be any partitioning of work areas or work assignments into hard territories. It is useful instead to think of a *focus* of work responsibility for each person. A focus has soft boundaries, and the work of different individuals can overlap.

The work must develop incrementally in such a way that all members of the team are participants in the work and in decisions about it. The work must proceed by persuasion and agreement; it cannot proceed well by voting.

If such collaboration is to succeed, there must be as much care for the process by which the work is accomplished as there is for the accomplishment of the work. Collaborative effort is never easy; it is often time consuming, but it is also sometimes essential.

4.4 THE PROFESSIONAL OFFICE ORGANIZATION

Most architectural design work is done within a hierarchic organiza-

Just as the designer must sometimes work in collaboration with other persons, he must also often work under the direction of other designers. Later in his career he must often guide the work of others. Just as collaboration in design has its unique difficulties, directing the design work of others has other, equal difficulties.

The greatest part of design work is done in a hierarchic organization. This is so because the architect, as a licensed professional practi-

4.4

tion. This is so because the licensed practitioner must, by law, take personal responsibility for his design decisions. He cannot delegate professional responsibility.

tioner, has personal legal responsibility for the quality of his work. If he is able to delegate some of his work for employees to do, he cannot also delegate the responsibility for the accomplishment of that work. He has a responsibility to review the quality of his employees' work to ensure that it is performed according to professional standards, and then to assume personal responsibility for that work as if it were his own. As a licensed practitioner, he is responsible, not only to his client, but also to the state for how his work affects public health, safety, and welfare.

The relationship between the architect and the client is often delicate. As he undertakes the design of a building, the architect must find a way to communicate with his clients about any degree of technical question the client wants to be concerned with. There has not been a full awareness in the design professions of the difficulty of communicating by means of drawings. The designer must become sensitive to these difficulties.

As the young designer moves through school and into his apprenticeship, he is initiated into a profession that has its own myths and its own separate culture. It is important for the designer to be aware of how he is affected by that culture.

4.4.1 Profession Responsibility

In professional practice the right to make a design decision is more a question of professional responsibleness than one of design competence.

As the young designer finishes school and moves into the professional office, he often has a difficult adjustment to make. If he has never worked in a professional office before, he must change from making his own decisions in design to having his work subject to another person's decision. Despite working for several very good architects, I disliked intensely having to submit work for their approval. A young graduate who worked in my office for a time continually forgot about decisions that I made that he disagreed with; he had to be reminded several times over to execute the decisions.

Most of this kind of behavior is ego related; indeed, it does not take into serious account the responsibilities that go with the right to make decisions. Most instruction in the schools does not deal adequately with problems of professional responsibility. It is a rather dull subject, one difficult to make interesting. This situation is unfortunate because a great part of professional practice is determined by questions of responsibility rather than of design ability.

Consider what happens when the architect wants to hire a consulting structural engineer. A first consideration is, not whether he is a brilliant structural designer, but whether he has professional liability insurance and whether he will accept financial responsibility for his work. If for some reason the structure fails, will he be able to fight the suit that will result, and does he have either a capital reserve or liability insurance that will enable him to compensate the owner for the failure?

4.4.1

When the architect uses consultants who stamp their own engineering drawings, he defers to their judgment; they accept the responsibility, and they therefore have the right to the decisions that attend that responsibility. By employing a consultant, the architect delegates both the *right* to a decision and the *responsibility* for it to the consultant. By contrast he cannot delegate either right or responsibility within his own organization. Legally he remains responsible. He might as a matter of trust and of working convenience delegate to an employee the responsibility for accomplishing a body of work, but he can never give decision right and fiscal responsibility by such a delegation. The employee is working under the professional architect's direction, and if not, they are both violating professional responsibility. The law assumes that the professional architect reviews the work of his employees in such a serious manner that he always has full responsibility for it.

4.4.2 Technical Decisions and Policy Decisions

Although the client cannot participate in every decision of the designer, his very interest in a decision makes it a policy decision. The only technical decisions are those in which the client is not interested.

One of the most difficult tasks in architectural design is the determination of critical choices. There is no way in which the client can participate in every decision of the professional; consequently the professional must save the client from trivial decisions and not usurp his right to participate in crucial ones. The judgment of what is trivial and what is crucial is sometimes difficult.

The professional has always been aware of this difficulty, but more often than not, the client was interested only in questions that had a clear and direct effect on the way he used the building. All the other questions were thought of as technical and to be left to the discretion of the architect. That balance seems to be changing. There seem to be fewer and fewer clearly technical decisions that remain within the discretion of the architect.

The trend toward greater client involvement in decisions has occured for two related reasons. First, clients are more variable in their needs than they were, and the buildings that have been designed for a "standard" client have often not been satisfactory. The client has insisted on having more say in the design of his building. Second, the architect has recognized how ill prepared he has been to understand the needs of remarkably different clients, and he has wanted more help from the client.

With this shift in client interest in design decision the architect must assume that any decision in which the client takes an interest is no longer technical. The interest of the client determines that the decision is a policy decision and thus one for the client to make.

4.4.3 The Effect of Presentation Techniques

The presentation of a proposal can disguise its quality. It is important that the proposal communicate the quality not only of its proposed product but also of its process.

Early in his school career the design student is amazed to discover the difference that appears between a project in its crude drawing stages and one in a finished presentation. What is more remarkable is that a scheme by another student that had seemed quite poorly worked out seemed reasonably good when drawn in an elegant way. The designer learns that drawings can mislead and that, if he is clever, they can actually be made to lie.

The manner in which different parts of the drawing are emphasized to communicate accurately can also be used in a different fashion to communicate inaccurately. Awkward parts of the building can be suppressed. Details in conflict with each other can be omitted. Tonal values can be used to give an apparent simplicity and clarity to circulation paths, even though the halls and lobby spaces would not have that clarity. The *entourage* of plants and people and automobiles can be used to conceal parts of the building (a friend once managed to get a cantilevered residence passed by a conservative local building board by concealing the cantilever behind a great deal of shrubbery), and so on.

When a designer has put more effort into his presentation than into his building design, his presentation effort is dubbed "eyewash." Unfortunately, more often than not, even with other experienced professionals, eyewash is successful. Sometimes, of course, an all-out presentation effort is entirely legitimate. A professional office in which I once worked was engaged in a competition for a major federal building. They were invited, paid participants in the competition, and only loose limits were set on the format of presentation. Enormous care had been taken with the building design, and an equal care was put into the presentation drawings. After the drawings had been executed in color on illustration board, the edges of the board were beveled, the beveled edge was gilded, and the drawings were taken to a local printing shop, where all the titles were set in letterpress and printed directly on the boards. The presentation reflected accurately the time and attention the building design had received. By contrast eyewash is a presentation effort that compensates for lack of effort in building design.

Another way in which a presentation can compensate for a lack of quality in the building is by what the designer says about his building. He can sometimes "talk" a good design when he is unable to execute one. I have known students who were extremely skillful in doing this. When the impact of Lou Kahn's philosophy was first being felt in the architectural schools, I observed a student begin his presentation in a seriously intended but unwitting parody of Kahn's own platform style. He was silent, apparently deep in thought. He held this reflective pose for a full three minutes before he raised his eyes to the audience to say, "I believe that this building wants to be. . . ."

In some ways the kind of formal presentation used in architectural schools is a bad form of training for serious presentation in practice. The young practitioner learns very quickly that he should do as little formal presentation as possible. The more quickly he can take the client into the back room and let him be involved in crude sketches, the more quickly he will be able to achieve an agreement about the design.

The designer can try out ideas in an early, formative stage before much work has been invested in idea development. Again in the manner of design collaboration, the client is able to participate in the development of the design in a way he cannot if he is shown only completed drawings. An incremental process of presentation is always preferable. If the client then requires an elaborate formal presentation for a public body, that can always be arranged.

4.4.4 The Architectural Profession's Values

During his career the architect becomes acculturated to his profession and acquires a consistent set of professional values.

If the architect is to perform as a professional practitioner, he must go through a number of stages that initiate him into his profession. Much of this initiation occurs in architectural school. The student takes great pride in his marathon performances. All students know which one has the record for the greatest number of sleepless nights *en charette.* I remember when one student had gone five nights without any sleep at all and when another had managed some three weeks with no more than two hours a night.

The student's survival through architectural school was considered something of an accomplishment, but to have participated fully in the student life was professional initiation. Extraordinary events are remembered and recalled when alumni meet. Stories are compared between students from different schools who are employed in the same office.

During his education (and his initiation) the student is introduced to the professional culture. He also acquires the beliefs that the profession has about itself. Some of these are true, but some are the purest myths. Whatever their truth, they form a substantial part of the self-image the profession has. Just as the doctor is inclined to think of himself as the noble, self-sacrificing healer, the architect is likely to think of himself as the liberally educated Renaissance man who is a master builder and artist.

The architect sees himself not only as a creative artist and "universal" man but also as a committed professional. It is not possible, I have heard, to be an architect only eight hours a day or forty hours a week; one must be an architect twenty-four hours a day. The architect is constantly looking at buildings and absorbing their architectural qualities. He has his sketchbook with him always to jot down design ideas he can use at some future time.

4.4.4

He does not understand architecture in any logical way that depends on words; instead, by experiencing it, he soaks it up through his skin and feels it directly in his bones. In fact he uses some group of deeper processes that are more direct and more vital than the verbal, logical processes that touch only the surface of the mind.

When he works at design, he does so by a visually presentive and integrative process that is more effective than verbal processes are. Because he is often not skilled in their use, he thinks that words are often not helpful and that they can indeed be downright treacherous. When challenged to say what the visually organized design process is based on and how it operates, the best he can offer is that it is "a way of thinking about things."

The fact is, of course, far different from the professional image and myth I have just outlined. The practitioner is typically a bright and a dedicated person well qualified in his profession. The reason the myth exists in the form it does is that there is no good, well-accepted explanation for what the architect does and how he decides what he does. Not many people believe the exact words I have used to describe the profession by its myths, but most do not have any better explanation.

Whether the school and apprenticeship experience provide a precise form of professional initiation or not, they do accomplish something else just as important. They define for the student and for the young designer what his profession is about. They cause him to ask the kind of questions architects ask and seek the kinds of answers architects seek. Whether that is a form of professional initiation, it is a form of professional acculturation and is vital to the existence of the profession.

5. Problem Formulation In Architecture

Participation in the architectural profession causes the designer to define problems in accordance with the solution processes he has learned. The professional designer has learned to solve standard problems by the use of standard solutions.

By all the experiences described in the first four chapters the young designer becomes acquainted with the architectural profession. As he completes architectural school and his professional apprenticeship, he is made aware of what architectural problems are and what architectural solutions can be. By repetition and exposure he learns what problems are brought to the practitioner's attention and what kind of solutions he can provide.

The experience of professional problem solution causes him to formalate problems in accordance with the solution processes he knows. Because he does this, clients bring him problems of that specific kind for solution. The process is circular. If the client comes to the architect for a building design, he will mistrust advice from the architect on personnel policy. The architect might have a need to know about the client's personnel policy, but if the client needs help in that area, it cannot come from his architect.

The architect bases his work on a group of professional canons. He works from an information and skill base. In fact standard solutions exist for standard problems. Since information about standard problems has not been strongly formulated, a good part of the architect's skill has been in his knowledge of standard solutions. His entire process can be assisted by better information about these standard situations.

A great part of the architect's difficulty and of the cost of his process has been that there was no standard body of material that could be referenced when he had a standard problem to solve. An obvious way to improve the architect's process is to make such standard material easily available to all practitioners. They should not have to reinvent these standard solutions each time they are needed.

When this standard body of information has been made available, it will be accompanied by a much stronger professional vocabulary. This vocabulary, or jargon, though it can be used to impress the lay person and prevent his access to the decision processes of the professional, also indicates that there is an intellectual content to the profession and that the profession actually has a set of learned ideas by which it can make decisions that the lay person cannot make. The design professions have for too long been professions of amateurs. If they knew how to design, they could not justify how they did so. The client has been able to assert, and with reason, that his judgments were equal to those of his professional advisers, and his adviser, the architect, was not able to argue otherwise.

If the architect has a special way of thinking about things, then he also has need of a way of talking about his way of thinking. The architect does have a broad way of viewing design. It is important that he maintain it, and he can do so by finding methods to explain and justify that way to those who do not understand it.

5.1 PROFESSIONAL CANONS IN ARCHITECTURE

An established profession is based on a knowledge of canon terms that describe typical problems and their typical solutions. The stronger the relation between a known problem and its known solution, the less freedom of choice the problem solver has.

When an architect has been in practice for some time, each word that describes a kind of building, room, furnishing, or a building component has a rich experience content. Because he has had considerable experience in designing these things, he knows most of the conventional ways in which they are designed. Each word evokes a series of standard solutions; in this sense these words are canonical terms. They are words that will be similarly understood and that will evoke similar groups of standard solutions across the architectural profession.

Although no formal procedure exists by which these standard solutions are tested or approved, there has apparently been some informal process by which some forms of solution are judged satisfactory and some unsatisfactory. The ones judged satisfactory are reused many times and become accepted within the profession as among the possible solutions to be taken into account.

The architectural profession has now reached a time when a need has arisen for a stronger codification and for a formal testing of these various solutions. Although work has gone forward in the formal testing of various solutions, in what is called building evaluation, no equivalent work has been done in the codification of solutions. The two are closely related. Evaluation cannot by itself contribute to a growth of knowledge in the field unless it is accompanied by a classification of what is being evaluated.

The greater the information about problems (especially about strongly structured behaviors for which the architect must design), the more likely there are to be standard solutions that will satisfy those problems. Strong knowledge of satisfactory solutions reduces the freedom of choice the designer has. In building areas where behaviors are not so strongly structured, the designer does not have strong decision criteria and consequently has greater freedom of expression.

When recorded standard solutions are available for building problems, the architect and his client can choose whether to accept the standard solution or to undertake a more original solution. When accompanying measurements of the impact of these solutions on building users have been made, the architect and his client can consciously select the degree of orderliness appropriate to their circumstance.

5.1.1 The Existence of Standard Solutions

There are well-known standard solutions to most architectural problems. A broad knowledge of possible solutions permits choice.

If an architect is concerned with the design of an elementary school, he knows the several patterns into which solutions will fall, for example, corridor plan, courtyard plan, finger plan, and open plan schools. Each has a number of possible variations according to the elements required in the plan and according to the size of the school and its site.

ARCHITECTURE, PROBLEMS AND PURPOSES

If the architect is selecting student seating for the classroom, he again chooses on the basis of available standard solutions. These solutions are not a strangling and stultifying influence on design; they are instead the very substance of design choice.

5.1.2 The Need for Better Records

Few of these solutions have been recorded in a consistent fashion.

At present no consistent record of the standard solution is available and consequently there is also no consistent evaluation of the quality of each solution. Whether one's interest is in the overall building scheme, the typical room layout, the available furnishings, or standard ways of detailing the arrangement of building components, no consistent records or comparative evaluations are available.

Some firms have undertaken a development of standard details and procedures according to their own experience, but except for building specifications, little standardization has been achieved across the entire profession. A clear need remains for profession-wide records of standard solutions.

5.1.3 Well-Recorded Solutions and Clearly Defined Problems

The best-recorded design solutions are for circumstances having clearly defined behavior requirements. Only strongly structured behavior sequences can generate clear requirements.

When full information is available about the solution appropriate to a particualr set of behaviors, those behaviors are likely to be organized and to occur in predictable patterns. Only when behavior is strongly structured in this fashion can one say what building forms will assist and support it, and only then are standard solutions available. To the degree that behavior is structured, to that same degree the architect's choice is constrained. The more the architect knows about the client's behavioral needs and what things will exactly satisfy those needs, the fewer his unconstrained choices.

The parts of the building where behavior is not so highly structured are those where the architect has greater freedom of choice, unconstrained by solutions known to serve structured behaviors.

5.1.4 The Relation between Knowledge and Choice

If design solutions are to be recorded, a distinction must be drawn between circumstances with well-defined behavior requirements, where the designer has little

One of the difficulties with practice as it now exists is that the architect cannot define what his areas of relatively unconstrained choice are and what they are not. Because no careful list of the successful solutions is on record, the architect is very unsure of his basis for decision. Typically he does not know whether he is producing a building that will be successful or not. Because no carefully organized typology of solutions and an evaluation of their use are available, the architect must choose without a basis for choice.

choice, and those with poorly defined behavior requirements,
where the designer has greater
choice.

Without adequate typologies the experienced architect has an in-adequate basis for evaluation. The less experienced architect has an inadequate basis for solution; he may spend a great amount of time in inventing schemes that are already recorded in the professional litera-ture but that are inaccessible to him. By an adequate recording pro-cedure the practitioner can have the standard solutions available to him. If for some reason he and his client judge that a standard solu-tion is not adequate, they will have a clear and strong basis for that decision. They can make a rational decision about the need for inven-tion in design.

A strong knowledge base provides a strong basis for control. A weak knowledge base prevents any possibility of control. Design needs a stronger base by the development of typologies and a record of design solutions.

5.2 THE DEVELOPMENT OF STANDARD SOLUTIONS

To organize a group of standard solutions in design, one must ad-dress the following subjects: (1) What are the recurring problems? (2) What are the available solution components? (3) What are the rules by which those components can be assembled? (4) What are the known successful solutions? (5) What is the process by which standard solutions are achieved?

To see more closely how a standardization of solutions can assist the design process, it will be helpful to examine what is required to record a group of standard solutions. Work is probably further along in the development of standard details than in any other part of building design. A description of what is required to achieve standardized details can serve as a model of the procedure and product necessary to develop a typology at any design level.

To organize a group of standard details, the following material will have to be developed: (1) a listing of the recurring problems in a build-ing that usually have to be detailed and the way these are different for different buildings, (2) a listing and organization of the available com-ponents that can be used in detail design, (3) a checklist of facts and principles affecting the way detail design is organized, (4) a record of the successful solutions to specific detail problems and the flaws in unsuccessful solutions, and (5) a description of the design and doc-umentation process by which the standard details are achieved.

The different parts of this article discuss each of these topics.

5.2.1 What are the Recurring Problems?

When larger problems are ana-lyzed, they consist of combina-tions of simpler problems that have been solved repeatedly.

In the design of buildings certain problems are encountered over and over again. Each must be solved, but each solution is not remarkably different from the solution to the other, similar problems. Every building must have a foundation. Every building must have doors that admit building users and that close out weather, or insects, or view into the building. Within severe climate zones every door must have a threshold. There are consistent ways in which walls intersect with roofs. There are accountably a large number of standard or common problems in the detail design of buildings.

Recently I worked with a group of graduate students in identifying where these problems occur in a building. To set a limit to their investigation, they studied only one building type, the elementary school. They examined a number of architects's drawings and listed the details that had been drawn. Their conclusion was that the problem sites that had to be detailed were at the intersections between major building components: walls, roofs, doors, windows, floors, foundations, and the like. It was clear that not all components intersect; a roof, for example, is not likely to intersect with a footing or foundation. But where intersections occur between these major components, ordinarily a detail is needed to show how the different components are to be joined.

To show which components intersect, the students prepared the adjoining diagram (Fig. 5.1). It is in the form of an interaction matrix that lists the major building components and those that intersect. Since each building component is given a number, the pair of numbers can be used to designate the detail of the intersection. Such a system forms a first basis for the orderly classification of construction details.

5.2.2 What are the Available Solution Components?

Information about available solution components can be organized in a way to relate to the problems these components can solve.

Although product manufacturers make a strong effort to provide information for design, the systems in use have organized the information more for the contractor than for the designer. Products have tended to be classified, not so much by their place and function in the building, as by the trade that would install the product.

Moreover, no attempt has been made until recently to provide a consistent and orderly arrangement of information about the various products. Often it is simply not possible to obtain information about costs, availability, delivery times, quantitites, pertinent dimensions, maintenance characteristics, durability, parts availability, and the like.

A need remains for information organized according to a hierarchic arrangement of components and according to the other components with which the product must fit. Where components could be used in a number of different assemblies, there is not always a close enough coordination between the different industries so that the sizes produced are compatible with each other.

To provide such information, it may be desirable to arrange construction products into "families" or systems of components, and several coordinated systems of components into a specific construction "vocabulary." The accompanying outline displays an orderly method of describing such a vocabulary (Table 5.1).

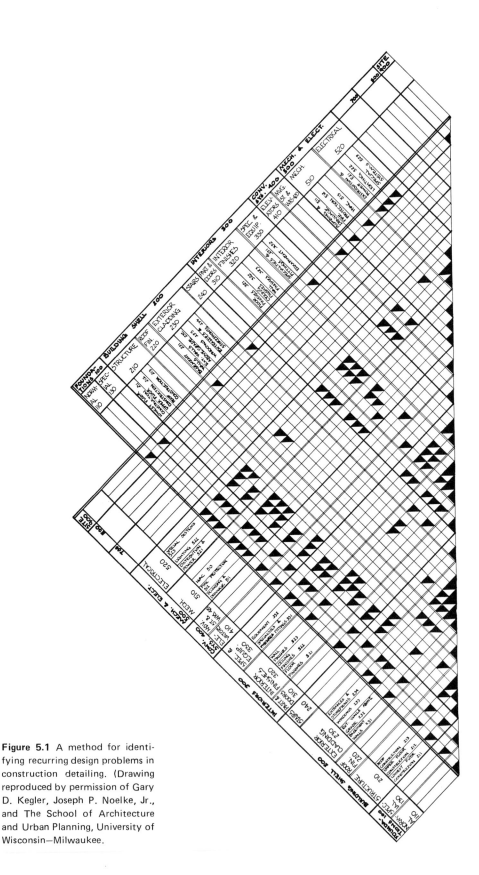

Figure 5.1 A method for identifying recurring design problems in construction detailing. (Drawing reproduced by permission of Gary D. Kegler, Joseph P. Noelke, Jr., and The School of Architecture and Urban Planning, University of Wisconsin—Milwaukee.

ARCHITECTURE, PROBLEMS AND PURPOSES

Table 5.1. Construction Vocabularies

---

1. Identification of Construction Vocabulary
   1.1 Systems Description, Standard Components
   1.2 Limits and Extent of System, Dimensions
   1.3 Special Components:
      1. Terminal conditions
      2. Junctures, connectors
      3. Joints and joining
      4. Attachments, connectors to other systems

2. Attributes and Performances of Vocabulary
   2.1 Attributes
      1. Structural properties
      2. Thermal properties
      3. Acoustical properties
      4. Optical properties
      5. Tactile properties
      6. Olfactory properties
   2.2 Performances
      1. Support
      2. Enclosure
      3. Exclusion, separation
      4. Penetration, access, control
      5. Utility circulation, delivery, collection
      6. Storage, ordering, classification
      7. Manipulation
      8. Specific operation

3. Development of Hierarchic System
   3.1 Design Unit under Consideration
      3.1.1 Component of design unit
         3.1.1.1 Subcomponent of design unit

4. Classification for Storage Retrieval
   4.1 Input
      1. Identify system in hierarchy
      2. Specify compatibility with adjacent systems and specify exposure
      3. Identify performances that must be provided
      4. Identify attributes of components that are required
   4.2 Output
      1. Systems having such attributes and performances
      2. Capability, range, and flexibility of each system
      3. Costs, availability, delivery, other specific characteristics, life
         expectancy, maintenence characteristics, hazards, installation
         characteristics, installation sequence, etc.

5.2.3 What are the Rules Affecting Relationships?

The information about assembly of components has scarcely progressed beyond the rule-of-thumb stage. That information can be organized into a set of facts and principles concerning component assembly.

The facts and principles that must affect detail design have in the past been learned as a series of pragmatic rules of thumb. A consistent or systematic body of fact or theory by which the arrangement and fitting of construction material can be undertaken, has scarcely been developed.

There are indeed principles that govern the appropriate attachment of one material to another; that govern the sequence of construction; that control the butting, or lapping, or fitting of materials; and that should affect the choice of sizes and the degree of continuity or change of materials. But because no significant body of these principles has been deduced, collected, and organized, the designer has never been able to make sure argument for the selection of one component over another in a particular situation.

The development of a body of fact, theory, and principle will have to comprehend the range of subjects shown in the following outline (Table 5.2).

Table 5.2. Facts and Principles of Construction Detailing

1. Construction Materials
   1.1 Forms of Materials: Linear, Planar, Mass
   1.2 Kinds of Materials: Mineral, Metal, Organic, etc.
   1.3 Performances of Materials
   1.4 Attributes of Materials

2. Materials Shaping
   2.1 Shaping Processes and Their Effects
   2.2 Influence of Materials Attributes
       1. Strength and cohesiveness
       2. Uniformity or homogeneity
   2.3 Influence of Size
       1. Length, area, volume relationships
       2. Handling problems vs. joint problems
       3. Size availability
       4. Grain size and density
   2.4 Influence of Shape
       1. Radius of gyration, section modulus, etc.
       2. Mass-surface relationships
   2.5 Characteristics of Linear Materials
       1. Ubiquity of linear materials
       2. Production of rectilinear forms
       3. Limitations in producing curved shapes
   2.6 Characteristics of Planar Materials
       1. Limitations on folding and bending
       2. Instability of flat surfaces of thin materials ("oil-canning")
   2.7 Characteristics of Mass Materials

3. Fitting Materials to Forms
   3.1 Space- and Surface-Filling Geometries
       1. Rectilinear, triangular, hexagonal
       2. Consistency between center and edge
       3. Relation to edge contour and unit variability
       4. Pattern continuity and unit cutting
   3.2 Units and Joints Between Units
       1. Unit standardization and joint variation
       2. Determination of joint size
   3.3 Supporting Frame and Panel Infill
       1. Structural considerations in frame size
       2. Frame continuity
       3. Controlling dimensions
   3.4 Joints Between Disparate Materials
       1. Reveal joints and painting out
       2. Cover joints
       3. Stepped cover joints

Table 5.2

3.5 Dimensional Control
  1. The sum of units and joints
  2. Modularity of units
  3. Dimensional stability
  4. Multiple unit flexibility
  5. Unit cutting

4. Influence of Manufacturing Processes
  4.1 Tooling Costs and Production Runs
  4.2 The size of markets, market stability
  4.3 Packaging
  4.4 Shipping methods and delivery times
  4.5 Quality controls

5. Assembly Processes
  5.1 Assembly Sequence
    1. Gravity and load considerations
    2. Curing times, other time periods in operations
    3. Scheduling for weather cover and enclosure
    4. Scheduling for one trip by one trade
    5. Scheduling for rough work before finish work
    6. Equipment size and opening size
    7. Order and lead times
  5.2 Fastening and Connecting Methods
    1. Types of connection: gravity, friction, pierced, bolted, etc.
    2. Replacement: disconnection and reconnection
    3. Access for repair
  5.3 Positioning and Configuring
    1. Lapping for closure against wind and water
    2. Arranging for drip
    3. Draining down and out
    4. Sealing or venting
    5. Sizing of separate parts
  5.4 Exposure Considerations
    1. Exterior ground contact
    2. Exterior
    3. Interior, dry but not heated
    4. Interior, dry and heated
    5. Interior, dry, heated, and out of reach
    6. Material incompatibility
  5.5 Finishing Processes
    1. Destruction and construction
    2. Trades interference
    3. Punch-listing
    4. Cleaning

6. Influence of the Construction Industry
  6.1 Organization of Contractors and Subcontractors
    1. Capability, capitalization, bonding
    2. Organization of trades
    3. Lines of authority and responsibility
  6.2 Organization of Materials Suppliers
    1. Franchises, dealerships
    2. Information distribution
    3. Standard specifications
    4. Organizations

7. Maintenance Considerations
  7.1 Materials Durability

Table 5.2

5.2.4 What are the Successful Solutions?

The successful solutions can be organized into systems of solution and into families of related systems.

Although no consistent, orderly subdivision of products into hierarchic arrangements has been made, there is, even within the present disarray, a grouping of products into consistent construction vocabularies. Consistent and traditional vocabularies are available in the following kinds of construction: wood frame, concrete block, post-and-beam, light steel, and precast concrete. Moreover, specific organized systems intended as complete construction vocabularies have recently been introduced. In all these consistent vocabularies, whether old or new, known successful solutions to the most commonly encountered problems are available.

Despite the existence of these successful solutions, an extraordinary amount of reinvestigation of the commonly encountered problems persists. This occurs in part because the architect has not been in the habit of thinking of standardization as a technique and in part because the detailing-by-drawing process is used to check the consistency and adequacy of treatment of the entire building design. The working drawing where details appear is often used, not just as a symbolic coded diagram of the relationship of one building part to another, but also as a pictorial representation during detail design. This double use results in a more laborious and costly representation than is required for construction.

At present no process for evaluating details exists that is sufficiently successful to set detailing standards for the profession. Beginnings have been made in that direction, but adequate criteria have not been adopted. Despite that difficulty it would still be possible to identify a number of commonly used successful solutions and accept them on a tentative basis as standard details. The successful solutions could be identified in the following ways:

1. Where a commonly recurring problem is solved by the use of standard components within a single construction materials system, a standard solution can be derived directly.

2. Where a commonly recurring problem is consistently solved by mating components from two materials systems, a standard solution can be derived that is a typical solution for the building vocabulary in question.

3. Sometimes in such a vocabulary there will be a successful solution based on a mating of components from three or more materials systems. These are probably not as frequent as the mating of two systems, but they exist.

What cannot be thought of as a standard solution in the bringing together of materials from several systems in a unique way to solve a problem that has little likelihood of recurrence.

5.2.5 What is the Design Process?

The design process can proceed in a systematic fashion. It must depend, in great part, on a method of classifying and retrieving successful pertinent solutions already achieved.

Detail design is the selection of mutually compatible components to solve some specific defined standard problem or some specific unique problem within a larger consistent design context. Given some specific problem with stated problem purposes, with defined spatial and configural limits, and with other limits or parameters stated, the step-by-step method for solution goes according to the following sequence:

1. Identify the elements of particular systems that are determined by the larger context or that have been preselected.

2. Select an element from the most pervasive or most basic system and position tentatively according to known facts and principles.

3. Provide supporting or stabilizing elements required by that placement.

4. Check for spatial compatibilities:

   (a) Is there an easy fit with the preselected elements?
   (b) Are auxiliary supporting elements reasonable?
   (c) Is there no interference with paths, continuities of other systems like plumbing, air ducts, etc.?

5. If *yes,* proceed to next most pervasive element. If *no,* revise placement until *yes* is achieved.

The most pervasive or most basic element is sometimes difficult to define; perhaps a better term might be the most constrained element, that is, the one that has the greatest number of external factors affecting its placement.

As details are developed (or where they already exist) for standard materials systems, thay can be recorded in an orderly fashion so that the designer does not have to redraw them again and again. There is no reason why the standard detail for a material system should not be referenced in the drawings the same way that federal and other standard specifications are referenced for a building. One can imagine a range of different degrees of standardization. Where the building relies only on standardized materials systems, very little special drawing would be required. Where there is considerable departure from standard systems of materials, more and more drawing of special details is required. The relationship between standardization and special detailing is shown in the accompanying diagram (Table 5.3).

What I have just described as a formal system for the development and use of standardized details is not unlike what occurs in today's architectural practice in an informal manner. That the detail internal to a system will be drawn is very unlikely; nobody is inclined to detail how one concrete block is joined to another; when not drawn, it is

Table 5.3 Relation Between Standardization and Drawing Requirements

Degree of Standardization	Drawings Required
1. The specification of a whole material system with the usual combination of elements. No variation.	1. No detailing required. The contract drawings need only reference the standard published drawings.
2. The specification of a whole material system but with variations to meet special conditions.	2. Similar to above, but drawings must be furnished to show deviations from standard conditions.
3. The specification of several material systems frequently used together and combined into a building vocabulary. No variations from usual intersections between systems.	3. No detailing required. Drawings would have to reference the systems specified and the published details that show the usual intersections between the several systems.
4. The specification of a whole vocabulary like 3, above, but with unusual intersections between the systems.	4. Reference the standard vocabulary. Draw only the unusual conditions. Note them as variances from the standard vocabularies.
5. The use of two or more standard systems not ordinarily combined into a vocabulary.	5. Reference the standard systems being used. Draw all of the intersections between standard systems.
6. No standard systems. Unique conditions and unique materials.	6. Draw everything. Use list of commonly recurring problems for required drawings.

understood to be according to the accepted practice within the industry. Details of the intersection between two systems are often taken directly form a manufacturer's literature or from a graphic standards, or else one of these sources is used as a guide for the development of a detail that will exactly supply the requirements of the situation.

5.2.6 Applications

Although this approach has gone furthest in organizing construction details, it can apply at any scale.

The considerations and procedures just described for detail design are similar to those that would be required in developing building and room typologies. There would be many differences in the kinds of constraints and considerations that would be employed, but the basic process would be similar.

Thinking about this process is important because a preponderance of design occurs informally according to this kind of pattern. Designers use prototypes as a guide to their design process. The difference between what I have described and the present process is in a matter of formality. The present design process does not rely upon formally recorded prototypes but on internalized prototypes drawn from the experiences the architect has of constructed buildings and from publications that describe constructed buildings.

These prototypes play an extremely important part in the architect's formation and statement of design problems.

5.3 A PROFESSIONAL VOCABULARY

When design process becomes more highly organized, it will develop a more highly organized professional vocabulary. The existence of such a professional "jargon" is evidence not only of the need for a specialized vocabulary but also of the existence of an intellectual content in that profession's process.

If design becomes more formally organized in the way I have described, that organization will be accompanied by a more formal and more strongly defined vocabulary. To the degree that a profession has information and insight different from that of the general public, to the same degree it has a professional vocabulary different from that of the public.

Architecture has not had as strongly different a professional vocabulary as law, medicine, or engineering, because it had considered that its basic vocabulary was visual and nonverbal. What it has failed to realize is the degree to which any visual vocabulary (if it is to be understood and under conscious intellectual control) must be accompanied by a corresponding verbal vocabulary. For these reasons the architect's statements about design sound more "amateurish" than "professional." By amateurish I do not necessarily imply that the architect's statements are inept but only that they do not seem to have a specific professional content. Not much about what the architect says causes a client to believe he has brought a substantial reservoir of professional insights and skills to his work.

5.3

I have had clients say to me that they did not see anything special about what architects do, and if they had taken the trouble to learn to draw, they could design buildings equally well. They were implying that no specific professional skill is required for design. Such a comment is unanswerable. It occurs precisely because no professional *jargon* impressive (because not understandable) to the lay person has been developed.

In ordinary conversation or writing jargon is considered undesirable; it is a perjorative term for obscure and sometimes meaningless language. I use the term here in a different and neutral sense. Professional jargon is obscure because its meanings are specialized to the profession; it is a private language because it requires considerable years of study and acquaintance to acquire. It exists because it is needed to express the specialized intellectual content the profession has.

As a design typology is developed, a series of terms will be developed with it that are precisely defined according to a professional usage. They will form a specialized professional jargon that will be evidence of an intellectual content in the architect's working process.

The architect uses now an extensive typology by which he organizes his problem statements and undertakes solutions. When he has also formalized that typology, he will have that much better a tool for problem statement and solution.

5.3.1 Participative Processes and Professional Competence

Deprofessionalizing design decision—giving greater choice to the building user—does not require less professional competence; it requires more. Participative processes will not help so much as a careful distinction by the designer between his responsibility for the "potential" environment and the user's responsibility for the "effective" environment.

Considerable discussion has occurred in the past few years about the proper role of the architect in designing for people. It has resulted from the architect's discovery of how little he has known about people's needs. One reaction to this discovery is to say the architect ought not design buildings but only assist people in designing buildings for themselves.

Much investigation has been put into the development of methods by which designers could do so. That seems to be a worthwhile effort, but it also seems to be an extraordinarily difficult thing to achieve. It requires, not a lesser but a greater degree of professional skill. Viewed offhand, a contradiction seems to exist when the exercise of fewer professional skills (because they have been delegated to the client-user) requires a higher level of professional competence. A reading of any of the literature with *participative design methods* will indicate the truth of what I have just said, because the terminology used is often more exclusive and obscure than that of the usual design method literature.

I believe very strongly in the need for the user to have a much stronger say in how his environment is organized, but I am not sure that what has been called participative design can accomplish this. A better approach may be a distinction drawn (by Herbert Gans, among others) between a potential and an actual environment.

According to this distinction the architect is responsible for the potential environment, and the clients-occupants-users are responsible for the actual environment. This has always been so to some degree or other. Difficulties have occurred because the architect has moved too far into an actualization of the environment—not leaving enough choice open to the users. If the architect makes only a potential environment, he need not worry about participative design. Even if participative design methods are used, the architect and the current and contemporaneous user run the same risk of overactualizing the environment; what will the *next* users prefer?

A potential environment is one that takes care of the basic physical factors that must be weighed in providing a tempered environment and that leaves the greatest possible choice open to the user who inhabits the environment *for the time.* A potential environment is thus likely to be a somewhat neutral, nonassertive, background environment that will not interfere with the assertiveness of the users. To say this does not imply that the buildings providing this environment are themselves necessarily neutral and nonassertive, but it does insist that the buildings provide that kind of environment at the personal level —in the immediate personal surroundings of the individuals who will inhabit them.

5.3.2 The Need for Professional Competence

Nobody can know better than a building's user *what* he needs; it is hoped that nobody can know better than the designer *how* to help the user achieve his needs.

No one can know better what is best for a person than the person himself; the client knows better than the architect what he needs. But knowing what is best is not the same as knowing how to achieve it. The fault and the guilt of the design profession spring from thinking it knows what is best at all levels of building detail. Overactualization is a result of arrogance.

Design has never been at fault when it has increased its skill in knowing how to achieve some preferred and desired result. Professionalization is in knowing how; it is not so much in knowing what.

Design must be as professional as it can possibly be to assist clients in achieving their aims. Whereas design can never be anything but a committed and a morally oriented profession, design as a professional orientation is also disinterested expertness. The greatest difficulty with architecture as with any profession is to know when its own moral point of view must prevail and when it must defer to that of others.

5.4 A WAY OF THINKING ABOUT THINGS

Design has been described as "a way of thinking about things." Although that description is nonspecific for the reasons described in this book, it can provoke thought about what the designer's way of thinking actually is.

At the Environmental Design Research Association's recent annual conference at Lawrence, Kansas, an interesting exchange occurred in one session between designers and behavioral scientists. A student designer, apparently troubled because the scientists were having more of a say in the conference than the designers were, asked why behavioral scientists were appointed to design faculties and employed as consultants to practitioners when there were no designers appointed to behavioral science faculties. After some discussion from the platform on what the behavioral scientist has to offer, one scientist asked the student what he thought the designer has to offer the behavioral scientist. After a bit of hesitation the student responded that the designer has "a way of thinking about things."

At some levels that is an extremely weak answer. I have heard it given before, and its difficulty is that it does not specify what that way of thinking is. It is nonspecific for all the reasons this book has discussed and especially because of the nonverbal orientation of the designer.

It will be extremely useful to attempt to provide some level of specificity to what that way of thinking is; it is a final element that must be considered in understanding how an architect formulates problems.

If the answer was weak, there is also some strength in the actual manner and attitudes that many architects bring to their work. The architectural profession is caught between the world of the arts and that of the sciences; as a result it suffers the disadvantage of belonging to neither and gains the benefit of an awareness of both.

5.4.1 A Humanitarian Way

A part of that way is humanitarian, concerned with conserving human life. Design consists in the application of a "tool ethic," a sequential set of criteria: (1) life support, (2) purpose, and (3) maintenance.

A great part of architecture is concerned with human life, not in the doctor's way with saving life but with conserving it (in a precautionary way). It is concerned with many of the things necessary to support human life, with providing shelter for the extraordinary range of human activities, and with public health, safety, and welfare.

During the student years these questions are addressed with an intensity sometimes difficult to bear without a release and a reaction. I remember during my own school years such an intense involvement with a redevelopment plan for a deteriorated part of a city that some antihumanitarian reactions occurred. Our class had been asked to develop a plan for rehousing the entire population of a section of the city, while providing for the development of amenities in the way of parks, open space, and lower housing densities. The requirements were contradictory, and the class was frustrated in finding how all requirements might be achieved. So while they seriously attempted to develop a policy and a plan, they also joked about a way that was sure to solve the problem by reducing the population. One group of students invented what they called a "Kiddie-Killer." All the elementary schools were to be located across major thoroughfares from the neighborhoods they were to serve, so that children had continually to cross the thoroughfare on their way to school. The thoroughfare would have a minimum speed limit of forty miles an hour, and each crossing was to be hidden. Only after the motorist had gone over a rise and around a sharp curve would he come upon a sign that said, "Careful, Children Crossing!"

Their *true* concerns were humane, and so intensely involved were they in trying to solve the city problem that they needed such an antisocial, and even antihumane, joke for release from the intensity of concern. The real tragedy is that what they invented as a joke often exists in reality in cities that have not been planned with the concern the students had brought to the planning problem.

All physical object design is organized from a life-supportive point of view. The first question in designing a building or any kind of object is whether it is supportive of human life or whether it is hazardous and nonsupportive. A second question in object design is whether the building or other object serves the specific purposes for which it is intended. A third is whether the object is durable and will continue to be available when needed. These three objectives form a set of sequential criteria in design: (1) life support, (2) purpose, and (3) availability. The importance of listing them here is to emphasize the priority of life support in design criteria. The architect's way and his concerns are humanitarian.

5.4.2 A Humanistic Way

Another part of that way is humanistic, concerned with the whole individual.

Architectural design is humanistic because it is involved with the total response of the human being to the building. If the architect is able to deal somewhat precisely with satisfying functional concerns, he has only the weakest of criteria for how he must deal with such things as the symbolic quality of buildings, or their emotionally affective quality, or their orderliness. Although he has weak criteria, he is also aware of the existence and importance of these qualities in producing the total human response to buildings. He attempts to deal with them in an intuitive way.

The architect's intuitive response is an inheritance from the arts. He usually has a specific and strong belief in an intuitive approach, sometimes focused on intuition itself and sometimes on some particular quality, such as nature, materials, form, contact with the physical world, resource conservation, economy of means, or any of a dozen other simplifying ideas. While he is constantly aware of the totality of human response, he is also constantly searching for some device that will simplify his task of dealing with it.

Each great design philosophy is just such a simplifying effort. Frank Lloyd Wright developed a number of such simplifying themes, of which one was something called "Truth to Materials." There have been various interpretations of Wright's idea, but perhaps the simplest is that materials are to be used in the way they occur in nature and that the materials of nature are to be guarded and respected.

One of my professors once told a story with tongue in cheek about architectural students and their sensitivity to materials. He said that he was constantly amazed at how great a respect architectural students had for the materials of building. He had entered the architecture building late one evening, shortly after a group of students had finished with a jury on a design problem. They had piled their building models in the middle of the marble floor, had set them alight as a bonfire, and were dancing around the fire like a group of wild Indians. "And do you know," he said, "when I told them that the fire could damage the marble floor, they put out the fire *immediately!*"

If those students were not especially sensitive, the development of such a sensitivity is encouraged by the continuing concern the architectural student has with materials. It is one element in his growing sensitivity to the totality of the building and to the totality of human response to it.

5.4.3 An Integrative Way

Another part of the way is integrative, concerned with synthesis as much as with analysis.

The totality of response that is a concern of the architect is reinforced by his need to bring things together. His proposal for a building is integrative. It brings together the multitude of concerns he has with the totality of building and of response.

Because it is not possible to describe articulately how a *proposal* is generated, the architect has come to rely on ideas of *intuition* and *creativity* for explanation. He tends to believe in a need for creative expression. The difficulty with these words, used in this manner, is that they seem to explain without doing so. If the architect attempts to say what they mean, he is back to describing the development of a *proposal*. His definitions are circular. He has not really provided explanations, only assertions.

Despite this difficulty the fact that the architect is oriented toward an integrative proposal is important. That he is consciously oriented toward integrating material into a totality causes him to approach design in a particular way. He tends to broaden the scope of his effort and to state his design problem in a more and more general way. Whereas he is likely to simplify his criteria for decision, he prefers to state his problem in the broadest, most encompassing terms.

This tendency can be stated in terms of the information spectrum described in an earlier part of this book and according to the heuristic power of the method used. The architect's tendency is to move toward the most general form of problem statement or toward the *person* end of the information spectrum. His tendency is to use the weakest method that can be applied to problem solution.

These two tendencies together result in an integrative, intuitive approach in design that attempts to incorporate as much material as possible into the content of the problem and relies on intuitive processes for relating the totality of material to a single solution.

5.4.4 A Tentative Way

Another part is tentative, aware that any solution proposed is never sure but is always subject to the preferences of other persons.

Since the architect uses such soft procedures for solution, he is constantly aware that his solution can only be tentative. A proposal is simply that, a proposal to be tested. If it fails, then another proposal can be developed.

Since the processes for developing proposals are so relatively mysterious, the process by which proposals are tested might be equally mysterious. The designer must always be ready for his proposal to be rejected. He becomes acutely aware that it is not usually possible for the client to state all of his criteria in advance; instead, when he has acquired some experience, he realizes that a solution proposal will often evoke new criteria from the client that he had not been able to express before.

Understanding this phenomenon, the designer must work always with a curious ambivalent attitude. He must *care* intensely about his work to incorporate all the essential material and to achieve a good solution. At the same time he must *not care* at all when his work is rejected. When this happens, he must be able to set it aside to achieve again another solution better suited to the client's needs.

It is this ambivalence, *caring* and *not caring*, that gives to the designer's work a tentativeness and that makes the tentative way an element in the architect's way of thinking about things.

6. A Theory of Design Process

Although description of the design process is complete, there has not been a coherent summarizing theory. Such a theory is presented in this final chapter.

Although the description of the entire design process is now complete, no coherent summary of the salient features of design has appeared yet in this book. Because the nontechnical narrative attempted to relate an understanding of design method to the practitioner's and the student's experience, no opportunity arose to develop a tight, summarizing, theoretical structure. This final chapter is intended to provide it.

The intent of this chapter is to provide an outline theory that makes a connection between all the parts of this book. Some of the parts to be connected appear in the nontechnical narrative, and others appear only in the supporting technical sections. For those who have read only the nontechnical parts, some new material will appear in this section.

This outline theory provides in order:

6.1 A discussion of problem awareness and identification; in the literature this area is called problem seeking.

6.2 A discussion of the representation process used in problem solution. Since the problem solver cannot always manipulate parts of the real world, he must find ways to perform equivalent manipulations on representations of the real world.

6.3 A description of a basic and general form of problem representation. This general form can then provide insights into different kinds of problems, and the strategies for solution that are most appropriate for the different kinds.

6.4 A description of the particular character of design problems. Special emphasis is placed on their concern with goals and with the controls available to the designer or problem solver.

6.5 The range of concerns that must be dealt with in determining the controls available; the resources and procedures available to the designer.

6.6 The closure process in determining goals. The use of typological information of image, and of invention in setting goals in design.

6.7 The process of adduction; problem decomposition, means-ends analysis, specification, and generation and matching as procedures of adduction.

6.8 The search process that produces solutions. The procedure by which demand and supply statements are used to determine the final arrangement for consideration and selection. The importance of identification to the selection process.

Since this theory statement is intended as an outline, the references are kept brief and without quotations.

6.1 PROBLEM AWARENESS AND IDENTIFICATION

Before problem solution can occur, there must be an awareness of the problem's existence. Problem solution is complementary with problem seeking and problem defining.

Before problem solution can begin, a problem must be defined. There is no way in which the mere collection of information can define a problem; the problem solver must bring some direction or preconceived idea to his effort (Ackoff, 1962, p. 25). As the individual engages in a variety of experiences from one moment to the next, either he makes decisions that move him more and more toward a certain goal, or he makes decisions that broaden his experience and increase the possibilities open to him (Kelly, 1963, p. 65). Which decision he makes at a particular moment is influenced by the level of stress he prefers (Wohlwill, 1966, p. 34), by the person or persons in whose interest he acts, by the kinds of criteria he applies to his decision (Parsons and Shils, 1951, p. 248), by the remoteness of the needs response from immediate availability, and by the severity and generality of the defined problem situation. Whereas the preferred level of stress determines the character of the needs, and whereas the "pattern variables" concerned with reference persons and reference criteria affect the response to those needs, it is the remoteness of a need response that defines a need situation as being also a problem situation. It is when an object to satisfy a need is not identifiable or not available that a problem exists.

6.1.1 Appropriate Tension Levels

The individual, according to his need, moves through a series of cycles that vary between problem-solving and problem seeking.

Every individual has both automatic and intentional mechanisms by which he maintains both his internal physical condition and his internal mental arousal. As an organism existing in an environment the individual exists in some condition of fit or nonfit with his environment (Henderson, 1958, p. 36). Under different circumstances the individual experiences different degrees of need or tension and corresponding multiple motivations (Maslow, 1970, pp. 53-54). But although deficit motives based on need constantly occur, there are also "growth" motives that maintain levels of tension in the individual in the interest of relatively distant goals (Allport, 1955, p. 68). Although it is usual to think of need and tension in association with a lack of "fit" with the environment and a motivation to reachieve the condition of fit, motivation toward a lack of fit and toward strife also exists (Klausner, 1968, p. vi). Indeed different individuals have different preferred levels of tension and preferred degrees of stability and predictability in their lives (Gans, 1962. p. 28).

As a result of these differences individuals seek different levels of tension for their immediate needs, for their long-range goals, according to the circumstance of the moment and their preferred lifestyle. When the means to a change in the level of tension is not immediately available, the circumstance can be defined as a *problem*

6.1.1

situation. Although both tension reduction and tension increase can be seen as *problem-solving* activities, under some circumstances it is also useful to speak of an effort to increase tension as a *problem-seeking* activity.

The individual moves through a series of cycles that vary between problem solving and problem seeking (Fig. 6.1). The best solution may be the one that leads to a new problem.

6.1.2 Variables in Action Decisions

The individual's actions are influenced by what he knows, what he desires, and what he values. His decision is influenced by whom he acts for, what principle he acts by, whether the object he seeks is an end or a means, and whether he views that object specifically or generally.

Any action within a need- or goal-determined problem situation is influenced by a number of different factors that can be grouped broadly according to cognition, cathexis (needing, desiring), and evaluation (Parsons and Shils, 1951, p. 5). Under cognition the individual is aware of the circumstance in which he finds himself. Under cathexis he is aware of the character of his need or desire. Under evaluation he relates his desire to the influences that affect his approach to the desired object.

Each of these evaluative influences can be thought of as a decision in relation to the action the individual takes. The decisions are : (1) whether to evaluate or not, (2) whom to act for, (3) what principle to act by, (4) whether to view the action object in terms of attributes or accomplishments, and (5) whether to deal with that object as specific to a particular need or in a broad, diffuse way (Parsons and Shils, 1951, p. 248). Undoubtedly some of these decisions are determined by the nature of the problem situation (whether or not, for example, the problem solver is working for a client), but others are determined by the nature of the problem. The problem solver's need determines whether he is dealing with an object in terms of its attributes or the capabilities it can provide. A narrowly defined problem forces an evaluation of the specific need that the object can fill, but a more broadly defined problem requires a more diffuse evaluation of the solution object.

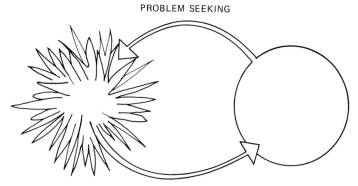

PROBLEM SEEKING

PROBLEM SOLVING

Figure 6.1 The problem cycle.

6.1.3 Remoteness of the Desired Object

A problem exists only when a desired object is not immediately attainable but is ultimately attainable. A design problem is the judgment that some imagined possible future condition is preferable to the present real conditon, along with a determination to convert the one into the other.

I observed that, when an object or a response is not immediately available for the satisfaction of a need, its lack of availability can be defined as a problem. To be consciously searching for an action appropriate to the achievement of some clearly imagined but *not directly attainable* aim is the essential definition of a problem (Polya, 1962, p. 115). If a person is in a situation where he perceives a problem, then the tensions cause him to move from the less structured problem situation to the more structured solution situation (Wertheimer, 1959, p. 239). If there is no difficulty—if the situation is structured instead of unstructured—there is also no problem.

The existence of a problem can then be determined by the separate existence of two different situations or states, a problem and a solution state. I should point out that, in addition to the solution states not being directly attainable, it must also be perceived as being *eventually attainable.* If it is perceived as *not* attainable, then again, it is not possible to say that a problem exists; not only must there be a difficulty to be overcome, but the difficulty must be of a kind that *can* be overcome.

If the problem state provides a stimulus for the problem solver, it must also provide a motivation by his perception that he can attain a solution.

A design problem can be described in these same terms; it is the comparison between a present reality and some imagined possible future reality, along with the judgment that the present is unsatisfactory by comparison. When attention is focused on the present reality, the focus is on a *problem condition;* when on the possible future, the focus is on a *goal condition.* Problem solution is a process of converting one condition into the other (Fig. 6.2).

6.1.4 Problem Severity

Problem severity is the distance between the real condition and the imagined condition. Problem generality is the frequency of repetive occurrence of a problem.

If two different states are being considered, a problem and a solution (or goal) state, it should be possible to compare them before any solution is attempted. I defined the lower limit of that difference as "not directly attainable." I defined the upper limit as "eventually attainable." How can problem difficulty between these two limits be measured?

On the one hand one can measure the differences between them by factoring and comparison. Each state could be divided into its elementary components by some orderly process, and the two could then be compared element by element (Newell and Simon, 1972, p. 428). On the other hand when a comparison is made between a problem concerned with the redesign of (say) an AM-FM receiver

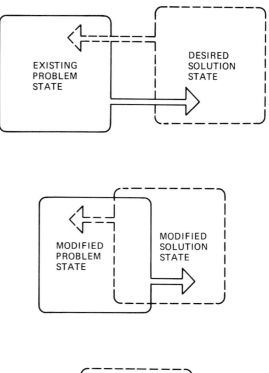

Figure 6.2 The problem solution process.

with the hypothetical problem of converting a sow's ear into a silk purse (Reitman, 1964, pp. 282 ff.), a possible measure is the distance between the two states; if the elements are dissimilar, just how dissimilar are they?

Since the real-world problem condition can undergo some degree of change, and since any imagined solution state can also change, it is important to realize that any measure of problem generality and severity (the number of elemental differences and the degree of those differences) will have to be a dynamic measure. The basis for such a measure is indicated in the accompanying diagram (Fig. 6.3):

REFERENCES

Ackoff, Russell L., *Scientific Method: Optimizing Applied Research Decisions,* Wiley, New York, 1962.

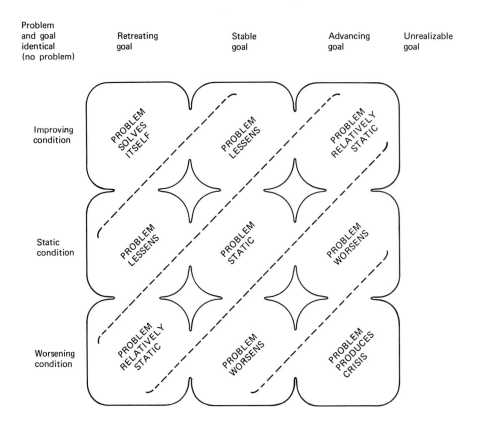

Figure 6.3 Problem severity.

Allport, Gordon W., *Becoming,* Yale University Press, New Haven, Conn., 1955.

Gans, Herbert J., *The Urban Villagers,* Free Press, New York, 1962.

Henderson, Lawrence J., *The Fitness of the Environment,* Beacon Press, Boston, 1958.

Kelly, George A., *A Theory of Personality: The psychology of Personal Constructs,* Norton, New York, 1963.

Klausner, Samuel Z., Ed., *Why Man Takes Chances,* Doubleday, Garden City, N.Y., 1968.

Maslow, Abraham H., *Motivation and Personality,* Harper & Row, New York, 1970.

Newell, Allen, and Herbert A. Simon, *Human Problem Solving,* Prentice-Hall, Englewood Cliffs, N.J. 1972.

Parsons, Talcott, and E.A. Shils, Eds., *Toward a General Theory of Action,* Harvard University Press, Cambridge, Mass., 1951.

Polya, George, *Mathematical Discovery,* Vol. 1, Wiley, New York, 1962.

Reitman, Walter R., "Heuristic Decision Procedures, Open Constraints, and the Structure of Ill-Defined Problems," in Shelly, Maynard W., II, and Glenn L. Bryan, Eds., *Human Judgments and Optialcty,* Wiley, New York, 1964.

Wertheimer, Max, *"Productive Thinking,"* Harper S. Row, New York, 1959.

Wohlwill, Joachim F., "The Physical Environment: A Problem for a Psychology of Stimulation," *Journal of Social Issues,* **22**(4), 1966.

6.2 PROBLEM ENCODING AND MODELING

Since the problem solver cannot usually manipulate parts of the real world, he must find ways to represent the essential parts of that world and perform equivalent manipulations on that representation.

Problem solution requires some form of manipulation if the solver is to achieve anything more than an amorphous sense of the solution state and the method of moving from the problem to the solution state. Typically it is not possible to perform these manipulations on the real world. In the interest of conserving time, or effort, or expense, the problem solver performs manipulations on some counterpart or representation of the real-world conditions (Raser, 1971, p. 15).

That representation is a pertinent translation of the problem situation. It is itself a system of components that symbolize the parts of the real-world problem situation. He then manipulates these symbols by processes of reasoning: deduction, inference, and the like. After such manipulation has achieved a bridge between representations of a problem and a solution state, he is then able to retranslate these manipulations into real-world processes, achieving in reality what his representations of reality had predicted (Craik, 1943, p. 50).

6.2.1 Simplification

Any representation is a simplification and an abstraction of the real world. Any problem solution based on a representation is only a solution with respect to the representation and may not be a real-world solution.

Although the accuracy of the representation is extremely important, it can be so only in the parts most pertinent to the solver's concerns. Every real-world problem is extremely complex, more complex than the problem solver can perceive and far more complex than he can actually represent. For that reason any representation he makes will be a simplification of the real situation (Wilson, 1952, p. 15).

Since the problem solver must reason with (or manipulate) a representation that is an idealization and a simplification of reality, no matter how well—no matter how accurately or comprehensively—he reasons with that representation, it is still only a representation. The results of his reasoning can apply with respect to the representation and not necessarily to the real world from which that representation was drawn (Shepard, 1964, p. 262). If his representation has been well drawn, pertinent to his chief concerns, then the result of his reasoning with the representation should be able to be transferred to the real-world situation. It is not surprising, however, to discover that modifications must be made in that reasoning to achieve a good fit with the real world.

6.2.2 Abstracting and Factoring

There are different degrees of simplification: decomposing, abstract-

Where the problem solver deals with the object of his concern sometimes narrowly and sometimes broadly (or specifically and diffusely), still at the broadest level of his thought some parts of the object are omitted. The very process of abstracting some attribute or performance factors out other attributes and performances. There are, however, different degrees of such omission.

ing, and factoring out. Each form of simplification omits some amount of detail.

The simplest such process is *decomposing;* there is no intention to omit but only to isolate for the moment to focus attention. A second level of omission is *abstracting,* whereby details are omitted to carry through a skeleton solution as a guide to a more detailed solution. A third level is *factoring out,* whereby details are omitted because they are not within the power of the problem solver to manipulate. At this third level the influence of those omitted details must be remembered and accounted for in the solution.

An example of the factoring out that occurs in the solution of a design problem can be seen in the diagram that appears as Fig. 6.4. The items shown to the right of the dashed line are usually factored out in the solution of a design problem.

6.2.3 Translations: Encoding and Decoding

Problem solution requires translation processes that *encode* problem conditions into problem statements and *decode* solution statements into solution condition.

To solve problems expeditiously within a given professional or disciplinary area, one develops a set of standard terms that refer to commonly recurring matters of concern. It is then the usual practice to convert information to that standard terminology or to that standard form. *Encoding* is a process the problem solver uses in interpreting his information input. External and sometimes internal information are coded so that they make sense and are related to the problem. Regardless of what transformations or manipulations the problem solver performs on the information (whether mentally or with external symbol processes), he must encode it to an appropriate form before he can perform the manipulations. *Decoding* is also essential if the problem solver is to externalize the information and place it in some communicatable form. Both processes are essential parts of any formalized problem-solving procedure (Best, 1969, pp. 151-152).

Both encoding and decoding are equivalent substitutions; information existing in one form is placed in another equivalent form that is more useful for the problem-solving circumstance. These equivalent substitutions can also be spoken of as translations.

6.2.4 Transformations

Problem solution also requires transformation processes that convert problem statements into inequivalent solution statements. Transformations are based on means-ends relations.

Problem solving cannot be accomplished by simple equivalent substitutions or translations. The usual solution requires some form of means-ends analysis that brings together information about some purpose, aim, end, or demand with other information about available resources, means, or supply. When a demand statement has been encoded, it is possible, from that encoded statement and a similarly encoded supply systems statement, to develop a specification for a means that will serve the end that generated the demand statement.

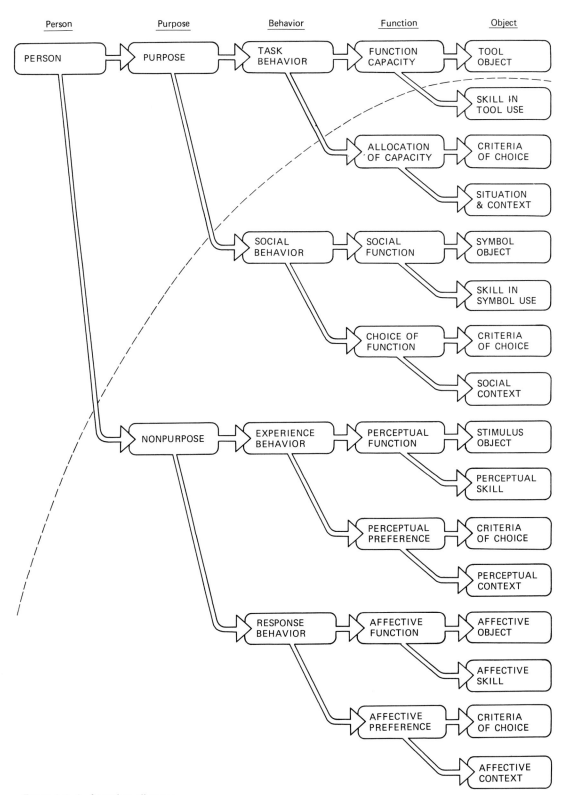

Person | Purpose | Behavior | Function | Object

PERSON → PURPOSE → TASK BEHAVIOR → FUNCTION CAPACITY → TOOL OBJECT

SKILL IN TOOL USE

ALLOCATION OF CAPACITY → CRITERIA OF CHOICE

SITUATION & CONTEXT

SOCIAL BEHAVIOR → SOCIAL FUNCTION → SYMBOL OBJECT

SKILL IN SYMBOL USE

CHOICE OF FUNCTION → CRITERIA OF CHOICE

SOCIAL CONTEXT

NONPURPOSE → EXPERIENCE BEHAVIOR → PERCEPTUAL FUNCTION → STIMULUS OBJECT

PERCEPTUAL SKILL

PERCEPTUAL PREFERENCE → CRITERIA OF CHOICE

PERCEPTUAL CONTEXT

RESPONSE BEHAVIOR → AFFECTIVE FUNCTION → AFFECTIVE OBJECT

AFFECTIVE SKILL

AFFECTIVE PREFERENCE → CRITERIA OF CHOICE

AFFECTIVE CONTEXT

Figure 6.4 A factoring diagram.

A THEORY OF DESIGN PROCESS

A transformation process uses different kinds of information in conjunction to generate another kind of information. Such a procedure results in a substition of information, but it is an inequivalent substitution.

6.2.5 Equivalent and Inequivalent Substitutions

An entire solution procedure requires encoding, transformation, and decoding.

The difference between equivalent substitution (or translation) and inequivalent substitution (or transformation) is shown by the adjacent diagram (Fig. 6.5), which also shows the relationship between symbols and events and between implications and causal actions (Craik, 1943, pp. 62-63). Solution depends on the existence of the relations described in this diagram.

REFERENCES

Best, Gordon, "Method and Intention in Architectural Design," in Broadbent, Geoffrey, and A. Ward, Eds. *Design Methods in Architecture,* Architect's Association, London, 1969.

Craik, K. J. W., *The Nature of Explanation,* Cambridge University Press, Cambridge, England, 1943.

Raser, John R., *Simulation and Society: An Exploration of Scientific Gaming,* Allyn & Bacon, Boston, 1971.

Shepard, Roger N., "On subjectively Optimum Selection Among Multiattribute Alternatives," in Shelly, Maynard W., II, and Glenn L. Bryan , Eds., *Human Judgements and Optimality,* Wiley, New York, 1964.

Wilson, E. Bright, Jr., *An Introduction to Scientific Research,* McGraw-Hill, New York, 1952.

6.3 PROBLEM DEFINITION

A generalized form of problem statement can provide insights into different kinds of problems and the solution strategies appropriate for each kind.

Several times in the prior discussion I have had occasion to speak of different states in the problem-solving process. I spoke of a problem and a solution state. I have also been speaking of the transformation of one such state into the other. So long as there was a parallel relationship between real-world and problem states, as occurs when the problem is to decide on a course of action, there is little confusion.

If, however, the problem solver is a detective asking how the murdered body came to be in the locked room, a difficulty exists; now the problem situation is the terminus of a series of prior real-world actions. As he moves forward toward a solution, he must move backward in the real world to the discovery of those initiating causal events.

A terminology is needed that will distinguish problem situation changes from real-world events and changes. To provide such a termin-

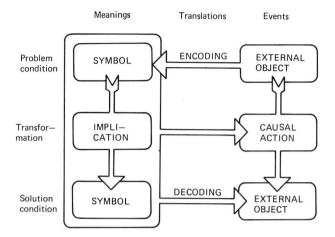

Meanings   Translations   Events

Figure 6.5 Relations between translation and transformation processes.

6.3

ology, think about a method of representing changes in the real world of events (Reitman, 1964, pp. 288-289). When the terminology has been proposed, it can be related to the thoughts on translation and transformation in the preceding article.

6.3.1 Problem Statement

A basic statement form must show a relation between an initial condition, some change process, and a terminal condition. $A \Rightarrow B$ is such a form.

Any real-world situation that undergoes some change can be described by taking into account: an initial condition, a transformation process, and a terminal condition. A statement describing such a change will be of the form, "the initial state (condition), when subjected to a specific transformation process, results in the terminal state (condition)." If the initial state is represented by A, the specific transformation process by $\Rightarrow$, and the terminal state by B, then the generalized statement of such a change process can be expressed by the form $A \Rightarrow B$. When all three terms in such a statement are applied to a particular situation, and when all three are adequately known, a description of the change in the particular situation results. When one or more of the terms are not adequately known, the statement form becomes the basis for a problem statement. The form is, of course, completely general, and for a useful problem statement to result, a measure of the amount of information the problem solver has about it must be associated with each term of the statement form.

When this form of coding has been developed to display the different classes of problems, only one other factor is needed to distinguish the full range of problem types. That factor must define where the present reality is in the problem situation. It must say whether the present reality exists in the initial state, in the transformation process, or in the terminal state.

6.3.2 Information Coding

For each term in the statement form a number coding can represent: (1) a known specific condition. (2) a range of possible conditions, and (3) an unknown condition. A logical expansion of this code for each term produces a problem typology.

To provide an information coding for each of the three terms in the statement form, it is possible to adapt the three-level measure of information used in decision theory (Ackoff, 1962, p. 13). These terms are certainty, risk, and uncertainty. Since these are concerned with the sureness that an action will lead to some known outcome, they can be modified appropriately to define levels of information that are *known* precisely, known as a *range*, or *unknown*. The coding for these levels is shown in Fig. 6.6.

As an example of the application of such coding think how it can be applied to the several kinds of problems referred to already in Sections 6.1.4 and 6.3. Such an application appears in Fig. 6.7.

The development of this form of coding in conjunction with the statement form can provide a method of problem classification.

When this number coding representing each of the three levels of information is entered into the problem statement forms, a unique *problem type* is described. If a *logical expansion* of the numerical coding is produced, it can become a guide to problem solution. When the problem types are grouped by the amount and degrees of information, they are also grouped according to the strategies that are effective for problem solution. A logical expansion of the problem types appears in Table 6.1.

The problem class designation is derived from the numeric sum of the information coding of each term in the statement form. The lower the value of the class designation, the greater the amount of information available about the problem situation.

Code	Term	Description
1	Known	Full information, adequate for description of state or process, or adequate without further development for input in a problem statement. Such an information level can be referred to as a "closed" condition
2	Range	The condition of the term is not fully known, but the full number of possible conditions of the term are known, and are small enough in number to be reviewed entirely. If necessary, for a problem solution process, a term having this level of information can be "closed" to a known condition by the assumption that one of the possible conditions exists
3	Unknown	Very little information exists about the term. The full number of possible conditions is not known; there are too many such conditions for the problem solver to review the entire set. If such a term is to be "closed" in a solution process, closure will occur by an arbitrary choice from among the possible conditions of the term

Figure 6.6 Coding the level of information an a problem statement term.

Problem description	A	$\Rightarrow$	B
The redesign of an AM–FM receiver functionally similar to the original but without radical retooling, and to meet the lower price of a competitor (Reitman, 1964)	1	2	2
The conversion of a sow's ear into a silk purse (Reitman, 1964)	1	3	1
The detective's problem of a murdered body inside a locked room	3	2	1

Figure 6.7 Examples of information coding in a problem statement.

Table 6.1. Problem Types Based on Information Coding

Problem Type	Problem Class	Class Description
1 1 1	3	Three knowns
1 1 2		
1 2 1	4	Two knowns &
2 1 1		one range
1 1 3		
1 3 1	5a	Two knowns &
3 1 1		one unknown
1 2 2		
2 1 2	5b	One known &
2 2 1		two ranges
2 2 2	6a	Three ranges
1 2 3		
1 3 2		
2 1 3	6b	One known,
3 1 2		one range, &
2 3 1		one unknown
3 2 1		
1 3 3		
3 1 3	7a	One known &
3 3 1		two unknowns
2 2 3		
2 3 2	7b	Two ranges &
3 2 2		one unknown
2 3 3		
3 2 3	8	One range &
3 3 2		two unknowns
3 3 3	9	Three unknowns

6.3.3 Solution Processes

Once a problem has been encoded, the solution process requires the following phases: (1) preparation, (2) adduction, and (3) search. Some (well-defined) problems are already prepared.

The earlier discussions of *endoding* and *decoding* of information being left aside, the transformation process in problem solution can have three separate phases: (1) *a preparation phase* (or a *closure* phase), in which the problem statement is placed in a form where adduction can take place; (2) *an adduction phase*, in which the remaining unknown term is adduced from the known terms by logical processes; and (3) *a search phase*, in which a real-world counterpart of the adduced term is sought. *Adduction* is concerned with what I have already referred to earlier as an inequivalent substitution; although two known terms are required for an adduction to occur, the occurrence is not so much related to the syllogism as it is to the Hegelian dialectic process; it is often in the form of a means-ends analysis.

I should point out that the phases described above are logical rather than temporal phases; although it is usual for the preparation phase to precede the adduction phase, and the adduction phase to precede the search phase, any solution process that is at all complex can have the phases occurring simultaneously or out of sequence. The iterative nature of problem solution, where the simultaneous fitting of many different elements requires the modification and adjustment of previously chosen elements, prevents any commitment to a hard, unvarying sequence in the process. The *logical* phases are summarized in Fig. 6.8.

With these phases in mind, we can now return to the problem typology developed earlier to add a further classification. The types of problem can be classified by the kind of *preparation* required (Fig. 6.9). This grouping is a guide to what procedure to follow in undertaking the solution of each kind of problem (Table 6.2).

In the problem-solving literature the kind of problem that requires closure is called ill defined. Clearly the kind of assumption or arbitrary choice the problem solver makes affects the kind of solution he achieves. I should emphasize that closure often occurs only gradually during an extended solution process (Reitman, 1964, p. 293). If a particular closure fails to yield an adequate solution, then the closure

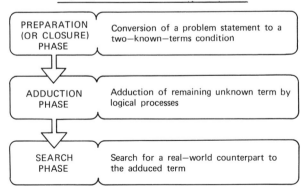

Logical phases in the transformation process

PREPARATION (OR CLOSURE) PHASE	Conversion of a problem statement to a two—known—terms condition
ADDUCTION PHASE	Adduction of remaining unknown term by logical processes
SEARCH PHASE	Search for a real—world counterpart to the adduced term

Figure 6.8 Logical phases in a transformation process.

ARCHITECTURE, PROBLEMS AND PURPOSES

Figure 6.9 Problem classes.

A'   Initial real-world state
⇒'   Real-world transformation process
B'   Terminal real-world state

A   Representation of initial state
⇒   Representation of transformation process
B   Representation of terminal state

(A')   Initial state, not in present reality
(⇒')   Transformation process, not in present reality
(B')   Terminal state, not in present reality

1, 2, 3   Information coding, as described earlier.

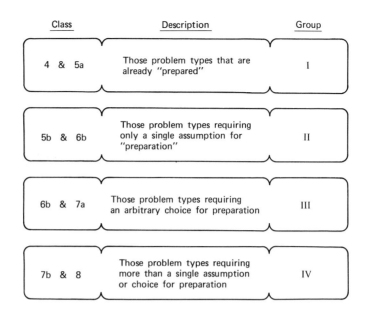

Class	Description	Group
4 & 5a	Those problem types that are already "prepared"	I
5b & 6b	Those problem types requiring only a single assumption for "preparation"	II
6b & 7a	Those problem types requiring an arbitrary choice for preparation	III
7b & 8	Those problem types requiring more than a single assumption or choice for preparation	IV

6.3.3

can be changed. All such closures occur from the problem solver's fund of information (Amarel, 1970, p. 182). To solve an ill-defined problem, the solver must deal with the vague information in that kind of problem (Newell, 1969, p. 411). Evidently he must deal with vagueness by assumption or by arbitrary choice.

6.3.4 World States and Problem States

A careful distinction must be made between changes in problem states during a solution process and changes in world states when a solution is put into effect.

Consider now the difference between real-world states (with the changes that occur in them) and problem states (with the changes that occur in them). In the accompanying diagram (Fig. 6.10) changes in real-world states are shown from left to right, and changes in problem state are shown from top to bottom. The problem whose solution is diagramed is the redesign of an AM-FM receiver, coded as a problem type 1-2-2.

6.3.5 Research, Management, and Action Problems

Research problems, management problems, and action problems differ in the location of present reality in their problem statement form.

Strategies for dealing with research problems, with operations (or management) problems, and with design problems are very different (Nadler, 1967, p. 16).

So far this discussion has dealt with problems only in terms of the amount of information available in the problem statement. It is also useful to look at the manner of distribution of the information in the problem to see what attitudes and emphases relate to such distribution. Without doubt, problems can be classified by the location of information about the present reality within the problem structure.

Table 6.2. A Problem Typology

Problem Type	Problem Class	Class Description	Problem Group	Group Description
1 1 1	3	Three knowns	◄━━━━━━ Set one term aside	
1 1 2 1 2 1 2 1 1	4	Two knowns & one range	I	Already "prepared"
1 1 3 1 3 1 3 1 1	5a	Two knowns & one unknown		
1 2 2 2 1 2 2 2 1	5b	One known & two ranges		Select two terms to close
2 2 2	6a	Three ranges		
1 2 3 1 3 2 2 1 3 3 1 2 2 3 1 3 2 1	6b	One known, one range, & one unknown	II	Requires single assumption for preparation
1 3 3 3 1 3 3 3 1	7a	One known & two unknowns	III	Requires arbitrary decision for preparation
2 2 3 2 3 2 3 2 2	7b	Two ranges & one unknown	IV	Requires more than a single assumption or decision for preparation
2 3 3 3 2 3 3 3 2	8	One range & two unknowns		
3 3 3	9	Three unknowns ◄━━━━━━ Obtain more information		

6.3.5

In tabular form (Fig. 6.11) appears a classification according to whether information about the present reality is the terminal state and the problem is a research problem, whether the information is in the process term and the problem is one of management and the use of technical capability, or whether the information is in the initial state and the problem is one of design or planning. This information placement implies that research problems are concerned with past events, management problems with present events, and design problems with future events. Although this implication is broadly true, Fig. 6.11 indicates that each kind of problem has more variety than such a simple statement would suggest.

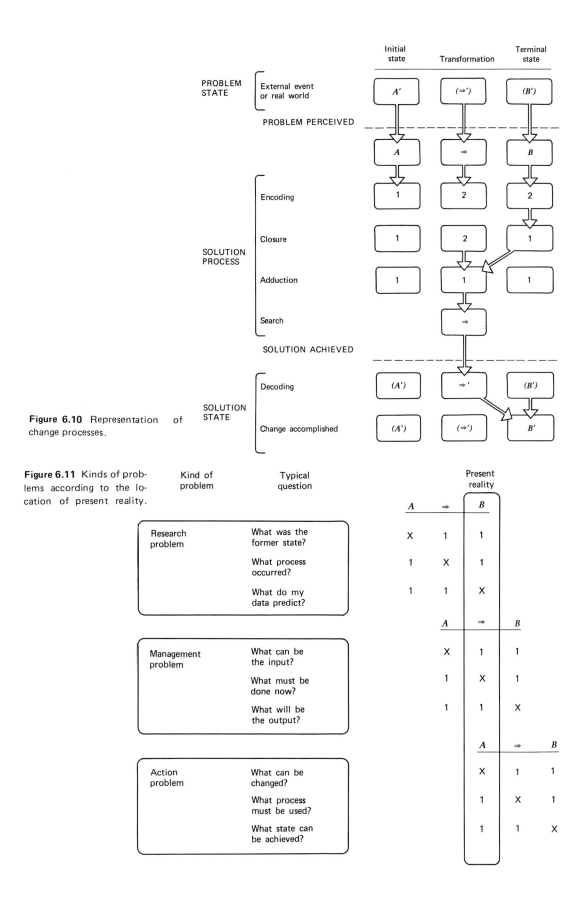

Figure 6.10 Representation of change processes.

Figure 6.11 Kinds of problems according to the location of present reality.

REFERENCES

Ackoff, Russell L., *Scientific Method: Optimizing Applied Research Decisions,* Wiley, New York, 1962.

Amarel, Saul, "On the Representation of Problems and Goal Directed Procedures for Computers," in Banerjii, R. B., and M. D. Mesarovic, Eds., *Theoretical Approaches to Non-Numerical Problem Solving,* Springer-Verlag, Berlin, 1970.

Nadler, Gerald, *Work Systems Design: The IDEALS Concept,* Richard D. Irwin, Homewood, Ill., 1967.

Newell, Allen, "Heuristic Programming: Ill-Formed Problems," in Aronofsky, Julius S., Ed., *Progress in Operations Research,* Vol. 3, Wiley, New York, 1969.

Reitman, Walter R., "Heuristic Decision Procedures, Open Constraints, and the Structure of Ill-Defined Problems," in Shelly, Maynard W., II, and Glenn L. Bryan, Eds., *Human Judgments and Optimality,* Wiley, New York, 1964.

6.4 DESIGN PROBLEMS

A design problem is an action problem that uses closure of the terminal state as its basic solution strategy. The *goal* established by this closure can be achieved only by *control* of the process for achieving that goal.

In a design problem the present reality is in the initial state and the concern is with some action applied to this present reality that will result in some preferred future state.

Although sometimes that preferred future state is more vivid or better known than the present reality, this is relatively rare. The more usual circumstance is for the present reality (as the initial state) to be fully "known." Ordinarily, in a design problem, the initial state is well defined, and the architect and his client know what they need to know about the initial state, or else they can find out.

What is not so well defined is the terminal state and the transformation processes to be used. Often the description of his needs the client provides for the architect is incomplete; often it is at a relatively high level of abstractness. Often the architect and his client are not clear about the resources available for use in achieving the needed or desired terminal state.

In sum the typical design problem is one that fits one of the forms described by the following coding:

1,2,2; 1,2,3; 1,3,2; 1,3,3.

6.4.1 Design Problem Closure

Closure of the terminal state in design converts a vaguely desired goal condition into a specific and detailed goal object. Such closure is conditioned by the processes available for goal achievement.

For a solution to be achieved on a problem in one of these forms, "closure" must be performed on either the terminal state or on the transformation process term. When it is performed on the terminal state, the architect and client are able to agree in detail on what changes should be accomplished in the environment. The closure then takes one of the following forms:

1,2,1; 1,3,1.

By contrast, if the architect and his client are not able to agree entirely on a terminal state, it is often possible to agree in detail about the resources available and the means to be used to achieve some mod-

6.4.1

ification in the initial state. Closure in the transformation process term can result in one of the following forms:

1,1,2; 1,1,3.

6.4.2 Decision Styles

There are strong and weak goals and strong and weak controls over process. Different combinations of control and goal strength "produce" different decision styles.

It is possible to speak of the terminal state as an objective and to think of strong or weak objectives; it is possible to evaluate transformation processes in terms of the degree of control the problem solver has over the process (Lynch, 1972). There is a relation between closure of the terminal state and a strong objective; there is some relation between closure of the transformation process term and strong control. When the objectives and the controls are evaluated as strong or weak, it is possible to describe the total decision (or design) style.

There are four such styles (Lynch, 1972, pp. 207-213):

1. **Determinate.** strong control, strong objectives.

2. **Strategic.** weak control, strong objectives.

3. **Open-ended.** strong control, weak objectives.

4. **Situational.** weak control, weak objectives.

By this terminology, closure of the terminal state can be thought of as a strategic design style. Closure of the process term can be thought of as an open-ended design style. Final solution results in a determinate process.

6.4.3 Circularity between Control and Goal

The processes to be used and the goal chosen for achievement are circular with each other.

The most usual procedure in design is the performance of closure on the terminal state. Although the closure of the process term is sometimes the more important to perform, the more usual circumstance, even when process is very important, is to let information about available processes and capabilities strongly influence the closure of the terminal state (Heider, 1958, p. 111). Although means or processes can become important in themselves (Maslow, 1970, p. 58), because the "irreality" of the terminal state is so much more easily manipulated than the reality of available process, that irreality becomes the medium for expressing needs, desires, and fears (Lewin, 1964, p.274). The choice of an objective (i.e., the closure of the terminal state) is also strongly influenced by the difficulty in achieving that objective (Lewin, 1964, p. 287).

When I commented earlier that in design both the terminal state and the process term were not well defined, I indicated that the purpose description providing information about the terminal state was often incomplete and highly abstract. If the designer (problem solver) is to "close" the terminal state, he must know how to complete and articulate the client's statement of purpose in a concrete form.

6.4.4 The Structure of Purpose

A description of purpose must take into account an ends-means spectrum as follows: person-purpose-behavior-function-object. It must also take into account a part-whole relationship at each point in this spectrum.

A number of statements can be made about *purpose* in relation to *action.* As the individual undertakes action, he uses two fundamental processes: *integration* and *allocation*; integration mediates the relation of the individual with his environment (Parsons and Shils, 1951, p. 108). Purpose implies the use of *resources* to achieve those purposes; resources are *mental* and *physical* (Nadler, 1967, p. 2). Action can also be seen as having two essential components, *capability* and *motivation*; capability also has two components, *opportunity* (which is another way of describing physical resource) and *power* (which is another way of describing mental resource) (Heider, 1958, pp. 98-100). To achieve purposes, the individual effects change; effecting change modifies the total situation, which includes *physical resources, mental resources, motivations,* and the *context.* When a group (instead of an individual) is acting to achieve some purpose, the total situation includes its materials, tools and techniques (physical resources); its internal system and norms (mental resources); its external system (motivations); and its environment (context) (Homans, 1950, p. 434). Since an appropriate description of behavior should take all levels into account (Miller, Galanter, and Pribram, 1960, p. 13), the relation between these various purpose and action elements can be seen in Fig. 6. 4, p. 301.

A purposive state can be described, not only in a spectrum from abstract to concrete, but also at each level of abstractness in terms of part-whole relationships. Each whole thing can be broken up into its component parts. Each purpose statement, each behavioral statement, each function capability statement, and each physical object description is not singular but consists of a number of related component objects. The diagram (Fig. 6.12) shows a typical hierarchic breakdown of the singular thing into its components. Note that, in viewing the physical object, any component at any of the hierarchic levels can be carried directly to the smallest part scale (labeled "piece" in the diagram) without having to break down through each of the intervening hierarchic levels.

REFERENCES

Heider, Fritz, *The Psychology of Interpersonal Relations,* Wiley, New York, 1958.

Homans, George C., *The Human Group,* Harcourt & Brace, New York, 1950.

Lewin, Kurt, "Behavior and Development as a Function of the Total Situation," in Cartright, Dorwin, Ed., *Kurt Lewin: Field Theory in Social Science,* Harper & Row, New York, 1964.

Lynch, Kevin, *What Time is This Place,* M.I.T. Press, Cambridge, Mass., 1972.

Maslow, Abraham H., *Motivation and Personality,* Harper & Row, New York, 1970.

Miller, George A., E. Galanter, and K. Pribram, *Plans and the Structure of Behavior,* Holt, New York, 1960.

Nadler, Gerald, *Work Systems Design: The IDEALS Concept,* Richard D. Irwin, Homewood, Ill., 1967.

Parsons, Talcott, and E. A. Shils, Eds., *Toward a General Theory of Action,* Harvard University Press, Cambridge, Mass., 1951.

6.5 PROCESS CLOSURE

The choice of process in problem solution is influenced by the skills and resources available to the designer and his client.

In design problem solving, whether closure is accomplished on the process term or on the terminal state, the process capability of the problem solver is a strong influence. Terminal-state closure, the choice of an objective, is influenced by the problem solver's aspirations; these in turn are influenced by what he believes himself capable of accomplishing.

Process capability is itself influenced by the manner in which the problem solver perceives the problem, whether as internal or external; by where he must direct his solution efforts; by his subsidiary goals and motives, whether, for example, he is more concerned with sureness or efficiency of accomplishment; by his resources and the value in exchange that he places on these resources; by the knowledge he has of available processes; and by the degree of control he has over his own processes.

The problem solver can perceive a problem as internal, requiring a reevaluation and a possible modification of his goals, his attitudes, and his aspirations, or as external and capable of solution by modification of the external environment. When the problem is identified as external, the next question is whether it is soluble by allocative processes, which reschedule activities, or by integrative processes, which require some modification in behavior capability. If the latter is required, then the question is whether the modification is toward known processes, or whether other processes have to be learned. In either instance those modified processes could require some change in the environment. An entire set of interlocked decisions and evaluations affects the performance or process capability of the actor (Parsons and Shils, 1951, p. 255).

6.5.1 Process Effectiveness

Solution processes vary in their power. Some are more likely to deliver a solution than others.

In addition to a knowledge of whether the processes are known, or whether new processes have to be learned, subtler distinctions can be drawn. Any process can be evaluated in terms of its power to deliver an accomplishment and of the generality of its application. The extent to which a problem solver can trust the effectiveness of the ac-

6.5.1

tions available to him is a strong influence on his selection of processes and objectives. When an action he takes produces only a probable outcome, he must behave differently from the circumstance when his action produces one specific and determinate outcome. To select combinations of processes, he must be aware of the effectiveness of a specific process and of the situations in which it can be applied.

6.5.2 Subsidiary Motives

The designer's choice of a process varies according to the power of the process and his subsidiary motives.

Since actions vary in their power and applicability, the problem solver's strategy in selecting a set of actions depends in part on his subsidiary goals and motives. He might, under different circumstances, place a high value on sureness of achieving a solution, efficiency in achieving it, or security against making errors or blunders in securing it. External forces can impose different motives; a problem that develops increasing importance over a long period of time might cause the solver to choose processes that are slow but sure; an emergency condition requiring quick action might cause him to gamble on a solution process that is not as sure but is more efficient (if successful). A severe emergency might provide time for only one kind of action under very limited information, and the problem solver might have to make any choice that appeared halfway appropriate. By contrast, under an extreme pressure to perform well, where a mistake might evoke extreme penalty, the problem solver might try process after process to select the very best. Strategies of solution are influenced by such subsidiary circumstances (Bruner, Goodnow, and Austin, 1956, p. 54).

6.5.3 Resources and Exchange

The designer's choice is also influenced by the resources he has and by the time constraints on his solution.

A major influence on the availability of a process lies in the resources available to the actor. Possession of or access to a plenitude of resources provides a wider choice of processes to the problem solver (Heider, 1958, pp. 93-96). The value the actor places on his resources affects his willingness to exchange them for others, whether of action or of object. Although the problem solver is sensitive to resource exchange when he deals with major exchanges of time and effort of of physical properties or of rights, he is less aware of this same exchange process when he makes decisions about undertaking simpler everyday actions. Exchange is, however, pervasive, and no decision favoring the use of a process for problem solution is undertaken without a weighing of the costs and benefits of using it. Often he is not able to quantify such a decision in any but very crude terms; still the equation is applied to any decision he undertakes regarding an action (Homans, 1961, p. 97).

6.5.4 Control and Feedback

Because design process typically requires a long sequence of steps, feedback from each step in the sequence is very important. Only by seeing the result of each step can the designer determine whether that step has moved him closer to a solution.

Finally an essential element in a decision on process is the control component and its accompanying feedback process. It is not possible to make effective use of any process or of any step in a process sequence without some gauge of the effectiveness of the just-accomplished action. A unique characteristic of any problem-solving process is that the output from one decision forms an input to the next; midway in such a sequence there is no firm evidence for evaluating any single decision in the chain (Eastman, 1970, p. 138). The only thing then that makes a problem-solving sequence possible is a feedback from each decision; although the problem solver cannot know whether a particular decision will eventuate in a solution, he can know whether it accomplished what he had hoped it might. He can know whether it moved him any closer to his goal.

The characteristic of a problem solution process is its goal orientation, what has been called "equifinality" (Heider, 1958, p. 101), the invariance of the end and the variability of means. This invariance in goal orientation provides the standard with which the result of an action is compared. It can occur in either of two ways: comparison can be made directly with the goal toward which action is directed, or it can be made with some derived intermediate objective that is a subgoal in a means-ends relation to the ultimate goal. Although the individual decision in a problem-solving sequence cannot always be evaluated directly and finally, still feedback provides an indication whether or not the decision moved the entire process toward or away from the final goal.

REFERENCES

Bruner, Jerome S., J. J. Goodnow, and G. A. Austin, *A Study of Thinking,* Wiley, New York, 1956.

Eastman, Charles M., "Problem Solving Strategies in Design," in Sanoff, Henry, and S. Cohn, *EDRA 1: Proceedings of the 1st annual Environmental Design Research Association Conference,* no publisher named, 1970.

Heider, Fritz, *The Psychology of Interpersonal Relations,* Wiley, New York, 1958.

Homans, George C., *The Human Group,* Harcourt & Brace, New York, 1950.

Parsons, Talcott, and E. A. Shils, Eds., *Toward a General Theory of Action,* Harvard University Press, Cambridge, Mass., 1951.

6.6 GOAL CLOSURE

Whereas the choice of a goal is strongly influenced by the processes available for goal achievement, choice is also strongly influenced by typological information and by the use of images.

In accomplishing problem preparation by a closure of the terminal state, a number of different factors are invariably taken into account. One basic to closure is that resulting from the availability of transformation processes. The selection of a goal is severely limited by what the actor is able to accomplish. An even more basic factor is the limitation on accomplishment by the very structure of the initial state; within the limitations of present technology and economics a sow's ear is not directly convertible into a silk purse. Within the existing road network the traveler cannot go directly from Fox Point, Wisconsin, to Florence, Alabama, without passing through a substantial number of other communities along the way.

6.6.1 Closure of Objective

The design process that uses closure of the terminal state is influenced by a great many different factors and events.

Among other factors that influence a closure of the terminal state is the process by which the problem solver generates an image of the terminal state. The solver is influenced in great part by his prior experience and the degree to which the components of that experience can be disassociated from their experiential context. In addition the selection of objectives and goals is strongly influenced by the aspiration level of the actor and the problem solver. In some problems, closure of a terminal state requires a very high level of invention, but in others the closure of a terminal state can be accomplished by the adoption of some ready-made totality. Sometimes the selection of an objective is hampered by a conflict between several nearly equally desirable objectives; it can also be hindered because all the available alternative objectives are repugnant. Finally it is influenced by the development of contrary arguments in favor of one objective or another; often a "sub-logic" case can be made with equivalent force from one point of view as well as another and often without any contradiction between them. Such situations are among the most difficult to close.

6.6.2 Problem Structure

The structure of a problem situation constrains the selection of solutions. The tensions that the situation evokes in the designer condition his choice.

Whereas the structure of a problem situation sets up tensions in the solver he is moved to resolve (Wertheimer, 1959, pp. 238-240), the structure also constrains the selection of solution possibilities. In some ways the steps toward solution are demanded by the problem's structure. A problem solver comes closest to an awareness of the structure imposed by a situation when he is faced with an accomplished event that is not reversible. He can cut his hair short, but he cannot cut it long; it must grow long in its own slow time. Situational structure can also be seen in such things as spatial and temporal continuities; a person cannot move himself at will or discontinuously except in the imagination (Kubler, 1971, p. 54).

ARCHITECTURE, PROBLEMS AND PURPOSES

6.6.3 Imaging

Design relies heavily on an imaging process that permits trial closures. These closures are first mental and subjective; they are made objective by drawings.

In accomplishing closure of the terminal state, the design problem solver relies heavily on an imaging process; it is not however, an arbitrary process but one intimately connected with a means-ends procedure. Closure is performed level by level according to the diagramed relations (Figs 6.4, p. 301, and 6.12). Since design is a social process, the imaging procedure is objective; it is essential that the image be displayed and thus shared so that all persons involved can agree about terminal-state closure and about objectives. Such an objective, shared imaging process is directly related to the process that occurs internally; it has a corresponding complexity (Boulding, 1966, pp. 47-48).

6.6.4 Typological Objectives

Imaging is guided by experience from the past. The designer organizes that experience in terms of problem types and successful solution types.

Imaging is guided in large part by experience from the past. The problem solver uses the information derived from that experience as it affects his conceptual structure in the review of possibilities and in the formation of a conceptual structuring of a terminal state. Because the terms he uses to represent those concepts are often common or standard to the design professions and often specifically to architecture, they can be thought of as canon terms, and the process of organizing solution ideas by them can be called encoding or canonization. This process results in a closure based on typological information, that is, information derived from former solution and former problem types (Colquhoun, 1972, p. 400).

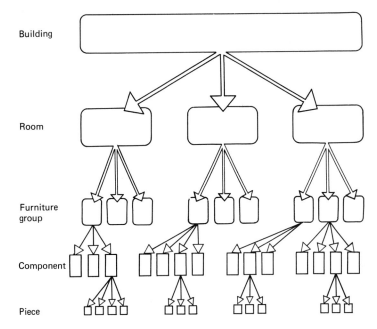

Building

Room

Furniture group

Component

Piece

Figure 6.12 A hierarchic breakdown of an object description.

6.6.5 Aspirations

Closure is influenced by the aspirations of the designer and his client.

The aspirations of the problem solver affect goal- or terminal-state closure in a very strong fashion. Careful social survey work has indicated that *hope* does "spring eternal" and that most individuals aim toward and expect to achieve a better state in their future than they have experienced in their past (Cantril, 1963, p. 43). Individual differences exist in the degree of aspiration, no doubt influenced by perceptions of life circumstance and individual capability; national differences also occur that are probably affected by the total political, social, and physical environment. I indiciated in an earlier article how the severity of a problem could be evaluated by examining the difference between the present problem condition and some preferred goal condition; the distance between the real and the imagined conditions could be seen as a measure of problem severity. That distance is strongly affected by the aspirations of the individual in that problem situation.

6.6.6 Invention

Some problem structures and some levels of aspiration do not permit solving by well-established typological solutions. Instead they require a high degree of invention.

When aspirations are high, sometimes nothing comparable with a previously experienced "typological" solution will be satisfactory as a goal. Closure of the terminal state then requires a more self-conscious process of invention than it might otherwise. To accomplish this, non-canon procedures must be employed. Such procedures are sufficiently different from anything in our discussion to this point that the invention process deserves a brief elaboration.

Although the great majority of image development occurs by the canon process described above (matters could hardly be otherwise since individuals have such strongly organized categories), other important processes also occur in the development of the image. There are two occasions: (1) in the development of wholes or parts at whatever scale for which there are no canon terms and (2) at the level of specificity for which there is no terminology. An example of the first is the invention of a room to serve a different combination of functions than presently exists; the first "family room" required an invention *process* instead of a *canon process.* An example of the second is the complete lack of terminology to describe combinations and juxtapositions of materials and objects that have a sensory affect in design; in such a *quality* process, parts and wholes are referenced to a spectrum of sensory qualities. Diagrammatically the *invention process* can be represented as shown in Fig. 6.13.

To notice the movement through a concrete-abstract spectrum and through a broad-term/narrow-term spectrum is not to say anything about how a particular new concept and configuration is achieved in a thought process. Little guidance for understanding that achievement has been available. The well-published sequence, preparation-incubation-illumination-verification, explains almost nothing; it says only that

6.6.6

the process leading to illumination or insight is hidden (Wallas, 1970, pp. 91-92). Since that has continued to be true, problem solvers should probably concentrate their interests on the preparation and verification stages, both of which require substantial amounts of organized work essential for the invention process to succeed (Ghiselin, 1963, p. 28).

The remaining thoughts that affect closure deal with the selection of alternates from among several possibilities for closure.

6.6.7 Goal Conflict

There are often conflicts between competing goal closures. It is possible to develop sublogic arguments in favor of the different goals.

Conflict can exist within a single goal or between competing goals (Lewin, 1964, pp. 260-261). A number of combinations of attractions and repulsions can occur, depending on what different goals are being weighed. The result of the powers or influences of these different forces with different strength determines the goal selection and the terminal state closure accomplished.

At the same time that strong affections or disaffections exist for particular goals, one can develop arguments from different points of view that can modify those basic affectional orientations. Without some thought given to conflicting points of view the actor and the problem solver may ignore viable alternatives, preweigh alternatives inaccurately, fail to gather adequate information, and ignore some goals for which closure must be provided (Churchman and Eisenberg, 1964, p. 51). By the development of sublogics, developed if necessary by different persons, some or all of these deficiencies can probably be avoided. When those sublogics are placed in competition, a more carefully organized and reasoned closure can be achieved.

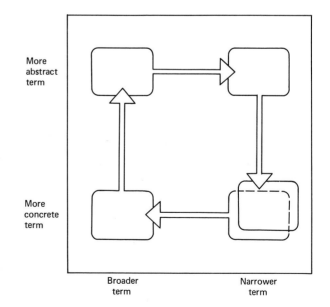

More abstract term

More concrete term

Broader term

Narrower term

Figure 6.13 An invention process.

REFERENCES

Boulding, Kenneth E., *The Image: Knowledge in Life and Society,* University of Michigan, Ann Arbor, 1966.

Cantril, Hadley, "A Study of Aspirations," *Scientific American,* **208**(2), 1963.

Churchman, C. West, and H. R. Eisenberg, "Deliberation and Judgment," in Shelly, Maynard W., II, and Glenn L. Bryan, Eds., *Human Judgments and Optimality,* Wiley, New York, 1964.

Colquhoun, Alan, "Typology and Design Method," in Gutman, Robert, Ed., *People and Buildings,* Basic Books, New York, 1972.

Ghiselin, Brewster, Ed., *The Creative Process,* the New American Library, New York, 1963.

Kubler, George, *The Shape of Time,* Yale University Press, New Haven, Conn., 1971.

Lewin, Kurt, "Behavior and Development as a Function of the Total Situation," in Cartright, Dorwin, Ed., *Kurt Lewin: Field Theory in Social Science,* Harper & Row, New York, 1964.

Wallas, G. "The Art of Thought," in Vernon, P. E., Ed., *Creativity,* Penguin, Harmondsworth, England, 1970.

Wertheimer, Max, *Productive Thinking,* Harper & Row, New York, 1959.

6.7 ADDUCTION

When closure has placed a problem statement into a "two-known-terms" condition, adduction processes are used to determine what the third term in the problem statement must be.

I have described in some detail factors that influence process closure and other factors that influence terminal-state closure. Before talking about adduction, I must review the relationship between closure and adduction.

In the use of the three-term statement $A \Rightarrow B$, to describe a problem situation, before solution can proceed, two of the terms must be known. When a problem statement is not in a two-knowns condition, it can be converted to it, that is, closed to such a condition, by assumption or by arbitrary choice, according to how much information is available to the problem solver. In discussing closure, I have been discussing influences on that assumption process or that arbitrary choice process.

6.7.1 Closure as a Subproblem

Closure of a terminal state can sometimes require the statement of a separate subproblem with its own processes of closure and adduction.

Adduction is a process for determining the third term in a problem statement from the two existing known terms. During the discussion of terminal-state closure, I have suggested the possibility of using some processes of reasoning, which can be appropriate in some parts of closure. Closure of a terminal state can become, in itself, a separate subproblem with its own processes of closure and adduction that occur before closure of the term in the major problem can be achieved.

6.7.2 The Adduction Process

Adduction is the derivation of a third term in a problem statement that is in a logical relationship with two already known terms. Adduction requires decompositon, means-ends analysis, specification, and generation and matching processes.

To restate, adduction is the process of deriving a third term of a problem statement in such a way that it is in a necessary and logical relationship with the other two known terms. Adduction ordinarily requires: (1) a degree of decomposition of the two known terms in such a fashion that some fit can be discerned between corresponding decomposed parts, (2) a means-ends analysis that uses the demand and supply counterparts from the known term components to determine a specific component of a third term, (3) the collection of those specific component descriptions into a specification for the holistic third term, and (4) a process for generating candidates for the third term and for matching those candidates against the specification.

6.7.3 Decomposition

Closure of the terminal state produces a set of demand statements. They evoke a set of possible supply system statements. Before these two systems of statements can be placed into relationship, they must be decomposed into component statements.

Decomposition and fitting requires an understanding of the manner in which different possible terms in a problem statement can be decomposed. In discussing the design problem, such decomposition and fitting can be best understood by thinking of the demand for functions, the systems by which functions are supplied, and the resolution between such demand and supply by detailed design. In one summary of design process there are three basic processes: layout, design of functional systems, and detail design (Honey, 1969, pp. 1389 ff.). Layout is a demand statement, design of functional systems is a supply systems statement, and detail design is a fitting of these statements with each other. The difficulties of design are produced because systems of demand and of supply do not ordinarily decompose into components that can be fitted to each other without some effort.

6.7.4 Means-Ends Analysis

Since demand and supply system statements do not ordinarily decompose along the same lines, they must be fitted with each other by a means-ends analysis.

Such a fitting procedure is accomplished by a *means-ends analysis.* A number of well-known means-ends chains are available that differ according to the context and the problem statement. Within design such a chain is ordinarily in the form: person-purpose-behavior-function-(designed) object. An element later in the chain is a means to an earlier element. An element later in the chain is in a supply relation to the demand of an earlier element.

6.7.5 Specification

A successful fitting produces a specification for a set of possible supply statements.

As a result of developing a fitted relationship between components in such a chain, a *specification* is generated for members of the set that form components of the third term in the problem statement.

6.7.6 Generating and Testing

The selection of an element that fits the specification requires a procedure that generates possible elements for consideration and tests those elements against the specification.

To complete adduction, a procedure is used to supply an element that actually fits the specification derived. It can be analyzed into two parts (1) a method of *generating* candidates and (2) a method of *testing* candidates. A number of procedures exist that differ by the manner in which these two parts are separated or combined and by the degree to which an orderly and comprehensive review of all the possible candidates can be considered. Apparently an inverse relationship exists between the efficiency of such a process and the comprehensiveness it provides.

6.7.7 Specific Choice

When such a procedure produces more than one successful candidate, additional testing criteria are needed.

Since the demand statements in a means-ends analysis are typically at a higher level of abstractness than the proposed elements to supply that demand, there is no way to ensure a determinate selection. The mapping from a more abstract to a more concrete level is usually a one-to-many mapping. Since this is so, a question arises about which of the logically equivalent specific candidates should be chosen. Specifics cannot be determined, they must be chosen.

As a candidate is generated that is more specific and concrete than the terms supplied in the problem statement, the only means to a selection is by reference to the authority that supplied the problem statement. Choice under such circumstance requires a question addressed to the problem authority (usually the client), "Is this (more concrete proposed thing), what you had in mind when you said. . . (your more abstract problem statement)?"

REFERENCES

Honey, C. R., "Information Flow in Architectural Design," *The Architect's Journal,* London, May 21, 1969.

6.8 SEARCHING

Different elements in a problem solution are generated by closure and by adduction. Every solution assembly uses both of these processes; what is known as synthesis consists of a proposal and its analysis. Final selection is by a process of identification.

Different elements in a problem solution are generated sometimes by closure (involving assumption or arbitrary choice) and sometimes by adduction; an interactive relation exists between the two processes, which are used in combination until a fitted group of elements fills the terms of the problem statement form $A \Rightarrow B$.

6.8.1 Solution Assembly

Solution assembly can occur as a step-by-step accumulation of already fitted components, or it can occur by a search for a completely configured solution.

The discussion to this point has passed over two important related parts of problem solution. The first is the *assembly* of a solution to any very complex problem, the second is the developed *interrelation* between the components in a solution.

I shall not attempt to deal with the second of these subjects in any detail in this basic discussion of theory. I shall simply accept at this point that the relation between the components is itself an important solution component and thus deal with the achievement of that relation as an essential part of problem solution without going into the detail of what those relations might be and how they are achieved. In discussing the assembly of a complex problem solution, please understand that I intend that this relationship is part of the requirement in such an assembly.

Several possibilities are available for discussing solution assembly. Closure and adduction can be seen as fully accomplished when all the elements of each term in the problem statement have been specified; in this view the search would be the process for finding the appropriate assembly of elements.

By contrast, closure and adduction can be seen as accomplished only when assembly of elements into a solution configuration has been fully defined; in this view search would be a more mechanical process that simply supplied the elements one by one to fit into the defined structure. In this view search could also be seen as a process of seeking the already combined elements whose configuration fitted the assembled solution definition.

6.8.2 Build-up and Purchase

Both processes are used. The first is known as "build-up"; the second can be called "purchase." The two are reciprocal.

Both views are useful, for both processes are used in problem solution. The first process occurs in the procedure known as *build-up*. Elements are added one by one, and the combination is then tested for its suitability. The second process occurs when a solution object has been so fully described that the problem solver can *purchase* or accept it as a whole thing itself; purchase can also occur when the assembled object is well enough defined to select individual elements in the assembled solution with a sure knowledge that they will fit together in the assembly.

Purchase and *build-up* are reciprocal processes. Where build-up adds elements one by one and tests at each stage of assembly, *purchase* examines whole objects for suitability and moves to examine parts only when a whole assembly is not available or is not appropriate.

Just as the translation from the more abstract to the more concrete involved a repeated question, "Is this what you meant when you

6.8.2

said. . .?'', so does the decision to move from a whole to the next parts level involve a question process. The question is, ''Do you see what you want at this singular or whole level?'' This question leads to an iterated two-part analytic process that leads level by level through each whole-part decomposition. Clearly this leads to an orderly, more and more detailed examination of the fit between an object or object proposal, and the image the client and his architect have of what the terminal state must be. The two-part repeated decision process appears in Fig. 6.14.

Whether the process is one of *purchase* or *build-up,* it tends to follow the set of canon terms available to the design profession for the particular solution type under consideration. A typical set of terms at different part levels (but dealing with only one component decomposition at each part level) appears in Fig. 6.15. *Build-up,* with the assistance of *planning,* the use of assemblies as elements (Eastman, 1970, p. 145), moves from the smaller components to the larger. *Purchase* moves from the larger components to the smaller.

Figure 6.14 A ''purchase'' algorithm.

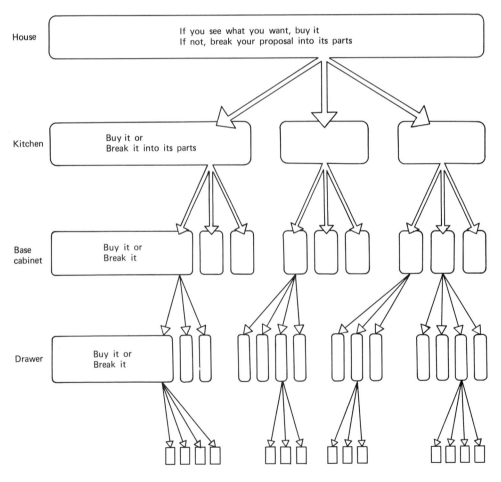

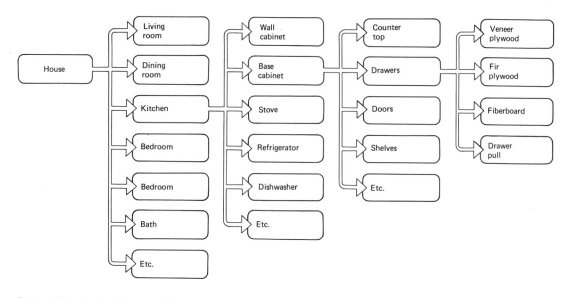

Figure 6.15 A typical set of canon terms in an object decomposition.

6.8.3 Solution Assembly Referencing

For any proposed solution the fit between demand and supply statements must be checked at each of the means-ends levels, whether person, purpose, behavior, function, or object. The fit must also be checked at each whole-part level.

I noted above that, as each more particular component was specified, a need arose to check with authority to determine whether the more particular component was an instance of statements at a higher level of abstractness. The process is even more complex than that simple checking; the demand statement might well have included statements at each of the levels of abstractness I have described. The client (or problem authority) might have imposed demands at:

1. The purpose description level.

2. The behavior description level.

3. The function description level.

4. The object level.

Solution assembly requires a referencing, not only from wholes to parts, but also from means to ends. Such a referencing can be represented in diagram (Fig. 6.16).

6.8.4 TOTE Units

These two checking procedures are interrelated by TOTE units into an entire linked chain of connections.

To see how a referencing occurs that incorporates both the part-whole and the concrete-abstract spectrum, one can use the mechanism known as a TOTE (Miller, Galanter, and Pribram, 1960, p. 26). The acronym TOTE stands for Test-Operate-Test-Exist (Fig. 6.17). A TOTE is, thus, a decision element that tests the congruity of some

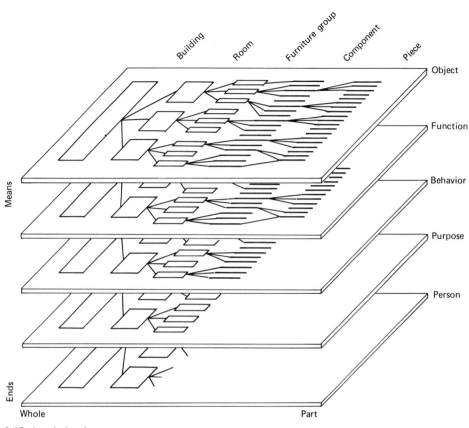

Figure 6.16 A relation between whole-part and ends-means spectra.

6.8.4

mental element against the purposes and structure of the decision situation. Its importance in understanding mental processes lies in the possiblility of the TOTE unit's being linked in its operate phase with other TOTEs. Each, in turn, can be linked to more remote TOTEs, so that the TOTE device can be used to represent the structure of decisions that reference different abstractness levels or different part-whole levels.

Figure 6.17 A TOTE unit. (After a diagram by Miller, Galanter, and Pribram, 1960, p. 26. Reprinted by permission of Holt Rinehart & Winston, New York.

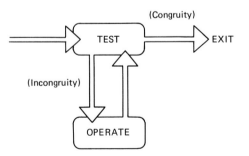

6.8.5 Cross-Referencing

Any checking of a whole-part relationship also requires a means-ends analysis; any checking of a means-ends relationship also requires a whole-part breakdown.

With the two spectra, whole-to-part and ends-to-means, described and joined in a diagram and with the TOTE element defined, it is possible to describe the decision process more accurately. During specification each change from a more abstract to a more concrete level involves a reference at the several parts levels. This reference process is indicated in the diagram, Fig. 6.18, by letting a single looped arrow represent a TOTE unit. The linked TOTEs at each crossover from an abstract to the next more concrete level represents the several linked TOTEs that occur in referencing the parts levels.

In a similar fashion the decomposition that breaks a whole into its several parts is referenced by linked TOTE units to the several levels of abstractness (Fig. 6.19). The diagram shows a TOTE at each level but, of course, there are varying degrees of referencing

Figure 6.18 TOTE units can connect parts of the ends-means spectrum via parts of the whole-part spectrum.

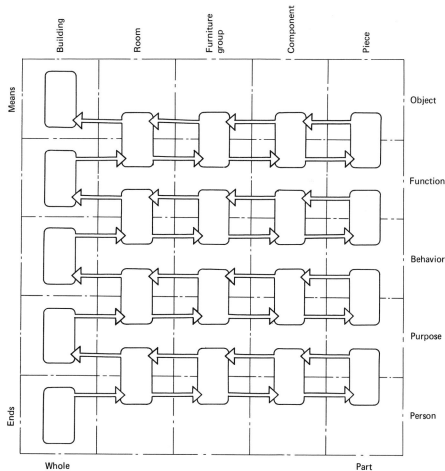

according to the particular decision situation. The direction of the arrows used in the TOTE units appears as in a *purchase* kind of assembly process. The direction of arrows in a *buildup* assembly process would be reversed. By the use of these two interconnected processes, solution assembly is made both specific and particular.

At appropriate stages in the solution process, the extent of TOTE linkage can be more limited. A "planning" heuristic abstracts a part of the problem and solves a less constrained problem as a guide to solving the more constrained total problem (Fig. 6.20).

As the solution process moves from programming through physical planning to design, there is also a tendency to move to a more detailed part consideration. Becoming more specific is interdependent with becoming more *particular* (Fig. 6.21).

Figure 6.19 TOTE units can connect parts of the whole-part spectrum via parts of the ends-means spectrum.

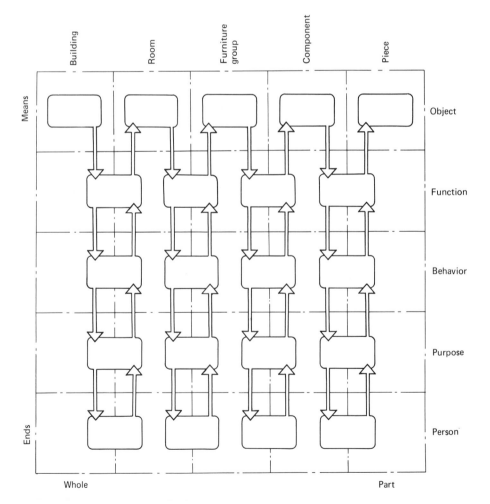

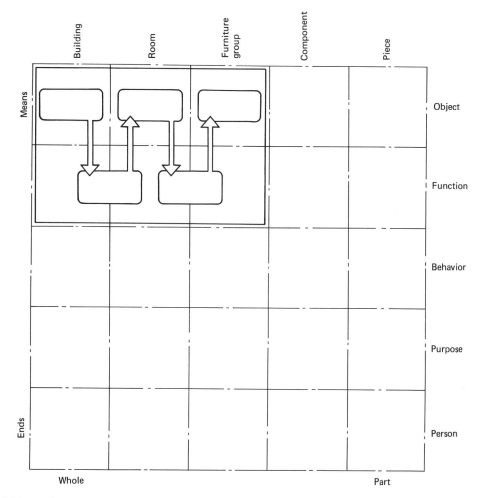

Figure 6.20 A "planning" heuristic reduces the range of consideration across the two spectra.

6.8.5

With a complete description of the solution assembly process it is possible to turn to other parts of the search process and the final selection of a solution. Solution assembly is not the same as solution selection.

6.8.6 Competing Solution Assemblies

It is possible to have solution assemblies that are in competition and conflict.

It follows from what was said earlier about goal closure that it is possible to have conflicting and competing solution assemblies. It also follows from the discussion of the difficulty in achieving a determinate choice of elements at a more specific level that there can easily be competing solution assemblies, even where full agreement occurs about goals and objectives.

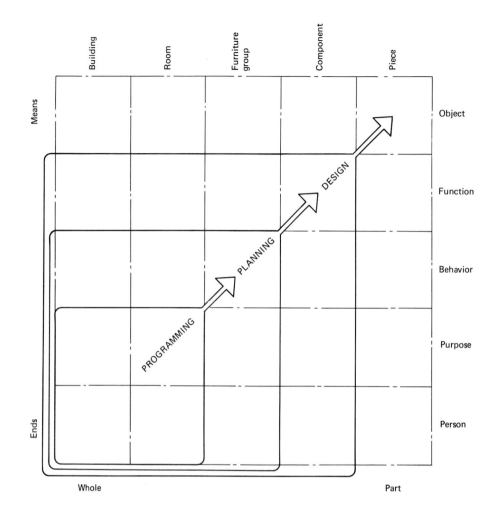

Figure 6.21 The solution process usually expands across the full spectra.

6.8.7 Hill Climbing and Parallel Development

The procedure known as "hill climbing" keeps the best solution so far achieved and modifies it when an improvement is found. Another procedure develops competing solutions in parallel.

Different methods are available by which alternative solution assemblies are developed and by which they are brought under review. Whatever assembly process is used, two primary methods exist for thinking about alternative solution assemblies: one is the parallel development (even from the initial assembly point) of different solution assemblies; the other is a process known as *hill climbing* whereby a single solution is brought forward by introducing changes in its various elements, the best achieved assembly being always kept until a next improvement is discovered. Hill climbing is ordinarily a less expensive procedure than parallel development, but it is not possible to make as explicit and careful comparisons between solutions as in parallel development.

Where parallel development is used, one can apply the same questions to the search for solution assemblies as those raised in the discussion of generating and testing—whether or not the search and selection criteria are to be combined and to what degree the search is to be comprehensive.

When a solution is assembled, or under parallel development when several solutions have been assembled, a substantial part of selection depends on a series of predictions:

1. That the proposed solution will be in accord with the context for which the solution is intended—that the problem solver has accurately predicted the circumstances for which he has provided a solution.

2. That, as the solution is decoded or enacted, the real-world counterparts to his solution will behave as his solution has behaved.

3. That the outcome of enacting the solution will fill his needs.

Such predictions can be tested only by placing the solution into effect. The solution can finally be tested only by being put into effect.

6.8.8 Checking

Selection in either procedure depends on a determination that all the stated problem requirements are met.

Before this time, however, the selection of a solution assembly depends on the degree to which all the problem requirements are met, the degree to which the subsolutions or subassemblies are compatible, and the degree to which the solution is compatible with the elements in the problem situation that were factored out.

6.8.9 Identification

Final selection is determined by an identification between the solution and the person doing the selecting.

Finally, in any selection process the decision is determined by whether the thing being selected is capable of being in a unit-formed relation with the person or persons doing the selecting. Only if the actor and the problem solver are able to identify themselves and their interest with the solution assembly is that solution assembly selected for enactment.

REFERENCES

Eastman, Charles M., "Problem Solving Strategies in Design," in Sanoff, Henry, and S. Cohn, *EDRA 1: Proceedings of the 1st annual Environmental Design Research Association Conference,* no publisher named, 1970.

Miller, George A., E. Galanter, and K. Pribram, *Plans and the Structure of Behavior,* Holt, New York, 1960.

Appendix A:
Author's
Resume

Appendix Author's Biographical Notes

John W. Wade
Professor,
School of Architecture and Urban Planning
University of Wisconsin—Milwaukee
Milwaukee, Wisconsin 53202

Born: Florence, Alabama 12/25/25
Married: Donna White Wade, 8/30/65

EDUCATION

Florence State College, 1943-1944
(now, University of North Alabama)

Harvard College, 1946-1949	B.A. (mcl)
Harvard Graduate School of Design, 1949-1952	B. Arch.
"Diploma Course," Department of Town Planning, University College, London, 1952-1953	. . .
University of Pennsylvania Graduate School of Fine Arts, 1963-1964	M. Arch.

ARCHITECTURAL REGISTRATIONS

South Carolina, #715	1960-1969
National Council of Architectural Registration Boards, #4246	1962-1969
Georgia, #1232	1962-1969
Alabama, #864	1964-1969
Wisconsin, #A-2977	1968-

AFFILIATIONS

American Institute of Architects (A.I.A.)	1961-
Association of Collegiate Schools of Architecture (A.C.S.A.)	1963-
Society of Architectural Historians	1964-1967
National Council of Architectural Registrations Boards (NCARB)	1968-1975
Construction Specifications Institute (CSI)	1968-1969

	Environmental Design Research Association (EDRA)	1973-
	Design Methods Group (DMG)	1974-
HONORS AND LISTS	Fulbright Scholarship (England)	1952-1953
	A.I.A. Homes for Better Living Awards, Honorable Mention	1967
	Who's Who in America	1974-
	International Directory of Behavior and Design Research	1974-
ACADEMIC EXPERIENCE	Lecturer, Mathematics Department, Armstrong College, Savannah, Ga.	1962
	Associate Professor and Head, Division of Architecture, Tuskegee Institute, Tuskegee, Alabama, (*Established new professional program* now accredited by NAAB)	1964-1968
	Professor and Dean, School of Architecture, University of Wisconsin—Milwaukee, Milwaukee, Wisconsin (*Established new school*, accredited June 1974 by NAAB)	1968-1974
	Professor and Dean, School of Architecture and Urban Planning, University of Wisconsin— Milwaukee (Initiated new urban planning program)	1974-1975
	Professor, Department of Architecture, School of Architecture and Urban Planning, University of Wisconsin—Milwaukee, Wisconsin	1975-
PRACTICE EXPERIENCE	Draftsman, North Alabama State Planning Board, Muscle Shoals, Alabama	1946 (s)*
	Draftsman, Turner & Northington, Architects, Florence, Alabama	1947 (s) 1949 (s)
	Draftsman, Paul W. Hofferburt, Architect, Gadsden, Alabama	1950 (s)

*(s) summer.

	Designer, Perry, Shaw, and Hepburn, Kehoe, and Dean, Architects, Boston, Massachusetts	1952
	Designer and Job Captain, Eero Saarinen and Associates, Architects, Bloomfield Hills, Michigan	1953-1956
	Job Captain, Hideo Sasaki and Associates, Landscape Architects, Somerville, Massachusetts	1956-1957
	Independent design practice, Hilton Head Island, South Carolina	1957-1960
	Independent architectural practice, Hilton Head Island, South Carolina, and Savannah, Georgia	1960-1963 1962-1963
	Architectural practice, Wade and Hight, Architects and Engineers, Tuskegee, Alabama	1964-1968
ADJUNCT ACTIVITIES	Member, Architect's Section, Examining Board of Architects, Professional Engineers, Designers, and Land Surveyors, State of Wisconsin	1968-
	Chairman of Examining Board of Architects, Professional Engineers, Designers, and Land Surveyors, Wisconsin	1970 1972 1974
	ACSA Councilor, School of Architecture, University of Wisconsin—Milwaukee	1970-
	Host for EDRA V, fifth annual meeting of the Environmental Design Research Association held at the School of Architecture, University of Wisconsin—Milwaukee	1974
INSTITUTIONAL CONSULTING	Member, Visiting Curriculum Advisory Committee for the Architectural Program, School of Architecture and Urban Planning, University of California at Los Angeles	1967
	Member, AIA New England School Advisory Committee (Visits to University of Massachusetts, University of Southeast Massachusetts, University of Connecticut, and University of Rhode Island)	1971
	Chairman, AIA New Jersey School Advisory Committee (Visits to Rutgers University	

	College at Newark, and Newark College of Engineering)	1972
	Chairman, AIA New School Advisory Committee— University of South Florida	1973
	Participant, U.S. Department of Housing and Urban Development Site Planning Evaluation Seminars	1973-1975
	Participant, U.S. National Bureau of Standards Architectural Research Seminar	1974
FUNDED RESEARCH (PRINCIPAL INVESTIGATOR)	"Planning and Design Services for Columbus, Indiana," Irwin-Sweeney-Miller Foundation, Columbus, Indiana, $119,000	1972-1973
	"Planning and Design Services for Columbus, Indiana, "Irwin-Sweeney-Miller Foundation, Columbus, Indiana, $14,770	1973-1974
	"Evaluation Study of Modular Coordination," Department of Commerce, National Bureau of Standards, $2,475	1973-1974
	A Study of Campus Planning for G. B. Pant Agricultural University, Pantnager, Uttar Pradesh, India," Midwestern Universities Consortium for International Activities, Co-principal investigator, (grant funded travel to India for one month for two faculty and four students) $13,000	1973-1974
	"The Classification of Design Methods," The Graduate School, University of Wisconsin—Milwaukee, $4,000	1974-1975
PROFESSIONAL ASSOCIATION PARTICIPATION	Member, AIA Education Committee	1971-1972
	Member, AIA Performance Criteria Task Force	1973-1975
	Member, NCARB New Exam Committee	1972
PUBLISHED DESIGN WORK	"Community Planning" (Unspoiled Oceanside Developed)," *House and Home*, August 1961, pp. 151-157.	

"Idea House, This House Set the Pattern at Sea Pines," *House and Home*, August 1961, pp. 158-159.

"Resort House, Hilton Head Island," *Review of Architecture* (South Carolina AIA publication) Spring 1963, pp. 24-25.

"Sea Pines Plantation, Hilton Head Island, South Carolina, Varied Land Use, Consistent Design," *Architectural Record*, November 1965, pp. 145-146.

"Homes for Better Living. Honorable Mention: A Low-Cost Prototype Designed for Row Housing," *House and Home*, September 1967, pp. 94-95.

"Architecture," *Wisconsin Architect*, July-August 1968, pp. 10-19.

"Photography," *Wisconsin Architect*, July-August 1968, pp. 24-28.

"Painting," *Wisconsin Architect*, July-August 1968, p. 29.

PUBLISHED ARTICLES

"Saarinen," *Review of Architecture* (South Carolina AIA, publication), 1961.

"An Architecture of Purpose," *AIA Journal*, October 1967, pp. 71-76.

"Disposal," *Industrial Design*, June 1968, pp. 54-57.

"Unity, Harmony, Balance, and Beauty," *Wisconsin Architect*, July-August 1968, pp. 20-23.

"Architecture: Goals and Goal Setting," *Wisconsin Architect*, September 1968, pp. 6-9.

"A Curriculum Structure," *Journal of Architectural Education*, March 1969, pp. 13-18.

"Architectural Curriculum for UW—M," *Wisconsin Architect*, April 1969, pp. 8-11.

"Communication from the School of Architecture," *Wisconsin Architect*, November 1969, p. 19.

"Manifesto," *UW—M Magazine* (University of Wisconsin—Milwaukee) Summer 1971, p. 2.

"An Institution for the Design Professions," *AIA Journal*, January 1972, pp. 37-39.

"A Service Institution for the Design Professions," *Engineering Education*, February 1972, pp. 460-462.

CONFERENCE PAPERS

Respondent to paper on Computer Use in Architecture by Michael Brill, *Architectural Researcher's Conference*, Wisconsin Dells, Wisconsin, September 1968.

"Architectural Education" (and participant in three-day symposium on education), *Arts Sixty-Nine*, University of Arkansas, Fayetteville, Arkansas, April 1969.

"Whole Problems and Partial Solutions," *Urbanology . . . New Approaches to Urban Revival*, University of Wisconsin—Milwaukee, June 1969, (in Proceedings, pp. 50-72).

"Education for the Professional," *Continuing Education—Urban Urgency*, University of Wisconsin—Extension, Milwaukee, Wisconsin. November 1969.

"Character Zoning in the Central Business District," *Rebuilding an American City*, Beloit College, Beloit, Wisconsin, January 1971.

"Clinical Instruction in Architectural Education," workshop theme paper, *ACSA Teacher's Seminar,* Yosemite National Park, March 1973.

"The Service Institution-Clinic Concept of the School of Architecture," *EDRA IV*, Convener of Workshop, Environmental Design Research Association Fourth Annual Conference, Virginia Polytechnic Institute, Blacksburg, Virginia, April 1973.

"A Measure of Order," (in Workshop 32, The Interpretation of the Environment), *EDRA IV*, Environmental Design Research Association Sixth Annual Conference, University of Kansas, Lawrence, Kansas, April 1975.

Author Index

A

Abercrombie, M. L. Johnson, 57, 58, 142
Ackoff, Russell L., 30, 35, 38, 97, 189, 231, 294, 304
Agnew, Neil M., 80
Alexander, Christopher, 112, 113
Allport, Gordon W., 294
Amarel, Saul, 82, 89, 90, 100, 307
Archer, L. Bruce, 34, 69, 114
Asimow, Morris, 68, 203

B

Barnett, H. G., 61, 62, 64
Berelson, Bernard, 250
Best, Gordon, 34, 82, 89, 135, 142, 190, 191, 300
Bierce, Ambrose, 39
Black, Max, 43, 66, 148, 180
Boulding, Kenneth, 167, 170, 176, 317
Braybrooke, D., 189, 198, 250
Broadbent, D. E., 102, 208, 233
Brooks, Cleanth, 31, 44, 58
Bross, Irwin D. J., 231, 232, 233
Bruner, Jerome S., 41, 47, 60, 61, 67, 118, 119, 170, 185, 215, 216, 232, 314
Bruyn, Severyn T., 30, 168

C

Cantril, Hadley, 318
Chernoff, Herman, 220, 231
Chomsky, Noam, 44
Churchman, C. West, 38, 48, 231, 254, 256, 320
Cohen, John, 45
Colquhoun, Alan, 101, 317
Craik, Kenneth H., 80
Craik, Kenneth J. W., 25, 40, 43, 91, 92, 98, 118, 119, 148, 217, 232, 299, 302

D

Denton, Trevor, 162
Denzin, Norman K., 168
Dewey, John, 172, 173, 175
Downs, Roger M., 117, 168, 174, 177
Duncker, Karl, 214

E

Eastman, Charles M., 25, 93, 112, 114, 202, 203, 210, 212, 219, 315, 324
Empson, William, 43

F

Fischer, David Hackett, 38, 58, 59, 93, 95, 98, 233

Lazarsfeld, Paul F., 39, 40, 42, 60, 173
Lee, Irving J., 178
Lewin, Kurt, 93, 116, 135, 148, 160, 174, 176, 214, 235, 255, 311, 319
Lindsay, Peter H., 24, 27
Lowenthal, David, 135
Lynch, Kevin, 188, 198, 249, 311

M MacIver, R. M., 95
Maldonado, Tomas, 101
Manheim, Marvin Lee, 115, 202, 218
Maslow, Abraham H., 294, 311
Mayall, W. H., 218
Meehan, Eugene J., 147
Miller, George A., 42, 67, 87, 92, 93, 116, 214, 312, 325
Miller, James G., 257
Minsky, M. L., 29, 33
Moles, Abraham A., 214
Murtha, Donald Michael, 30, 110, 200

N Nadler, Gerald, 30, 68, 307, 312
Nagel, Ernest, 59
Newell, Allen, 25, 29, 32, 33, 59, 100, 112, 114, 131, 209, 210, 212, 214, 216, 220, 247, 257, 296, 307

O Olsen, Leonard, Jr., 109, 112, 257
Osgood, Charles E., 172, 250

P Paige, Jeffrey M., 80
Parkinson, C. Northcote, 105
Parsons, Talcott, 68, 129, 131, 132, 246, 248, 294, 295, 312
Peirce, C. S., 145
Peltz, Richard, 38, 41, 174
Pepper, Stephen C., 172
Perin, Constance, 66
Polanyi, Michael, 41, 143
Polya, George, 27, 28, 29, 59, 66, 109, 113, 248, 296

Q Quiller-Couch, Sir Arthur, 171

R Rapoport, Amos, 135
Raser, John R., 148, 299
Reitman, Walter R., 31, 88, 89, 90, 97, 98, 99, 297, 303, 306
Restle, Frank, 93, 143
Rosenthal, Robert, 46
Ross, W. D., 170

S Sennet, Richard, 136

Shelly, Maynard W., II, 90
Shepard, Roger N., 32, 33, 89, 92, 189, 190, 235, 236, 299
Sherif, Carolyn, 171
Simon, Herbert A., 112, 114, 131, 209, 210, 211, 212, 214, 220, 296
Sommer, Robert, 136
Sorokin, Pitrim A., 235
Steinitz, Carl, 136
Stretton, Hugh, 137
Studer, Raymond G., 65, 135

V

Venturi, Robert, 136.
Vickers, Geoffrey, 258

W

Wallas, G., 144, 145, 319
Walter, W. Grey, 67, 146, 170
Wehrli, Robert, 25, 201
Weinland, James D., 57, 176, 177, 208
Wertheimer, Max, 57, 61, 88, 141, 142, 202, 296, 316
Wilson, J. Bright, Jr., 27, 28, 108, 188, 299
Windelband, Wilhelm, 70
Wohlwill, Joachim F., 135, 294
Wolf, A., 142
Wright, Frank Lloyd, 288

Subject Index